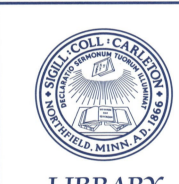

Nazis and Good Neighbors

The United States Campaign against the Germans of Latin America in World War II

Based on research in seven countries, this international history uncovers an American security program in which Washington reached into fifteen Latin American countries to seize more than 4,000 German expatriates and intern them in the Texas desert. The crowd of Nazi Party members, antifascist exiles, and even Jewish refugees were lumped together in camps riven by strife.

The book examines the evolution of governmental policy, its impact on individuals and emigrant communities, and the ideological assumptions that blinded officials in both Washington and Berlin to Latin American realities. Franklin Roosevelt's vaunted Good Neighbor policy was a victim of this effort to force reluctant Latin American governments to hand over their German residents, while the operation ruined an opportunity to rescue victims of the Holocaust. This study makes the very contemporary argument that security measures based on group affiliation rather than individual actions are as unjust and ineffective in foreign policy as they are in law enforcement.

Max Paul Friedman is Assistant Professor of History at Florida State University and a former Woodrow Wilson Postdoctoral Fellow in the Humanities. His work has been published in *The Americas* and *The Oral History Review*. Before entering academia, he was assistant producer for National Public Radio's "All Things Considered" and a freelance writer published in the *Washington Post, New York Newsday, Atlanta Constitution, Cleveland Plain Dealer, Orlando Sentinel*, and other newspapers and magazines. He earned his Ph.D. from the University of California at Berkeley in 2000.

Publication of this book has been supported by the generosity of the Lucius N. Littauer Foundation.

Nazis and Good Neighbors

The United States Campaign against the Germans of Latin America in World War II

MAX PAUL FRIEDMAN

CAMBRIDGE
UNIVERSITY PRESS

PUBLISHED BY THE PRESS SYNDICATE OF THE UNIVERSITY OF CAMBRIDGE
The Pitt Building, Trumpington Street, Cambridge, United Kingdom

CAMBRIDGE UNIVERSITY PRESS
The Edinburgh Building, Cambridge CB2 2RU, UK
40 West 20th Street, New York, NY 10011-4211, USA
477 Williamstown Road, Port Melbourne, VIC 3207, Australia
Ruiz de Alarcón 13, 28014 Madrid, Spain
Dock House, The Waterfront, Cape Town 8001, South Africa

http://www.cambridge.org

First published 2003

Printed in the United States of America

Typeface Sabon 10/12 pt.   *System* LATEX 2_ε [TB]

A catalog record for this book is available from the British Library.

Library of Congress Cataloging in Publication Data

Friedman, Max Paul.
Nazis and good neighbors : the United States campaign against the Germans of Latin
America in World War II / Max Paul Friedman.
    p.   cm.
Includes bibliographical references and index.
ISBN 0-521-82246-7
1. World War, 1939–1945 – Deportations from Latin America.   2. Germans – Relocation –
United States.   3. Jews – Relocation – United States.   4. World War, 1939–1945 –
Concentration camps – United States.   5. National security – United States.
6. United States – Relations – Latin America.   7. Latin America – Relations – United States.
8. Anti-Nazi movement – United States – History.   9. Anti-Nazi movement – Latin America –
History.   I. Title.
D769.8.A5F75   2003
940.53′17′0973–dc21   2002041424

ISBN 0 521 82246 7 hardback

For My Father

Contents

Prologue

San Francisco, California, April 1945. Werner Kappel lies in his hospital bed, his cheek full of shrapnel, his jaw broken, clutching his newly awarded medal, a Purple Heart. He has plenty of time to reflect on the strange course of events that brought him to this point.

Werner was the sixteen-year-old son of German Jewish parents in 1938 when his father Fred Kappel, a leather wholesaler in Berlin, was threatened by the Gestapo and ordered to leave Nazi Germany. Father and son slipped out to Denmark and made their way to Panama, where they earned a living as bus drivers. Then, on December 7, 1941, Japan attacked Pearl Harbor, and the U.S. government put into motion an obscure operation to secure its southern flank. Identified by U.S. intelligence agents as possible Nazi subversives, Fred and Werner Kappel, along with more than four thousand other Germans from Latin America, were deported to the United States and interned in camps in the Texas desert.

For the next year and a half, from behind barbed wire, Fred wrote frantic letters to everyone he could think of: the State Department, the White House, the Justice Department, American Jewish organizations. His campaign, and protests by some of the other eighty Jewish refugees interned in camps for "dangerous alien enemies," eventually secured their conditional release on parole in late 1943. Werner Kappel went to St. Louis, where he found a job as a baker's apprentice – and was drafted into the U.S. Army.

Shipped to the Philippines, Werner was seriously wounded in fighting on Luzon. Six months of hospitalization followed. His earlier petition for U.S. citizenship was denied on the grounds that he had entered the country illegally – a cruel irony for someone seized and brought to the United States by force. But his congressman took an interest in his case, and by the end of June 1945, he would take the naturalization oath before an immigration judge. It would take another six months for Werner Kappel, decorated war veteran and U.S. citizen, to be released from the supervision of the government's Alien Enemy Control Unit.

"The whole thing was very unfair," Werner recalled many years later. "We had nothing to do with Hitler, because we were chased out by the Nazis. We didn't even feel like Germans anymore, and the Germans didn't think we were Germans – only the Americans thought so." Time has allowed him to forgive, if not forget, what happened to him and many others seized in Latin America in the Second World War. "When you left Germany to get away from Nazism, and then you get thrown into a camp for Nazis, it was idiotic," he says today. "When I think about it, I get angry right now!"[1]

Acknowledgments

To finish a manuscript is to acknowledge unpayable debts. I am indebted for years of sagacious counsel and encouragement from Diane Shaver Clemens, David Hollinger, and Victoria Bonnell of the University of California at Berkeley. I owe more than I can say to longtime friends and mentors Steve Volk of Oberlin College and Seymour Hersh, who taught me that there are no secrets.

At the History Department at Berkeley, I had the good fortune to be surrounded by colleagues who were generous with their friendship and their criticism. Dirk Moses, David Engerman, Phil Soffer, Jim Cane, and Chaela Pastore all offered sustaining measures of both. My thanks as well to Professors Anthony Adamthwaite, Jon Gjerde, Leon Litwack, Gerald Feldman, the late Jim Kettner, and the resourceful Mabel Lee. At the University of Colorado at Boulder, my gratitude goes to Jeffrey Cox and Paula Anderson of the Center for Humanities and the Arts, and Tom Zeiler and Bob Schulzinger of the History Department, for all their support.

Broadening a foreign relations study beyond the records of the policymakers to consider its impact on the individuals and nations that are its object; finding evidence not easily available in the United States; and considering the perspectives from abroad and from below – these goals make multinational archival work an imperative. My research and interviews overseas would not have been possible without the support of the following institutions: the Society for Historians of American Foreign Relations, the Woodrow Wilson National Fellowship Foundation, the Institute on Global Conflict and Cooperation, the Mellon Foundation, the Franklin and Eleanor Roosevelt Institute, the Rockefeller Archive Center, the American Historical Association, the Lucius N. Littauer Foundation, and at Berkeley, the Institute of International Studies, the Center for German and European Studies, the Center for Latin American Studies, the Graduate Division, and the Department of History.

More than forty people involved in this murky corner of history agreed to speak with me about their experiences (their names appear in the Bibliography). Our conversations were not always easy for them. They already have my thanks, to which I add my respect and appreciation for their willingness to wrestle with the past.

Archivists, those unsung heroes of historical research, provided useful guidance through often obscure collections of documents, especially at the Politisches Archiv des Auswärtigen Amtes in Bonn, Bundesarchiv Berlin-Lichterfelde, Bundesarchiv Koblenz, Schweizerisches Bundesarchiv in Bern, Ibero-Amerikanisches Institut in Berlin, and Archivo Nacional de Costa Rica in San José. Special thanks to Rocio Rueda at the Archivo Histórico de Quito and to Margarita Vanegas at the Archivo del Ministerio de Relaciones Exteriores in Bogotá; to Bill Walsh, Ken Heger, and John Taylor at the National Archives in College Park; and to the NA's Cary Conn for graciously expediting my Freedom of Information Act requests.

I am grateful for the advice, ideas, leads, and support provided by the indefatigable Roger Daniels, as well as by Haim Avni, Bart Bernstein, León Bieber, Enrique Biermann, Jean-Pierre Blancpain, Friedhelm Boll, Tico Braun, Jürgen Buchenau, Michael Buddrus, Marta Calderón, Judy Ewell, Norbert Finzsch, Edith Friedman, Mark Gilderhus, Marcel Hawiger, Carmen Janssen, Elisabeth and Kathryn Jay, Ines and Gerd Kaiser, Arnold Krammer, Walter LaFeber, Michel Laguerre, Tom Leonard, Mercedes Muñoz, Hugo Murillo, Monica Navarro, Ronn Pineo, Rocio Rueda, Rosemarie Sambrano, Bettina Sassen, Chris Scholl, Daniel Schorr, Friedrich Schuler, Elena Servi, Ilka-Maria and Klaus Vester, Regina Wagner, and Patrik von zur Mühlen. My editor, Lew Bateman, has been an amiable motivator throughout the process, and I thank my readers, Tom Schoonover, David Schmitz, and William O. Walker III, for their excellent suggestions. Many hands have helped to shape this work, but the responsibility for it is mine.

This book is dedicated to my father, Martin Friedman, who cared for the manuscript with a quiet grace, as he has done with me all my life.

From that golden summer afternoon in Berkeley when I first saw Katharina to the cold Berlin winters we've spent working at one desk while arguing in two languages, I have been entranced by her sharpness of mind, the pleasure she takes in irony, and her unmasterable spirit. *Sine te nihil.*

INTRODUCTION

Nazis and Good Neighbors

Washington, September 1941. President Franklin Delano Roosevelt, determined to coax a reluctant public into a necessary war for a just cause, takes to the airwaves to warn Americans that "Hitler's advance guards" are readying "footholds, bridgeheads in the New World, to be used as soon as he has gained control of the oceans. Conspiracy has followed conspiracy" in Latin America, where, the president intones, German agents are at that very moment carrying out "intrigues...plots...machinations...sabotage." The most recent sign that the Nazis are coming, the president informs his rapt national audience, is the discovery of "secret airlanding fields in Colombia, within easy range of the Panama Canal."[1]

In Bogotá, the response is pandemonium. U.S. Ambassador Spruille Braden, astonished that "the President has gone out on a limb with this statement," sends his staff scrambling across the farms and rice fields owned by local Germans, trying to produce evidence for the assertion ex post facto. Colombian President Eduardo Santos scoffs at Roosevelt's unprovable claim, telling Braden, "in the final analysis all of Colombia is a great potential airport." An indignant Colombian Senate votes unanimously that no such airfields exist – that Colombia has fulfilled its responsibility to defend against the Axis menace. Back in Washington, Secretary of State Cordell Hull is forced to call in Colombia's Ambassador Gabriel Turbay to express "the very deep regret of the President, of myself and of our Government for the unintentional reference."[2]

Turbay takes it in stride. For a year he has reported to his foreign ministry the "marked tendency of the United States to exaggerate the dangers of Nazi penetration" in Latin America – whether "deliberately or unconsciously." Why should the president be immune to such fears?[3]

THE GERMAN MENACE

How 4,058 Germans, 2,264 Japanese, and 288 Italians came to be deported from Latin America and interned in the United States has remained one of the lost stories of World War II.[4] Understanding it requires us to take a step back in time, to the years preceding American entry into the war, when the most immediate security threat perceived by the Roosevelt administration was the possibility of German destabilization of Latin America. Over a million and a half ethnic Germans lived in the region, concentrated in southern Brazil, Argentina, and Chile, and dispersed in small, tightly knit communities throughout South and Central America. Overseas agitators for the NSDAP – the Nazi Party – made a few converts and a lot of commotion in these communities during the mid-1930s; by the war's eve, most German citizens in the region, although still unwilling to join the Party, enthusiastically celebrated the achievements of their homeland regime. Inept Nazi spies contributed little to the German war effort but much to the menacing images. British propagandists, amateurish intelligence agents, and overheated news reports further stoked this activity into a fevered vision prevalent inside the U.S. government and among the public at large that a Nazi takeover of the continent by a "fifth column"* could be imminent.[5] FDR believed it, and his military prepared for it.

Of the nearly 100 meetings of the joint planning committee of the State, Navy, and War Departments in 1939 and 1940, all but six had Latin America at the top of the agenda.[6] U.S. military strategists considered most likely the possibility that German airborne forces would cross the Atlantic at its narrowest point, from Dakar in the French colony of Senegal to the Natal province of Brazil. "When ready to send armadas of bombing planes from Africa," FDR explained to his friend and ambassador to Mexico Josephus Daniels in 1939, German residents would start "a civil war...and German planes will swoop down from Africa on Brazil to decide the war in favor of the side that Germany has taken."[7] In May 1940, when the British warned that this nightmare might be at hand, the President ordered his military to draw up a hurried plan – operation "Pot of Gold" – to send 100,000 U.S. troops to Brazil. Unassimilated German immigrants played a starring role in this and all other scenarios of the anticipated Nazi assault. By blacklisting and expelling them, Washington hoped to destroy "the nuclei of Axis infection" and keep the continent safe.[8]

Although Germans in the United States were registered and thousands watched by the FBI, the alarm centered on the Germans of Latin America, because they were unassimilated, because rumors of Nazi involvement in

---

* The term "fifth column," used in everyday parlance in this period, stems from the Spanish Civil War, when fascist General Emilio Mola was asked how many soldiers he had available for an attack on Madrid. "We have four columns on the march outside the city," he said. "In the city we have a 'fifth column.'"

coup attempts were taken as gospel in the late 1930s, because Nazi propagandists claimed the allegiance of every German, and because of an essential aspect of U.S.–Latin American relations that went back to the Monroe Doctrine and forward to the present day: many in the United States thought Latin American countries could not manage their own affairs without paternal guidance from Washington, and assumed that the hidden hand of a European power lay behind any significant unrest or discordance with U.S. plans.[9]

This view precipitated a hasty series of measures that evolved into a program for the deportation and internment of thousands of people. The operation was carried out during the heyday of Roosevelt's Good Neighbor policy, an era customarily depicted as a rare period of harmony, when the United States promised not to interfere in the internal affairs of Latin American countries and brought about the finest hours of the inter-American system. This turns out to be a serious overstatement, a myth sustainable for so long only by the remarkable omission of the entire deportation program from existing histories.

As this book will show, officials in Washington were able to prevail upon their Latin American counterparts to collaborate in the program only by violating both the letter and spirit of the Good Neighbor policy. Although it has somehow escaped notice, the deportation program – which was the most direct manifestation of wartime anti-Axis policy in Latin America, and which heralded the return of interventionism – should be at the center of any history of the war and Latin America, and especially of U.S.–Latin American relations in this era.

Why did fears over the Nazi gains in Europe lead to very disparate measures against German residents of North and South America? Why were Germans who were taken into custody within the United States granted hearings and the majority released before internment, but those seized in Latin America at Washington's behest denied hearings? Why were less than one percent of all German citizens in the United States interned, while the U.S.-orchestrated deportation program led to the expulsion of perhaps 30 percent of the Germans in Guatemala, 25 percent in Costa Rica, 20 percent in Colombia, more than half in Honduras?[10] It was not because Germans in Tegucigalpa or San José were more enthusiastic partisans of the Third Reich than those in Manhattan's Yorkville or in Milwaukee. There were some eight thousand members of the Nazi Party in all of Latin America, most of them in Argentina, Brazil, and Chile (countries not involved in the deportations).[11] There were ten thousand to twenty-five thousand members of the U.S. equivalent, the German-American Bund.[12] Twenty-two thousand people packed a Bund rally at Madison Square Garden in February 1939 to cheer Nazi speechmakers.[13] The evidence does not indicate that Germans in Latin America outdid their fellow citizens in the United States in their support for Hitler.

The difference lies elsewhere. The U.S. government pursued two different policies toward German alien enemies depending upon where they lived because of the U.S. view of Latin America as a vulnerable, dependent region where latinos are helpless and foreigners are the real actors; because of the poor quality of the intelligence operation that was supposed to find subversives to the south; and because Germans living in Latin America presented another challenge: they were making important inroads into Latin American markets.

In the mid-1930s, with worldwide depression and high protectionist tariffs leaving Latin Americans with few places to sell their goods, Germany began a vigorous campaign of exclusive trade agreements, barter exchange, export subsidies, and inflated prices for Latin American products that led to a spectacular expansion of German trade – at the direct expense of the United States. It was a bitter conflict. "Germany exports or dies," proclaimed Adolf Hitler, who also needed raw materials for his war machine. "We must sell abroad more of these surpluses," Secretary of State Cordell Hull declared while on a trip to Latin America. President Roosevelt's efforts to spur a domestic recovery could rise or fall with foreign trade, and the news from Latin America was worrisome. In the first year of its aggressive new trade strategy, Germany's exports to the region doubled, while U.S. exports declined. The trend continued into the late 1930s, while U.S. manufacturers and chambers of commerce pleaded for government assistance to hold their ground.[14]

As with the fear of military invasion, U.S. officials believed the German economic offensive depended upon the collaboration of Germans residing in Latin America. German immigrants, far more willing to settle down than the typical sojourning Yankee, applied "their undeniable efficiency and business acumen" to create a distribution network second to none, explained a State Department analysis; it was their presence on the ground that gave Germany an advantage over the United States. As hostility between the two great powers increased, it would not have occurred to most people in Washington to draw a distinction between military and economic aims in the quest for national security. Latin American "interests" will follow trade routes, Secretary of War Henry L. Stimson warned Congress. Roosevelt economic adviser Bernard Baruch predicted that "German economic penetration could bring [Latin America] under her control without firing a shot."[15]

For those entrusted with guaranteeing the safety of the United States, then, German economic competition was a security issue, and they believed its commercial success rested on the work of its expatriates. Yet as the threat of a military attack on the Western Hemisphere receded after Stalingrad and Midway, the deportation program came to focus increasingly upon individuals who could in no way be tied to Nazi activity, but had acquired significant economic positions. Economic issues gradually replaced security concerns near the midpoint of the deportation program, almost entirely supplanting the early notion of removing subversive Germans with an unsentimental drive to commandeer market share from the Germans who remained. This process, again, required the violation of the principles of the Good Neighbor policy, through such measures as the threat of economic devastation, to overcome Latin American attempts to preserve a measure of the German presence as an alternative to the often unhappy reliance on U.S. capital. Deporting and interning people who posed no security threat in order to improve the economic position of the United States may have served certain U.S. interests, but it further diminished the credibility of earlier rationales for the highly disputed program, and it increased resentment at such hegemonic behavior.

Lack of knowledge about – often coupled with utter disdain for – Latin America has been the source of much of the regrettable history of U.S. policy toward the region. However, in this era, the United States was not alone in its beliefs about the Germans of Latin America: the view from Berlin was equally blurred. Party organizers in the overseas department who lacked any important role in the Third Reich exploited a tradition of pan-Germanist sentiment among the emigrants to try to turn patriotism into allegiance and allegiance into material support. Their hopes for the German expatriates faintly echoed U.S. fears: both sides misconstrued expressions of group solidarity and ethnic and national pride among the Germans of Latin America as a sign of their readiness to collaborate in war. If U.S. policy was objectionable, German policy was disastrous: the Nazis' ineptitude and bullying tactics further damaged Germany's standing, alienated potential converts, and provoked a destructive backlash against the communities they were supposedly fortifying. That did not prevent Ernst Bohle, head of the *Auslandsorganisation* (foreign organization) of the Nazi Party, from parading his ignorance when he boasted in 1939 that "today, the Reich can rely on Germandom abroad much more securely than in 1914."[16]

Most of the German emigrants themselves knew better, as did their Latin American neighbors. But to uninformed outsiders, whether in Washington or Berlin, the Germans living in Latin America seemed to be the key to Nazi aspirations for dominating the region by military, political, or economic means. The perceived threat – or false hope – was located in their persons. This view became conventional wisdom by 1941, so that by the time the United States entered the war, although there was no specific plan to expel thousands of German civilians from their homes in Latin America and intern them in camps in the United States, no such plan was needed. The deportations were the consequence of misplaced security concerns and an economic struggle that focused on the German inhabitants themselves.

If many of the internees were wholly blameless, the enthusiasm for Hitler some of them exhibited makes sympathy stick in the throat. But that repugnance should not distract us from an accurate assessment of the other factors at work – ethnic prejudice, wartime fears, a belief in Latin American inferiority, and economic opportunism – that helped bring them and their less enthusiastic compatriots into the camps, nor prevent us from recognizing the damage caused to inter-American relations.

Misperceptions of the kind that propelled the campaign to remove Germans from Latin America also made U.S. officials anxious to defend against another imagined threat: that allegedly posed by the arrival in the Western Hemisphere of Jewish refugees fleeing Europe. The rejection of European Jews seeking asylum in the United States is well known. Less so is the story of the several thousand Jews placed in a special holding facility at Bergen-Belsen by the Nazis, in order that they might be traded for German civilians held by the Allies. Such an exchange could have taken place, involving Germans from Latin America who were willing to be repatriated. This book explains for the first time how the Latin American connection could have saved thousands of lives, and how the State Department frustrated attempts to bring the project to fruition.

The deportation and internment program was, by any calculation, a net loss. It worsened U.S.–Latin American relations in a period of elevated hopes for long-term improvement. It deprived many people who posed no threat to U.S. interests of their livelihoods and property, and in the absence of due process forced them to spend the war years imprisoned behind barbed wire. It diverted precious resources that could have been used to fight the real war. It required the violation of international and national law. It encouraged corruption within Latin American countries, while tightening unofficial collaboration between U.S. and Latin American police and intelligence establishments, fostering the kind of extralegal approach to internal security throughout the region that proved so harmful during the latter half of the twentieth century. It even played a direct role in the failure to rescue several thousand people who were endangered, and then murdered, by the real Nazis in Europe. And it accomplished all of this while doing very little to enhance U.S. or regional security.

NAZIS AND GOOD NEIGHBORS

In this book, while the history of the deportation program is a central concern, it also serves as a point of departure for examining larger themes implicit in four readings of the title.

"Nazis and Good Neighbors" refers to the foreign policies of Germany and the United States toward Latin America during a time when the tenures of Adolf Hitler and Franklin D. Roosevelt happened to coincide. The years between Roosevelt's inaugural in 1933 and the onset of the war represented the high-water mark of U.S.–Latin American relations. But the Nazi menace, both the real one emanating from Europe and the largely imaginary one in Latin America, placed that system of cooperation under stress and would bring the abbreviated period of U.S. noninterference to an end, as

Washington backed its demands for the expulsion of local Germans and the expropriation of their property with diplomatic and economic tactics that belied its self-description as a good neighbor. Latin Americans complained vigorously, and U.S. officials admitted privately: the deportation program made the Good Neighbor policy a casualty of the war.

The second reading of the title divides the Germans of Latin America into two separate camps: the "Nazis" and the "good neighbors." The U.S. government tried and failed to make this distinction. The difference was never clear to the officials running the deportation program, whose conflicting instructions sometimes called for them to target dangerous Nazis and leave peaceful Germans alone and, at other times, declared that all Germans were dangerous simply by virtue of their national origin – a principle that helped fill the camps with many good neighbors. So, too, did the realization by several Latin American leaders that seizing the property of their German neighbors could be greatly simplified by calling them Nazis and handing them over to the United States. Concretely, this study uses archival records from seven countries, including 531 postwar reviews conducted by the U.S. government and analyzed in this book for the first time, to establish that only a minority of the deportees conceivably warranted the label of "dangerous enemy alien."

Third and most controversially, from the point of view of some Latin Americans (and most Germans), one could be both a "Nazi" and a "good neighbor." Germans, even nationalistic ones, had long enjoyed an admiration in Latin America that sometimes verged on idolization. Though this perplexed their U.S. rivals, Germans had earned a place in the hearts of many Latin Americans by putting down roots, learning the local language, and making a contribution to economic development out of all proportion to their numbers, without seeking the dominance over Latin American affairs exerted by the United States. Many Latin American officials doubted whether any local Germans, Party members or otherwise, actually posed a threat of any kind, political or economic, and were persuaded to expel some of their most favored residents only reluctantly. After the war, they fought to get them back. While Nazi racial views offended many latinos, the largely white ruling elites of countries from Cuba to Chile believed that they, too, sat atop a natural racial hierarchy. Nor was the United States a society free of official and unofficial racial discrimination, as latinos who had been there knew all too well. Despite the sharp differences between the two great powers competing for their sympathy and support, Latin American leaders saw themselves not as participants in a clash between good and evil, but as leaders responsible for pursuing their own national interests by playing off one great power against the next.

Finally, the title raises a question that is at the heart of any attempt to understand the fascist era, whether in Germany or elsewhere. How could good neighbors – good people – become Nazis?* Except for a small number of activists and a smaller number of spies, the Germans of Latin America who joined the Party were not nationalist fanatics. Patriotism, opportunism, and group pressure, rather than zealotry or racism, led many to sign membership cards. Expatriates who had grown up in the Germany of Kaiser Wilhelm before World War I, and who believed the tenuous interwar democracy of the Weimar Republic was responsible for Germany's decline, welcomed the advent of a strong leader promising economic renewal and national greatness. It is doubtful that anyone living in Germany after 1933 could have failed to be confronted with the hatred and violence inherent in Hitler's methods. For those who lived an ocean away, it could be another matter. At that distance, they were often unable "to see the true state of affairs in a society organized for total war and ridden by the Gestapo," as a U.S. intelligence report put it.[17] The activities of local Nazi groups were far from benign – they included social boycotts of Jews and the suppression of dissident views within the German communities – but many members experienced their meetings as an extension of the nationalist spirit and group solidarity they had long nurtured in their emigrant enclaves. The very fact that good people could be lured into the ranks of the Nazis should offer more cause for concern than the blithe assurance that every German who supported Hitler was simply evil and thus utterly unlike ourselves. They may not have been so different. Such a conclusion is, if anything, more troubling.

WHAT THIS BOOK IS NOT ABOUT

This book is not about the experience of the Japanese internees from Latin America, nor that of the Italians.

The effort to combat the influence of Axis nationals in Latin America and to remove them physically from the region was developed almost entirely as a response to the German threat, which loomed much larger in the eyes of anxious U.S. officials. Germans lived in every Latin American country and had achieved a level of social standing and financial success far beyond that of the more recent and less numerous Japanese arrivals. In the nightmare scenarios of subversives taking over Latin American countries, they were "Nazis," not "Japs." As Secretary of State Cordell Hull remarked, "The problem of the Japanese is in most countries relatively small."[18] Except in Peru and to some extent in Panama, Japanese who were seized and deported to U.S. camps were swept up almost as an afterthought by a program put in place to collect Germans.[19]

---

* Here the term "Nazi" refers to Germans in Latin America who enrolled in Nazi organizations or openly supported Hitler, not to participants or collaborators in the Holocaust and other war crimes; the subjects of this book were too remote to be involved in any of the horrors perpetrated in Europe.

The smaller number of Italian internees seized in Latin America – 167 cases plus family members – were mostly captured merchant sailors and repatriating diplomats plus a few suspected fascists, along with unfortunate victims of poor intelligence work. There was never any discussion of an "Italian fifth column." Italians were easily assimilated into Latin American society because of linguistic, cultural, and religious affinity, and support for fascism among the largely working-class Italian expatriates, often more sympathetic to anarchist movements, was low. President Roosevelt, like most in his government, was not worried about them. "I don't care so much about the Italians," FDR told his attorney general, Francis Biddle. "They are a lot of opera singers, but the Germans are different, they may be dangerous."[20]

This book is not principally about the wartime policies of Argentina, Brazil, Chile, and Mexico, nor about U.S. relations with their governments, nor about the experience of the large German communities in those countries, for one reason: the ABC countries and Mexico did not agree to deliver German nationals for internment in the United States. Less beholden to U.S. influence than the fifteen smaller countries that did cooperate with the U.S. deportation program, each had reasons of its own to choose an alternative policy. Argentina, influenced by historically close ties to the German military and determined to maintain its strong self-image as an alternative pole to the United States, pursued an independent policy during the war that was inclined to pro-fascism and included minimal interference with its German population. Chile, with nearly three thousand miles of indefensible coastline exposed to potential attack, sought while strongly tilting towards the Allies to remain officially neutral in the conflict for as long as possible, comparing its policy to that of the United States towards Britain from 1939 to 1941; the Chilean judicial system dealt with those German residents the government believed to be dangerous. Brazil and Mexico, allied with the United States at an early stage, created their own internment facilities for dangerous Axis nationals and firmly refused U.S. requests to let Washington handle their internal security programs.[21]

The smaller countries of the Caribbean basin and northern South America were correspondingly more vulnerable to U.S. pressure. The largest number of German deportees from Latin America came from Colombia, Guatemala, Costa Rica, and Ecuador; for that reason, the experience of these countries is emphasized.

Although U.S. intelligence practices are analyzed here, this book does not focus on espionage and counterespionage in Latin America. Nearly all of the German spies actually at work in the region were in the ABC countries and Mexico, and the successful U.S. countermeasures have been well described elsewhere.[22] With only eight of the 4,058 German deportees even allegedly involved in espionage, and the record of sabotage "practically nil" according to the FBI, spying and sabotage were red herrings as far as the internments were concerned.[23]

THE CHAPTERS

The book is organized into chapters as follows. Chapter 1, "Contamination," depicts the German communities of Latin America as relatively autonomous outposts of Germanness, dedicated to maintaining a cultural identity firmly rooted in the homeland, but with independent interests that did not always mesh with plans emanating from Berlin. The manipulation of national symbols, outright coercion, and the backing of a popularly acclaimed regime brought the expatriates into line, but their support for Nazism was not profound. Publicly offensive Nazi Party activities tarred the whole community with the same brush, setting the stage for the far-reaching deportations to follow U.S. entry into the war, despite Germany's lack of interest in the region.

Chapter 2, "Assessment," examines the hopelessly inadequate attempts by a U.S. intelligence system still in its infancy to identify dangerous Nazis, the contribution of yellow journalism to the distorted impressions conveyed to U.S. officials, and the pivotal role played by a few refugees and German exiles practicing amateur counterespionage, whose experience with Nazism in Europe made them predisposed to believe the worst about their German neighbors – and to report the worst to their US contacts.

Chapter 3, "Blacklisting," examines the first major violation of the Good Neighbor's promise to respect Latin American sovereignty: the decision to pursue unilateral economic warfare by blacklisting companies and individuals residing in Latin America without consulting the governments concerned. The protests by Latin Americans at this intimate interference inside their countries call attention to some of the damage done to the Good Neighbor policy by the campaign against the region's Germans.

Chapter 4, "Deportation," describes the rapid evolution of an unplanned regional deportation program from its origins as a limited security measure. The chapter follows the diplomatic maneuverings undertaken to persuade Latin American rulers to hand over their German residents, measures that sometimes reverted to pre-Rooseveltian pressure tactics. But Latin American leaders were not merely "puppets on a string" controlled by Washington.[24] Pursuing their own national or personal interests, some resisted, evaded, or creatively interpreted U.S. demands, even turning the anti-German pressure into an opportunity to expel political opponents and seize valuable property. The chapter reveals the mechanisms of arrest, deportation, and transportation to the United States and provides detailed information about many of the internees, showing how insubstantial were the accusations that they threatened national security.

Chapter 5, "Internment," recounts the conditions in the camps of the United States and Latin America, which ranged from the filthy, overcrowded state prison at Stringtown, Oklahoma, to the well-kept lawns and colonial-style buildings of Seagoville, Texas, built to resemble a college campus.

Family separation led to protests by the male internees and their newly politicized wives, leading to a change in policy to permit family reunification. Special attention is paid to the experience of the more than eighty Jewish refugees taken from Latin America and interned in the United States; along with the astonishing fact of their internment in camps designed for their enemies, their statements support the conclusion that only a small minority of the internees were active Nazis who used coercive methods and the backing of the German regime to try to enforce control over a compliant majority – just as they had done in the Latin American expatriate communities from which they came.

Chapter 6, "Justice," recounts the gradual discovery by civil rights-minded Justice Department officials that they were holding many inoffensive civilians as security cases, leading to vehement disputes with the Department of State. Hitherto unpublished testimony from a U.S. official with unique inside knowledge of the deportation program throughout the hemisphere confirms documentary evidence that the internees, for the most part, posed no danger to the United States.

Chapter 7, "Expropriation," considers the economic aspects of the deportation program, which devastated the German commercial presence in a region where the United States had long believed itself naturally entitled to preeminence. A preoccupation with a potential military threat set the deportations in motion, but they were extended and expanded well after such concern had faded, in order to ensure the permanent elimination of a major trade rival. The position of Latin American leaders in this regard varied considerably from one instance to the next: some resisted U.S. economic warfare policies as interference in their internal affairs, and sought to protect German investment as an alternative to overdependence on the United States; others turned U.S. insistence on expropriating German property to their own advantage, doling out confiscated farms to their cronies, and balancing their national budgets with seized German assets.

Chapter 8, "Repatriation," examines the German government's response to the deportation program and recounts the stop-and-go attempts to repatriate many of the deportees to the Third Reich. Initially, Washington planned to remove dangerous Germans from Latin America and ship them to Germany, to be exchanged for Americans held in Europe. Britain, on the front lines, objected to supplying the enemy with any more men – especially those who might be useful to the war effort. Disappointed with the "quality" of the impoverished, largely foreign-born American citizens brought home in an early trade, the U.S. government decided to keep potentially dangerous Germans in internment camps and terminated the exchanges. When German officials were unable to find many nationals of the American countries to use as bargaining chips, they offered to release thousands of Jews from concentration camps instead – a genuine opportunity for rescue thwarted by the U.S. government.

The Epilogue, "The New Menace," recounts the disillusionment of officials who had spent the war trying to extract Nazis from Latin America only to realize when it was over that the people they had interned were not the dangerous agents they had imagined. As the U.S. government shifted its focus from hunting Nazis to fighting Communists, some of the same faulty practices established in the anti-German campaign were redirected toward the new enemy – producing even more ineffective foreign policy and a sanguinary record that fueled further conflict with the rest of the Americas. The campaign against the Germans living in the region not only ruined the temporary gains of the Good Neighbor policy and failed to achieve its central goal of improving hemispheric security; it also created a precedent for the excesses of the anti-Communist crusade that obsessed the United States over the next fifty years of relations with a Latin America it seems never to be able to perceive with clarity.

I

Contamination

"Gott beschütze uns vor   "God protect us from
   Sturm und Wind,   the storm, the breeze,
  und vor Deutschen,   and from Germans who are overseas."
  die im Ausland sind."   –German sailors' proverb

Guatemala City, February 1936. Gerhard Hentschke, a 41-year-old sales-man, has achieved a renown unattainable back home. His official post as German commercial attaché is mere cover for far more important duties: chief of the Nazi Party in Guatemala, self-styled "personal representative of the *Führer*." Even in this remote corner of Germandom, Hentschke and his disciples work tirelessly, "pervaded by the true national socialist spirit, to carry out our part in the erection of the New Germany, of the Third Reich." Party membership is growing, especially among younger men. Members who profane the race by marrying Guatemalans are expelled. An organized social boycott, soon to be enforced by block patrols in the German neighborhoods, pressures local Germans to break with their Jewish friends and fire their Jewish employees. The Nazi takeover of the German Club's executive board is not yet complete – older, established Germans are putting up surpris-ingly tenacious resistance – but even Hentschke's own followers cannot dis-suade him from hoisting, in violation of Guatemalan law, a swastika flag on German flag day.[1]

Not every stratagem is successful. The unhappy German minister to Guatemala, Erich Kraske, unable to soothe the many conflicts sown by Party activists, frustrates Hentschke's bid to edit his invitation lists for of-ficial events. (Representing Guatemala's discordant German community "is indeed an honor, but not a pleasure," Kraske will grimly inform his succes-sor.) President Jorge Ubico, whose jails are filled with his critics and whose palace is crammed with busts of Napoleon, takes a benevolent view of the affluent German community. But he rejects Hentschke's startling demand for personal veto power over all unknown foreigners requesting an audience with the Guatemalan president.[2]

Now, while his revered Führer dispatches troops to occupy the Rhineland, Hentschke undertakes a struggle on his own modest scale. A group of prominent German citizens has petitioned Minister Kraske to restrain the Nazi boss, since he is disrupting German unity and disturbing the business climate, so dependent on good relations with the host government. Members of the board of directors of the *Colegio Alemán*, the best school in the country with a majority of Guatemalan students, are threatening to resign over the nazification of the curriculum and the introduction of the Hitler salute. Hentschke and the teachers, most of them Nazis imported from Germany and paid by Berlin, continue their indoctrination program and fight openly for control of the school board.

President Ubico, a man of short temper and brusque decisions, has had enough of the Germans' squabbling and the propagandizing of students. He orders the school closed. Hentschke's infuriated response – "who does that Indian think he is?" – speaks eloquently to the scrawny growth of the Nazi weed on Latin American soil.[3]

THE GERMAN COMMUNITIES

If Latin America has been all too often the stomping ground of the Ugly American, racist Nazi activists who appeared on the scene in the 1930s provided a comparable archetype in the Ugly German. Thuggish upstarts like Gerhard Hentschke, not only in Guatemala but elsewhere in the region, offended many a long-established immigrant and sparked a backlash that ultimately devastated the same German communities they claimed to champion. While recruiters for the Nazi Party were not typical of German expatriates, their mobilization attempt, although not very successful in Latin America, was partly responsible for provoking an anti-German response in the form of the deportation program that is at the center of this study.

Large-scale German migration to Latin America began in the middle of the nineteenth century. Even before then, German volunteers had sailed with Cortés and Magellan and served in the revolutionary army of South American independence hero Simón Bolívar.[4] But the first significant wave of German immigration followed the failed liberal revolutions of 1848, and larger waves followed in the 1880s and 1890s and after World War I.

Of all European immigrants to Latin America, Germans received the warmest welcome. The influential writer and future Argentine president D. F. Sarmiento in 1860 praised "their proverbial honesty, their tireless devotion to work, and their pacific character."[5] A Chilean government report in 1865 found Germans to be the most preferable kind of immigrant.[6] Germans benefited from enduring Latin American affection for the scientist-explorer Alexander von Humboldt, exalted by Bolívar as "a great man who, with his eyes, pulled America out of her ignorance, and with his pen, painted her as beautiful as her own nature."[7] Until Chancellor Otto von Bismarck's unification of the separate German states in 1871 created the modern German nation, German arrivals had a special appeal, because they had the backing of no powerful imperial state, no France, Spain, Great Britain, or United States ready at a moment's notice to send gunboats to Latin American ports to enforce the claims of one of their nationals. Latin American political leaders tended to embrace European immigrants in general for bringing "sobriety" and "culture" as a necessary corrective to local "creole indolence" – a kind of racial flattery that would make German expatriates that much more receptive to twentieth-century racist appeals.[8]

Most of the immigrants retained a powerful sense of their identity as outsiders in the Catholic, *mestizo*, Romance language-speaking societies of Latin America, far more so than did their counterparts in the United States. The newcomers were mainly Protestant, and they founded their own churches to practice their faith. German was spoken at home and passed down through generations. Germans in South America defended their language against the intrusion of modern vocabulary taken for granted in the old country – *Feuerwagen*, not *Lokomotive*; *Lichtfett*, not *Petroleum*.[9]

In many parts of Latin America, Germans often married within their own community. Among the more bizarre examples of the separatist trend were the isolated "colonies" of Tovar in Venezuela and Nueva Germania in Paraguay, the latter founded by Friedrich Nietzsche's crusading, anti-Semitic sister Elisabeth. These virtually autonomous little outposts were bound by a rule requiring the expulsion of any German who married a native – a foolhardy scheme by the master race, against which biology was the best revenge, as inbreeding led to feeblemindedness and birth defects among the settlers' descendants.[10] But these were exceptionally extreme cases. Elsewhere the standards were more relaxed, and German polite society would sometimes accept intermarriages as long as the non-German spouse, usually the wife, kept a German household, and the children received a German education.

At exactly what point one ceased being a "German" and became a "Latin American" was anything but clear. Unlike most countries of the world, citizenship in Germany rested on the principle of *jus sanguinis*, the right of blood, which attributed nationality according to ancestry rather than birthplace.[11] The principle was codified by the Delbrück nationality law of 1913 (still in force as late as 1999). The result was not a little confusion over the status of second-generation immigrants and an exaggerated emphasis on language as a marker of national allegiance. Latin American governments and populations therefore did not always distinguish between *Reichsdeutschen*, German citizens, and *Volksdeutschen*, persons of German descent who were no longer citizens of Germany. (The two groups together were the *Auslandsdeutschen*, Germans abroad.)

1. The range of emigrant experience. Prosperous German emigrant farmers, still wedded to their old-country style of dress, pose with their bumper crop of cabbages in Paradiestal Kolonie (Paradise Valley Colony) near Monterey, Mexico, in 1923. Credit: Deutsches Auslands-Institut, 137/7883 Bundesarchiv, Koblenz.

A vast array of separate cultural institutions hardened the immigrants' sense of their difference. "The first thing that two Germans do when they meet abroad is to found three associations," wrote an observer, and the Germans of Latin America proved this with enthusiasm, creating a profusion of *Vereine*, clubs or associations for recreational, educational, cultural, and charitable purposes. There were singing clubs, sports clubs, beer-drinking clubs, mutual aid societies, reading circles, volunteer fire brigades. German emigrants recognized their clannish propensity by jokingly accusing each other of being *Vereinsmeier*, joiners. The *Vereine* were sanctuaries of familiarity and the focal points of community, cementing the ties that linked expatriate Germans to one another and to the homeland they had left physically but not mentally. Their flourishing numbers attest to their vital role in the life of the German abroad: by the 1930s, there were 130 associations in Ijui, Brazil, alone; 48 in Valdivia, Chile; 160 in Buenos Aires.[12]

The emigrants' contact with the homeland tended to wane over time, vitiating any truly energetic nationalism on their part. What remained was a strong cultural identification, and a patriotic regard for Germany's successes and regret over its failures. In contrast to the later Nazi era, the German regime made no substantial demands on the expatriates. They knew, of course, where their own interests lay: in maintaining friendly relations

2. An impoverished German family dries tea in Paraguay's isolated Colonia In-dependencia. 1920s. Credit: Deutsches Auslands-Institut, 137/17333 Bundesarchiv, Koblenz.

with their Latin American neighbors, customers, and governors. Nurturing a German identity was no impediment to this – not yet.[13] Most German immigrants occupied an in-between space, loyal but apart, welcomed but unincorporated, in Latin America but not of it.

YANQUIS AND ALEMANES

U.S. observers acknowledged the concord achieved by the German immigrants, as opposed to the conflicted relationship between U.S. citizens and Latin Americans. Nelson Rockefeller, whose youthful curiosity and investor's concern for Latin American affairs grew into years of travel and government service in the region, lamented that the image U.S. citizens projected in Latin America was of "a dollar-conscious group of people who had no interest but making money." He liked to tell the story of attending a dinner party in 1939 in an unnamed Latin American country, seated between the country's president and the wife of a U.S. businessman. She had lived in Latin America for eighteen years, but Rockefeller found himself translating for his dinner companions even though his own Spanish was still poor. After dinner, Rockefeller asked the woman why she didn't speak Spanish after so long. Her response was emblematic of attitudes he often encountered among U.S. citizens: "Why should I learn – who would I talk to if I did?"[14]

In contrast, even the FBI acknowledged that "the Germans are generally well-liked. . . . They came to the territory and worked hard, proved to be

3. Charley Hirtz was one of those German farmers who, by settling in the Amazon, acquired "the halo of the jungle" – the respect of Ecuadorians for enduring harsh conditions and fulfilling the terms of an agricultural visa instead of giving up and moving to the city. (One of Hirtz's compatriots, recounting the many years of insect plagues and failed harvests, calculated that he had survived thirty years of Amazon existence partly by eating ten thousand bananas.) The remoteness of his homestead did not prevent Hirtz from joining Ecuador's Nazi Party. Nor did the lack of important sabotage targets in the area deter U.S. officials from arranging Hirtz's deportation and internment in the United States. Credit: Courtesy Foto Hirtz, Quito.

4. Hirtz and his friend Bio Beate are paid a visit by their neighbors in 1934. Credit: Courtesy Foto Hirtz, Quito.

progressive colonists and honest businessmen. They lived moderately and unpretentiously, learned the language and married into the local families."[15] They also tended to be involved in small-scale retail trade, as opposed to the big North American extractive industries like oil, mining, and agribusiness, and they therefore depended on fostering good relations with local consumers and enjoying the benevolence of local rulers.

The popularity of the *Auslandsdeutschen* in Latin America rose and fell with Germany's imperial ambitions. At the turn of the century, Germany greatly expanded its navy, unsuccessfully sought a naval base in the Caribbean, and made plans for an anticipated conflict with the United States in its effort to gain markets in Latin America. The U.S. yellow press and the navy and shipbuilding industry played up the German menace as an incentive for bigger budgets and to diminish resistance to U.S. expansion in the region. The high point of tension came in 1903, when German, British, and Italian warships shelled Venezuelan ports, demanding repayment of loans. The Venezuelan crisis ended with a negotiated settlement in 1904, and Germany returned its attention to Europe – although two decades would pass before alarm over the "German peril" in Latin America subsided in North American public discourse.[16]

World War I provided the first serious challenge to the delicate poise of the *Auslandsdeutschen*, balancing fidelity to their origins against loyalty to their new home. Expatriate communities of many stripes were swept by war fever, as French, British, and German nationals sailed back across the

Atlantic to join their enthusiastic compatriots signing up to fight in Europe. Five hundred Germans in Chile volunteered for enlistment. One hundred fifty-six Germans from Argentina died in the trenches, and many more served. German businesses in Latin America imposed a voluntary war tax on themselves; in Chile, this netted 2.5 million marks by 1918.[17] This was an active form of transnationalism, with the members of the diasporic community giving their wealth or even their lives for the cause of the homeland. Still, with all European communities involved in similar fashion, and most Latin American countries remaining neutral, expatriate jingoism did not seem to pose a security threat to the host states during World War I.

Britain had imposed blacklists on German businesses abroad in 1915, and when the United States entered the war two years later, it too issued "Enemy Trade Lists" so broadly conceived they could include anyone with a German surname. In South America, resentment against this form of U.S. intervention in the internal affairs of other states – especially when the distant European war seemed to have so little urgency – provoked a backlash of sympathy for Germany. The blacklists were in this sense counterproductive, because they encouraged neutralism among Latin Americans whose fear of Yankee domination was greater than their suspicion of their German neighbors.[18]

A lesson could be drawn from the First World War experience. U.S. officials examining this record twenty years later would try to avoid making the same mistakes by narrowing the scope of the blacklist developed in World War II, but it, too, would have a similar effect.[19]

THE NEW EXPATRIATES

The end of the First World War and the economic collapse and political chaos that followed in Germany pushed a huge wave of demoralized and impoverished people out of the country. Branded as aggressors by the Treaty of Versailles, Germans were personae non gratae nearly everywhere, except on "the last free continent," as Latin America was called among those seeking a route out of national isolation. A hundred thousand new immigrants arrived in Latin America during the decade following the war.[20] These despondent veterans, embittered nationalists, and jobless drifters changed the character of the expatriate communities they joined, opening the way in the 1930s to a seductive ideology that would fill old pan-Germanist bottles with an intoxicating, virulent new wine.

The new immigrants were as diverse as the population of Germany itself, but the postwar wave was characterized by its high proportion of young men alienated from the frail democracy of the Weimar Republic they had left and unimpressed by the societies they were joining. They included cashiered military officers and members of the *Freikorps*, right-wing veterans' clubs responsible for much of the brutal postwar violence in Germany.[21] Some of the post–World War I emigrants published travelogues, often printed in the hundreds of thousands of copies, laced with language that revealed a racist disdain for their Latin American neighbors. Werner Hopp blamed the "idiocy" of the Quechua Indians on their "only very low mental capacity" and innate inferiority to whites, which rendered them incapable of participating in modern life. Other writers routinely referred to *indios* as "louts" and "wild savages" with "eyes close together like apes." They dubbed *mestizos* "half-breeds" and described them as lazy, thieving, superstitious, and cowardly.[22]

Meanwhile Germans long residing in Latin America could hardly conceive of the changes taking place in their distant homeland. If anything, they were more surprised by defeat in war than Germans who had witnessed firsthand the long stalemate in the trenches or the relentless decline of morale on the home front. In Argentina, the most widely read German-language paper, the *Deutsche La Plata Zeitung*, was still predicting German victory two weeks before the armistice of 1918. The shock of defeat helped create the legend of the "stab in the back" so central to the Nazis' later claim of national betrayal by Jews and Communists; most of the German-language press adopted this myth as the only way to account for the humiliation of Versailles. Far less radical than the new immigrants, the established Germans were nevertheless more loyal to the Kaiser they knew than to the new democracy they did not. The expatriates demonstrated their hostility to the new German government by flying the old black-white-red imperial flag from their homes and businesses and *Vereine* instead of the new black-red-gold flag of Weimar, a protest so emotionally charged and widely staged that it perplexed German diplomats and overshadowed official community events for years.[23]

The radicalism of the new immigrants and the disconsolation of the old made both groups more receptive to a harsh, revanchist form of pan-Germanism when it arrived at the end of the decade. There was no shortage of messengers to import this new ideology. Reinhold Wulle, a right-wing, ethnic chauvinist politician, made a speaking tour of Latin America in 1927. General Karl Litzmann, a war hero and Nazi deputy in the Reichstag, made his lecture tour in 1932. The writings of Oswald Spengler and other antidemocratic authors were widely disseminated by German-language publications in Latin America.[24]

THE NAZI OFFENSIVE ABROAD: THE AUSLANDSORGANISATION

The first Nazi group overseas was founded by Bruno Fricke (who later left the Party) in Paraguay in 1929. Small, isolated Nazi organizations sprouted in several Latin American capitals in the next four years. But most German emigrants tried to ignore these first coarse, noisy national socialists. It was not merely their grating style that kept the Nazis from making many early converts. The conservative *Auslandsdeutschen* abhorred the disorder, the acid partisan rivalries that hobbled the Weimar government and regularly spilled onto the streets of Germany's cities. Shrill local Nazi groups now threatened to import the same conflicts to the staid overseas communities. Local leaders of the NSDAP (*Nationalsozialistische Deutsche Arbeiterpartei*, or German National Socialist Workers Party, official name of the Nazi Party) had no social prestige in the German colonies; their extolling the supremacy of German culture and calls for maintaining the purity of German blood, even if they matched the discreet beliefs of some emigrants, seemed in extremely poor taste where maintaining respectful relations with latinos was crucial to continued social and financial success. The Party's insistence on absolute obedience to hierarchical authority, the *Führerprinzip*, did not go over well among expatriates accustomed to congenial discussions. The Nazis quickly made powerful enemies by launching fierce public attacks on established community leaders for inadequately defending German values. Where Nazi leaders moderated their tone and cooperated with the German establishment, as in Chile, they received a commensurately warmer welcome – and slightly higher enrollments.[25]

Hitler's rise to power in 1933 changed the equation, and the influence of the Nazi Party in Latin America began to grow. Previously a small collection of boisterous troublemakers, the Nazis moved to back up their transnational organizing efforts with the machinery of the state. The first targets were the *Vereine*, the centers of community life for the *Auslandsdeutschen*. In country after country, NSDAP officials marched into meetings with the boards of directors of German schools and German clubs to demand control as the true representatives of the Führer. They were backed by a newly empowered division of the Party tasked with converting overseas Germans to Nazism: the *Auslandsorganisation* (AO or Foreign Organization).

The AO had a precursor in the *Auslands-Abteilung* (Foreign Department), established in April 1931 under singularly infelicitous leadership. Hans Nieland, a Nazi Reichstag deputy, spoke no foreign language and had never been outside Germany when he was charged with recruiting overseas Germans to the cause. As his first move, he hired his father and sister to run the office. Tiny Nazi cells were organized in some thirty countries over the next two years. In the fall of 1932, Nieland's department was renamed the *Abteilung für Deutsche im Ausland* (Department for Germans Abroad), and despite his meager achievements he was awarded the prized title of *Gauleiter*, the highest rank for a Party official.[26]

Nieland's ineffectiveness and nepotism had already driven one of his most talented aides, Ernst Bohle, to resign in disgust, and when the stakes were raised in 1933 with the Nazis' takeover of government, a bureaucratic power struggle broke out. By May, Nieland was out and Bohle was in, shepherded by his mentor, Hitler's deputy Rudolf Hess. Unlike Nieland, Bohle had substantial foreign experience. He was born in 1903 in Bradford, England, the son of a university professor and future Nazi Party stalwart who would serve as *Landesgruppenleiter* (NSDAP country chief) in South Africa. With support from Hess, another German born abroad (in Egypt), Bohle moved to strengthen the Party's hold over Germans in other countries. His department was renamed a final time in February 1934 as the *Auslandsorganisation*, responsible for all Party work outside Germany.[27]

Even under Bohle, however, the AO never achieved real influence within the Nazi party-state apparatus. In Berlin, he was something of a bad joke, possessing rank but not power; he was never a part of the inner circle of officials close to Hitler. But his organization did have jurisdiction over the Party-related activities of NSDAP members abroad.[28] Ambitious in his own fief, Bohle ordered his overseas cells to pursue three goals: to enroll more members, to win sympathy for Germany through propaganda, and above all, to seize control of the *Vereine*, carrying overseas the process of *Gleichschaltung*, the bringing into line of German institutions.

In Uruguay, Nazi recruiters were frustrated by an urban emigrant bourgeoisie satisfied with and protective of its success. In Chile, imported Nazis were expelled from the executive committees of the associations and German-Chileans resigned en masse when the AO attempted to take over the German-Chilean Chamber of Commerce in Santiago.[29] German consular dispatches from the early Nazi years reveal bitter resistance to the AO's effort to force the *Vereine* to conform to Nazi policies.[30] Not only the left-leaning but even nationalistic Germans fought back against the attempt to bring the cultural and business life of the communities under the thumb of Nazi officials. They complained that the AO was threatening the internal harmony of the German community and its relationship to the rest of the population, and that AO meddling was bad for business.

When they were denied the right to lead, the Nazis employed other strategies. One way to take over an association was for the Party to order its members to flood the membership rolls, as when seventy members of the NSDAP entered the Deutscher Verein of Santiago all at once. The principal German union in Chile, the *Deutsch-Chilenischer Bund* (DCB), fought off Nazi encroachment for two years, losing its director and its subsidy from Berlin in the process. But by late 1935, it was under Party control and started promoting national socialism in its publications. The Nazis also forced out the director of the *Deutscher Volksbund für Argentinien*, replacing him with a Party member who urged all Nazis to join. A third of the old membership resigned, thereby indicating their displeasure – but also consolidating Nazi control.[31]

The local Nazi groups were able to get large numbers of *Auslandsdeutschen* to join demonstrations, festivities, and holiday celebrations once the foreign service was nazified, because the participation of German diplomats gave these events an official character and association with national German holidays made these nonpartisan events in the eyes of the participants.[32] In Colombia, Ambassador Dittler issued a call to all *Volksgenossen* (a term often translated as "racial comrades," members of the German ethnic group), not just German citizens, to "demonstrate anew their belonging to the German *Volksgemeinschaft* ['racial community']" by participating in the German national holiday celebrations on 1 May and by displaying the German flag.[33] Many Germans in Brazil made a sharp distinction between the activities of the local NSDAP, which they found disastrous, and their enthusiasm for their Führer and the renewal of Germany. In 1935, there were rival May Day rallies in the German community at Curitiba in southeastern Brazil. The established German associations refused to provide the Nazis with a hall or to organize a joint celebration, so the Party held its own celebration. It was far less well attended than the traditional community event. Still, an outsider could be forgiven for missing the distinction: both events featured toasts to the new Germany, paeans to Hitler, and the singing of "Deutschland über Alles."[34]

By 1937, the disputes over control of the *Vereine* had largely been resolved in favor of the local Party groups. Only about 10 of the 350 German-Brazilian societies in Rio Grande do Sul were free of Nazi control. The hundreds of highly regarded German schools were dependent on Berlin for their budgets. Only one of them, the Pestalozzi-Schule in Buenos Aires, managed to avoid nazification of its faculty and curriculum.

Coercive measures and the backing of the Nazi regime played a significant role in persuading expatriate Germans to toe the Party line. Many workers employed by German firms were told to join the Nazi union, the *Deutsche Arbeitsfront* (DAF), or face losing their jobs. Professionals and shopkeepers were threatened with boycotts if they made trouble. AO fundraisers used extortionist techniques to extract "contributions" from German businesses and even required payroll deductions from workers' salaries. The money was supposed to aid charitable operations in Germany via the *Winterhilfe* (Winter Help Fund) and other campaigns, but a high proportion of the funds were drained off for local Party work. Embassies could refuse diplomatic protection to wayward German citizens or withhold passports, birth certificates, and other necessary documents; stubborn expatriates were threatened with confiscation of their property in Germany and reprisals against relatives there.[35] More violent methods were not unknown. Party members physically attacked the independent-minded director of the German School in Quito, Wilhelm Sacklowski, because he refused to expel Jewish pupils and tried to strike a balance between national socialist teachings and the traditional curriculum.[36]

Throughout Latin America's German communities in the late 1930s, the old ideal of expatriate solidarity and group amity gave way to suspicion and distrust. Snitches wrote letters to the AO denouncing neighbors or rivals who behaved in an "un-German" manner. Repatriates and travelers to Germany sometimes turned in the names of dissenters to the Gestapo.[37] Party courts, the *Uschla*, enforced extraterritorial compliance with the new rules of the German state among AO members.[38] Everywhere, anyone with relatives in Germany was vulnerable. "Even some who were not Nazis pretended to be," recalled an Ecuadorian who married into a German family. "Because they knew that looking over the shoulder of every German [in the Reich] was an SS man. And remember that many of these people had to travel to Germany or had relatives there."[39] Family ties were perhaps the strongest transnational links uniting expatriates to the homeland, and the Nazis exploited those ties ruthlessly.

OPPOSITION IN EXILE

There was an alternative to going along to get along, of course: breaking completely with the homeland regime and its local minions, becoming a dissident. A courageous few among the longtime German residents of Latin America did join the antifascist organizations founded by political exiles and refugees fleeing the Third Reich. Exile members of the German Communist Party (KPD) formed a popular front organization in Mexico to resist Nazism, *Freies Deutschland* (Free Germany). Weimar republicans and social democrats opted for the most part for the larger *Das Andere Deutschland* (The Other Germany), founded in Buenos Aires in 1937 by exiles grouped around a newspaper of the same name.[40]

In addition to offering social services, locating jobs and holding Spanish language classes, these groups performed valuable political and cultural

5. The many forms of Nazi efforts to mobilize allegiance to Germany among the expatriates. A singing lesson at Guatemala's German school (attended by German and Guatemalan students) takes place under a portrait of Adolf Hitler side-by-side with a poster and stuffed version of the quetzal bird, Guatemala's national symbol. Credit: Deutsches Ausland-Institut 137/58865, Bundesarchiv, Koblenz.

6. Guatemalan dockworkers load sacks of coffee donated by German plantation
owners for the *Winterhilfe* program designed to aid the poor in Germany – while
building ethnic solidarity across the Atlantic. Credit: Deutsches Ausland-Institut
137/40539, Bundesarchiv, Koblenz.

work. *El Libro Libre* (The Free Book), an exile press in Mexico, brought
out the writings of banned and exiled German authors. Anna Seghers, Egon
Erwin Kisch, and other notables created journals to provide publishing opportunities for exiled writers with no other way to make a living – and as a
way of getting critical information about Nazism into the public sphere.[41]
Exile activists in several countries tried their hand at counterespionage, passing intelligence on the "fifth column" to U.S. and British embassies. These
efforts were highly uneven, bringing erratic results. (See Chapter 2.)

Estimates of the total membership of the opposition are hard to come
by. The *Anti-Nazi Freiheitsbewegung* in Colombia, affiliated with *Das Andere
Deutschland*, had 250 members at its peak – compared to 300 in Colombia's
NSDAP. Most were exiles. The flagship paper of *Das Andere Deutschland* had
a circulation fluctuating between two thousand and five thousand. With total
Nazi Party membership in Latin America reaching about eight thousand,
it might be tempting to draw some facile conclusions about the relative
strengths of the movements for and against Hitler.[42]

That would be a mistake. To be sure, labeling the *Auslandsorganisation's* campaign of nazifying Latin America's Germans a "failure" or a "fiasco," as some authors have done, rightly points out how counterproductive were AO efforts to improve the standing of Germany and its expatriates.[43] Without a doubt, Bohle's office failed to meet any of its own goals. Party membership rarely exceeded 3 to 9 percent of German citizens in the principal Latin American countries.[44] Nazi activities created distrust and hostility toward Germany and the Germans, rather than drawing sympathy for the Nazi cause. The AO's wartime goal of promoting neutrality among Latin American states failed everywhere save Argentina, and a good case can be made that Argentina acted out of consideration for strategic relations with the great powers and a long-standing desire to resist U.S. dominance in the Western Hemisphere; local Party pressure was insignificant. On its own terms, then, the Nazi Party never came close to achieving its ambitions in Latin America.

THE PARTY ORGANIZATIONS

But just as US officials were wrong to portray the Germans as a monolithic bloc ready to march at a signal from Berlin, later writers were perhaps too ready to interpret raw membership figures and early incidents of resistance to AO takeover attempts as evidence that the AO also failed to gain influence among the *Auslandsdeutschen*.[45] The number of Party members should not be confused with the extent of support for Nazi Germany. Comparing Party lists to the total population of German citizens yields the figures of 3 to 9 percent for the most often-studied countries of Argentina, Brazil, Chile, and Mexico. However, in the German communities of the smaller countries, the percentage of Party members could be somewhat higher: around 10 percent in Guatemala, over 20 percent in Honduras, 30 percent in Haiti.[46]

Moreover, when one considers that becoming a Party member often entailed a serious commitment to organizing and attending meetings, perpetual fund-raising, and submission to party discipline, it seems possible that some people who were in agreement with the party's goals did not join for lack of time or interest in activism.[47]

One might try to gauge support for Nazism by adding to the NSDAP figures the members of Nazi-affiliated organizations such as the DAF workers' union, the *NS-Frauenschaft* (National Socialist Women's Union), and the *Hitlerjugend* (HJ, the Hitler Youth). But such a figure, too, would be misleading. Dedicated antifascists would not have been caught dead in such company, but the apolitical and the tepid might well have been attracted by the DAF's free Spanish, English, and accounting courses, its job-placement services, the regular afternoon coffee klatch and singing events of the *NS-Frauenschaft*, and the hiking and camping trips of the HJ.[48] Werner Ascoli, a second-generation Guatemalan whose German Jewish grandfather immigrated at the turn of the century, attended the Colegio Alemán and went on Hitler Youth camping trips as a boy. "This was the kind of thing you did because everyone in the school did it," he said, recalling "having to listen to a bunch of speeches" but being far more interested in the weekend soccer games.[49] They sang invigorating songs together, remembered Otto Luis Schwarz of Ecuador: "They took advantage of our youth, our enthusiasm and energy for that sort of thing."[50] AO officials might have asserted that all the members of the affiliated organizations were true believers, and U.S. officials might have swallowed that claim, but many of these were troops of dubious commitment.

The issue is a subtle one. One may acknowledge that not all members of the Party, and even less so of its affiliates, were prepared to do battle of any kind for their *Führer*, without forgetting that these organizations were suffused with Nazi ideology. The extent to which that doctrine was welcomed, absorbed, or ignored by the membership is impossible to quantify. At any rate, the intent of the organizers was unmistakable. Consider the ideas transmitted by something as apparently benign as a singing club, with these lyrics taken from the songbook of the Nazi recreational group *Kraft durch Freude* (Strength through Joy) in Costa Rica:[51]

"Volk ans Gewehr"	"People, To Arms!"
Viele Jahre sie zogen dahin	Year after year
gefesselt das Volk und betrogen	The people were bound and deceived
Verräter und Juden hatten Gewinn	Traitors and Jews made their profits
sie forderten Opfer Legionen.	And demanded legions of victims.
Im Volke geboren erstand uns ein Führer	Born of the people, our *Führer* arose
Gab Glaube und Hoffnung	Restored our faith and hope for
an Deutschland uns wieder	Germany
Volk ans Gewehr! Volk ans Gewehr!	People, to arms! People, to arms!
(. . .)	(. . .)
Jugend und Alter und Mann für Mann	Young and old and every man
umflammen das Hakenkreuzbanner.	Rally round the swastika banner.
Ob Bürger, ob Bauer, ob Arbeitsmann,	Whether burgher, or farmer, or workingman
sie schwingen das Schwert und den Hammer.	They swing the sword and the hammer
Für Hitler, für Freiheit, für Arbeit und Brot	For Hitler, for freedom, for work and for bread
Deutschland erwache, und Juda den Tod.	May Germany wake, and may Judah be dead.
Volk ans Gewehr! Volk ans Gewehr!	People, to arms! People, to arms!

It is doubtful that one could sing such lines aloud for pleasure without embracing their meaning to some degree. That does not make the singer a soldier, but it does show how thoroughly the Nazis corrupted the culture of organized German social life. (For indications that the Germans in internment were generally unwilling to follow Nazi dictates, see Chapter 5.)

NAZISM ON LATIN AMERICAN SOIL

The specificities of the Latin American context worked for and against the spread of Nazi ideology. Those immigrants whose worldview rested on social Darwinist and racial determinist assumptions often saw their prejudices reinforced by the stratification of the Latin American societies they joined. They took their places in the *pigmentocracia*, a hierarchy in which those with lighter skin tone advanced further up the social ladder, where many elite families boasted openly of their *limpieza de sangre* ("clean blood" or racial purity, a concept that goes back to Spain's expulsion of Muslims and Jews in 1492), where some national government redesigned immigration policy to "whiten" their populations, and deferential locals sometimes asked white foreigners for counsel, imitated their fashions, offered them the best seats on the bus.[52] Some Germans managed rapidly to create sizeable plantations or thriving businesses, tangible achievements which some of them – and not a few of their latino neighbors – interpreted in the pseudoscientific racial terms fashionable since the late nineteenth century, managing to overlook the advantages of education, technical skill, and access to German capital and markets that they brought along with their renowned work ethic.

Of course, those Germans who intermarried or had close social connections with Latin Americans were less likely to welcome an ideology based on strict racial hierarchy. One reason the AO failed to achieve an ideological monopoly over expatriate Germans is because of the incompatibility of its racist fundamental principles: unlike the broader embrace of all ethnic Germans that predominated in the expatriate communities, Nazi standards explicitly rejected a large segment of the German population – those who married non-Aryans, who did not speak German in daily life, who dedicated themselves to local political issues, who adopted Latin American citizenship. For this reason, the AO alienated many Germans and wound up becoming not the unifying pan-Germanist force it aspired to, but a divisive faction.[53]

The expatriates' response to Nazism was determined by other factors as well. Distance from the conflicts of home reduced the sense of perpetual combat that characterized the Nazi Party's organizing efforts in Germany, softening its edge, making the NSDAP appear to some as just another political party. For decades, members of the German communities had held the ideal of an expatriate solidarity cutting across class lines, as they placed (or claimed to place) Germanness above other social distinctions. The Nazi promise of an ethnonational community or *Volksgemeinschaft* appealed to this ideal. If the wide discrepancy between propaganda images and the Third Reich's actual achievements was not always apparent to observers in Germany, those an ocean away with limited access to information saw a picture that was even more disconnected from reality. Even U.S. State Department analysts acknowledged that Germans in Latin America were simply too far away to be aware of "the true state of affairs in a society organized for total war and ridden by the Gestapo."[54]

Nazism's violent hostility to communism struck a chord with German landowners in Latin America, for whom the possibility of worker agitation, peasant revolt, and the loss of property through land reform were a constant anxiety in many countries – especially during a decade that began with *La Matanza*, the massacre of tens of thousands of peasants to put down an agrarian uprising in El Salvador and ended with the Mexican nationalization of oil production. Anticommunism therefore was a major theme in Nazi propaganda tailored for Latin American distribution.[55]

The German Protestant churches helped to encourage a positive reception of Nazi ideas, sometimes quite directly. One of the founders of the early AO group in Guatemala, Otto Langmann, was a pastor who traveled the country to tend his flock – and to sign up new Party members.[56] Asunción's pastor Richert sympathized with Nazism and cooperated with the AO in holding meetings and organizing special events.[57] Many Lutheran pastors greeted the Nazi rise to power as a kind of historico-theological event that would restore the honor of the German people. Fully two-thirds of the German pastors in Brazil joined the Nazi pastors' organization and were members of the AO.[58]

Old-fashioned, religious strains of anti-Semitism detectable throughout Latin American society differed from the biological theories of national socialism, and publicized incidents of Nazi anti-Semitic attacks – the boycott of Jewish businesses in 1933, the Nuremberg laws of 1935, and the so-called *Kristallnacht* of November 9–10, 1938, the "Night of the Broken Glass," when Jewish synagogues and shops across Germany were burned and thousands of Jews were beaten or marched off to concentration camps – were not celebrated. Until the 1930s, the few German Jewish immigrants to Latin America were integrated into the *colonias alemanas* as completely as Jews were assimilated into German society before Hitler: German Jews and non-Jews worked together, lived side by side, made lasting friendships. Anti-Semitism was therefore not the obvious instrument of choice for Party organizers seeking to broaden their base. Patrick von zur Mühlen notes that the "Third Reich"s *Auslandspropaganda* [propaganda for distribution abroad] ... spread less Nazi ideology than patriotically-draped claims for German international standing and greatness."[59]

A reading of the *Karibischer Beobachter*, a thirty-page biweekly published in Barranquilla by Colombia's Nazi Party organization, generally supports this assessment, although "less Nazi ideology" is relative. A typical issue reproduced articles from the Nazi Party flagship paper, the *Völkischer Beobachter*, along with a two-page photo spread depicting Hitler speaking to huge crowds, the latest-model Focke planes and Mercedes trucks, the construction of the Autobahn, and the like, designed to dazzle overseas readers

7. Published by Nazis in Colombia, the biweekly *Karibischer Beobachter* was designed to showcase Germany's accomplishments and exploit expatriate Germans' strong sense of community. Innocuous local-interest stories shared these pages with racist propaganda sent from Berlin. Credit: Ibero-Amerikanisches Institut, Preussischer Kulturbesitz zu Berlin.

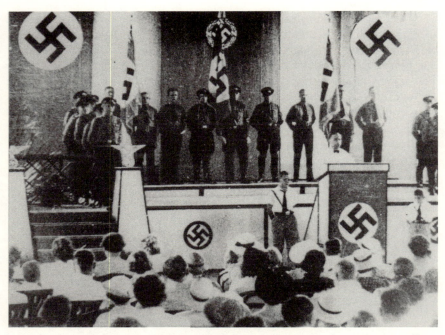

8. Colombia was home to a Nazi organization with 300 members. Here, a rally in Barranquilla. Credit: Vallejo Sánchez to Director Policía Nacional, 13 Jan 1942, "Actividades Nazis 1940–42," Archivo del Ministerio de Relaciones Exteriores, Bogotá.

with Germany's accomplishments. Local-interest sections for Bogotá, Cali, and Barranquilla were used as bait to widen the circle of readers; this was the only German-language publication in which one could read stories about community dances or tennis matches, some of them sponsored by *Kraft durch Freude*. Positive, rather than negative, propaganda was at the forefront, but no issue of the magazine was without its anti-Semitic article, from a warning that world Jewry was conspiring to start a war against Germany to editorials urging German parents not to give their children Jewish-sounding names. In the issue published after *Kristallnacht*, one article, written by Joseph Goebbels' Propaganda Ministry in Berlin, warned, "Jewry holds its fate in its own hand. . . . It is possible that one day the patience of the German people will come to an end. Then Germany will be able to give Jewry a blow from which it will never recover."[60]

The Nazis tried to spread their message elsewhere as well. The propaganda chief in Germany's Mexico City Embassy, Arthur Dietrich, provided anti-Semitic printed matter to the fascist "gold shirts" of the *Acción Revolucionaria Mexicanista* (ARM). In Argentina, the German Embassy printed fifty thousand anti-Semitic pamphlets in Spanish for general distribution.

9. A nighttime bonfire. Both were favored elements of Nazi pageantry, which created an image of militancy that far exceeded the actual capacity of the local organization. Credit: Vallejo Sánchez to Director Policía Nacional, 13 Jan 1942, "Actividades Nazis 1940–42," Archivo del Ministerio de Relaciones Exteriores, Bogotá.

The Colombian government seized imported Spanish-language propaganda reprinting Hitler's speeches, "documenting" Polish atrocities against ethnic Germans, and decrying British imperialism. The texts were unencumbered by subtlety, tending toward such lines as "Adolf Hitler, Paladin of universal peace."[61]

The harmonious relationship between Jewish and non-Jewish Germans could not survive the tension created by the outrages in Germany and the assiduous indoctrination campaign by the local Nazi groups. In his study of German Jews who sought haven in Latin America, von zur Mühlen reported that destitute refugees could not count on local Germans for support because the latter had absorbed Nazi propaganda about the refugees and sometimes greeted them with open enmity. "If private contacts between many non-Jewish *Auslandsdeutschen* and Jews continued, and a few courageous persons opposed the official policy of Nazi officials in German associations and institutions, these were exceptions," von zur Mühlen writes. "The [refugees] experienced the established Germans as a hostile, or at least cold, phalanx."[62]

GERMANS AND JEWS: GOOD NEIGHBORS?

Eric W. Heinemann, longtime leader of Guatemala's Jewish community, bitterly recalled the shift in mood. "It is difficult to understand how rapidly our close acquaintances and so-called friends converted themselves 100% into rabid Nazis, who prohibited their wives from having any relations with Lilly [Eric's wife]; who walked past without greeting us; who threatened me that if I didn't buy merchandise from German salesmen, they would take revenge on my family in Germany." Only "a few" Germans continued to behave *correctos*, Heinemann wrote, naming four families.[63] Interfaith relations seem to have suffered more in Guatemala than in other countries, because of the exertions of the local Nazi boss, Hentschke, to enforce a social boycott of Jews; he even organized block wardens to spy on Jewish homes and report the names of visitors. In Guatemala City, a Jewish woman's good friend came to her one day in tears. "I want to visit you," she wept, "but Hentschke is patrolling the streets, and if he sees me, my relatives in Germany are in danger."[64]

The long arm of the Nazi state reached into the long-standing business relations between Germans and Jews in Latin America. The Foreign Trade Office of the AO and the *Lateinamerikanischer Verein* worked with nazified German chambers of commerce in Latin America to carry the "Aryanization" program overseas, compiling long lists of contracts held by Jewish importers in Latin America who distributed German products. This information was used to terminate the contracts and transfer the business to non-Jewish German import-export firms.[65]

In countries where the local Nazi leadership was not quite so zealous, relations might be strained but could still be courteous. "I never knew a single German here who was anti-Semitic," said Ilse Grossman, a Jewish doctor who came to Ecuador in 1939. "Except for [Party leader Walter] Giese and [AO organizer Heinz] Schulte, maybe." Grossman read down a list of Party members in Ecuador, and recognized many as friends of hers and her husband, a Jewish professor of physics who had arrived in Quito in 1925. "Good people," she commented. "Giese signed them up, and they went along, without knowing what they were doing. . . . It was a kind of a men's club, maybe they sang the Horst-Wessel song [the Nazis' unofficial national hymn] or something, but who thinks so much about such things anyway?" Roberto Hahn, who fled to Guayaquil as a refugee in 1935 and retains an encyclopedic knowledge of the local German community, reacted in a like manner to the Party list: while identifying a few names as people who were active in Party affairs, most he believed to be "totally apolitical . . . totally harmless . . . guaranteed not a Nazi." Hans Ungar, founder of the antifascist *Vereinigung Freier Österreicher* (Union of Free Austrians) in Colombia's capital, was unimpressed by reports of Nazi activity in Bogotá. Asked about acquaintances who were on the Party list, he shook his head. "I would put my hand in the fire that he's not a Nazi," Ungar exclaimed at one name.[66]

The Party membership of their friends and acquaintances named on the lists is not at issue. The *Auslandsorganisation*'s central card files in Germany were saved from destruction at the end of the war by a paper mill owner ordered to turn them into pulp; perhaps to curry favor with the occupation authorities, he delivered them instead to the U.S. Army. The names were catalogued and published in two versions by the Army and the U.S. Senate. The originals were microfilmed and can be viewed at the Berlin Documents Center and the National Archives in Washington.[67] Nor are these anecdotes intended to contradict the bald fact that there were at least sixty Party members in Ecuador, for example, and some three hundred in Colombia, including a number of dedicated Nazi ideologues.

But the testimony of these Jewish refugees, some of whom lost their families in the Holocaust or were active in anti-Nazi organizations, is intriguing evidence that many of Latin America's Germans, even some of those who joined the AO, did not fully embrace the ideology propagated by the Party leadership. These Jews in particular have nothing to gain by exculpating their former neighbors; on the contrary, they have compelling reasons to harbor intense, abiding resentment toward anyone who might have contributed to their suffering or that of their families. It is possible, of course, that their Party member friends led a double life, showing one face in public and another in select company. It is even conceivable that these lukewarm national socialists were actually adept spies who somehow went undetected by the U.S. counterintelligence agencies monitoring virtually all radio traffic to Berlin.[68] But it is not likely. These statements tend to corroborate the assertions of some former Party members interviewed that their decision to join came not from any interest in promoting a violent political movement, but out of patriotism or social instincts. Hans Kolter, then a young athlete who excelled in the sports competitions at Guatemala's German Club, looks back today with sorrow. "Unfortunately, I was naturally with the majority in those times. Lamentably," he added. "You know how it is – as a young man, you want to go along with all your friends."[69] Walter Held, a Colombian-born German who studied in England and the United States, joined the AO in Barranquilla because it was seen as "good form" among the prosperous German merchants there. At meetings, he remembers, they discussed economic developments in Germany. Those who wore brownshirts were more fervent, but there was no pressure to join. "If you weren't in the Party, you weren't looked at badly, but everyone said 'We're all doing it, why don't you come too?' "[70] Party membership, in the period before the war and before the Holocaust, clearly held a different meaning for some members in Latin America than it did in the European context or than it does to us today. "Even those in Germany didn't necessarily know the worst that was coming – that Hitler would unleash the Second World War, that he would cause the barbarities against the Jews," said Carlos Gehlert, a former Guatemalan congressman of German descent. "So how could someone over here know?"[71]

Acknowledging the variety of ordinary reasons that could lead someone to join the Nazi Party enables one to better assess the level of the threat posed by Latin America's German communities. If even some of the Party members were innocuous, it is likely that the larger number of those unwilling to enroll constituted still less of a danger. One can also see how Ilse Grossman's "good people" – not demons, not the deranged, not only the malevolent – could be manipulated by clever propaganda and appeals to their nationalistic and social impulses into lending their names to the most vicious, destructive movement in human history. Since party and state had fused, Germans who lacked the courage or political commitment to express their patriotism via acts of resistance embraced national symbols that were now Nazi symbols. Alfredo Brauer, born in Ecuador, explained his father Leopold's behavior this way: "He was a German. As a German, he raised the German flag on his hacienda. And what was the German flag in those days? The swastika! What other flag was he going to raise?"[72] That several alternatives come to mind – the older versions of the German flag so hotly contested in the Weimar era, the Ecuadorian flag, no flag at all – merely underlines the extent to which the Party used the state to try to control potential outlets for patriotic expression.

THE QUALITY OF CONSENT

Scholars have tried to comprehend the "soaring popularity of Hitler, contrasted with the massive unpopularity of the Party and of so many aspects of the daily experience of Nazism" within Germany itself, where the Party's association with hatred, violence, and the loss of personal freedom somehow did not tarnish the image of "a Führer who seemed to stand aloof from political infighting and the grey daily reality of the Third Reich."[73] In Latin America, where many Party officials were particularly brusque or inept, and where Hitler's image was burnished by distance and nostalgia for the Kaiser, many expatriates could be unhappy at the activities of the AO without changing their positive opinions of the homeland regime.

The case of Costa Rica brings this apparent contradiction into focus. The German Club in a suburb of San José was one of the centers of social life, not only for Germans but for prominent Costa Ricans and even many North Americans, who flocked to its swimming pool, its tennis courts, and the only bowling alleys in the capital. In November 1934, after an unsuccessful bid to take over the board of directors, Party boss Herbert Knöhr ordered all NSDAP members to resign from the club. Instead, some club members quit the Party. Richard Kriebel, a respected German dentist, wrote in his letter of resignation that the German Club had flourished over a half-century precisely because political differences were always checked at the door. Kriebel and Minister Kraske (whose responsibility included all of Central America) exchanged sympathetic letters regretting Knöhr's boorish, divisive tactics; Kriebel noted that even among Party members there were many who were unwilling to follow such a leader. As for himself, Kriebel said, he had resigned his membership in the German School Association and withdrawn his son from the Hitler Youth, because he believed his son "should be raised as a good, free, honest German patriot." Were Knöhr to be replaced, Kriebel concluded, "we would all be again, as before, of one heart and one soul."[74] Clearly, this conflict was not about the legitimacy of Nazi rule at home, or about loyalty to Germany. As in many other cases, it was the behavior of the local Nazis that was unwelcome.

In 1938, club members with voting rights – Germans only – elected Karl Federspiel their president. Federspiel was a known antifascist, a bookstore owner and printer living in Costa Rica since 1912. After he published an anti-Nazi article in a Catholic magazine and displayed a book by an anti-Nazi exile in his shop window, Federspiel was threatened with the loss of his German citizenship by the local Nazi group and the new minister for Central America, Otto Reinebeck (who replaced Kraske in 1937). Federspiel promptly became a naturalized Costa Rican. His election by a majority of the *colonia alemana* as late as 1938 – which the FBI found "difficult to understand" – indicates the Nazi grip was far less secure than U.S. officials believed. Paradoxically, it came in the very year that Costa Rica's Germans voted overwhelmingly in favor of Hitler's leadership in what appeared to be a remarkable extraterritorial demonstration of transnational allegiance.[75]

THE SHIPBOARD VOTE

In April 1938, following the *Anschluß* or annexation of Austria, Hitler ordered a plebiscite to be held among the Austrians and all German citizens. The *Auslandsorganisation* eagerly undertook a massive, costly effort to demonstrate the unity of all Germans everywhere. To avoid creating a diplomatic incident by actually holding an election within the territory of another state, German expatriates were encouraged to go to designated ports and board one of a hundred ships dispatched around the globe for the purpose. The vessels then steamed out into international waters and provided a venue for the plebiscite on the high seas.[76]

These arrangements proved too unwieldy for countries with very large German populations. No vote was held in the United States due to "technical difficulties." Most Germans in Brazil were unable to attend when governors of the states with the highest German populations refused to allow the ships to be boarded. (In contrast, Panamanian officials made the most of the opportunity, permitting the plebiscite to go forward, then charging the voters $10 a head to reenter the country.) In Argentina, the Party and the Embassy found it impossible to organize enough funding and transportation to get tens of thousands of Germans to the ports of embarkation and back to their homes. Instead, Party members collected voluntary *signatures of support* for the *Anschluß* – thereby giving the lie to the fiction that this was a genuine attempt to ascertain the will of the German people. Minister Reinebeck in Guatemala tried the same gambit with this request to the Foreign Office: "Please permit voting, *or at least declarations of agreement*, via a signature at the Legation."[77] (A legation is a diplomatic post below the status of embassy.)

Where polling did take place, Bohle triumphantly informed Hitler, the vote ran 99 percent in favor – just as in Germany and in Austria itself. This result was taken at face value by the U.S. government and has been repeated by historians ever since as a demonstration of Germany's transnational reach and the unanimity of the *Auslandsdeutschen*. But it did not have the same meaning for all the participants at the time. Voters interviewed years later played down the political significance of the event, saying that the shipboard plebiscite was a welcome diversion from their dusty, sometimes quite isolated lives in Latin America – a festival with free admission. Private photographs of the event in Guatemala depict German men and women in bathing suits, sunning themselves on the ship's deck. A tourist's 8mm film footage of the shipboard vote off the Ecuadorian coast shows scenes of accordionists playing, couples dancing, men playing cards, passengers napping on deck after a big meal, children scampering around, and much quaffing of beer. After a full day of this, passengers lined up to vote and turned in their ballots to the ship's captain. "Everyone was thinking about the *Volksfest*, nobody was thinking about the meaning of the vote," said Hugo Droege, whose farm was a day's horseback ride away from his nearest neighbors. "Everybody went. There was German beer, good German cheese and German black bread. We hadn't seen that in years. Of course," he added, "in those days support for Hitler was one hundred percent, we had a whole picture of how it was at the beginning, that everyone got work again and it was all fantastic. No one thought about war." Inge von Schröter of Costa Rica, twenty-one years old at the time, recalled the day sixty years later with some nostalgia. "Of course I went," she said. "I got to go out on a ship, there was – I even remember there was green pea soup with sausages. And I voted for Austria. At the time, we were all excited about Austria. It was like a *Volksfest*. You should be able to imagine it, since you are a young man, that we all had such a good time, we came back at nine o'clock at night, all sleepy on the train."[78]

For people who had left Europe to make a living in the relative solitude of farming and trade in the smaller Latin American countries in the 1930s, the attraction of a large social gathering seems to have been a stronger draw than ideology; that Nazi organizers knew this and took advantage of it to make a propaganda point does not mean we should automatically accept their assessment of the significance of the response. The optimism and political consensus was not as universal as these participants suggest, and there were inducements beyond the convivial and the culinary for homesick expatriates. True to character, the Nazis could not resist injecting an element of coercion, a hint of menace into the invitations. "Your right to vote is a duty to vote!" growled the circulars prepared by the *Auslandsorganisation*. U.S. intelligence believed that "all Germans...were virtually forced" to board the ships, a fact confirmed in interviews. Just in case the expatriates might be unsure which way to cast their votes, the physical appearance of the ballot itself made crystal clear what the "duty" entailed: at the top was the question, "Do you support the reunification of Austria with the German Reich, and do you support...our Führer, Adolf HITLER?" Below was a big circle right in the middle, labeled *Ja*, and, off to the side, a little circle labeled *Nein*.[79] (In distant areas where the ballots could not be shipped directly from Germany, Bohle's instructions on the preparation of ballots on site made clear that this visual cue was no accident: "7th line, middle: *Ja*. Underneath goes a circle 35 millimeters in diameter. Next to this circle, to the right, at the same level, place a small circle 20 millimeters in diameter. Over this circle, lower than the *Ja*, place the word *Nein*.")[80] With their customary subtlety of a wrecking ball, the Nazis ensured there was to be no confusion over what a correct vote would be.

Yet despite all the precautions, in order to achieve its "landslide," the *Auslandsorganisation* still had to cook the books. It was true that only one percent of the ballots were marked "Nein," but of the 58,628 votes cast overseas, nearly 8,000 were "invalid." That is an astonishing number given that the ballots were so simple and participation was officially voluntary, suggesting a possible hidden protest vote via blank or defaced ballots, or, at minimum, significantly less complete support than Bohle asserted.[81] Once again, the degree of conformity or resistance is difficult to measure precisely, but the unanimity claimed by the Nazis and credited by U.S. officials is clearly overdrawn. Still, Germany proclaimed its achievement with pride, and the vote was taken very seriously by the host countries. Public opinion and local governments objected to this display of extraterritorial influence by a foreign power. And the plebiscite became a key piece of evidence in the eyes of those U.S. officials who viewed the German communities of Latin America as nests of Nazi intrigue.[82]

BROAD, BUT NOT DEEP

This was transnational mobilization on a grand scale, and it generated a kind of surface response commensurate with the effort that went into it. Up until the late 1930s, the German communities of Latin America had remained relatively autonomous outposts of Germanness, dedicated to maintaining a cultural identity firmly rooted in the homeland, but with independent interests that did not always mesh with plans emanating from the metropole. While accepting only a certain kind of German as legitimate and thereby creating divisiveness, the Nazis tried to unify the German communities from outside with state power, force, and authoritarian leadership. This was a sea

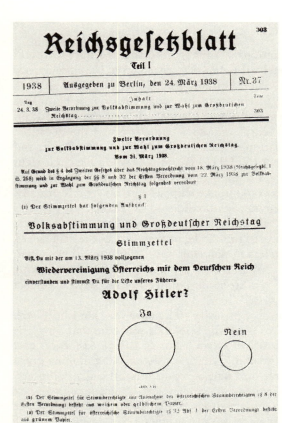

Reichsgesetzblatt 303

Teil I

| 1938 | Ausgegeben zu Berlin, den 24. März 1938 | Nr. 37 |

Tag
24.3.38 Zweite Verordnung zur Volksabstimmung und zur Wahl zum Großdeutschen
Reichstag. 303

Zweite Verordnung
zur Volksabstimmung und zur Wahl zum Großdeutschen Reichstag.
Vom 24. März 1938.

Auf Grund des § 4 des Zweiten Gesetzes über das Reichstagswahlrecht vom 18. März 1938 (Reichsgesetzbl. I
S. 258) wird in Ergänzung der §§ 8 und 32 der Ersten Verordnung vom 22. März 1938 zur Volksabstimmung und zur Wahl zum Großdeutschen Reichstag folgendes verordnet

§ 1

(1) Der Stimmzettel hat folgenden Aufdruck:

Volksabstimmung und Großdeutscher Reichstag

Stimmzettel

Bist Du mit der am 13. März 1938 vollzogenen

Wiedervereinigung Österreichs mit dem Deutschen Reich

einverstanden und stimmst Du für die Liste unseres Führers

Adolf Hitler?

Ja

Nein

....

(2) Der Stimmzettel für Stimmberechtigte mit Ausnahme der österreichischen Stimmberechtigten (§ 8 der
Ersten Verordnung) besteht aus weißem oder gelblichem Papier.
(3) Der Stimmzettel für österreichische Stimmberechtigte (§ 32 Abs. 1 der Ersten Verordnung) besteht
aus grünem Papier.

Reichsgesetzbl. 1938 I

10. THE 1938 SHIPBOARD VOTE *What it meant to the German government...* A ballot for the 1938 plebiscite in support of the annexation of Austria. The Nazi Party claimed the vote demonstrated total unity of Germans abroad. To be certain that voters knew which way to vote, the authorities issued explicit printing instructions centering the circle for "Ja" and making it three times larger than the circle for "Nein." Even so, a significant number were defaced. Credit: "Volksabstimmung vom 10. April 1938," R46292, Rechtsabteilung, PAAA, Bonn.

11. *What it meant to the participants...* Voters described the day as a *Volksfest,* a rare holiday on the water. They wore their Sunday best and spent most of the day enjoying food and beer brought from Germany, dancing to accordion music, and sunbathing on the ship's deck. For expatriates living in relative isolation, the attractions went well beyond politics. Credit: Courtesy Hans Kolter, Guatemala City.

12. Participants in the voting day at sea. Credit: Courtesy Hans Kolter, Guatemala City. (Kolter is seated, second from right.)

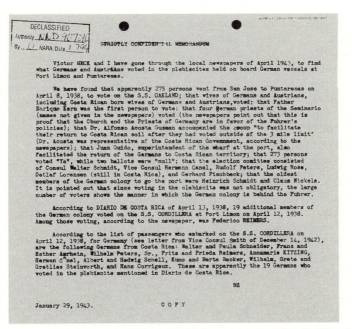

DECLASSIFIED
Authority N.N.D 957016
By ... LL NARA Date 1 7 96

STRICTLY CONFIDENTIAL MEMORANDUM

    Victor HECK and I have gone through the local newspapers of April 1943, to find what Germans and Austrians voted in the plebiscites held on board German vessels at Port Limon and Puntarenas.

    We have found that apparently 275 persons went from San Jose to Puntarenas on April 8, 1938, to vote on the S.S. OAKLAND; that wives of Germans and Austrians, including Costa Rican born wives of Germans and Austrians, voted; that Father Enrique Kern was the first person to vote; that four German priests of the Seminario (names not given in the newspapers) voted (the newspapers point out that this is proof that the Church and the Priests of Germany are in favor of the Fuhrer's policies); that Dr. Alfonso Acosta Guzman accompanied the group "to facilitate their return to Costa Rican soil after they had voted outside of the 3 mile limit" (Dr. Acosta was representative of the Costa Rican Government, according to the newspapers); that Juan Guido, superintendent of the wharf at the port, also facilitated the return of the Germans to Costa Rican territory; that 273 persons voted "Ya", while two ballots were "null"; that the election comittee consisted of Consul Walter Schmidt, Vice Consul Hermann Canel, Rudolf Peters, Ludwig Rose, Detlef Lorenzen (still in Costa Rica), and Gerhard Fischbeck; that the oldest members of the German colony to go the port were Heinrich Schmidt and Claus Nickels. It is pointed out that since voting in the plebiscite was not obligatory, the large number of voters shows the manner in which the German colony is behind the Fuhrer.

    According to DIARIO DE COSTA RICA of April 13, 1938, 19 additional members of the German colony voted on the S.S. CORDILLERA at Port Limon on April 12, 1938. Among those voting, according to the newspaper, was Federico REIMERS.

    According to the list of passengers who embarked on the S.S. CORDILLERA on April 12, 1938, for Germany (see letter from Vice Consul Smith of December 14, 1942), are the following Germans from Costa Rica: Walter and Paula Schneider, Frans and Esther Amrhein, Wilhelm Peters, Sr., Frits and Frieda Reimers, Annamarie KITZING, Herman C nel, Albert and Hedwig Schell, Kuno and Berta Becker, Wilhelm, Grete and Gretlies Steinvorth, and Hans Corrigeux. These are apparently the 19 Germans who voted in the plebiscite mentioned in Diario de Costa Rica.

BZ

January 29, 1943.   C O P Y

13. *...and what it meant to U.S. intelligence.* U.S. officials, like their Berlin counterparts, considered the vote to be proof of broad support for Hitler in the German communities in Latin America. Participation in the plebiscite was grounds for deportation and internment in the United States. Credit: 29 Jan 1943, folder A8-5 (1-Costa Rica) Germans, Naval Attaché – Guatemala City, Personality Files 1940–6, Box 45, Office of Naval Intelligence, RG38, National Archives. (The date "April 1943" in the first line is one of the common errors in such reports; it should read "April 1938.")

change from the old pan-Germanist ideal of natural internal unity based on blood, or language, or culture. Public activities such as the extraterritorial vote and displays of Nazi insignia obscured continuing variances between the regime and its expatriates. Acceptance of the Nazis among the Germans of Latin America, then, can be characterized as broad, but not deep. Had more of them been more enthusiastic, they would have expressed it not merely with occasional symbolic acts that can be read in different ways but through the concrete commitment of time and resources – such as joining the Party and working for its goals. That more than 90 percent were unwilling to do so is telling.

In spite of an energetic campaign by Nazi organizers to capture the allegiance of German expatriates, important elements of ambiguity and ambivalence persisted within a generally positive response to Hitler's rise to power – allowing for enough resistance to Nazi Party demands and enough variety among Latin America's Germans to refute the notion that they formed a unified, menacing bloc. They did not sign up in large numbers to join the Party, and those who did enroll often did not display the kind of fanaticism associated with the Party faithful in Germany, a zealotry trumpeted by Party leaders, feared by the United States, but largely absent in Latin America. Symbolic demonstrations of unity organized by the AO were marred by subtle acts of dissent, as in the 1938 vote. The *Auslandsorganisation* was not able to complete its project of transnational incorporation of the *Auslandsdeutschen*, many of whom resented the Nazis' contamination of their long-standing good reputation, but its highly visible conduct did create the impression – so fundamental to shaping U.S. policy – of having brought all Germans abroad into line. Like so many actions taken by the Nazis, it was a ruinous, self-defeating strategy. Ultimately, the most tangible outcome of this attempt to unify expatriate Germans for the Nazi project was to provoke a broad-based rejection of their tactics in a backlash that swept throughout the Americas.

THE NAZI DECLINE

Ironically, U.S. concern grew most acute in the very years, mid-1938 through early 1942, when Nazi influence in Latin America had passed its peak and was steadily eroding. The April 1938 shipboard vote not only set the high-water mark of AO influence but also directly precipitated its decline. The Nazis' transnational claim on the allegiance of the *Auslandsdeutsche* offended governments throughout the Americas, whether by extraterritorial loyalty tests, like the vote, or the parades of brownshirts in public. Chile had already banned the nazified German youth organization in November 1937. Following the 1938 vote and the *integralista* coup attempt in Brazil, Nazi organizations came under attack throughout the region; the Party was banned outright in Brazil and Venezuela in 1938, in Argentina and Guatemala the following year.[83]

The pressure was so intense that Ernst Bohle ordered an end to parades and other demonstrations by the AO groups in Latin America, and the heads of the German diplomatic missions in South America held an emergency meeting at Montevideo in July 1938 to consider their plight. The envoys sent a letter to the German Foreign Office (*Auswärtiges Amt* or AA) urging an immediate reduction of AO activity because of the harm it was causing to German–Latin American relations. They asked that Party members in Latin America dispense with all outwardly visible symbols, including the Hitler salute and the wearing of uniforms and swastikas, and that the German schools, clubs, official trade union and women's organization and especially the youth organizations all be rapidly depoliticized. With the American nations scheduled to meet shortly at Lima, the diplomats warned, Nazi activity was strengthening pan-Americanism at Germany's expense.[84]

Berlin summoned the diplomats for a showdown meeting with the AO in the Foreign Office on June 12, 1939. It was attended by Bohle; State Secretary Ernst von Weizsäcker, Foreign Minister Ribbentrop's cautious deputy; the German ministers – von Thermann of Argentina, von Schoen of Chile, Langmann of Uruguay, Reinebeck of Central America, and others; and the Nazi Party chiefs for each country.

The meeting demonstrated typical Nazi hostility toward the softness and gentility of the diplomatic service. ("'What *does* a legation counselor do all day long?' Hermann Göring had rhetorically inquired of a Foreign Office official in 1935. 'In the morning he sharpens pencils, and afternoons he goes out to tea somewhere.' ")[85] The ministers opened the meeting by complaining that the AO's obstreperousness was leading to Party bans all across the continent. Nor were they winning any more converts among the *Auslandsdeutsche*, said von Thermann. "Whoever has not found their way to us yet will not do it in the future either," he asserted, arguing for an end to recruitment even among German citizens.[86] Von Thermann's observation that Party enrollment had flattened in Latin America is confirmed by AO membership figures showing sluggish growth from 1937 to 1939 of about 2.5 percent per year – with more than 90 percent of German citizens still choosing to remain outside the Party.[87] Von Schoen demanded that public relations work be taken away from the Party officials and given to his embassy, and that the Party stop publishing materials in Spanish, because their propaganda had been so counterproductive. Even Otto Reinebeck, loyal water carrier for the Nazis in Central America, stated his belief that continuing camouflaged Party work would lead to the expulsion of German residents.

Bohle's response showed that the AO's collapse in Latin America had hardly registered with its leadership in Berlin, which continued to push for its transnationalist project of incorporating German expatriates into the ranks of the Nazis. "The party can on no account abandon the view that every drop of German blood abroad must be preserved," he declared, calling for resistance against the assimilationist efforts of the Latin American countries. He flatly refused to relinquish control of the press department. Moreover, he declared, "the recruitment of *Reichsdeutsche* can in no way be considered to be closed.... The Germans overseas should not only become national socialists, they should remain national socialists. It is the duty of the party to place a disciplined community of Germans overseas at the disposal of the chief of mission in case of an emergency. The AO gets the credit for the fact that today, the Reich can rely on Germandom abroad much more securely than in 1914." Bohle wanted to preserve the momentum of the Party by going underground wherever it was banned, and by maintaining control over the German community via a special AO representative inside each diplomatic mission. At all costs, he concluded, the Party and the Foreign Office must unite to ensure that "the old bourgeois club life not be resumed abroad, because otherwise there will be nothing left of national socialism."[88]

Once again, the Nazi leadership proved itself out of touch with Latin American reality, bent on a course that could only harm the German communities whose support it hoped to gain, whose cause it claimed to uphold. Bohle's hostility toward both the established ("bourgeois") German residents and the nationalistic Latin American governments typified the Nazi approach, and ensured its failure.

After a second fruitless meeting in August, the group dispersed without reaching agreement. But even the ambitious Bohle eventually had to face the fact of defeat. By 1941, the governments of Guatemala, Nicaragua, Honduras, Colombia, and Peru had taken measures to ban Nazi propaganda and symbols in their countries; El Salvador and Ecuador expelled German diplomats accused of distributing Nazi propaganda.[89] In April 1941, Bohle instructed his subordinates in Latin America to avoid any unnecessary activity at all, even abstaining from frequent correspondence with Berlin.[90] Together with the Party bans, this spelled the end of the AO in Latin America.

The minutes of the AO-AA conferences on policies for Latin America make clear the quite limited goals of Nazi Germany in the region: rally the *Auslandsdeutsche* behind the Nazi banner, arouse sympathy among the Latin Americans. The AO was inadequate to the first task and failed utterly at the second. There was no talk of subverting governments, or confronting the United States, or conquering the hemisphere. By the end of the 1930s, the AO was playing a defensive game in Latin America – and losing.

HITLER'S VIEW OF LATIN AMERICA

The decline of the Nazis' fortunes in Latin America coincided with their seemingly unstoppable series of gains in Europe, and therefore did little to reduce U.S. alarm. No one in Washington could know exactly what Germany was planning in secret, and in the absence of reliable information, the Roosevelt administration assumed Hitler might use the *Aus-landsdeutsche* to pave the way for a German invasion of the Americas. No record of any such planning by the German military has been found. Other evidence of trans-Atlantic military intentions – an on-again, off-again project to construct large battleships and long-range bombers, the search for naval bases on or near the North African coast – suggests Hitler expected to challenge the United States eventually, although he sometimes remarked that the confrontation might take place decades in the future, even as late as the 1970s.[91]

Hitler had plenty of opinions about the "degenerate" U.S. democracy "enfeebled" by its influential population of Jews, but he evinced no interest in Latin America. He openly conceded that the region belonged properly in the U.S. sphere of influence and referred often to the Monroe Doctrine, asserting a comparable sphere for Germany under a "European Monroe Doctrine."[92] In strong contrast to his habitual micromanagement of foreign policy toward nations he was interested in, Hitler and his top aides left policymaking toward Latin America to the *Auswärtiges Amt* – so often cut out of important decisions elsewhere – and the foreign ministry left it to department heads.[93] Hitler took only rare notice of the potential of German-Latin American trade. Conquest of the USSR under Hitler's plans would make Germany practically self-sufficient in raw materials, so any contribution from Latin America would be unnecessary. He did make remarks to foreign diplomats in 1940 and 1941 suggesting that a German-dominated Europe could eventually displace the United States as principal trading partner with Latin America, but there were no concrete measures undertaken after the erosion of German export gains began in 1938.[94]

Accounts in the U.S. press warning of Hitler's military designs on Latin America regularly referred to statements contained in the best-selling *Gespräche mit Hitler*, published in London as *Hitler Speaks* in 1939. The author, Hermann Rauschning, was Danzig senate president and a former member of the NSDAP who reluctantly broke with the Nazis over financial issues. He claimed to report the content of Hitler's bombast delivered at luncheons where he himself had been a guest, although he wrote the book years afterward. It presented dramatic statements purporting to be Hitler's, on the order of "if ever there is a place where democracy is senseless and suicidal, it is in South America" and "our conquistadores have a more difficult task than the original ones, and for this reason they have more delicate weapons."[95] Rauschning is still cited as a key source in nearly every publication that argues that the Nazi regime sought to take over Latin America. Unfortunately for proponents of this view, *Hitler Speaks* was demolished by subsequent investigations that showed that Rauschning had invented the quotations.[96]

When Hitler did make a rare reference to Latin America in a late edition of *Mein Kampf* and in his so-called second book, it was merely to dismiss the region as the epitome of racial mixing; he did not even remark upon the large

German presence in South America – a telling omission, given his fervent interest in the *Auslandsdeutsche* of Eastern Europe and the Soviet Union, and his oft-mentioned vision of a worldwide German racial community.

Hitler's disdain was matched by the ignorance of other top Nazis, who manifested the dismissiveness exemplified by the common German remark, "*das kommt mir spanisch vor*" (roughly, "it's all Greek to me"). Foreign Minister Joachim von Ribbentrop could not tell the countries of South America one from another. Hermann Göring believed that cosmopolitan Argentina was populated by Indian natives (to which the Argentine ambassador retorted that his country had as many Indians as Sweden had Laplanders).[97] Ernst Bohle had no interest in Latin American affairs and felt at a loss at diplomatic functions for visiting Latin American dignitaries; not only could he not understand Spanish, but he also could not remember the odd-sounding names of the diplomats, and resorted to addressing them all as "Excellency." Bohle even felt alienated from the *Reichsdeutsche* of Latin America, who on visits to Berlin would spend their time at the South American Club and speak Spanish among themselves. He complained that German citizens who settled in Latin America "tended to take on a very different outlook than was generally considered fitting for good Teutons – they became much more lively and light-hearted, and often assumed a rather Latin attitude toward life which made them rather hard to handle at times."[98]

Rather than deploy German residents as a fifth column to take over Latin America, top Nazi officials may actually have been planning to call many of the region's Germans back to Europe after the war was over, so that their experience working in underdeveloped areas could be applied to help "settle" the more important territories in the East. Only Germany's defeat, apparently, prevented the scheme from being tried.[99]

Nazi Germany's attitude toward Latin America can thus be summed up largely as one of neglect. The prejudices of top Nazis made the region uninteresting to them, and geopolitical considerations held their attention elsewhere. Neglect became an explicit policy of disinterestedness as part of Hitler's strategy to avoid provoking the United States. His subordinates expressly forbade any sabotage or interference in local politics in the region for fear of alienating Latin American leaders and angering Washington – and their agents followed orders throughout the war.[100]

It was too late. The AO had already managed to contaminate the image of the German communities. Besides, trying to read Hitler's intentions from his public statements would have been as ineffective as analyzing the most logical path for Nazi Germany to take: neither was a good guide to predicting behavior when a megalomaniac was in charge. Instead, Washington assumed Hitler, and the German emigrants, were capable of anything – and that Latin Americans were incapable of meeting the challenge. U.S. officials therefore moved to create a unified hemispheric response to the threat from Germany that their sources and cast of mind told them was urgent and real.

2

Assessment

"Somebody in the Cabinet said, 'Columbia? Columbia? Columbia, that is in South America, isn't it?'"
— President Franklin D. Roosevelt, January 1940[1]

Panama, November 1941. War looms ever closer to the Americas. The Canal Zone, under U.S. military jurisdiction, swarms with soldiers and construction workers laboring in the wet tropical heat – laying mines at the entrance, stretching antisabotage nets across the locks and spillways, setting up antiaircraft installations on all sides. Lieutenant Jules Dubois, chief of the Intelligence Branch of the U.S. Army's Panama Canal Department, sits at a table in the unassuming little restaurant run by German immigrant Wilhelm Heinemann. Dubois, a self-confident future anticommunist crusader whose taste for the mixed metaphor will emerge in his memoirs, knows that Heinemann arrived from Europe only two years before. "With their sights trained on Latin America, the Axis powers began to groom puppets and sympathetic groups in every republic to seize the reigns [sic] of their governments' machinery," he will write after the war.[2] It makes no difference that Heinemann is a Jewish refugee with a heart condition who fled Hitler in Germany, Franco in Spain, and Mussolini in Italy before finally finding asylum in Central America. The U.S. government – even President Roosevelt himself – has often enough issued public declarations and private memoranda warning of the danger that Jewish refugees might serve as Nazi spies, and Dubois is a fervent believer.[3]

The intelligence chief takes his job seriously; his handiwork leads to so many cases of German civilians interned as dangerous enemy aliens that postwar investigators will label him "the ubiquitous Dubois."[4] His memoirs reveal his assumptions: "There were approximately three million Axis nationals residing in Latin America then, each of whom could have been made available to form part of a militant striking force capable of implementing the plans of the Axis at the appropriate time."[5] That this figure can be reached only by including every last Italian grandmother and Japanese toddler does not deter the newly minted intelligence agent from seeing evidence of a fifth column under every rock. Swallowing the dregs of his coffee, the lieutenant peers into the bottom of the cup and sees a twisted piece of straw in the shape of a numeral 4. Convinced it is a secret code signal, Dubois denounces Heinemann as a Nazi spy, and the refugee is arrested and interned in the United States.[6]

ARENA FOR THE GREAT POWERS

For too many U.S. officials, from intelligence agents to ambassadors and cabinet members, failure to understand Latin America and Latin Americans begins at the fundamental level of not being able to speak their

14. "My, How You've Grown!" Leaning across the backyard fence, Uncle Sam praises a fair-skinned, female Latin America while a bearded Europe – complete with Germanic monocle – takes a sudden, covetous interest. U.S. political discourse, expressed in the statements of government officials, in news reporting, and in editorial cartoons, consistently represented Latin America as vulnerable, in need of protection, and requiring the tutelage of the United States. Credit: Sykes, *Philadelphia Ledger*, 1923. Reprinted by permission of the *Philadelphia Inquirer*.

15. "Cutting a Switch for a Bad Boy." Pre-Rooseveltian images of Latin American countries typically represented them as misbehaving children in need of parental discipline. Credit: McKee Barclay, *Baltimore Sun*, 1910. Reprinted by permission.

languages, and runs the gamut of stereotype and prejudice. In two hundred years of relations, there has been a remarkable consistency in the quality of the U.S. gaze southward, determined by a constellation of beliefs that have proven highly resistant to change and that form the filter through which meaning is attributed to events. This history of misunderstanding, reflected in the words of presidents and the sketches of cartoonists, in the conditions placed on loans, and in the language of Hollywood screenplays, presents Latin Americans as inferior and childlike, feminized and vulnerable. Passive objects of history, their countries become mere stage sets for the real actors, exotic backdrops for the playing out of great power rivalries. If this attitude was sharply evident during the Cold War and still persists in some quarters today, it suffused the culture of U.S. policymaking on the eve of the Second World War and, together with alarming news from Europe, created a predisposition to see a Nazi plot behind every incident of

16. "Not as Bad as Painted." Herbert Hoover's first steps toward improving relations are here presented as an instant success: a female Latin America patiently awaiting her suitor is smitten by her first glimpse of "the *real* Uncle Sam," and the views of Latin American observers (the absent portraitists) are dismissed as an unfair caricature. Credit: Thiele, *Culver Citizen*, 1928. Reprinted by permission.

political unrest, a German hand pulling the strings of so many Latin American puppets.

In the period from 1938 until Pearl Harbor, these convictions went all the way to the top. President Franklin D. Roosevelt, in his private messages and his public statements, regularly warned of the danger. Several of his closest aides – including top assistant Harry Hopkins, Treasury Secretary Henry Morgenthau, and Assistant Secretary of State Adolf Berle – believed Nazi subversion in Latin America was likely. Even officials as well acquainted with the region as Undersecretary of State Sumner Welles and his deputy Laurence Duggan would come to share this perspective for a time. If Latin Americans were too immature, too insignificant to make important things happen, responsibility and blame must lie elsewhere.

In this period, coup attempts and other forms of political unrest were routinely ascribed to Nazi machinations, despite the absence of evidence for such

17. "Neighborly Call." FDR's new policy toward Latin America contributes to its representation as a grown man, rather than a child or a coquette. Nonetheless, the Good Neighbor's principles of respect and sovereign equality are not self-evident; they are gifts to be given out of generosity and received with gratitude. Pease, *Newark Evening News*, 1934. Courtesy of The Newark Public Library.

a link and the presence of local actors with their own agendas.[7] In Brazil in May 1938, a fascist group called the *integralistas*, led by Plinio Salgado, tried to overthrow the government of Getulio Vargas. U.S. officials believed the Nazis had planned, funded, and orchestrated the plot. These claims were not based on evidence of German involvement, which was lacking; the presence of a few ethnic Germans at the lower ranks of the *integralistas* was enough to convince the U.S. government that the Nazis called the tune. But an alliance between Nazis and *integralistas* was highly unlikely, because their goals were in contradiction: integralism stood for Brazilian nationalism and virtually forced assimilation of minority groups, while the NSDAP believed in German superiority and urged the immigrants to guard their German identity zealously. This conflict was apparent to the Brazilian press, which ascribed to the Nazi *Auslandsorganisation* a practice of *desnacionalização*, denationalizing, as opposed to the Brazilian nationalist program of *nacionalização*, the creation of a homogeneous, culturally united nation.[8] *Nacionalização* was actually the name for President Vargas's own policy of Brazilianization, not the program of the *integralistas*, who wished to carry it further. Both Brazilian positions were in direct conflict with Nazi aims; indeed, German Ambassador Karl Ritter, afflicted by his own version of great power blindness to small power initiative, assumed Vargas's policies were instituted at the behest of the United States. To representatives of both Berlin and Washington, the facts – that this was a conflict among Brazilians over Brazilian issues – did not fit their assumptions of Latin American inferiority and malleability.

The following September, a Chilean fascist organization with the evocative name of the *nacistas* attempted its own coup, with disastrous results: more than sixty of the seventy-one putschists were shot dead by police. The founders of the *Movimiento Nacional-Socialista de Chile*, Jorge González von Marées and Carlos Keller, both came from German-Chilean families. Unabashed partisans of fascist and racist ideology, they named their movement after the preeminent fascist party in the early 1930s, hoping to capture some of the reflected limelight. There the connection ended. Their hero and model was not Hitler or Mussolini but Diego Portales, the authoritarian Chilean leader of the nineteenth century. Their intellectual inspiration came from Chilean authors who celebrated the Chilean "race," and they rejected the NSDAP program.[9] In return, the AO in Chile criticized the *nacistas* for being insufficiently anti-Semitic and for making the same demand that prevented any alliance between the Nazis and the Brazilian *integralistas*: urging German-Chileans to abandon their German ethnic identity and assimilate into Chilean culture. This helps explain why the *nacistas* "never received any support, financial or otherwise, from the German government."[10]

As the Hitler-Stalin pact would notoriously demonstrate, the Nazis were capable of temporary alliances with incompatible ideologies for tactical gain. And their influence was palpable inside the military establishments of Argentina, Chile, and Bolivia historically trained by German officers. But in the absence of any evidence of German involvement in the coup attempts, it made little sense to ascribe to the Nazis responsibility for an action carried out by their rivals – unless one believed that Latin Americans never acted independently, operating only at the behest of one or another great power.

FEAR OF A FIFTH COLUMN

Washington reacted similarly to reported coup attempts in Argentina in 1939,[11] Uruguay in the summer of 1940,[12] and Colombia[13] and Bolivia in August 1941.[14] "Conspiracy has followed conspiracy," intoned President Roosevelt.[15] British disinformation specialists made the most of these opportunities to warn the Americans that they faced a common enemy. And lurid press accounts transformed the whispering campaigns into conventional wisdom.

In each case of supposed external subversion, U.S. assumptions made up for the lack of evidence of German involvement. The anxieties over Nazi intrigue stemmed not only from the well-publicized AO activities in Latin

America but were provoked by events occurring in an area U.S. officials habitually accorded far more importance. Between April and June 1940, Germany invaded Denmark, Norway, the Netherlands, Belgium, and France, subduing them more rapidly than expected. Each collapse produced a wave of rumors that German success on the battlefield was produced not only by military superiority, but by a fifth column of traitorous German residents – including German Jews. FDR's friend and ambassador William C. Bullitt, recalled from Paris after the fall of France, told a Philadelphia audience that "more than one-half the spies captured doing actual military spy work against the French army were refugees from Germany."[16] Bullitt repeated his warnings about the "diabolically efficient organization of Germany as to its Fifth Column" to the White House.[17] President Roosevelt, cabinet officials, and members of Congress joined the U.S. press in blaming the disaster of 1940 on German infiltrators and warning of a similar threat at home. Assistant Secretary of State Adolf Berle recorded in his diary the "shattering experience" of listening to a Hearst Newsreels reporter describe "the way the Fifth Column was already in control of New York...it frightened me completely," Berle wrote, until he checked with the FBI, learned that the situation was not nearly so grave, and was able to "begin to pull myself together."[18]

A calmer look at the evidence later would show a much more limited role for any fifth column. In Norway and Yugoslavia, some German inhabitants did serve as interpreters for invading troops and identified anti-Nazi German citizens there. But the contemporary reports of German expatriate farmers across Europe scything their crops into arrows pointing bomber pilots toward their targets, or putting on uniforms and directing the invading armies, were greatly exaggerated.[19]

Nevertheless, the myth of the "mysterious omnipotence" of the fifth column captured the imagination of the public, not only in Europe but in the United States as well.[20] In early 1940, isolationist Senator Robert R. Reynolds of North Carolina announced that the FBI was receiving more than 217 reports of sabotage a day and urged that every person in the United States be fingerprinted. "Alien enemies, members of the 'fifth column,' are coming from across the Atlantic," Reynolds declared. "They are entering the United States from across the Canadian border; they are coming north across the Rio Grande from the south, and other members of the 'fifth column' are already here by the hundreds of thousands.... The 'fifth column' is here and the Trojan horses in great herds are grazing upon the green, tender grasses of the pastures of America."[21] The public's receptiveness to these images was confirmed by their eager consumption of an outpouring of films, comic books, radio programs, and pulp fiction on the fifth column theme. Newspapers reported that such diverse sectors of society as the American Legion, Navajo tribes, and Midwestern college campuses all were mobilizing locally against fifth column infiltrators.[22]

Latin America held a prominent place in the nightmare. FDR wrote to Ambassador Claude Bowers in Chile in May 1940: "I think there is no doubt that in the event of a continued German victory in Europe, German agents in many Latin American countries will immediately undertake activities with the view to overthrowing existing governments."[23] Roosevelt took seriously information he received even from nonexperts outside government, such as the unnamed friend with "exceptional connections in South America" who offered Roosevelt this sophisticated analysis of the security situation there: "the power boys in the army, navy and the political cabal are pro-Hitler because under Hitler the army, navy and the big muscle men get the money." Forwarding the letter to Secretary of State Hull, FDR penned a covering note: "Please let *no one* see this. Please talk to me about it, at your leisure."[24]

The concerns over Latin America's helplessness were shared across the political spectrum. Congressman Martin Dies, chair of the House Un-American Activities Committee, warned in August that a million German settlers were "organized in companies and battalions" to "invade South America from within."[25] Muckraker Carleton Beals set aside his years of protesting U.S. intervention in Latin America (he had written the first sympathetic dispatches from Augusto Sandino's rebellion against the Marine occupation of Nicaragua) and transformed himself into a one-man campaign on the issue, bringing out a barrage of widely read articles and books, including *The Coming Struggle for Latin America*, which went through six printings, and an adventure novel, *Dawn over the Amazon*, depicting a fascist conquest of Brazil.[26] *The Coming Struggle* asserted that the pleasure excursion boats used by the Nazi Strength through Joy organization were "easily convertible into airplane carriers" and that "the equivalent of strong Nazi regimes exist in several countries."[27] An *American Mercury* article on Nazi intrigue in "lovely little Costa Rica" warned of easy pickings for outside aggressors, using typical gendered language: "[The] most white and Spanish of all the Latin-American republics, Costa Rica is the most vulnerable."[28] To drum up support for international antifascist struggles, the Lawyers Committee on American Relations with Spain also indulged in rumor mongering about the threat to the south, describing a mythical German naval base in Peru in which "German warships and submarines go in and out and rows of Nazi sentinels guard the concession boundaries."[29]

Many people in the United States learned what little they knew of the countries to the south by reading popular travel writer John Gunther's 1941 book, *Inside Latin America*. Gunther's geographical determinist explanations for our neighbors' behavior ("One cannot expect advanced political development from people who live perpetually at 12,500 feet") were a secondary theme, the principal subject being Nazi infiltration of the continent – and Latin Americans' puzzling nonchalance about it. Gunther seemed equally baffled to encounter cultured Latin Americans. "I sat down at my first dinner party hoping to hear about the Fifth Column and the Panama Canal,"

Gunther wrote with amazement of his arrival in Bogotá, "but no one would talk about anything except Marcel Proust."[30]

Government officials contributed their share to the disinformation that worked its way into conventional wisdom in the United States. Secretary of War Henry L. Stimson told a press conference in August 1940 that eighty-one Axis agents working in the Canal Zone had been detained and faced deportation. The next day he acknowledged his error: they were not "agents," but "aliens," emigrants arrested because their papers were not in order. But corrections are never as widely read as sensational headlines, and the story became a fresh piece of evidence of Nazi intrigue.[31] Stimson generally took a more measured view of what he called "Hitler's so-called fifth column movements in South America," which he considered "attempts to frighten us from sending help where it will be most effective" – meaning Europe.[32]

Within the region, agitation over the Nazi threat never reached U.S. levels, partly because of Latin Americans' greater familiarity with their German neighbors, and partly because government officials there, relying on their own sources of information and eager to show they were in control, denied the danger existed. But some Latin Americans with political agendas of their own did worry about the fifth column. The Costa Rican Communist Party newspaper *Trabajo* printed "a convenient blank form, which the reader could clip out, fill in with the name and address of the suspected 'quinta-columnista,' and mail to the newspaper."[33] A young professor of philosophy at the University of Montevideo, Uruguay, Hugo Fernández Artucio, Socialist Party official and tireless radio campaigner against the Nazis, gave a lecture tour in the United States and wrote the widely read *Nazi Underground in South America* (published in London as *The Nazi Octopus in South America*). He regularly overstated Nazi influence in each country, claimed incorrectly that the *Auslandsorganisation* had taken over the *Auswärtiges Amt* (AA, German Foreign Ministry) and warned that "the soldiers of the Third German Empire ... have been distributed by the thousands throughout the political underground of this continent."[34] Ernesto Giudici, soon to join the Communist Party's Central Committee in Argentina, wrote a series of sensationalist articles for *Crítica*, the largest-selling Spanish language daily in the world; in 1938, he published the collected pieces as a book titled *Hitler Conquista América*.[35]

YELLOW JOURNALISM

The reporters sent by U.S. newspapers to write about the German threat in Latin America contributed directly to the impressions held by policymakers in Washington. Many government officials and Roosevelt himself read the *New York Times* every morning.[36] There they saw their suspicions confirmed by a cycle of disinformation, as off-the-record briefings of correspondents by

U.S. embassies later appeared as dramatic, unsourced stories in papers sold in the United States – and the articles duly made their way into government reports. COLOMBIA'S NAZIS ARMED FOR ATTACK blared the headline of a piece by *Times* reporter Russell B. Porter, who traveled through Latin America in 1940 writing overheated dispatches on the Nazis' ambitions. One of his stories reported that Germans had smuggled armored cars into Colombia disguised as tractors (a rumor then circulating in Braden's embassy) and estimated Nazi Party membership at 1,500 – a 500 percent exaggeration.[37] On another occasion Porter claimed that Germans could use their airline in Ecuador, SEDTA, to launch an attack on the Panama Canal – a most unlikely scenario given the defenses that would have to be overcome by the two lumbering, obsolescent JU-52 transport planes that made up SEDTA's entire fleet.[38]

When the United Press reported that a U.S. citizen flying over Haiti had discovered a German air base there, President Roosevelt forwarded the clipping to Sumner Welles with the question, "What do you know about this and what are we doing?" Welles immediately sent an embassy official to visit the site, who discovered that the "airfield" was a mineral water bottling plant run by refugees.[39]

But when a reporter who actually knew something about air power – the Associated Press's Aviation Editor, Devon Francis – toured South America to appraise the threat posed by German-owned airlines in Colombia, Ecuador, and Peru, he was unimpressed by the handful of militarily useless old aircraft and more struck by the "spirited competition" between the German lines and Pan American Airways. It was a perceptive insight, since Pan Am took over the routes when the German lines were closed under U.S. pressure. The rivalry between SEDTA and Pan Am's Panagra line was often personal, as Francis recounted in the following anecdote:

Unable to get a seat in one of his own planes, a Panagra employee the other day bought one on SEDTA. "How many passengers do you have?" asked the American. "Seven passengers and two pigs," replied the German pilot.

"I looked around," says the American in relating the story, "for the other Yankee."

But there really were two pigs. SEDTA carries everything. That is one of the secrets of its success in Ecuador.[40]

Other news organizations exposed nothing so much as their taste for sensation and outdid one another in parading their own ignorance. Readers of the *New York Herald-Tribune* were treated to investigative reporting by the paper's drama critic, Richard Watts, who returned from a visit to Bogotá (then, as now, a center for innovative theater) to describe mythical secret airstrips and to cite such popular Colombian newspapers as "*Il Tiempo*" and "*Il Commercio*," thereby revealing a greater familiarity with Italian opera than with the Latin American press.[41] Documentary producer Alan Brown asked the State Department for assistance with his upcoming *March of Time*

18. Half the fleet of Germany's SEDTA airline, an outdated JU-52 transport plane, lands in Loja, Ecuador, drawing the interest of locals more accustomed to other forms of transportation. The *New York Times* claimed that SEDTA's two aircraft put the Panama Canal at risk. Credit: Courtesy Foto Hirtz, Quito.

newsreel on Axis subversion in Argentina, Brazil, and Uruguay; Ellis Briggs of the Latin American Division noted dryly that "Mr. Brown speaks neither Spanish nor Portuguese and has never been in South America before," but was not to be dissuaded from his project.[42] Cornelius Vanderbilt, Jr., breathlessly warned readers of *Liberty Magazine* that "German officers are training natives with German guns" in both Colombia and Costa Rica. "No one knows exactly how many Germans there are in either country," Vanderbilt wrote, "but all I talked with are sure that at least one tenth of the inhabitants have come from the Reich, and that fully 80 per cent of these are Nazis."[43] (Actual figures for Colombia were 0.04 percent and 7.5 percent, respectively, and 0.1 percent and 6 or 7 percent for Costa Rica.)[44]

The Colombian embassy in Washington regularly decried such "sensationalism." Ambassador Gabriel Turbay complained that "here in the United States, deliberately or unconsciously, official and semi-official declarations have exaggerated . . . the dangers of Nazi penetration."[45] Elsewhere, too, U.S. alarmism – and the underlying assumption that Latin Americans could not be trusted to handle their own affairs – provoked resentment among the people best able to judge local conditions. As one scholar wrote, "Washington's fascination with subversion in Latin America quickly became annoying to most governments below the Rio Grande, who argued that the real menace was the 'Sixth Column' of people who believed in the Fifth Column."[46]

BRITISH DECEPTION

Pulling back the curtain of disinformation often revealed the wizards of British intelligence at work. From a skyscraper in Manhattan, a chemical lab in Canada, and a postal censorship station in Bermuda, William Stephenson's British Security Coordination (BSC) engaged in extensive propaganda and forgery to create a climate of public support for aid to Britain and to try to bring the United States into the war.[47] BSC agents took their counterintelligence campaign to Latin America as well, where the priority of the British was not so much to amass verifiable information on the Nazi menace in Latin America as to fabricate such information in order to persuade the U.S. government of the urgency of the threat – using artifice whenever necessary. In June 1940, BSC agent Fred Stagg forged a letter implicating Major Elias Belmonte in a German coup plot in Bolivia; revelation of the alleged plot gave the Bolivian government an excuse to jail its domestic opponents, and the Belmonte affair became fodder for a host of U.S. reports on German subversion in Latin America.[48] A year later, Stagg turned up in Colombia, where he boasted openly to Ambassador Braden about his success with the Belmonte forgery and offered to repeat the ruse there. Braden declined. In early 1942, Stagg would return with a more ambitious proposal: the United States and Great Britain should jointly assassinate the eccentric, anti-Semitic and independent-minded Colombian foreign minister, the physician and writer Luis López de Mesa. Braden, horrified by the suggestion, reported it to the State Department, which persuaded the British Foreign Office that Stagg was unfit for further service in Latin America. Yet the FBI continued for some years to countenance his forgeries and to circulate them in official reports; the Belmonte affair would have a lingering impact on U.S. policy toward Bolivia throughout the war. (See Chapter 4.)[49]

President Roosevelt was not always immune to the influence of British deception, especially when it suited his purposes. It seemed essential to evoke the danger of a German threat to the south in order to persuade a somnolent American public that the war concerned them directly. In a speech on Navy Day, 27 October 1941, FDR dramatically announced the discovery of a secret map revealing Germany's plans to conquer South America and divide the continent into five satellite states under Nazi control. The map was reportedly seized from a German agent, although evidence suggests that it came from the BSC.[50] Roosevelt also urged his aides to read an astonishing report by the British Secret Intelligence Service warning of imminent German takeovers in Argentina, Brazil, Chile, Peru, Colombia, Venezuela, and Ecuador. The British recommended nothing less than staging preemptive coups against all seven governments, using "bribery," "elimination of key personnel," and "drastic action against certain intractable elements" to install compliant regimes, all at an estimated cost of $1.6 million. The project went nowhere, but it was typical of British efforts to convince the

U.S. government of the gravity of the threat, and of the need to engage in joint action.[51] Despite some skepticism from Berle, who warned Hull in September 1941 that "British intelligence has been very active in making things appear dangerous" in South America and that the U.S. government should "be a little on our guard against false scares," the disinformation campaign contributed to an overall impression.[52]

Fear of a fifth column grew to alarming proportions in the U.S. mind in the summer of 1940, when the specter of Germany's seizure of French colonies in West Africa and the possibility of British defeat seemed to increase the likelihood of an invasion of the Americas. Until then, the officials who knew Latin America well believed that these stories of Nazi plots were much exaggerated. Laurence Duggan, head of the American Republics Affairs Division (ARA), thought the press was exploiting such fears to sell newspapers, and that U.S. businessmen were issuing dire warnings in order to gain commercial advantage over their German competitors. Selden Chapin, assistant chief of ARA, believed – correctly – that the Nazis' maximum strategic goal was to persuade Latin Americans to remain neutral in regard to the European conflict. Welles and Berle were more suspicious, but they did not become alarmed until Western Europe began to fall.[53]

That crisis, with the possibility that the French navy would wind up in German hands and that Great Britain might be next, leaving the Atlantic undefended, brought about several parallel developments inside the U.S. government that greatly increased the amount of intelligence reporting on subversion in Latin America. Berle directed all U.S. missions in Latin America to submit information on the fifth column threat. Laurence Duggan sent a long memorandum on Nazi activities (prepared by German exile Tete Harens Tetens) to Cordell Hull, warning of extensive Nazi paramilitary preparations in South America.[54] And the collection of intelligence in Latin America was systematized for the first time.

INADEQUATE INTELLIGENCE

These first concerted attempts to determine the extent of the German threat began as an ad hoc effort, because, until World War II, the United States had only a rudimentary foreign intelligence service dependent on embassy cables, reports by G-2 (military intelligence) and ONI (naval intelligence), and information volunteered by private citizens. Assistant Secretary of State Dean Acheson remarked that the State Department's information-gathering methods "differed only by reason of the typewriter and the telegraph from the techniques which John Quincy Adams was using in St. Petersburg and Benjamin Franklin was using in Paris." General George Marshall complained that most "intelligence" was "little more than what a military attaché could learn at a dinner, more or less, over the coffee cups."[55] In Latin America, the problem was especially acute. Sumner Welles lamented the fact that the most-talented U.S. military officers shunned assignment to Latin America because such backwater postings were "prejudicial to their promotion."[56] The military attachés unable to avoid these posts became the source of much of the intelligence reporting on the Nazi threat; in carrying out their duties, they often amply confirmed the deficiencies that got them assigned to such undesirable positions in the first place.

In Bogotá, Ambassador Braden regarded his military attachés with contempt. Colonel John Walton Lang, brought in to help Colombia start its own intelligence service, was "just too utterly dumb" to get one going and soon left the country. Lieutenant Wesley P. Cox had a predilection for drunken brawling in nightclubs. In one memorable incident, Cox and a prostitute attracted the attention of police when they tussled in the street, half-dressed and shrieking at each other. It emerged that Cox had refused to pay the woman for her services, claiming "diplomatic privilege." (The lieutenant was eventually court-martialed.) Braden had another military attaché, Colonel Carl Strong, transferred for exceeding his authority and all but ordering President Eduardo Santos to intern every German in the country. When the aristocratic Santos heard that, Braden recalled, "the President nearly fell off his chair."[57] (Colombia, at the time, was a neutral country.) Strong's knowledge of the region's geography was exemplified by his warning that German planes would attack Colombia "via Dakar and Nepal."[58] Despite his "erratic and undependable judgment," Strong was nominated by the War Department to become head of military intelligence for all of Central and South America; the State Department managed to get him banned from further assignment to Latin America altogether.[59]

Credulity combined with regional ignorance encouraged Colonel Joseph Pate, military attaché of the Guatemalan Legation, to warn in 1940 that "the German Government could arrange for the overthrow of this Government and all the other Governments in Central America at a moment's notice" by using local residents loyal to Hitler. This message was dutifully conveyed to the State Department by the chargé d'affaires, John Moors Cabot, with the caveat that he did not believe it likely to succeed, since the German community in Guatemala "could scarcely muster 500 men of military age" who were in any case scattered around the country, not known to have trained or stockpiled arms, and were under surveillance.[60]

Some of the naval officers were more capable. In Guatemala, all five Office of Naval Intelligence staffers could speak some Spanish and were careful to keep a healthy distance from notoriously unreliable informants.[61] With seventy-nine personnel in U.S. missions in Latin America by 1938, ONI was the largest U.S. intelligence network in the region until the FBI arrived two years later. The head of the ONI's Latin American Department, Colonel Robert Blake, was a University of California graduate who had visited every major Latin American port and spoke fluent Spanish. Blake thought that reports of secret Nazi bases were so much "hot air" stirred up by the *New York Times*, and some of his agents were circumspect in their reporting.[62]

But not all of them were careful. The naval attaché in Cuba wrongly claimed that all German men between the ages of 16 and 65 living in the Americas were subject to conscription into a secret auxiliary force of spies and saboteurs.[63] Ambassador Edwin Wilson in Panama found frustrating the "red-tape, professional jealousy particularly as between ONI and G-2, and an amazing amount of amateurishness" that characterized the army and navy intelligence officers his embassy dealt with.[64] U.S. officials in charge of collating commercial intelligence for Latin America decided not to rely on naval or military intelligence reports because "experience" had shown "it is not safe" to do so.[65]

With the entire bureaucracy on the lookout for subversives, errors could creep into the record at many points. The State Department's Central America chief, John Moors Cabot, remembered keeping a close eye on the reports of the postal censors "because they contained an amazing amount of *mis*information. The censors simply didn't know what they were talking about." He cited a censorship excerpt headed "American lady visits notorious Nazi *finca*," which named two friends of his, both pro-Allied, but confused the name of their property with another German-owned ranch. "I stormed down to see the officer handling censorship and set the record straight in this and many other cases," Cabot wrote. "But I wonder how often I failed to catch some unjust comment and how many people are still branded as notorious Nazis because of mistakes of this kind?"[66]

The FBI's J. Edgar Hoover had been lobbying for an intelligence role in Latin America ever since the limelight began to fade for G-men catching gangsters and shone instead on those protecting national security in a time of crisis. Hoover engaged in a struggle for authority in Latin America with his chief bureaucratic rival, William J. ("Wild Bill") Donovan, who headed the Office of the Coordinator of Information (COI), later the Office of Strategic Services (OSS). Meanwhile, the military intelligence agencies sought to defend their own preeminence in the region. In June 1940, the blitzkrieg in Western Europe heightened the stakes, and Roosevelt settled the squabbling with a telephone call ordering that the FBI be responsible for intelligence gathering in the Americas and the ONI and G-2 watch the rest of the world.[67] Hoover and Adolf Berle proposed the creation of a "Special Intelligence Service"* under Hoover's control, to operate with U.S. diplomatic missions to combat financial, economic, political, and subversive activities detrimental to the security of the United States. By 1941, FBI agents were posted at U.S. embassies throughout Latin America, designated as "legal attachés" or liaison officers to national police forces, supposedly working

---

* The SIS label was rarely used, perhaps to avoid confusion with the British Secret Intelligence Service, and because the operatives were simply FBI agents working abroad.

undercover. One of their primary duties was to compile lists of suspected Axis nationals and sympathizers.[68] That the FBI's mandate was domestic investigative work was no obstacle to snooping in "America's backyard": before the war was over, Hoover would have 360 agents based in Latin America, spending a budget of over $5 million.[69]

The agents Hoover rushed to Latin America generally made up in enthusiasm and imagination for what they lacked in competence and experience. Most were new recruits with little training beyond a crash course at the FBI Academy at Quantico, Virginia. Agent Donald Charles Bird recalled later that, in August 1941, he was given two weeks of language instruction – in Spanish – before being sent to Brazil.[70] Their work did not impress the old hands at the State Department. The FBI's claim that 77 percent of Colombian military officers were pro-Nazi struck the desk officers in ARA as "somewhat exaggerated" and the embassy as false. To be sure, Germans had provided training to the Colombian army for years, and the German Legation did mail a weekly propaganda sheet to some officers. But the statistic turned out to be based on reports by one or two informants, who had classified every Colombian officer as either pro-United States or pro-Nazi – with no allowance for neutrality, indifference, or garden-variety Latin American distrust of the United States.[71] Hoover also forwarded such gems of intelligence work as the warning that "1400 airplanes and 50 submarines are near readiness at Martinique for an attack on the Panama Canal, Puerto Rico, Florida or the Florida Keys, and Cuba."[72] As evidence of Nazi military preparations in Colombia, the FBI offered the ominous discovery of "tractors" and "signs for directions" on German farms, as well as the threatening presence of "rice fields" and "large storage tanks."[73] In its principal document on Bolivia, circulated widely at the highest level of the bureaucracy, the FBI fell for Fred Stagg's Belmonte hoax (already debunked by Braden and Berle) and printed a menacing-looking graphic displaying the twelve thousand German residents of Bolivia – men, women, and children – lined up like so many storm troopers. This fearsome image masked one detail: 8,500 of these Germans on the march were actually Jewish refugees from Germany and Austria – unlikely footsoldiers for Hitler.[74]

State Department officials were quick to object to the FBI's new role, especially when the agents began to claim instant expertise in their new stomping grounds. In October 1941, in a remarkable gesture, foreign service officers meeting in Havana unanimously condemned the State Department's practice of transmitting reports on local political conditions labeled "from an unnamed but responsible Government source." ARA chief Laurence Duggan endorsed the protest: "If these reports come from the FBI the officers wish to know it," he wrote to Berle and George A. Gordon, head of the Division of Foreign Activity Correlation. "The officers at the conference seemed to be fully aware that there are under-cover FBI operatives in many countries. Many of them gave the impression that these operatives stand out like sore

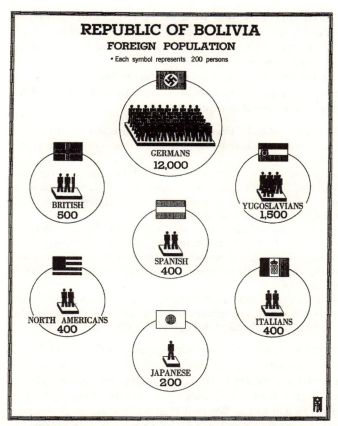

19. Urged on by a J. Edgar Hoover eager to retain the spotlight during the war, the FBI issued warnings such as this illustration from a report on Bolivia, depicting that country's 12,000 German residents in military formation under a swastika. The only catch: 8,500 of them were Jewish refugees. Credit: Hopkins Papers, Box 141, FDR Library.

thumbs. Their representation and objectives become quickly known."[75] The State Department's response was to send a "read and destroy" note to all U.S. chiefs of mission in the region, telling them that the phrase "from a confidential source within the Government" would henceforth signify that the data came from the Bureau – to be treated with caution.[76]

The tension endured. FBI Agent Robert Dreher, sent to the Dominican Republic under the cover of factory representative for the Smith-Kirkpatrick tractor company, caused consternation among the diplomats because he liked to brag about his embassy contacts while trying to bribe potential informants.[77] Embassy chiefs in Colombia fought a running battle with the FBI's Richard C. Godfrey, who drafted reports dependent on informants the embassy considered unreliable, and then sent the memos (warning of imminent coup attempts and the like) directly to Washington without clearing them with the ambassador. Eventually, both Dreher and Godfrey were recalled, but not before damage was done.[78]

In its first year on the job, the FBI compiled what it had learned into a broad memorandum on "Axis Aspirations in South America." The ARA's Selden Chapin wrote a devastating critique:

[D]ealing with possibilities and probabilities of this sort is a grave and delicate matter requiring qualities of judgment not too well displayed in the selection of material for use in this memorandum. . . .

As an instance, the statement may be cited on page 16: "It has also been reported that Germany is constructing a fleet of submarines, approximately 1,000 in number, with a carrying capacity of 25 to 50 tons, which fleet will reportedly carry Nazi expeditionary forces to Colombia and Venezuela."

Without going into the technical difficulties of such a project and disregarding the fact that such a force, if available, might presumably be used more effectively in the campaign against merchant shipping, it is noteworthy that the original report to this Government was in the form of an example of the kind of exaggerated rumors which were current in South America. . . .

Other instances of exaggeration, or erroneous evaluation, based upon incomplete knowledge of conditions in the field and upon insufficient background as to general conditions in these countries, could be cited throughout the document.[79]

In another survey, the FBI presented its understanding of the "geopolitical theory" behind Nazi purposes in Latin America: the Germans planned to unite with Spanish fascist disciples of Francisco Franco in the region to bring about the return of Spain's former colonies to the mother country.[80] The feebleness of Spanish fascism in the Western Hemisphere aside, the notion that after more than a century of independence anyone in Latin America would collaborate in such a project would be laughable if it did not indicate the profound naiveté of a major government agency dabbling in foreign affairs.[81]

The implications of all of this for the deportation program were clear: the FBI, directly responsible for identifying suspects for deportation and internment, was home to some of the most poorly informed U.S. officials working in Latin America.

COUNTERINTELLIGENCE

There were also some capable investigators among the U.S. intelligence agents sent to Latin America to counter the Nazi threat, but they were not speculating about imperial conspiracies, and they were not involved in the deportation program. Instead, posted to the largest countries, and armed with a secret weapon, they were busy catching real spies.

In 1935, Admiral Wilhelm Canaris took command of the *Abwehr* (German military intelligence) with the aim of expanding the number of agents abroad who could supply information of military value to the Reich. In a covert counterpart to the public efforts of the AO, Canaris's organization recruited expatriates from business and commercial circles and built up a network of spies in Argentina, Brazil, Chile (the ABC countries), and Mexico. Some of them were equipped with wireless communications kits.[82] Latin America was not a priority for the *Abwehr*, and its agents' main task there was to relay information from agents in the United States. Meteorological and geomagnetic interference impeded east–west radio transmission across the Atlantic but did not affect north–south transmissions. Thus South America became the main radio link between Germany and its operatives in the United States.[83]*

The *Abwehr* agents provided estimates on U.S. war production figures and other data compiled from press clippings and agents' reports from the north. Once the war was on, they sometimes signaled the departure of ships from Latin American ports; this does not appear to have contributed to any actual submarine sinkings.[84] Captured records show the *Abwehr* did make a serious attempt to map and spy on the Panama Canal, but the German agents assigned to the task complained that Canal security was so tight that they could not get close enough to observe ship movements. One assessment describes the *Abwehr* as "a plodding, utilitarian and rather mild-mannered organization whose plots and stratagems seemed – and often were – naive and diffident."[85] At any rate, the spies might have caused more damage if they had not been so easily defeated by their own flawed security practices. The secret weapon British and U.S. intelligence agencies wielded was a copy of the German code: they had been listening in on the *Abwehr*'s radio transmissions since 1940. As a result, they could warn the convoys, identify the agents, and ensure their arrest.[86] Where radio intercepts were insufficient, inept German agents often revealed themselves through lavish spending, drunken indiscretions, or disclosure of their secret missions to lovers who promptly went to the police.[87] The FBI's work in Argentina, Brazil, Chile, and Mexico, despite its "critical deficiencies," and assisted by local law enforcement agencies, contributed significantly to the sorry record of *Abwehr* spying.[88]

One of the main success stories of counterintelligence work in Latin America was the joint effort by the Colombian government and the FBI to restrict the smuggling of platinum during the war. Colombia was one of three main world producers of the metal, essential to the aircraft industry.

---

* The *Abwehr*'s rival agency, the *Sicherheitsdienst*, sent a few agents to Argentina and Brazil; some of their reports are in "Südamerika: SD-Meldungen," Fiche 2973, Inland IIg, PAAA. Ribbentrop's personal intelligence service, the Dienststelle Ribbentrop, apparently achieved nothing in Latin America. See Rout and Bratzel, *The Shadow War*, 10–15.

The FBI helped Colombia identify smugglers, and the United States offered to purchase the entire output of the strategic material. Estimates vary on the effectiveness of the crackdown, but it was significant. (The six people deported from Colombia to the United States for platinum smuggling comprised two Syrians, a Spaniard, a Russian, an Austrian, and an Egyptian Jew. So much for national identity as a reliable indicator of dangerousness.)[89]

With only a handful of exceptions, Germans involved in espionage were confined to the ABC countries and Mexico, countries that did not participate in the deportation program. Postwar FBI summaries of its campaign in Latin America name exactly six individuals – Heriberto Schwartau-Eskildsen, Hermann Heinrich Rullhusen, and Ernest Gustav Max Vogel of Colombia; Hans Christoph Von Buch and Ferdinand Enrique Paul Hans Westhoff of Peru; and Heinrich Loeschner of Ecuador – who spied for Germany among the four thousand German deportees sent to the United States. In addition, Ingo Kalinowsky of Costa Rica and Georg Nicolaus of Mexico admitted to spying for Germany.[90] Thus the successful counterespionage work of Allied intelligence did not overlap with the program for interning enemy aliens. Few of the legal attachés compiling lists of dangerous enemy aliens in the other countries displayed much skill, and they did not have the benefit of being able to listen in on the conversations of their targets. Undertrained and inadequately sensitive to local conditions, they played a crucial role in the development of the deportation program: first, by contributing to exaggerated assessments of the danger posed by German residents, and then by selecting those individual Germans to be deported and interned in the United States.

LOCAL POLICE

With no reliable sources of their own, the FBI agents established close working relationships with local police forces, thereby intensifying support for the enforcers of regimes that were often corrupt to the core, especially in Central America and the Caribbean. (See Chapters 3 and 4.)

This reliance on local law enforcement brought mixed results. Asking police or military leaders in countries ruled by dictatorships for the names of dangerous Germans often yielded a list of the dictator's personal enemies, or the owners of attractive real estate coveted by his friends. And the local police officers did not necessarily display the requisite talent or honesty needed for effective investigation.

Douglas Henderson, U.S. Vice Consul in Cochabamba, Bolivia, employed as his principal informant – "Source A" – the former assistant police chief, Esau Peñaranda. Henderson had to defend Peñaranda against the charge by Bolivian embassy employees that he was "known to drink, go to parties and not pay the bill. They also said that he orders merchandise and supplies for his personal use and never pays for it and is generally considered a bad hombre."[91] Henderson retorted: "I don't think that the stated criticism affects his efficiency," but soon had to hire a replacement.[92] Henderson had high hopes for the new "Source A," Angel Anzoleaga, a former police officer. But again the embassy found his reports "a little disappointing, inasmuch as they apparently contain only information which source A has received from the police files and represent absolutely no independent investigation on his part." Indeed, Anzoleaga's reports were usually limited to providing the name and residence address of German nationals, with the occasional notation "owns a radio receiver."[93] The source hired to replace Anzoleaga, Julio Eguino, openly bragged about his connection to the consulate and tried to extort money from Cochabamba residents by threatening to place them on the U.S. blacklist if they did not pay him off.[94]

Ex-cops were not the only Ecuadorian officials turning the anti-Nazi campaign to their own purposes. In March 1944, Major Vernet L. Gresham, the U.S. assistant military attaché, attended a secret meeting of the "Ecuadoran Committee for the Political Defense of the Continent" at which police officials and immigration authorities blamed ongoing political unrest and strikes on Axis fomentation and promised strong measures in response. Major Gresham suspected that the committee's intention was "to strive rather for the maintenance in power of the Arroyo administration than on behalf of hemispheric defense" – a pattern widely repeated throughout the region, as U.S. pressure and assistance in cracking down on Nazi subversives was transformed into a useful tool for repressing domestic dissent.[95]

The Colombian Policía Nacional and its director of investigation and identification, Arturo Vallejo Sánchez, were among the more effective and judicious forces keeping an eye on potential subversives. (It was perhaps no coincidence that Colombia was at the time among the most democratic of Latin American countries.) The Colombian police shadowed suspected Nazis, obtained photographs of their meetings, tapped their telephones, and read their mail. President Santos's government not only kept tabs on suspect Germans within Colombia, but Colombian diplomats in Quito pressured the Ecuadorian government to be stricter with its own local Nazi Party.[96] As the publisher of Colombia's largest newspaper *El Tiempo*, Santos was very well informed about national affairs, and he took a balanced view of the potential danger from local Germans. Forwarding a police report on Nazi activity in Medellín to his foreign minister, the president wrote in a covering note: "Even though I think there is a little literature here, I also think there is some truth."[97]

INTELLIGENCE FOR SALE

Unfamiliar with local society and unable to speak Spanish or German, most U.S. agents could think of nothing better than to accept the word not only of the local police but also of any informant who showed up at their offices. There was no shortage of volunteers. "The embassies took all comers," recalled Justice Department troubleshooter Raymond W. Ickes, who traveled throughout Latin America to investigate faulty U.S. intelligence reporting during the war.[98] In Guayaquil, Ecuador, word on the street said the going rate for denouncing a Nazi to the U.S. consul was $50.[99] The bartender at the Roxy Night Club earned a retainer of $7 a month for passing on saloon gossip. The consulate paid an official in the Ecuadorian Immigration Office ten *sucres* (about sixty cents) for every photograph and short biography of German Nazis he could provide. The enterprising bureaucrat then discovered eighty-three Nazis in Guayaquil, thereby quadrupling his monthly salary. (German documents captured at the end of the war reveal a maximum of twenty-six Party members in Guayaquil at the time.)[100]

In Ecuador's capital, Quito, imported whiskey may have lubricated the flow of denunciations. FBI agent Clarence Moore was in charge of drawing up lists of dangerous Germans and pressuring President Carlos Arroyo del Rio to deport them. Ecuadorian customs receipts show that Moore ordered fifty cases of whiskey in his first year on the job, well beyond the far more modest personal requests of his colleagues or the official stock for Embassy functions.[101] Some agents in dusty Latin American posts did prefer to do their investigating through the bottom of a glass, but it is impossible to know whether Moore's private stock went to slake a powerful thirst, served as inventory for a sideline enterprise or, most likely, purchased information. Whatever the truth, the deportation lists prepared in Moore's office were based on "a large number of confidential informants."[102]

All intelligence agencies relied on paid informants as a matter of course. The ONI, arguing that "judicious bribery" in Mexico would "obtain more information and greater cooperation...than anything else," funneled fees of $10 to $50 to the informants hired by their man Holland McCombs, contributing editor to *Time* and *Life*. Maynard Owen Williams, Foreign Editor of *National Geographic*, also provided his services. Archaeologists, prospectors, and businessmen received monthly retainers of $100 to $400 for amateur spy work.[103]

The trouble with paid informants is that they are paid only if they have material to provide – a structural incentive to invent information that contributed greatly to the inflation of the German threat in U.S. assessments. This fundamental weakness in the system was recognized by Ambassador Josephus Daniels in Mexico City, who complained to his diary in April 1941:

Almost every day we have a call from some Mexican who tells us of the existence of Nazi organizations.... Of course the Military and Naval Attachés have sources and are able to employ people who are reliable to get them information, but my experience is that most of the people who apply for positions of this character and wish compensation are inclined to exaggerate the situation in order to make us believe that their services are more valuable than I think they are.[104]

Spruille Braden, who moved on from Colombia to become ambassador to Cuba in 1942, brought with him a healthy disdain for the military attachés and their favorite sources, and ordered them to stop buying intelligence. "You may get an informant who gives you one good piece of information, but then if you take him on permanently he thinks he's got to earn his pay," Braden explained later. "Then he begins to invent stuff in order to earn his stipend."[105] Braden recalled that the head of Cuban Intelligence, Colonel Mariano Faget, "once assured me he would coach the worst stumblebum in Havana for fifteen minutes in my presence, send him to my Naval and Military attachés, and guarantee that he would come out with not less than twenty dollars."[106] Braden's order to the attachés to cease and desist immediately sparked a formal protest by the heads of all three intelligence agencies – Hoover of the FBI, Major General George V. Strong of G-2, and Rear Admiral Harold C. Train of ONI – and made no impact on the business of paying cash for "positive information" about Nazis.[107] "Negative information" (i.e., that an individual German or the German community in general was *not* engaged in subversive activities) was not held to be worth paying for. The implications for balanced reporting are clear.

THE AMATEURS

As an alternative to paying "stumblebums," Braden turned to an apparently incorruptible source: the writer Ernest Hemingway, whose passionate hatred of fascism and connections among Cuba's Spanish exiles made him an ideal candidate. The ambassador approved Hemingway's scheme to create what he called his "crime shop" or "crook factory," staffed by "a few wharf rats, some down-at-heel *pelota* players and former bullfighters, two Basque priests, assorted exiled counts and dukes, several Loyalists and Franquistas." In exchange for their reports, Hemingway asked Braden to equip his fishing yacht, the *Pilar*, with a bazooka to blow holes in German submarines and machine guns to mow down the crews. In Braden's telling, he skirted regulations and provided the weapons. The ambassador evaluated Hemingway's success differently on different occasions: in 1953, Braden declared that Hemingway never found a sub and "we never got anything that was of any particular import" from his exile network. By 1971, Braden had apparently changed his opinion, for he wrote in his memoirs: "[Hemingway] built up an excellent organization and did an A-One job." That did not include sinking any submarines.[108]

Outside of Cuba, in several key countries, the principal paid informants emerged from among the thousands of Jewish refugees in Latin America, who spoke German, hated Nazis, desperately needed a source of income, and thus seemed perfectly suited for the job.

Little has been written about the German Jewish informants who provided intelligence to Allied diplomatic missions.[109] They should not be confused with antifascist refugee activists who performed valuable work in other ways, publishing the writings of exile intellectuals and presenting an accurate picture of Nazi Germany to the Latin American public (in organizations such as those described in Chapter 1). The record of the much smaller group of amateur informants is equivocal and suggests that some of the most energetic could also be the least effective.

In Guatemala, Alfredo Schlesinger took payments from the British Embassy to print pamphlets denouncing alleged Nazis, and he named names to the British and U.S. embassies directly. Schlesinger sometimes extorted money from his targets to keep them off his personal blacklist, leading one U.S. embassy official to remark, "I wouldn't trust him around the corner with a red-hot stove."[110] A consensus among ONI, the Military Intelligence Division (MID), and State Department officials that his information was "unreliable" did not prevent FBI agents posted to Guatemala from using Schlesinger's lists as a principal source of information on dangerous Germans.[111]

In Bolivia, as the FBI admitted after the war, although some of the refugees providing denunciations of Nazis "were known to be absolutely reliable, . . . others undoubtedly reported all of their personal enemies to be Nazis."[112] The most egregious example of the latter category was Ernst Schumacher, publisher of the antifascist German-language newspaper *Rundschau vom Illimani*, who spied for both the Bolivian police and the U.S. Embassy. Schumacher impressed his patrons by breaking into the German legation to steal documents, but he also used his connections to denounce his former landlord, with whom he had quarreled, as well as a rival émigré who was also active in anti-Nazi circles. Schumacher's targets wound up on U.S. deportation lists until 1943, when a delegation of Jewish refugees went to the U.S. embassy to protest that Schumacher had created problems for at least a dozen of his coreligionists and should be restrained.[113] "Statements from anonymous sources and from members of anti-Axis organizations" provided nearly all the evidence the U.S. embassy used to identify Germans it wished to have deported from Bolivia once the war began.[114]

French and British nationals and Jewish exiles living in Ecuador joined together in 1938 to form the *Comité Interaliado*, headed by the French citizen Pierre Lafargue. At first they worked to distribute anti-Nazi publications, and soon they were spying on local German residents. It was not hard to identify the leading members of the Nazi Party; Ecuadorian newspapers published a photograph of thirty men and boys in brownshirts, posing proudly in front of the German Club in Quito.[115] But the Inter-Allied Committee was more ambitious. Arturo Weilbauer, a Jewish lawyer who fled with his family from Germany in 1939, recounted in his memoirs that the Committee investigated every family whose children attended the German School, placing him and other refugees under suspicion. Lafargue paid a visit one day to German political exile Armin Huber, whose wife was Jewish, and surprised him with the news that the Committee believed he was sheltering a member of the SA (*Sturmabteilung* or Storm troopers) and had been in contact with a German submarine.[116] When the U.S. embassy sought candidates for deportation in early 1942, the committee drew up a list of several hundred dangerous Germans and Italians. The embassy pared it down to 122, but noted that Ecuadorian officials "thought it ridiculous to suggest they put out of the country old men who had lived here for a long time, some from forty to fifty years, who, in official opinion, had long since lost contact with their homelands, hence had little interest in isms, their main desire being to conserve what they had and remain unmolested."[117]

The most highly developed exile informant network arose, appropriately enough, in Colombia, a country that also had one of the most significant local Nazi Party organizations. Erich Rath, a German Jew and left-wing opponent of fascism, fled Germany for Colombia in 1936, where he landed a job as motor transportation adviser to the Colombian army until other German advisers prevailed upon the army to cancel his contract in 1938. Rath loitered amongst the refugees and exiles in Bogotá for the next two years until the U.S. naval attaché suggested "that he might best serve his native country by organizing the known anti-Nazi Germans in Colombia and systematically obtaining information about the Nazi organization and activities there."[118] Rath called together his contacts in the *Anti-Nazi Freiheitsbewegung* (ANFB, Anti-Nazi Freedom Movement), founded by exiles Otto Wiland and Erich Arendt as a united front, according to the ANFB platform, for anti-Nazis from "far right to far left, that is everyone except the Nazis," although Communists and Social Democrats predominated.[119] Rath's initial reports to the embassy so impressed Braden that the ambassador arranged a dummy position at the Texas Oil Company paying Rath the healthy salary of $400 per month. Rath "did a perfectly magnificent job for me in the way of intelligence," Braden wrote in his memoirs, temporarily forgetting his concerns over the hazards of regular payments for information. Rath became the embassy's chief supplier of information on the Germans.[120] He was not above using threats and intimidation to get what he needed. His organization's newsletter, distributed among the exiles of Bogotá, warned that "those who have sufficient contacts [in the German community], but who never find information, prove that they themselves are either dopes or saboteurs."[121] Rath pressured other Jews to make denunciations even when they insisted they had no information to provide.[122]

Like other Jewish refugees from Nazi Germany, Erich Rath's perception of German expatriates was shaped by his experiences at the hands of those who had driven him into exile. It did not require a great deal of imagination to see in the patriotism and clubbishness of the German community, along with the real Nazi sympathies of many of its members and the exaggerated claims of Party organizers, a nascent movement threatening to replicate German Nazism in Colombia.

Fearing the worst from Nazis in their newfound place of refuge, Erich Rath and his network of exile informants reported the worst to their U.S. contacts. As a result, the quality of their intelligence was uneven. In one list, Rath identified no fewer than twenty-three people as "Gestapo official" or "one of the chiefs of staff of the local Gestapo."[123] (In fact, the Gestapo did not have operatives in Latin America, except for a few agents attached to embassy staffs to keep tabs on the German diplomatic corps.)[124] On another occasion, Rath warned the embassy's FBI agent of an imminent uprising by thousands of armed supporters of Laureano Gómez, a conservative politician. The agent rushed to try to send the information to Washington but was dissuaded by level-headed Chargé d'Affaires Gerald Keith. No uprising took place.[125] Rath was able to identify the leading members of the local Nazi Party – as the Colombian police had done on their own – but he also provided the embassy with an overwrought report on German paramilitary units that would play a starring role in major State Department and FBI documents on the Nazi threat for the next four years.

The Rath report purported to reveal the internal structure of a secret German paramilitary strike force. It included a detailed chart depicting infantry; air, mechanized, and storm troop sections; field surgery groups; communications troops; demolition teams; even a chemical warfare unit.[126] The legend of the paramilitary organization would persist in U.S. government circles into the first years of the war, gaining credibility through FBI Director Hoover's enthusiastic endorsement and by sheer repetition, despite the logical improbability that enough trained specialists would be found among the four thousand German men, women, and children in Colombia to form such attack units – not to mention that any such specialists would have been asked to return home to join the war effort by 1939.[127] "Some of the embassy people tried to show me [the paramilitary report], but I was never convinced of it," recalled the Justice Department's investigator Ickes. "There were clubs where some young men were militants and held military exercises up in the boondocks every now and then. . . . I think Hoover painted with too garish colors."[128] Reference to the paramilitary groups was notably absent from Colombian police reports and from postwar FBI summaries of its efforts in Colombia.[129]

The U.S. embassy distanced itself from Rath's organization after Braden's departure in 1942, and the United States would come to have quite a different opinion of the anti-Nazi activist over the course of the war; he himself ultimately wound up in a U.S. internment camp alongside the people he had denounced (see Chapter 4). (Braden may have been expressing ruefulness over his decision to keep Rath on the payroll when he later bemoaned the problems inherent in offering cash for information.) But Rath and the other informants paid by U.S. officials throughout the region became a primary source of data for the reports warning of high levels of Nazi activity in Latin America – and for the production of lists of individual Germans dangerous enough to be deported and interned in the United States.

Taken together, all these ingredients – the inflated intelligence estimates, the unreliable informants, the sensationalist press reports, and the British disinformation campaigns, which proliferated from a small number of actual, generally ineffective acts of German espionage – made for a disorienting cocktail readily swallowed in Washington. Fierce commercial competition with the Germans of Latin America in the 1930s had already primed the United States to fight back. Despite the occasional dissenting voice, the prevailing view on the eve of American entry into the war was unmistakable: the Germans of Latin America posed an unacceptable risk to national security. Something had to be done.

3

Blacklisting

> "It is a policy designed by us to secure the commercial and financial annihilation of persons resident in and doing business in accordance with the laws of the American republics."
> –Division of American Republic Affairs chief Philip Bonsal, describing the U.S. blacklist of Axis nationals, January 1942[1]

Santo Domingo, 1939. The Good Neighbor to the north, seeking to reduce costs and improve its image at home and abroad, has withdrawn its soldiers from Latin American soil. The departing marines did not abandon their posts before training and equipping domestic armed forces, the *guardias nacionales*, who could put down unrest in their absence. Throughout Central America and the Caribbean, U.S.-backed dictatorships are fully able to maintain order on their own. A Latin American historian will later make this point by reeling off the names of the dictators of Nicaragua, Guatemala, El Salvador, Honduras, the Dominican Republic, and Cuba: "Somoza, Ubico, Hernández Martínez and Carías were, like Trujillo and Batista, better guarantors of the *Pax Americana* than the marines themselves."[2]

Twenty years earlier, in 1919, Rafael Leónidas Trujillo was a promising young second lieutenant trained by the marines for the Guardia of the Dominican Republic, with a reputation for jailing his countrymen to extort ransom from their relatives and expertly extracting confessions from his captives. Once, while on patrol duty, he seized a peasant family to use as human shields against the guerrillas he was supposed to be hunting. Instead, he locked the family in a church for three days, raping the 17-year-old daughter once a day. Her mother found her bloodstained and weeping. "Three times implies consent," Trujillo's defense lawyer told a marine investigating commission. The officers agreed. Praise from his U.S. superiors would lead Trujillo to command of the Guardia, and to rule over the country.[3]

The self-appointed Generalissimo now completes his apotheosis by renaming his capital after himself and filling it with 1,800 statues of his likeness.

The official newspaper announces Trujillo's decree, "taking into account his services," promoting his son Ramfis to colonel in the army – a few weeks before the child's fourth birthday. In the better neighborhoods of Ciudad Trujillo, plainclothes police loiter outside foreign embassies with standing orders to shoot, and kill, anyone rushing in to claim asylum. The palace staff includes an official whose sole duties consist of procuring Trujillo his thousands of "conquests," preferably virgins. Near the end of his life, the dictator will weary of traveling to exercise his feudal *droit du seigneur* and instead choose his bedmates from "selections" of forty women presented to him three times a week. The palace official in charge of the selections is rewarded with a fee of 10 percent of all public works contracts. In other ways, too, Trujillo is magnanimous: he sends cash payments and condolences to the widows of opposition figures assassinated on his orders.[4]

In 1939, Trujillo is still basking in the warmth of his friendships. The head of the U.S. Army's Caribbean Defense Command, Lieutenant General George H. Brett, is his latest admirer from the North. When Trujillo asks the visiting commander for a photograph, Brett sends his official plane to Panama to get it – a round trip of some 1,600 miles.[5]

Trujillo's impetuous massacre of ten thousand Haitians, although it provokes a brief international outcry, has proved no obstacle to his latest honor: an invitation to Washington, with red carpets, twenty-one gun salutes, and a Marine honor guard for a most reliable ally. The festivities are outdone by the reception accorded Nicaraguan dictator Anastasio Somoza that year, when for the first time since 1933 President Roosevelt leaves the White House to welcome a foreign head of state at Union Station while five thousand troops stand at attention and military planes fly overhead in formation. Of such stuff good neighborhoods are made.[6]

THE GOOD NEIGHBOR POLICY

The Good Neighbor policy was made possible partly because of the extent to which much of Latin America was ruled by men willing to go along with the strategic goals and fundamental demands of the United States. With the exception of a corrupt elected government in Costa Rica and a restive Panama still dominated by a large U.S. military presence controlling the Canal, the countries of Central America and the Caribbean were in the hands of a collection of dictators of whom Trujillo was merely the longest-lived. This lack of democracy made possible the withdrawal of U.S. troops, since popular unrest seeking a change in labor conditions or land tenure could now be put down by the local army. Support for dictatorship and military rule thus made it possible for the United States to behave in a more "neighborly" fashion.

President Roosevelt's stated determination to abstain from overt intervention in Latin American affairs whenever possible, known as the Good

Neighbor policy, seemed to represent a historic shift. In the past, U.S. conduct toward the region had displayed a remarkable consistency going back to the declaration by President James Monroe in 1823 that the Americas were closed to future colonization and that the United States would oppose any further European intervention in the region. The Monroe Doctrine was tantamount to the premature declaration of a sphere of influence. It evolved into the unstated principle – broadened by Secretary of State Richard Olney's claim to "sovereignty" and "fiat" throughout the hemisphere in 1895 and then by President Theodore Roosevelt's 1904 "Corollary" to the Monroe Doctrine claiming the right to act as a police power – that the United States would intervene at will in Latin America in response to disorder or any development that threatened U.S. interests.

U.S. military interventions in the region reached their peak in the first quarter of the twentieth century, when Marines routinely landed on Latin American shores, often with disastrous outcomes. U.S. intervention was followed by the installation of some of the most violent militaries and oppressive dictatorships in the hemisphere, breeding widespread resentment in Latin America and negative publicity in the United States. By the end of the twenties, the State Department was ready to abandon President Theodore Roosevelt's aggressive interpretation of the Monroe Doctrine. Calvin Coolidge and Herbert Hoover took the first steps in that direction, the former by addressing conflicts with Nicaragua and Mexico through diplomatic channels, the latter by withdrawing the marines from occupation duty in Nicaragua, where their war against rebels led by Augusto Sandino had long hurt the U.S. image throughout the region.

Franklin Roosevelt thus was not the first president to veer from longstanding tradition, but his administration went farther than any other in seeking to abstain from direct intervention in Latin American affairs. He removed the last U.S. forces from Haiti and the Dominican Republic and abrogated the Platt Amendment, dating from 1901, which had asserted the right of the United States to intervene in Cuba. This withdrawal of the direct U.S. military presence was made easier by the fact that the dictators now kept order with their own forces, but the new policy was not merely rhetorical. When Mexico nationalized U.S. oil installations in 1938, Roosevelt, anticipating the coming clash with Germany, wisely neither dispatched troops nor backed the oil companies, forcing them instead to accept a settlement amenable to Mexico. Like other presidents, FDR sought to defend the Monroe Doctrine by the means adequate to the moment; in this period, ordering in the marines seemed neither necessary nor likely to be effective.

The Good Neighbor policy was developed and implemented by three principal figures in the State Department. Secretary of State Cordell Hull, who claimed credit for developing the policy, focused his attention on obtaining reciprocal trade agreements with Latin American countries. Undersecretary

Sumner Welles, after a misstep in 1933 when he recommended sending gunboats to Cuba to enforce a change of government, became "the inspiration and guide of our policy," according to its third architect, Welles's deputy, Laurence Duggan.[7]

Under their guidance, in the mid-1930s, the State Department officially abandoned its use of nonrecognition as a diplomatic sanction against regimes that came to power through revolutions. In April 1936, State Department officials instructed U.S. diplomats in Central America, formerly kingmakers, to "decline comment" and "abstain from offering advice on any domestic question," even should their counsel be sought by local politicians.[8]

At inter-American meetings at Montevideo in 1933 and Buenos Aires in 1936, the United States relinquished its claim to any form of intervention. The protocol signed at Buenos Aires was definitive: the signatories "declare inadmissible the intervention of any one of them, directly or indirectly, and for whatever reason, in the internal or external affairs of any other of the Parties."[9] Instead, external threats to the hemisphere would be answered through mutual consultation and cooperation. This resolution went well beyond a pledge not to invade.

Such pronouncements were greeted at first with skepticism in many quarters. The repeated interventions of the previous decades made some Latin Americans wary that imperialistic motives lay behind U.S. calls for pan-American unity. The Argentine author and critic Manuel Ugarte thought a pan-American system with the United States at its head would be "a congress of mice presided over by a cat."[10] But the withdrawal of U.S. troops from occupation duty and the unprecedented U.S. pledges of nonintervention made an impact, together with another factor not to be underestimated – the charismatic personality of FDR. When Roosevelt visited Buenos Aires in 1936, he was greeted by huge cheering crowds lining his route. By 1937, even the dubious Ugarte concluded the U.S. president could be trusted.[11]

The shift from nonintervention to noninterference meant that the Good Neighbor policy would not be limited to acknowledging the sovereignty of other states merely by not invading them. It was a policy that promised an end to paternalistic behavior and the beginning of mutual respect. As such, it was a welcome corrective to the conduct Latin Americans had come to expect from the "Colossus of the North."

Thus when Washington called for summit meetings to discuss a common response to the Axis menace, Latin American governments readily participated in the hope that these would mark the beginning of true partnership. In December 1938, the foreign ministers of the American countries came together at Lima. As the German chiefs of mission had feared, the conference resolution, the "Declaration of Lima," included a provision denying minority rights to foreign ethnic groups and opposing political activity by foreigners. It also called for a consultative meeting of foreign ministers to be held in the event of any threat to the peace and security of the Americas.[12]

The outbreak of war in Europe led to the first such meeting at Panama City in the beginning of October 1939. The American nations affirmed their neutrality in the conflict, agreed to joint patrols to ensure the neutrality of their coastal waters, creating a so-called chastity belt extending 300 miles out to sea around the Americas, and established a committee to discuss economic questions stemming from the crisis.[13] In the two years that followed, Latin American countries tended to adhere strictly to the policy of neutrality established at Panama, while the United States tilted increasingly toward open assistance to Great Britain.

In July 1940, after German defeat of the Netherlands and France, the foreign ministers met at Havana to affirm their opposition to the transfer of European colonies in the Western Hemisphere, a warning to Germany not to seize Dutch or French possessions in the Caribbean basin. In typical fashion, the German minister to Central America, Otto Reinebeck, sent threatening diplomatic notes hoping to intimidate Latin American leaders from supporting the resolution. The effort backfired, causing such resentment that Reinebeck had to disown his messages, blaming a poor translation for their bullying tone.[14] The episode contributed to Latin American solidarity, for the foreign ministers responded by proclaiming the principle of collective security: that an act of aggression against any one of their nations would be regarded as an act of aggression against all.[15]

LATIN AMERICANISTS VERSUS INTERNATIONALISTS

By mid-1940, many in official Washington were concerned with responding to the German presence in Latin America. They differed somewhat in their assessment of the gravity of the threat and diverged even more on their approach to obtaining Latin American cooperation.

State Department officials with influence over Latin American policy divided into two camps, which Randall Bennett Woods has labeled the "Latin Americanists" and the "internationalists."[16] The first group was led by Welles, and its members were characterized by years of service and travel in Latin America, sophisticated understanding of inter-American affairs, respect for the sovereignty of Latin American nations, and a tendency to emphasize local conditions and actors when analyzing the causes of political developments. Welles's friendship with Roosevelt, and the President's respect for his intelligence and decisiveness, gave him easy access to the White House. Despite the lapse on Cuba, his competence as director of the evolving Good Neighbor policy was unquestioned. Foreign service officers believed that "no man in Washington understood so perfectly or sympathetically the problems of Latin America, and no one was so familiar with the personnel and the psychology of the various nations."[17] In Latin America he was held in equal, if not higher esteem. Carlos Lleras Restrepo, Colombian treasury minister during the war and later president of Colombia, spoke for many when he declared in 1983: "Of all the North American public officials of this century, none has known Latin America better and wished to serve her with such sincerity as Sumner Welles."[18]

Laurence Duggan, Welles's closest aide, also belonged to the "Latin Americanists." Chief of the Division of American Republics Affairs and later State Department political adviser, Duggan had already devoted himself to furthering inter-American understanding before joining the government, when his father, Stephen Duggan, who directed the Institute of International Education, sent Laurence on a tour of Latin America to organize scholarly and professional exchange programs. Fluent in Spanish, widely traveled, and personally dedicated to improving hemispheric relations, Duggan advanced quickly after joining the State Department in 1930 and was considered "the ablest officer in Latin America."[19] (He was also one of the most cherished contacts of Soviet intelligence. Motivated by his "romantic radicalism," Duggan passed documents to the NKVD from 1937 until his distaste for Stalin's purges and fear of exposure led him to try to distance himself from the Soviets in 1939. They repeatedly tried to reenlist his services even after the war was over, notably just before he fell or jumped to his death from a Manhattan office tower in 1948.)[20]

Other officials who shared Welles's and Duggan's sympathy for Latin America included Duggan's assistant, Philip Bonsal; John Moors Cabot, Central America desk officer; and the ambassadors Jefferson Caffery and Arthur Bliss Lane. Such men were thoughtful exceptions in a blue-blood department still largely in thrall to its tradition of interventionism and instinctive disdain for Latin Americans.[21]

More widespread in the bureaucracy was the approach of Secretary Hull and his loyalists, led by Assistant Secretary Breckinridge Long. Hull, Long, their assistants, and many foreign service officers were Wilsonian internationalists, who recognized that an action like that of the former president who landed troops in Mexico in 1914 to "help her adjust her unruly household" was no longer tenable in the Good Neighbor era.[22] But their slight knowledge of Latin American affairs did not reduce their ingrained sense of superiority to these neighbors, nor did it diminish their tendency to view important hemispheric events as the product of great power rivalry. Hull's habit of mispronouncing Spanish names – he called Chile's Foreign Minister Miguel Cruchaga "Mr. Chicago" and Argentina's Carlos Saavedra Lamas "Mr. Savannah" – hinted at his unfamiliarity with the countries they represented.[23] Welles later wrote that Hull was "devoid not only of any knowledge of Latin American history, but also of the language and culture of our American neighbors."[24] Ernest Gruening, appointed to the U.S. delegation at the 1933 conference at Montevideo, met with Hull to urge him to support a resolution renouncing intervention. Recording the incident in his memoirs, Gruening tried to be faithful to Hull's speech patterns:

"Ah'm against intervention," Hull said, "but what am Ah goin' to do when chaos breaks out in one of those countries, and armed bands go woamin' awound, burnin', pillagin' and murdewin' Amewicans? How can I tell mah people that we cain't intervene?"

"Mr. Secretary," responded Gruening, "that usually happens *after* we have intervened."[25]

With the help of Gruening and eloquent Latin American delegates at Montevideo, the Secretary of State did come to see that abjuring military intervention was essential to good hemispheric relations, and he signed several inter-American accords to that effect. Nevertheless he viewed wartime disputes with the governments of Argentina and Bolivia as indirect confrontations with the Axis – and quickly turned them into personalized vendettas. ("It was a regular old Tennessee feud," State Department economic counselor Merwin Bohan said of Hull's protracted quarrel with Argentina, "and every time he could sneak around the tree and see an Argentine in the sights of his musket he'd let go at him.")[26]

For an ambassador, Spruille Braden exerted an unusual amount of influence on the evolution of anti-German policy, partly because of his imperious personality and willingness to push his own agenda; Dean Acheson once remarked that Braden was the only bull to carry around his own china shop.[27] Partly it was because from 1939–42 he was posted to Colombia, a country at the heart of U.S. concerns over Nazi influence. Braden had many years of Latin American experience, but his outlook was much closer to Hull's than to Welles's. Explaining why negotiations to end the Chaco War between Bolivia and Paraguay were so difficult, Braden turned to racial stereotyping: "They're great little bluffers, both the Bolivians and the Paraguayans. They're largely Indian and they've got some Indian tricks up their sleeve."[28] His family business in Chile, the Braden Copper Company, was notoriously paternalistic in its treatment of Chilean employees. Single women who became pregnant were fired. Supervisors frequently sent company police to search workers' lodgings late at night; any miner found with a woman in his bed was ordered to marry her or leave his job.[29] His policy prescriptions were based on the fundamental need to protect the unequal status quo between North and South America. When Colombia's foreign minister López de Mesa raised the idea of developing light industry to make Colombia less dependent on imported motors, drugs, and chemicals during a time of wartime scarcity, Braden wrote that such a program would harm U.S.-Colombian relations because it would reduce U.S. exports; even worse, Colombian industrialization "would nurture unsound nationalistic programs in commerce" and induce Colombians to invest their financial resources locally to the detriment of repaying debts to U.S. banks.[30] As he pressed for agreement on a series of anti-Axis measures, Braden complained privately that the Colombians were not falling rapidly into step with U.S. plans. "We can only lead these people slowly," he wrote in frustration, blaming the Colombians' hesitation on the "fundamental deficiencies of Colombian character – innate suspiciousness, inefficiency and dilatoriness."[31] If these private words did not strike the respectful tone that had become de rigueur in official statements, Braden was not alone in maintaining the assumption of U.S. superiority over the neighbors to the south. Even FDR was not immune. "They think they are just as good as we are, and many of them are," Roosevelt told a news conference.[32]

Braden played an important role in producing intelligence on the Nazi threat; not only did he hire Erich Rath, the influential head of an amateur spy network, but he claimed to have originated the idea of bringing FBI agents to Latin America.[33] ("God knows the Colombians are able to do little themselves in the way of investigating Nazi activities," he grumbled – although the evidence suggests they did a more accurate job than he did.)[34] His embassy was the first to begin collecting data on German commercial operations in preparation for blacklisting, well before Washington issued a general request for such information.[35] His alarmist reports of a Nazi paramilitary threat to the Panama Canal helped draw the attention of the State and War Departments to the German presence, and he was the first U.S. diplomatic representative to lobby the government to which he was accredited to deport its German residents to the United States.[36] Through his actions, Braden demonstrated the combination of lack of confidence in Latin Americans and the assumption of northern superiority that made the German threat loom so large.

Assistant Secretary Adolf Berle, among the most brilliant and irascible of the Brain Trusters, was the main force behind the initiation of the deportation program, and in some ways he embodied the apparent contradictions of the Roosevelt administration's evolving attitude toward Latin America. A fluent Spanish speaker, Berle was pledged to ending armed intervention ever since he visited the Dominican Republic in 1918 and saw firsthand what he termed "atrocities" perpetrated by the Marine occupiers there, in a "shocking invasion of rights."[37] He was a strong supporter of the Good Neighbor policy and participated as an adviser at inter-American summit meetings held at Buenos Aires, Lima, and Havana.

In the 1960s, however, Berle would champion both the marine invasion of the Dominican Republic and the war in Vietnam. His biographer has described this as the end of Berle's antiinterventionism.[38] In fact, Berle's role in the deportation program in World War II reflects a continuity in his thinking and a broader continuity in U.S. policy, summed up as an ongoing defense of the Monroe Doctrine by the means adequate to the moment. The Berle who supported the landing at Santo Domingo in 1965 and the Berle who pushed through anti-German measures over Latin American objections during the war were both responding to what seemed to him to be an external threat to the Americas. The threat from the Nazis in the 1940s was more credible than that of the Communists two decades later, and the interference in internal Latin American affairs in World War II less flagrant than later outright military invasion. The principle, however, was the same: U.S. commitment to staying out of Latin American affairs was always a lower priority than combatting great power rivals in the region.

LATIN AMERICAN NATIONALISTS

Under the influence of such thinking, Washington was quick to place Latin American leaders who showed signs of resisting U.S. policies in the pro-German camp. When the War Department in 1941 sought to obtain seventy "little Canal Zones" with 999-year leases on small plots of land in Panama for air defense of the Canal, the populist government of Arnulfo Arias bargained hard. U.S. officials thought the demands were delaying tactics, a Nazi-inspired scheme to obstruct Canal defense. But Arias, for all his xenophobia and fiery rhetoric, was not a Nazi but a nationalist, whose goal of *panameñismo* – Panama for the Panamanians – sought to reduce the massive U.S. influence in his country. He made Spanish the legal language of business transactions, and Panamanian government officials irritated their U.S. interlocutors by asking them to speak in Spanish instead of English. And Arias sought to extract whatever advantages he could in exchange for the thousand-year concession of Panamanian territory. But in this era, Latin American nationalism could only mean pro-Nazism to Washington (as it would come to be seen as pro-Sovietism after the war). President Roosevelt "told Hull to try some strong arm methods on him," Secretary of War Henry Stimson recorded in his diary, and in October, Arias fell victim to a coup Washington may have condoned and certainly welcomed. It was "a great relief for us," Stimson wrote.[39]

U.S. officials had similar apprehensions over León Cortés of Costa Rica and Maximiliano Hernández Martínez of El Salvador. And they fully expected Guatemala's strongman, Jorge Ubico, to be a partisan of the German cause. After all, had Ubico not been an early admirer of Spain's fascist leader Francisco Franco, had he not ordered his diplomats to quit the League of Nations when it criticized Italy's aggression against Ethiopia, had he not bestowed a medal on Mussolini? Even worse was his apparent willingness to allow German coffee planters to turn the highlands of Alta Verapaz into a Teutonic colony, where Germans held title to 80 percent of the land and grew rich from the labor of the *indios* who helped them produce 40 percent of the Guatemalan coffee crop. Germans bought up and exported another 30 percent of the total crop from smaller farmers for a 70 percent share of the country's principal product. The U.S. embassy dubbed the region "Little Sudetenland," and if that was a bit much, the *Auslandsorganisation* did have more success there than anywhere else in Central America. Of Guatemala's 6,000 Germans, 260 joined the Nazi Party, and they tried to extend their influence by boycotting anti-Nazi businesses and shunning Germans who married Guatemalans.[40] German plantation owners and bankers maintained warm relations with the president. He was "the only good president that Guatemala ever had," remembered coffee planter Hugo Droege: "Ubico was very German-friendly, because he knew that we were the main producers in his country. And we brought capital from Germany. . . . He was a colossal help to us. The country was clean and there was no corruption under him."[41]

But appearances could be deceiving, both to Germans and to U.S. officials. Beneath the militarism and emulation of the fascist style, Ubico was neither pro-Germany nor pro–United States; like any head of state, he pursued his own interests and those of his country as he saw them. Washington's either-or inclination to categorize Latin Americans into one of two camps missed the point that Ubico made decisions based on an entirely different set of considerations. He recognized Franco's government in 1936 because of an abiding, anticommunist abhorrence of the "red" Spanish Loyalists. The timing of Guatemala's withdrawal from the League of Nations was coincidental; it came after his advisers decided they could no longer afford to pay League dues. He sent a medal to Mussolini at the same time that he decorated the presidents of France, China, and neighboring Central American states – all attempts to obtain favorable trade agreements through flattery. Meanwhile, he gratefully permitted German residents to continue making their contribution to the Guatemalan economy, provided they did not indulge in excessive celebration of Adolf Hitler, that "peasant," as Ubico scornfully called him. He cooperated in the pan-American conferences designed to respond to the German threat, and the closely controlled Guatemalan newspapers printed anti-Nazi material throughout the late 1930s. In 1939, he banned the Nazi Party.

At the same time, Ubico engaged in a series of pro-U.S. acts. He hired a U.S. officer to run his military academy and put Franklin Roosevelt's picture on a postage stamp. Privately, Ubico told his German friends that he was exaggerating his fears of a German threat to placate the Americans, and he would not worry about a German invasion until he saw submarines in Lake Amatitlán. But the game of playing both sides was coming to an end. In January 1941, he forbade any public statements in favor of the Axis. In April, he declared a German diplomat suspected of working for the Gestapo, Christian Zinsser, persona non grata. In October, the Central Bank took over the sale of coffee produced or marketed by Germans and deposited the proceeds in blocked accounts. After Pearl Harbor, Ubico froze all Axis assets, restricted travel for foreigners, outlawed the speaking of German on the telephone, and placed all bases and military facilities in the country at the disposal of the United States.[42]

During the war, while the experienced Latin Americanists in the State Department paid attention to indigenous political conditions and were tactful in their efforts to build support for U.S. strategy, the internationalists around Hull would evaluate Latin American countries almost exclusively according to the degree of their ready acquiescence to U.S. demands. They were inclined to interpret any resistance by a Latin American government as de facto evidence of pro-Axis sympathy, rather than considering that the factors influencing each country's response to a new policy might be as complex as they were in the United States, where policies emerged from the interplay among the rival executive branch agencies, the fractious Congress, the caprice of public opinion, and the enigmatic FDR.[43]

The extreme pressure of war and the need to respond to the perceived Nazi threat in Latin America brought the two camps closer together. The internationalists prevailed, as the most dedicated defenders of Good Neighbor noninterference set aside their qualms to achieve the expulsion and expropriation of Germans from Latin America – even when it required reverting to techniques the Good Neighbor had supposedly relinquished.

U.S.–GERMAN TRADE RIVALRY

The first steps would be taken in the economic field. The Nazi rise to power brought a change in German trade policy toward Latin America in the 1930s. The worldwide depression and the loss of its colonies severely limited Germany's access to raw materials and export markets. To fill these needs, Nazi Germany came up with a scheme that would boost its share of Latin American trade at the direct expense of the United States. Before war came to seem inevitable, what concerned U.S. officials was not any potential military threat but rather Germany's economic challenge in an area Washington considered an integral part of its own trading system.

In 1934, a German trade delegation toured the continent making offers the cash-strapped, market-deprived Latin American countries could not refuse: they could receive inflated prices for selling their agricultural goods in Germany and buy German industrial products without spending scarce foreign exchange. There was a catch: the Germans refused to pay cash. Instead, they created four systems of payment to obviate the need for foreign currency to change hands. Direct barter transactions under compensation agreements were the simplest: a quantity of imports would be traded for exports of equal value. Clearing accounts were established for indirect barter so that importers could pay in and exporters could withdraw in equal amounts without any currency leaving the country. Under payment agreements, any foreign exchange earned by one country on an unequal trade was set aside for purchases or debt service within the other country to balance the accounts. Finally and most notoriously, Germany paid the Latin Americans for their goods with a special currency, the *Ausländer Sonderkonto für Inlandszahlungen* or "Aski mark," redeemable only in Germany on terms set by Berlin.[44]

This was a raw deal for the Latin Americans, especially as Germany repeatedly devalued the Aski, but they had few alternatives. Markets were closed and tariffs were high all over the world in the Depression era. The United States, already paying some of its own farmers to destroy their crops, was unable to absorb more agricultural surplus. Faced with the choice of selling coffee to Germany for Aski marks or burning the harvest, a Brazilian agriculturalist observed that "compensation marks are worth much more to us than ashes."[45]

It was a "cutthroat trouble-breeding method of trade," grumbled Secretary Hull, then trying to negotiate a series of reciprocal trade agreements with Latin American countries to lower tariffs on each side. Hull's fears were confirmed as Germany's program brought immediate results. The share of total German exports bound for Latin America doubled in 1935, the year after the trade mission. Germany surpassed the United States as Brazil's major trading partner in 1936. Only in the sheltered markets of Cuba, Mexico, and Panama, and in Peru, could the United States hold its own; everywhere else U.S. trade declined relative to German gains.[46]

The United States had $5 billion invested in Latin America by this time, and the region was absorbing a third of U.S. industrial exports; in the key sectors of cotton textiles and steel-mill products, more than half of U.S. exports went to the region.[47] U.S. manufacturers begged Washington for help against the "damned compensation mark" that was eroding "their" markets. The National Foreign Trade Council in 1936 wrote to the State Department: "We trust that our Government will find a direct means for checking the growing menace of this form of vicious bilateral trade practice."[48] In the long term, Germany's gains might threaten much more than corporate profits. Sumner Welles had declared in December 1934 that regaining foreign trade was essential to the success of the New Deal.[49] And when a military conflict began to seem possible toward the end of the decade, the United States worried that as Latin Americans accumulated millions of marks in Aski accounts (partly because Germany was not making promised deliveries), they might prove unwilling to risk offending the nation that could hold their payments hostage.[50]

A FALSE CHOICE: ECONOMIC OR SECURITY INTERESTS?

Conventional accounts of this era by the "realist" school of historians have played down or ignored the economic considerations that affect foreign policy choices, arguing that national security always comes first.[51] Revisionists, following William Appleman Williams, have given economic factors pride of place.[52] But protecting the nation's security and encouraging economic expansion abroad are not necessarily mutually exclusive aims – certainly, they were not in the minds of New Deal policymakers. Roosevelt and his subordinates drew no fine distinctions between protecting the United States from outright military attack from the south, reducing the effectiveness of German propaganda or potential subversion, and diminishing the German market share. As FDR told a group of senators in 1939, the "whole threat" from Germany was wrapped up in an attempt to dominate world trade and put an economic fence around the United States.[53] Later, when the progress of the war came to eliminate Germany's capacity to pose a military threat to the region, economic considerations would again predominate – especially in broadening the scope of the program of expelling German civilians to encompass those involved in unwelcome commercial rather than political activities.

Hitler's planners may not have realized how seriously Washington would react to Germany's trade offensive. Nazi officials held a different, more aggressive view of foreign policy, in which the goals were to extend military and political power and seize territory. Since they did not plan to do any of that in Latin America, at least not in the foreseeable future, they did not expect the barter and Aski system to provoke the United States as much as it did. To North American officials raised on the Monroe Doctrine, the creation of exclusive bilateral trade agreements in a region they claimed for their own was unacceptable. Hitler misread the Good Neighbor policy as a commitment by Roosevelt to abstain from exercising any kind of pressure in Latin America. These misjudgments led the Nazis to believe that they could try to capture the Latin American markets without offending the United States.[54]

Instead, the success of the German trade offensive led directly to increased U.S. concern over the German communities in Latin America, whose commercially adept members seemed to be the essential links making such trade expansion possible. Worse still, Washington believed, successful German retailers were bringing Latin America under their sway. "German merchants [in Latin America] are essentially cogs in the economic machine of Germany," claimed a key State Department report on the Nazi threat. "The interior parts of many countries are serviced commercially only by Germans, and it is safe to say that the whole commercial structure, private and official, is an open book to German commercial agents. By various connections, they are allied to native financial and political personages. It is a web of influence, from the water's edge to the far boundaries of practically every state."[55] Such logic, although disproved by the alignment of most of Latin America on the side of the Allies when war came to the Americas, shaped the policies the United States would deploy against the German residents of the region.

ECONOMIC WARFARE

Relying on compliant dictators of Trujillo's and Ubico's mold and harvesting the fruits of the goodwill earned by the Good Neighbor policy, Washington set about organizing a pan-American response to the Nazi threat.

The first campaign was aimed at canceling the contracts of Germans working for U.S. companies. Among the Germans living in Latin America were capable businessmen with good contacts, and since many spoke excellent English as well as Spanish, they had been hired in droves by U.S. companies seeking local managers or sales agents in overseas markets. In these positions, the Germans sometimes had access to confidential trade information and, more importantly, they were suspected of using the profits generated by U.S. exports to support the distribution of pro-Nazi propaganda. The Roosevelt administration resolved to get them fired, to stop U.S. companies from putting money in German pockets.[56]

U.S. policy explicitly called for boycotting and blacklisting Germans without regard to their activities, political stance, or loyalties: "Persons of the German race (whether or not pro-Nazi) and concerns controlled by such persons contribute, voluntarily or involuntarily, a certain percentage of their salary or profits to local Nazi organizations," explained Nelson Rockefeller's Office of the Coordinator of Inter-American Affairs (CIAA).[57] There was no need in principle to investigate individual cases; Germanness was sufficient, defined so loosely ("race") as to make even citizenship irrelevant.

Thus the two most important elements of economic warfare directed against German individuals in Latin America, the cancellation of representation contracts and the subsequent blacklisting of businesses and private persons, did not require substantive investigations.

There were risks in this decision, as a State Department economic warfare official, Harley Notter, acknowledged. "Some of the German agencies – it may be a great many of them – are staffed by Germans who have long since been naturalized as Latin American citizens," Notter worried. "This necessitates great care to avoid collision with the unquestionable rights of the citizens of the Latin American country to conduct business under the laws of that country. . . . It will be called 'yankee imperialism,' and our firms may be for a time regarded unfavorably as a spearhead of that alleged imperialism." The best way to avoid such charges, Notter argued, was to make the program appear voluntary: "This Department should be in a position to say that the American firms should take such action . . . of their own patriotic and helpful free will."[58]

When appeals to patriotism did not prove sufficient to induce U.S. firms to cut their long-standing and profitable ties with their German agents, in January 1941 Rockefeller's office put 17,000 U.S. businesses on notice that the government wished them to dismiss their German agents. Those that did not comply saw their export licenses revoked.[59] As with other wartime policies, security and economic concerns went hand in hand. Josephus Daniels approved Rockefeller's campaign to remove the Germans on the grounds that "such men might, after the war, use their contacts to promote German goods at prices below America's ability to compete."[60] Ambassador Braden noted with favor that eliminating the lucrative contracts "will benefit American commerce after the war."[61] Certainly no one in Washington objected to the idea of running the German sales agents out of business and finding substitutes who would deal exclusively in U.S. brands, hurting German exports in the long term. It was a two-birds, one-stone policy, benefiting U.S. economic interests, while weakening actual or potential sources of Nazi influence.

THE PROCLAIMED LIST

The Proclaimed List of Certain Blocked Nationals (PL) was issued by the State Department on July 17, 1941, to carry the economic warfare campaign to all businesses suspected of being pro-Axis. It was based on information collected by U.S. diplomatic missions, Rockefeller's CIAA, and data supplied by the British government. A special unit within the State Department, the Division of World Trade Intelligence, compiled the PL under the authority of Dean Acheson. Technically, as U.S. diplomats assiduously assured their Latin American colleagues, the list was simply a domestic regulation of U.S. firms: it prohibited companies and persons under U.S. jurisdiction from trading with listed firms and individuals. In practice, since any Latin American company that did business with a PL firm would itself be listed and thereby excluded from trade with the United States and other local firms, businesses of any nationality in all countries were forced to shun PL firms or risk their own demise.[62]

The Proclaimed List Clearance Committee in charge of the program decided not to blacklist all Germans, partly because such a measure in the First World War had caused serious economic disruption in Latin America, and also because of an aversion to sweeping measures based on ethnic identity alone: "The placing of any impediment upon trade with certain individuals merely because they are present nationals of or were born in an Axis country," stated the Committee, "partakes too much of the nature of policies of the Axis countries."[63] Instead, U.S. officials developed a long list of criteria to determine whether a particular individual or firm was "dangerous" enough to warrant blacklisting. The criteria were so broad, however, that in practice, they could apply to anyone of German origin. One could be listed for being a member of the Gestapo, but also for having family members in Germany or sending one's children to a German school.[64] Nor was the list restricted to Axis nationals. Latin Americans who had served as lawyers or accountants for Axis nationals, or even rented housing to them, were also subject to blacklisting. By May 1942, there were nearly six thousand listings for Latin America.[65]

The Proclaimed List, neglected by historians, fostered some of the most intense of the inter-American disputes the Good Neighbor policy was supposed to have abolished. While the dictators complied, the more democratic among Latin American leaders vociferously protested the extraterritorial

20. Propagandists working for Nelson Rockefeller's wartime Office of the Coordinator of Inter-American Affairs tried to rally Latin American sentiment against the Axis powers by promoting certain Hollywood films, censoring others deemed offensive to latinos or overly critical of U.S. society, and producing posters such as these. The artist's image of the Latin American is true to convention: barefoot, powerless, voiceless, in need of rescue from an outside menace. Credit: CIAA, 229-PG-7, National Archives.

reach of the PL, arguing that it was not the act of a Good Neighbor to exercise such power within their countries. Chile's ambassador to the United States told Sumner Welles that his government considered the list a "form of unwarranted interference by the United States in the domestic affairs of Chile in derogation of Chilean sovereignty."[66] Brazil's foreign minister, Oswaldo Aranha, reacting to a barrage of protests from his fellow citizens, told Ambassador Caffery that the U.S. imposition of the Proclaimed List might reduce Brazilians' desire to cooperate in the war effort, and asked, "How can you expect us to acknowledge your list when you do not blacklist undesirable firms in the United States?"[67] Costa Rica's foreign minister, Alberto Echandi, advised Costa Ricans simply to ignore the Proclaimed List and continue to do business with blacklisted Costa Ricans.[68] Colombia's foreign minister López de Mesa, decried the "economic excommunication" inflicted by the Proclaimed List, while his minister to Costa Rica publicly

21. In this poster, a miniscule Latin American tries to rig a defense against the inexorable advance of Nazism toward the Americas. Clearly, he needs a bigger ally. (Despite his Mexican outfit, he stands in Ecuador.) Credit: CIAA, 229-PG-7, National Archives.

compared the blacklist, based as it was on secret denunciations, to the Spanish Inquisition.[69]

At first, Washington stuck by its program, convinced that the blacklisting of some German companies that had been funding the production of Nazi propaganda in Latin America was worth the political cost of including innocent individuals by mistake. U.S. officials were unwilling to relinquish the listing of Latin American nationals and their businesses, because experience had shown that German companies such as chemical giant IG Farben deliberately "cloaked" their enterprises abroad by placing them under the nominal ownership of foreign nationals while retaining control through secret protocols. This practice was not limited to the large cartels. In the United States, the Alien Property Custodian discovered some sixty German enterprises engaged in cloaking attempts.[70] But Latin Americans saw the problem differently.

The Ecuadorian minister of finance, Vicente Illingworth, and Ecuador's ambassador to the United States, Colón Eloy Alfaro, went to the State

Department in August 1941 to protest the unilateral nature of the Proclaimed List. Illingworth acknowledged the necessity for having effective controls over Axis capital but argued that some 25 percent of the names on the blacklist for Ecuador were based on false information and urged that the United States seek Ecuador's consent before publishing more names. He came away empty-handed.[71] Ecuadorian citizens lodged protests after finding their names in the blacklists published in their newspapers. In Quito, foreign ministry officials requested the removal of names they believed to be included in error; the embassy refused. Direct appeals from President Arroyo del Rio had no better success.[72]

The Chilean ambassador to the United States went to see Philip Bonsal, deputy and friend of Laurence Duggan and a staunch defender of the Good Neighbor policy, to propose converting the Proclaimed List, as Bonsal recorded, "from a unilateral measure on our part to a cooperative venture in which all the American republics would participate." In a message to Sumner Welles, Bonsal warned that despite the usefulness of the PL as a tool of economic warfare, it was, "unless very carefully handled, apt to affect unfavorably the long-term development of our relations with the other American republics." Bonsal expressed his hope that "we will continue to give considerable weight" to the opinions of Latin American governments concerning blacklists affecting their countries.[73] The Chilean proposal went nowhere.

On November 7, 1941, the Colombian Senate unanimously adopted a resolution denouncing the Proclaimed List as interference in Colombia's internal affairs and for being the product of espionage in friendly countries. The resolution demanded that the names of Colombian firms not be listed without first being submitted to the Colombian Government, "before receiving the sentence of condemnation of a foreign power." Most disturbing to U.S. officials, the Senate voted that the resolution be sent to the chancelleries of the other American republics. Ambassador Braden managed to get the Senate report suppressed, but not before it had reached several other countries.[74]

In Brazil, Foreign Minister Aranha kept up his vigorous and frequent protests to Ambassador Caffery that the Proclaimed List seemed to be a pretext for replacing genuinely Brazilian firms with British or U.S. companies. Most of the 265 firms in Brazil, which were initially blacklisted, were either Brazilian-owned or had operated there for many years. One company, Brahma, employed two thousand Brazilian workers and the majority shareholders were Brazilian; it was blacklisted because some of the minority stockholders were Germans. Aranha demanded its delisting, saying that he had "no sympathy" for the Proclaimed List, that it favored U.S. companies, and that its operation was undercutting support for the Allies because "we will have no arguments to defend our American friends... nor in explaining to the other American countries an intervention of this nature in our internal economy." The PL was "contrary to the spirit and the letter of the pan-American conventions," Aranha declared. Unable to obtain satisfaction, the Brazilian government finally prohibited the publication of the PL in the newspapers.[75]

From the perspective of U.S. officials conducting economic warfare, ensuring hemispheric security and promoting U.S. economic interests went together in the anti-German campaign. In November 1941, James Hill of the Sterling Products Corporation called at the State Department to report that a Brazilian firm was importing 20,000 kilos of aspirin powder, and to say that only two companies in Brazil made aspirin tablets: his own and the German company Chimica Bayer Limitada. Sterling had not ordered any of the 20,000 kilos, so the entire shipment must have been destined for Bayer. Hill offered his opinion that "the only effective means of preventing aspirin powder from getting into the hands of the German firm (which is one of the most important German units in Brazil) would be to make all of the ingredients subject to export license." Aspirin powder was placed on the export control list the following month. The U.S. government struck a blow against German economic potency in Latin America, the region's consumers did without twenty-two tons of aspirin, and the Sterling Corporation's only serious competition in Brazil was eliminated.[76]

Since Bayer – a subsidiary of IG Farben – and other large firms owned by parent companies based in Germany often collaborated with Nazi efforts to spread propaganda and sometimes provided cover or payments to espionage agents working for the *Abwehr*, hurting Bayer also made sense from a strictly security-related point of view. The intelligence agencies of any nation would have faced a much more difficult task without such arrangements. Out of patriotic or self-interested service to the U.S. government, U.S. corporations also supplied cover and payments for FBI agents and freelance informants in Latin America. (Erich Rath and Robert Dreher, mentioned in Chapter 2, are but two examples.) Of the German firms, the shipping companies Hamburg-American and North German Lloyd were particularly effective in maritime espionage, transmitting information on ship movements and cargoes. U.S. intelligence agencies considered IG Farben to be "so active in the services of the Nazis that the mere employment of an individual by IG Farben has come to be accepted as possible evidence of intelligence activities."[77]

Such arguments could not as easily be made for blacklisting the many smaller, locally owned hardware stores, farms, and restaurants, ruined by the PL, although they were hardly the likes of IG Farben. Not only did the PL eliminate businesses and livelihoods without Latin American consultation. It also placed an acute stigma on those who were listed, especially once war was declared. U.S. Ambassador Pierre Boal in Nicaragua described the case of Adolfo Altamirano Browne, a newspaper owner and member of the Nicaraguan Congress who was placed on the PL in mid-December 1941 even though he had voted in favor of Nicaragua's declaration of war against the Axis. While "Altamirano Browne has not been above suspicion and cannot very well be classed as friendly to the United States," Boal noted, "there is a long step between his adopting such an attitude while his country was not at war and our branding him as a traitor to his country now that his country is at war."[78] For such embarrassing or politically delicate cases, the State Department eventually put five thousand names on a gray list, the "Confidential List of Unsatisfactory Consignees," which was not published externally, but served to deny export licenses, for example, of newsprint to Latin American newspapers that criticized the United States.[79]

The Proclaimed List began as a tool for blocking the return of capital to Germany and the availability of funds for the dissemination of Nazi propaganda. Carl Spaeth, U.S. delegate to the Committee for Political Defense (CPD), the standing inter-American security organization based in Montevideo (see Chapter 4), stated that "the original and, in fact, continuing purpose, of the Proclaimed List is to cut off sources of revenue that might be used to carry on subversive activities."[80] But the list rapidly extended its reach from firms engaged in international commerce to cover "any person or organization which appeared to be identified with Axis interest. This has been necessary in order to identify such persons and thus *restrict their influence in the local communities*," Acheson explained. The broad objective became "the elimination from positions of economic and social importance of those whose political ideas and policies rendered them undesirable." This was both a broader and more long-term goal than the denial of funds for subversion. Acheson acknowledged that "the list has not, of course, been popular with most of the governments," but in making decisions related to economic warfare, the Department of State must decide "purely on the basis of determining, under the particular circumstances, what action would best serve the war interests of the United States."[81]

After months of receiving Latin American complaints over the operation of the Proclaimed List, Philip Bonsal, one of the more sympathetic listeners, again proposed turning the blacklist into a genuinely multilateral operation, as called for by the inter-American resolutions. In a memo to Sumner Welles in January 1942, Bonsal clearly laid out the contradictions between the exigencies of war and the principles of the Good Neighbor:

There is little to be gained by rehearsing the arguments pro and con the Proclaimed List. Suffice it to say that the policy behind the list is more consonant with ruthless economic warfare regardless of consequences than with the long range development of international relations and particularly relations with the other American republics along lines involving a scrupulous respect for sovereignty and an abstention from interference with internal concerns.

It is a policy designed by us to secure the commercial and financial annihilation of persons resident in and doing business in accordance with the laws of the American republics and against whom we feel that those republics will take no action.

... The question which arises is this: Are we going to continue to be the arbiters of what constitutes Axis financial and commercial activity in the Republic which has now declared war on or severed relations with the Axis or are we going to take the declaration of severance at its face value and at least share the control function [with] the country in question. It seems to me obvious that the relationship must be placed as soon as possible on a cooperative rather than the present unilateral basis....

It is indeed difficult for the average citizen of one of the American republics to understand how we are able to ferret out dozens if not hundreds of undesirable firms in his country while, so far as he is aware, none such have been discovered in the United States.[82]

This last point was a particularly sensitive one. To be sure, the U.S. government did discover some undesirable firms in the United States. Under the authority of the Trading with the Enemy Act, the Treasury Department's Division of Foreign Funds Control and the Alien Property Custodian froze or seized their assets and denied them export licenses. But the investigative standards for such action were stricter, and the application much narrower, than was the case with the Proclaimed List. There was no blacklist of U.S. citizens who had past dealings with Axis nationals when such transactions were legal. Enemy aliens residing in the United States were neither blacklisted nor subject to financial or commercial restrictions, except in selected cases. And, of course, all such restrictive measures were wholly internal.[83] To Latin Americans, the unilateral operation of the Proclaimed List not only implied a lack of trust in their ability to manage their own affairs and hinted at a U.S. desire to eliminate its competitors in the region while leaving productive German nationals undisturbed in the United States, it was also a clear violation of the commitment made at Buenos Aires in 1936 not to intervene "directly or indirectly, and *for whatever reason*, in the internal or external affairs of any other of the Parties."[84] While Bonsal and other defenders of the Good Neighbor policy tried to preserve that promise not to interfere "for whatever reason," they could not prevail; the appearance of an external threat to U.S. control in the region proved to be reason enough.

IMPACT OF THE PROCLAIMED LIST

Because the guidelines for the Proclaimed List were so broad and the investigative procedures of the U.S. diplomatic missions so inadequate, its impact was sometimes felt by those least likely to contribute to the German war effort. Max Brill left Germany for Ecuador in 1937 with his wife and two sons. A Jew and a Social Democrat, he had watched the Nazis burn his factory, lost his property, and spent two months in a German prison before managing to emigrate. He found work as an electrician in Guayaquil and soon opened a pub he called the Salon, but he saw his business dry up after the U.S. placed his name on the Proclaimed List. Brill appealed to the U.S. consul "more than twenty times" for a meeting but was able to see only younger consulate employees. To them, he offered his thick dossier of "proofs that I was never a Nazi": photographs of his factory in flames, a copy of the sentence issued against him by a Nazi judge, documents confirming his religion, eighteen character references supplied by prominent Ecuadorians. The documents made no difference. Brill believed that some former friends, among them unemployed fellow refugees, had denounced him in order to collect payments from U.S. intelligence. A friend with embassy connections told Brill there was a report that one of his sons had been seen driving through Quito with a swastika flag flying from his car, which Brill called "laughable." Meanwhile, the newspapers were rejecting his advertisements, and Ecuadorian businesses refused to sell food to his restaurant because to do so would mean landing on the Proclaimed List themselves. His family's life had become "impossible," Brill said in an appeal to the Ecuadorian Ministry of Foreign Affairs. "Often I do not know how to pay rent or salaries," he wrote. "I spent all of my money building the Salon, and now nobody wants to set foot in the Salon because of the blacklist."[85]

Other targets were more plausible. Antonio Lehmann's publishing house in San José was blacklisted although he was a native-born citizen of Costa Rica. But his citizenship did not prevent him from participating actively in Nazi Party events and printing all the propaganda distributed by the German legation and nazified organizations in the country.[86] Heinrich Schulte's large bakery landed on the PL because Schulte organized the brownshirts in Quito and ran the DAF and other Party organizations.[87] The large hardware-importing company Casa Helda in Barranquilla, Colombia, was blacklisted because two of the owners in the Held family were in the Party, and senior partner Emil Prüfert was *Landesgruppenleiter* of the AO in Colombia.[88]

The case that most offended Colombians was the blacklisting of Laboratorios Román, an important pharmaceutical firm founded in 1835 and owned by Colombians. After Braden's embassy got wind of a drunken incident in which the proprietors of Laboratorios Román, Henrique and Rafael Antonio Román Vélez, tore up a photo of FDR and made pro-German utterances, they were placed on the Proclaimed List. Several senators, the Cartagena Chamber of Commerce, and President Santos himself intervened with the embassy, asking that the long-established firm, which employed fifty Colombian workers and distributed tropical medicines throughout the country, be removed from the list.[89] U.S. Ambassador Arthur Bliss Lane, Braden's successor, argued that "the attitude of the President towards us is so much more important than the fact whether Román is or is not on the Proclaimed List, that I cannot turn a deaf ear to the President's request. . . . Whether Román is kept on or off the List will not affect the course of the war."[90] Lane and the Colombians were unsuccessful. So were the fifty-eight employees of the Hotel Astoria who petitioned, in the name of their families, for the hotel to be removed from the blacklist so they could keep their jobs.[91]

U.S. officials on the ground, even those who were unsympathetic to the objects of blacklisting, could not fail to see the hostility that it produced. "The Proclaimed List in Costa Rica is undoubtedly cluttered with the names of many persons who are neither dangerous, important, nor powerful, who own no property, and whose continued control not only fails to serve a useful purpose but may actually be detrimental to our interests," wrote the chargé d'affaires in San José, Edward G. Trueblood, himself an advocate of strong anti-Axis controls. "The net effect of their inclusion in the list is that they are unable to secure any employment, and they are faced with the alternatives of being driven to complete dependence upon others in order to subsist, or of seeking clandestine ways of earning their living. This results in ill will toward the United States for what appears to be a policy of persecution against individuals who cannot be regarded as dangerous to our interests."[92]

Sustained Latin American resistance produced a minor change in U.S. policy. At the end of January 1942, Secretary Hull instructed U.S. diplomats to consult with the governments to which they were accredited over future additions to the PL, provided the government had broken relations with the Axis.[93] This would seem to have been in line with Bonsal's heartfelt proposal made at the beginning of the month. However, it took more than a year before the first formal consultative bodies were created, and even then, the United States continued to reserve the right of unilateral action, as Hull made perfectly clear: "It should be stressed that the final decision with respect to additions and deletions in the Proclaimed List, which relates to controls established by this government, must rest with the Interdepartmental Committee in Washington."[94] Hull rejected any preliminary screening of Latin American nationals by their own governments; nor was he willing to include any Latin American representatives as members of the Interdepartmental Committee. Instead, he instructed that the new consultative commissions created in Latin American capitals in the summer of 1943 be given expanded powers to supervise economic and financial anti-Axis controls there. In other words, the mechanism created for consultation was transformed into an instrument for furthering, not lessening, U.S. oversight of Latin American economic affairs.[95]

The consultative bodies, for all their weakness, do reveal that Washington's assumption that Latin American participation would cripple economic warfare was incorrect. The review committee in Bogotá consisted of the head of Alien Property Control in the Colombian Treasury Ministry, an officer from the Commercial Department of the Foreign Ministry, two Proclaimed List officials from the U.S. Embassy, and one from the British Embassy. Their meetings were lively, as the Colombians questioned the inclusion of Colombian citizens on the PL whose businesses had already been taken over by the government and thus posed no further danger. They also raised practical objections to other listings; for example, firing German power plant engineers in some Colombian towns would have meant closing the plants and cutting off electricity to the community. However, the Colombian representatives also recommended other individuals for listing because they were known Nazis or were "cloaks" for Nazis. Although in practice, the U.S. Embassy and the Interdepartmental Committee in Washington made all the decisions, the discussions in the consultative committee should suggest the kind of cooperation that might have taken place had the United States been willing to consider a genuinely multilateral effort.[96]

Instead, the U.S. government closely held the power of delisting. Under its review process, Latin American firms requesting to have their names removed from the list were not told what negative information had resulted in their blacklisting. Instead, "the burden of proof must be carried by the firm in question" to show that "the unsatisfactory conditions which resulted in the firm's inclusion have been remedied" and that "the future conduct of the firm can be expected to be satisfactory."[97] In issuing these requirements, the Good Neighbor perpetrated a deeper intrusion into Latin American economic affairs. The U.S. commercial attaché in Bogotá, like his colleagues in other countries, offered some Colombian businesses the chance to avoid blacklisting, provided the owner sign a form promising not to engage in commercial transactions with anyone on the PL or anyone specified by the embassy, and to fire any employee considered undesirable by the embassy. Among other things, the signatory had to agree to this demand: "At any moment that it may be required by the American Embassy, to allow its books, accounts, and correspondence to be examined by auditors designated by the Embassy, with the costs of such examinations borne by the undersigned."[98]

In July 1942, representatives of the American nations came together in Washington for an Inter-American Conference on Systems of Economic and Financial Control. Feelings ran so high at the intimate interventionism of the blacklisting procedure that the State Department found it necessary to avoid making any mention of the Proclaimed List – the program at the center of economic warfare in the Americas – in the conference resolutions. Raising the issue at all, according to Acheson, would have sparked unwelcome opposition and requests for deletions.[99]

Washington's unilateral blacklisting of Latin American citizens created one source of friction over the Proclaimed List. The practice of intrusive intervention in internal Latin American economic affairs was another. Three other factors made the list arbitrary and unfair in Latin American eyes: a lack of discrimination among individuals chosen for listing; the way U.S. officials expanded the list to prove their effectiveness to their superiors; and the fact that blacklisted firms were not deleted from the list even after they were removed from German control.

In Bogotá, Ambassador Lane ruefully watched the conflicts over the Proclaimed List wear away a decade's worth of goodwill. His aides were passing along complaints from Colombians in all parts of the country. His economic counselor, Robert J. Derby, explained that Latin American bitterness over the list was based not on principle alone but on concrete effects. "Inclusion of a business on the Proclaimed List now means that sooner or later it will have to liquidate," he wrote. "When this occurs, the employees of that concern blame the United States Government.... When they are denied the opportunity to earn a living because of our economic sanctions, it creates a feeling of hatred on their part toward the United States." The larger listed firms routinely had their assets frozen, their profits diverted to blocked government accounts, and their management taken over by Colombian authorities. Still, that action – effectively de-Germanizing the firm for the duration of the war – did not change its status as far as U.S. policy was concerned. "The officials and people of Colombia resent the fact that when a Proclaimed List firm is placed under Government administration, its removal from the PL does not follow," Derby wrote. "They feel that it is an arrogant attitude on our part which refuses to recognize that administration by the Colombian Government will prevent enemy interest from doing any harm to the cause of the democracies."[100]

"Sooner or later we will have to decide how far we are going to let the Proclaimed List policy affect our post-war economic and political relations with Latin America," Lane warned.[101] He wrote to Sumner Welles asking that the State Department bring him to Washington for consultations so he could make his case in person. Welles turned down the request, asking Lane to prepare a memo instead.[102]

Arthur Bliss Lane was a serious diplomat. A career foreign service officer with an excellent record, he served in Mexico from 1925 to 1933, then as minister to Nicaragua. After Anastasio Somoza used the U.S.-created National Guard to seize power, Lane called the Guard "one of the sorriest examples on our part of our inability to understand that we should not meddle in other people's affairs."[103] His commitment to noninterference made him one of the staunchest defenders of the Good Neighbor policy. At the same time, Lane was not pollyannish about the German threat. As ambassador in Belgrade during the German occupation of Yugoslavia, he returned home with an abiding suspicion of Nazi fifth column activities.[104]

Thus it was especially significant for Lane to complain in his report to Welles that "inadequate investigation" and a "too great readiness to accept accusations against a given firm or person, often based on hearsay, unfounded on facts" had resulted in many mistaken blacklistings. Some of the fault lay with informants who denounced their "personal enemies or business competitors" to credulous U.S. officials. Lane also blamed the "understandable enthusiasm and energy on the part of young officers" working on the PL who were eager "to make an outstanding showing on the number of recommendations presented for listings." As an example, Lane mentioned a case in which "the word of two virtually unknown European nationals was accepted ... despite the fact that the President of the Chamber of Deputies, a former Minister of Public Works, and a leading Conservative Senator, the leading exponent in his party of friendship for the Allied cause, and the Embassy's Legal Adviser indicated that the subject's political views are not inimical to the United States."[105]

Lane further noted that the embassy and U.S. consulates were receiving regular and insistent protests from Colombians. The problem was not merely one of fairness, Lane concluded, but "will serve to create a spirit of bitter antagonism against the United States which can only result in our losing markets and political friendship when the war is finished."[106]

If he was wrong about the markets – Europe was far too devastated by the war to offer much of an alternative to U.S. products – he was right about the degree to which the Proclaimed List abraded the amicable feelings so recently attained.

A VIEW FROM THE SOUTH

Alfonso López Michelsen, son of the Colombian president and himself future president of Colombia in the 1970s, wrote a novel about this era dedicated to portraying sympathetically the victims of the Proclaimed List in his country. Presented as the memoir of a German refugee of Jewish descent, the book describes the travails of the protagonist, "B. K.," after he is blacklisted. He is shunned by his friends, who fear getting blacklisted themselves; then he is evicted from his boarding house because the owner is not allowed to do business with anyone on the PL, and he finally winds up in an internment camp.

At one point, a Colombian character remarks that U.S. citizens who come to Colombia arrive with a salary from home and do not risk investing their own money in businesses unless they are subsidiaries of U.S. companies that will repatriate the profits. "In contrast, the Germans here created many important things through their individual efforts: aviation, ranches, hardware stores, beer and cigarette factories," the Colombian says. "Why should we be against these Germans, who have made us prosper, simply because in their country, which they left thirty years ago, a dictatorial regime has been established?"[107]

As his life falls apart, B. K. seeks a meeting with "Muir," a thirty-year-old U.S. embassy official in charge of the Proclaimed List for Colombia. Muir is a haughty, insolent drunkard who merrily reduces people to ruin:

He would arrive late to his office, often drunk, and gaze deprecatingly at his victims or their lawyers, who had had appointments to see him two or three hours earlier.

"I'm busy and can't see anybody. Come tomorrow at three o'clock." And, without further ado, this son of privilege, who in peacetime had no idea how to earn a living and in wartime ran no risk of losing his own life, sent away men who had struggled twenty or thirty years to build up their businesses and had come to wait for him, to

ask him not to ruin them, because it was not their fault that they were Germans and
they did not get involved in political affairs.

"No. I'm very busy. Come back some other day."

And he went out to a dance club.[108]

López Michelsen accurately conveyed the sentiments of many of the
Colombian elite toward their German neighbors and toward the economic
warfare policies of the United States. His account is marred by its partiality,
the first sign of which is the title of the book. *Los Elegidos* ("The Chosen
Ones") refers to the selection of those placed on the blacklist, but it also
draws an obvious parallel between the suffering of the German expatriates
in Colombia and the suffering of the Jewish people. Such a comparison is
unconscionable, the more so in a work about the Second World War written
after the fate of the Jews of Europe was well known. While many of the
Germans blacklisted or interned were, like B. K., longtime residents with
no connection to Nazi Germany, others were devoted adherents of that very
"dictatorial regime" established in their homeland – especially in Colombia,
home to Latin America's strongest Nazi organization outside the ABC countries and Mexico. When the embassy's Muir callously dismisses B. K.'s appeal
with the remark that there is a life or death struggle against the Axis going
on, he is speaking a truth otherwise missing from the rest of the book.[109]*

That the struggle in question seemed so remote to some Latin Americans
helps explain why the fact of German responsibility for starting the war,
and the real existence of local Nazi activity (supported in important ways
by some of the larger companies on the PL), sometimes faded from their
understanding of such *yanqui* intrusions as the Proclaimed List. But most official Latin American objections were raised in the context of overall strong
support for the Allied cause and the desire to make their contribution as
effectively as possible. By the same token, a U.S. government fighting total
war against a vicious foe paid little attention to the Latin American perspective. Having inflated the German peril in the region and exaggerated Latin
American vulnerability, Washington then took the German threat very seriously, while it did not take Latin American opinion or desire for mutuality
very seriously. The Proclaimed List thus contributed both to the weakening
of the German economic presence in Latin America (with a commensurate
strengthening of the U.S. position) and to the long-term souring of inter-
American relations, so recently and ephemerally restored during the brief

---

* There is more to the story. The author was not just the president's son. López Michelsen was
  also an attorney who represented stockholders in the blacklisted German-owned (and Dutch-
  named) firm Handel Industrie Maatschattij. When their assets were frozen during the war,
  López Michelsen bought up the securities at fire-sale prices, keeping the profits for himself.
  When the scheme became publicly known, it caused a scandal that led to the resignation of
  his father, President Alfonso López Pumarejo. Some Colombians today believe that López
  Michelsen wrote the book to atone for stealing from his German friends.

peacetime application of the Good Neighbor policy. The Proclaimed List helped revive Latin American cynicism toward U.S. promises and suggested that the appearance of a foreign menace, whether real or imagined (or both), made the Good Neighbor policy a parenthesis of good intentions in good times – masking an underlying continuity in the U.S. approach to the region when there seemed to be anything at stake.

The inter-American disputes over the Proclaimed List would be extended into conflicts over the selection of German deportees to be sent to the United States. And the weaknesses of the Proclaimed List, with its reliance on hearsay, denunciation, and inadequate intelligence work, would continue to characterize the deportation process, as the blacklist became one of the principal sources for establishing the lists of deportees.

4

Deportation

In the United States, "[a]n enemy alien, if at liberty, must constitute a threat to the internal security of the United States before his internment is ordered."
–U.S. Department of State[1]

In Latin America, "all German nationals without exception . . . are all dangerous and should be removed from their present sphere of activity as rapidly as possible."
–U.S. Department of State[2]

San Pedro Sula, Honduras, April 1942. Tiburcio Carías, like his fellow despots who rule over most of Central America in the age of the Good Neighbor, is no stranger to the exercise of arbitrary force. He brought "blessed peace" to Honduras, in Carías's favorite phrase, and has maintained it for a decade by killing or jailing labor leaders and opposition activists. A constitutional ban on self-succession does not prevent him from extending his term in office every four years. The official newspaper, *La Epoca*, praises this practice of *continuísmo*, observing that there are "three great *continuistas* in the world: Carías, Roosevelt, and God – in that order."[3] Hondurans neatly sum up his domestic policies as *el encierro, el destierro, y el entierro*: lock 'em up, throw 'em out, and bury 'em.[4]

The U.S. Legation acknowledges that Carías's regime is unusually corrupt "even for Central America." Public officials with nominal salaries amass six-figure fortunes. The typical army commander pads his rosters with fictitious names, pocketing the phantom soldiers' pay, dressing his friends in uniform for rare inspections. Carías bestows upon his Ministry of Development an annual budget of $400,000 for road building – an activity practically unknown in Honduras. The amount of bribery required to do business in the country is "incredible," groan U.S. businessmen accustomed to more moderate levels of palm-greasing.[5]

San Pedro Sula is a center of economic activity, German settlement, and resistance to Carías's rule. In July 1944, the president will suppress a pro-democratic uprising in the city, sending troops to fire on demonstrators, most of them women, engaging in a peaceful demonstration. OSS officials describing the event will remark that "the brutality of the police and army in suppressing the anti-Carías manifestations has greatly increased hostility toward the government.... Some 50 persons were killed and the wounded were literally dropped from dump trucks at the hospital."[6] ("Of course there was blood on San Pedro's sidewalks," scoffed the head of Carías's rubberstamp Congress. "The women demonstrators must have been menstruating.")[7]

Carías can order such treatment of Honduran protestors with impunity. Citizens of powerful foreign countries, however, can demand satisfaction from their diplomatic representatives. Thus the bringer of blessed peace treads more carefully when confronted by opponents holding European citizenship.

Germans dominate the import–export trade, but they are hardly a threat to the nation's security. Only thirty-nine people in all Honduras make it onto the U.S. Proclaimed List – no Latin American country has fewer blacklisted names.[8] The local Nazi Party numbers fewer than fifty members, a disappointing total to German officials, one of whom later recalls that the "AO could never get on its feet in Honduras."[9] U.S. military planners organizing joint patrols and air bases to protect neighboring Central American countries do not even bother with Honduras.[10] But to a leader always alert for an occasion to promote his own interests, the war and the anti-German campaign provide a perfect opportunity.

The Tennessee newspaperman-turned-diplomat, U.S. Minister John Draper Erwin, requests a meeting with Carías to ask for his cooperation in expelling the leading Germans from his country. Erwin happily reports Carías's "keen desire to cooperate fully in this undertaking.... He informed me that he had no ties of any description with the Germans; that they had always opposed him politically and that he felt no reluctance in taking whatever action is deemed best for continental defense and the safety of his own Government."[11]

Erwin produces a list drawn up by his small intelligence staff, including the military attaché, Colonel Austin, a man with "the unfortunate habit of listening to everybody who came into his office and sort of reporting what was said to him verbatim, sending it off to Washington without much attempt to verify whether this was true or not."[12] Collaboration between Carías's police and the Legation's intelligence personnel produces mixed results. They deport the most obvious targets, such as Detlev Paysen, German Consul and a leading Nazi, and Robert Rossner, owner of the largest German business in the country, who paid for the printing of pro-German propaganda. Twenty-six of the 144 Germans deported from Honduras during the war are members of the Nazi Party; an equal number of their Party comrades remain behind unmolested.

U.S. and Honduran officials also deport Heinz Bernhard Wettstein, who had lived in the isolated town of Mosquitia since 1921, selling the occasional Detroit-made automobile. Postwar investigators will find "not a whisper of a charge against him." He is joined by Rudolf Andrzsjewski, a Jewish emigrant who will wind up joining the U.S. Army; Franz Hoffmann, an anti-Nazi informant who provided "considerable evidence" on local Nazis to the U.S. Legation, only to be deported alongside the people he turned in; and Leon Fuerst, a Jewish refugee and former inmate of a concentration camp.[13] At least six other deportees, postwar investigators will conclude, are political opponents of Carías, "undoubtedly the chief reason for [their] arrest and deportation." They have lived in Honduras since the 1920s. Not one is a Party member. There is no negative information about any of them.[14]

The U.S. deportation program has handed Carías an opportunity, and he has seized it in order to "lock up" and "throw out" troublesome Germans simply by telling the U.S. Legation they are Nazis. Seizing their property follows naturally thereafter.* Minister Erwin will later claim that the Legation made an independent inquiry in "a great majority" of the cases before anyone was deported, and that there was a substantial reason for internment in "practically" all of them. Given the evidence to the contrary, this can only mean that the U.S. investigations were inept, or that the Legation endorsed Carías's practices. Both are probably true.[15]

THE PATH TOWARD EXPULSION

The Honduran episode exhibits some of the unexpected consequences of a policy designed to combat dangerous Axis subversion and ensure the security of the Western Hemisphere. Whatever the real danger from German nationals residing in Latin American countries, the war transformed them into a kind of currency of inter-American relations, demanded by the United States as proof of pro-Allied cooperation and offered by Latin American governments seeking to placate Washington and to gain material advantages. In practice, the program largely lost its putative security value and came to serve an array of other purposes that varied according to the political conditions of the individual countries involved.

When the Japanese bombing of Pearl Harbor brought the United States into the war on December 7, 1941, and Hitler declared war on the United States on December 11, the goal of eliminating the German menace to the south became more urgent than ever. Reports flooded into Washington that submarines had been spotted in the Caribbean, that the disciplined Germans

* See Chapter 7, "Expropriation."

of Guatemala and Ecuador were planning to seize power, and that those of Colombia were preparing an assault on the Panama Canal.[16] U.S. officials in or with responsibility for Latin America moved quickly to prevent such a development before it could begin.

A regional deportation and internment program was not foreseen before U.S. entry into the war. Rather, the removal of Latin America's Germans evolved rapidly out of three related currents of policy.

The first was the endeavor by the U.S. government to identify and neutralize dangerous Axis nationals in Latin America. With war coming, the United States pressed Latin American governments to control their populations of "alien enemies" through surveillance and internment of those on the Proclaimed List. U.S. officials had no confidence that Latin American governments were able to discipline their own Axis nationals and believed that local internment would be inadequate.[17] Dissatisfaction with the effectiveness of local controls would provide a rationale for transferring the aliens to United States custody.

The second current flowed from the desire of the United States to destroy German power and of some Latin American leaders to turn the anti-Axis campaign into political or financial gain. To be sure, some Latin American governments opposed U.S. pressure to deport their residents (and in some cases their citizens) of German origin. But others, especially the more autocratic among them, took advantage of the opportunity created by the U.S.-driven anti-German campaign to offer up unwanted Germans as Nazis and confiscate their property. This was most easily accomplished after sending the owners out of the country so they could not offer resistance. Thus venality and the tactics of economic warfare came together under unrelenting diplomatic pressure from Washington, creating additional momentum in favor of deportations.[18]

The third current emanated from a traditional wartime practice under which belligerents agree to repatriate enemy diplomats and bring their own diplomats home. For logistical reasons, the United States offered to collect Axis diplomats from Latin American countries that declared war on or broke relations with the Axis powers, and to place them all together on neutral ships sailing from New York to Lisbon.[19] This operation created the infrastructure for removing many other, nonofficial Axis nationals from Latin America to the United States.

By early fall of 1942, the deportation and internment program was in place and had acquired a certain momentum, as U.S. intelligence agents sought to identify more candidates for deportation, and U.S. diplomats pressed Latin American governments to relinquish them. In most countries involved, the arguably threatening Germans – leaders of the Nazi organizations or individuals involved in propaganda work – were taken away in the initial waves of expulsions, together with many inoffensive individuals. By the end of the first year of the operation, a shift can be detected. In 1943 and 1944, the receding German threat and ever-widening U.S. demands provoked disputes over U.S. interference in Latin American internal affairs, as what had begun as a security program generated by the fear of a German menace and tied to an exchange of civilians broadened into the opportunistic expulsion of Germans to facilitate the seizure of their property. Wherever the United States had to exercise extraordinary pressure to bring about the deportations, the program was surrounded by accusations that the Good Neighbor was backsliding.

PRECEDENTS FOR INTERNMENT

While internment of enemy aliens inside one's country was a universally accepted practice, the seizure of enemy aliens in foreign nations was new. There were two precedents for removing Germans from Latin America established in the year before the United States entered the war, and both were the work of Assistant Secretary of State Adolf Berle. A freelancer in the State Department on a wide variety of political and economic issues, Berle was "more directly involved in intelligence coordination for the New World than any other administration official."[20] With the assistance of Fletcher Warren in the Division of Foreign Activity Correlation (FC), and Warren's aide Frederick B. Lyon, Berle made it his mission to counter German influence in Latin America wherever possible.

In May 1940, after renewed German offensives in Europe, Berle and Ambassador Spruille Braden decided to move against the German airline in Colombia, Sociedad Colombo-Alemana de Transportes Aéreos (SCADTA). Founded in 1919 by Colombians, Germans, and Austrians in Barranquilla, it was the oldest airline in South America and the first commercially successful airline in the world. Pan American Airways purchased a majority financial interest in 1931, but Germans retained control of management, and all the pilots were Germans. Colombians looked upon the airline with pride and gratitude, for it had linked together a country whose mountainous topography made overland travel a grueling, time-consuming experience: the advent of SCADTA cut travel time from Bogotá to the principal port of Barranquilla from a week-long drift along the Magdalena River to a three-hour flight.[21]

Defense planners in Washington were much more impressed by the implications of German pilots – some of whom were reserve officers in the *Luftwaffe* or members of the Nazi Party – flying aircraft within range of the Panama Canal. Colombian officials believed the pilots were loyal and most of them too old for combat, and thought that by placing Colombian military co-pilots on every flight, they were able to eliminate any risk.[22] But Braden believed that borings on the underside of some of the planes were intended for attaching bomb racks, and U.S. newspapers printed alarming scenarios.[23] After protracted negotiations, Braden and Berle persuaded

Pan Am to fire SCADTA's German personnel and replace them with U.S. pilots, even, to President Santos's dismay, at the cost of disrupting service. Pan Am filtered the U.S. pilots and mechanics into Barranquilla two at a time and then, on June 10, 1940, moved suddenly, firing all the Germans that night.[24] SCADTA became Avianca (Aerovías Nacionales de Colombia), with a Colombian president and Pan Am the principal shareholder.

The action clearly had the goal of eliminating a potential threat. However, as with much of U.S. anti-German policy in Latin America, security and economic goals fit together well. The United States had been hostile to SCADTA since long before the Nazi rise to power. A French diplomatic report in 1928 suggested that U.S. hostility to SCADTA even at that early date indicated the existence of a North American plan "to monopolize the major aerial communications lines in South America."[25] Indeed, with the demise of SCADTA and the other German- and Italian-owned airlines in South America in the first years of the war, that is exactly what happened.[26]

Some of the unemployed pilots tried to return to Germany, to the consternation of the British, who were already fighting the war Americans were still preparing for. Berle described the dilemma in his diary. "The British protested," he wrote, "without basis in law, but naturally enough, since these men will probably be used to bomb London. They wanted us to send them back to Colombia if we couldn't keep them here. I pointed out that they would then probably be used to bomb the Panama Canal. The British were, in their usual imperturbable way, quite philosophical on that point." Berle's solution was to route the passenger liner carrying the pilots past a Canadian cruiser waiting on the high seas to stop, search, and remove the Germans for internment in Canada.[27] The episode, with its elements of genuine security concerns, accompanying commercial advantages, inter-American disagreement, and British-inspired internment, anticipated the contours of the broader deportation program to come.

Berle acted more directly in the case of forty-eight sailors of the German ship *Eisenach*, seized in a Costa Rican port. In March 1941, the crew heard that the Costa Rican government was planning to impound the ship, so they burned it. The government interned the crew and then expelled them so that they could return home by way of Panama and Japan. Berle's division arranged for the sailors to be detained in Panama and turned over to U.S. officials, who sent them to internment camps in Montana and South Dakota, without the approval of the Costa Rican government. This precedent would later be cited by State Department officials organizing the first deportations of German civilians from other countries after Pearl Harbor.[28]

PROTECTING THE CANAL

Panama, home to the Western Hemisphere's single most strategic asset, was at the forefront of planning and the site of early negotiations over the treatment of Axis nationals. Shortly after the overthrow of President Arnulfo Arias in October 1941, the Panamanian government agreed to a U.S. proposal to establish camps for interning the Panamanian Japanese in the event of war. Panama's Foreign Minister Octavio Fábrega was at first reluctant to include Germans and Italians in the plan as requested by the United States, since many of them had become naturalized citizens of Panama.[29] By October 31, U.S. Ambassador Edwin C. Wilson had obtained the agreement in principle to cover Germans and Italians, with a caveat: "there might be a very few exceptions in the case of Germans or Italians married to Panamanians concerning whom the Government could give assurances that they would constitute no danger (the [Foreign] Minister's aunt is married to a German)."[30] This allusion to family ties augured future disputes over well-connected Germans both in Panama and elsewhere.

Ambassador Wilson must have felt the full weight of his responsibility as U.S. representative in a country harboring the vital passageway linking the Atlantic and the Pacific in what was likely to become a two-ocean war. In his previous post in Uruguay, he showed that he had been prepared to expect the worst from local German inhabitants: in May 1940, he warned the State Department of an impending Nazi coup in Montevideo and asked for fifty U.S. warships to be dispatched immediately. The Uruguayan minister in Washington discounted the danger, but Socialist Party activist Hugo Fernández Artucio was broadcasting urgent radio appeals for resistance, which Wilson took seriously. President Roosevelt sent two ships, and several local Nazis were arrested and then released when police found no evidence of a plot.[31]

Wilson was not going to stand by and wait to see if such an attempt might take place with the Canal as a target. As the *USS Arizona* settled to the bottom of Pearl Harbor, Panamanian authorities began arresting Germans, Italians, and Japanese throughout the country, beginning before the official declarations of war and rounding up a thousand of them by December 15 – most of the Axis nationals in Panama. That the arrests were the product of U.S. initiative was asserted clearly by the U.S. Embassy: "The request to have these enemy aliens in the Republic of Panama detained and interned was made by the United States Government, because of reasons connected with the defense of the Panama Canal."[32] Roundups also took place in several other countries that week, including Costa Rica, Guatemala, Nicaragua, and the Dominican Republic.[33] Meanwhile, the nine Central American and Caribbean countries all declared war on the Axis. Mexico and Colombia broke relations, and Brazil, Bolivia, Ecuador, Paraguay, Peru, Uruguay, and Venezuela declared their solidarity with the United States. "If ever a policy paid dividends, the Good Neighbor policy has," Adolf Berle wrote with pleasure.[34]

Guatemala's President Ubico went a step further, asking the U.S. Legation if it would assist him in expelling Nazis of military age from his country.[35]

Top State Department officials including Berle and Assistant Secretary Breckinridge Long agreed by December 12 – and began to consider broadening the project to include all Central American countries.[36] Discussions proceeded for the next week among officials in the State Department's Special Division (SD), Division of American Republics and Division of Foreign Activity Correlation. On December 16, John Moors Cabot, the Central America desk officer in the State Department (who would later protest the excesses of the program), summed up the arguments favoring a regional effort to intern the Germans in the United States:

I feel that it is wise to clear as many young Nazis out of Central America as possible, because (1) it will definitely diminish the danger of subversive activities in Central America and the indirect threat they represent to the Canal, (2) it will give us hostages who will serve as a brake on any measures taken against our citizens in enemy-occupied territory, (3) it will please the governments of countries which are anxious to get rid of the Axis nationals, and will be considered by them an act of practical cooperation, (4) it may serve as an inspiration for other countries which seriously fear subversive activities, (5) it will build up a vested interest in Germany's defeat in the countries concerned, particularly if any property is seized.... While I do not think we should *urge* any government to deport Axis nationals, I see no harm in discreetly pushing the matter when an opening is given.[37]

It is worth noting that the distinction between the categories of "young Nazis" and "Axis nationals" is elided here, reflecting the consensus at this time that principally Germans – and *all* Germans – were dangerous. Opinion within the relevant State Department divisions was unanimously in favor of removing them, and by December 20, a policy of "discreetly pushing" individual Latin American governments to send their Axis nationals to the United States was in place.

U.S. Ambassador Wilson suggested to the Foreign Minister that he reconsider the desirability of keeping the internees in Panama, given the difficulties of housing, feeding, and caring for so many prisoners. On January 13, the Panamanian government agreed "that they should be transported to the United States and interned there as Panamanian internees."[38] To maintain a sense of its sovereignty over its own residents, Panama insisted it would not relinquish jurisdiction over these Axis nationals, who were explicitly not to be repatriated; instead, they were to remain in temporary custody of the United States.[39]

The Germans sent up from Panama formed a motley crowd. They included Herbert Jabs, head of the Nazi trade union DAF, who distributed propaganda in Panama and joined the Nazi clique seeking to exert authority inside the internment camps;[40] August Karl Westermeier, a leading Nazi in Colón;[41] and an assortment of Germans who were or were believed to be members of the Party.[42] But they were joined by such men as Josef Ursprung, a gold prospector the AO considered an "apolitical tramp" who rarely came out of the bush unless he had nuggets to sell;[43] Georg Karlinger, a brewmaster termed "politically indifferent" by the AO, although he was a Party member;[44] and Max Kaufmann, a Jewish refugee, interned solely because "a group of Germans always requested him to be their waiter."[45] The evidence used to prove dangerousness was typically very slight, if there was any. In the case of Carl Bald, a bartender and musician, postwar investigators found "no indication of any charges against Bald" except that "in 1934 one C. Bald made a contribution of $2 to the German Consulate in Colon for the '*Spend der Arbeit*' (Unemployment Relief Fund)."[46]

Some cases among the Germans deported from Panama aroused the sympathy of postwar investigators. Hans Bartsch had a silver plate in his skull ever since he was badly beaten by Nazi storm troopers breaking up a meeting of the Center Party in Germany in 1933. Interned because "his lack of funds might make him susceptible to Axis agents," Bartsch would volunteer to join the U.S. Army. (He wound up in the U.S. Forest Service.)[47] George Karliner, a Jewish refugee, was no stranger to barbed wire; he had been imprisoned in Buchenwald in 1938 along with his father, who was killed there by Nazi guards.[48] Again and again, postwar reports turned up "no evidence of any charges," "no indications of any reason" for individual deportations. Such was the case of Walter Wolff, a Jewish butcher whose only offense was that he reportedly had "many German customers."[49]

Of the 247 Germans deported to the United States from Panama from 1941 to 1945, approximately 150 were "cases" and the others were family members.[50] Of the 150 cases, there is detailed information on 85: 76 from postwar U.S. investigations, and 9 from information collected on repatriated Germans by the *Rückwandereramt* (return migration bureau). In addition, the membership list of the AO's Nazi Party organization in Panama can be compared to the names of all Panamanian deportees.

Cross-checking these records reveals that the Panama group included twenty-one Nazi Party members and thirty Jewish refugees, five of whom had spent time in Buchenwald, Oranienburg, or other Nazi concentration camps before fleeing to Central America. There was also a handful of "drunks," "cranks," and "beachcombers." In forty-nine cases, there were no allegations, let alone evidence, of any subversive activity.[51] On the other hand, thirty-seven out of fifty-eight of the members of the local Nazi organization were left behind in Panama.[52] Clearly, as a program intended to select dangerous suspects, the deportations were worse than unjust: they were ineffective.

The record makes clear that many of those deported were not individually targeted, but were picked up in mass sweeps. One shipment of Germans was sent to U.S. camps not for what they had done or said, but because of where they worked: "because they were employed in bars and cabarets or had hotels where American subjects frequently stayed, it was thought that because of possible indiscretions by American subjects and soldiers, these

Germans could obtain dangerous information. To avoid this danger, the American authorities preferred to intern them in the United States."[53] After nearly two years of deportations, Justice Department officials discovered that the illogical cases such as most of those just described were not accidents but the result of set policy – a policy that differed significantly from practices the U.S. government mandated for its own domestic internment program. For Germans residing in the United States, selective internment was the order of the day: as Secretary Hull wrote, "In dealing with the problem of enemy aliens, this Government is not resorting to mass arrests of individuals on the sole ground of their enemy nationality but is detaining specific persons who are actually suspected of subversive activities."[54]* But in Latin America, the rules did not apply. Investigators from the Justice Department found that the Panamanian government and U.S. military officials in the Canal Zone were, as a matter of course and at the initiative of the US Legation, cooperating to intern Axis nationals "without inquiry as to the loyalty or danger of the particular alien."[55]

Of course, protecting the Canal was a vital goal. But the measures taken to ensure its safety went beyond the official U.S. policy of selective internment for its own German residents to embrace the notion that any German in Latin America might be considered dangerous. That this approach was not successful in a key country is made dramatically clear by the fact that it led to the internment of more Jewish refugees than Nazi Party members, while the majority of the Nazis were left behind in Panama. The record is similar for the four thousand deportees as a whole. Only about every fifth deported adult male was a member of the Nazi Party; four out of five were not. Adding women and children internees lowers the figure to between 10 and 15 percent overall.[56]

CENTRAL AMERICA: THE FIRST ARRESTS

Elsewhere in Central America, Nazi leaders and activists were rounded up in the first wave of arrests and sent out with the first transports to the United States. In Costa Rica, thirty-five Germans and one Italian were arrested over the New Year's holiday. They included the best-known Nazis in Costa Rica: Party leaders Otto Krogmann, whose brother was the mayor of Hamburg; the fanatical Ingo Kalinowsky, dueling scar on his right cheek, who wrote regularly for the local NSDAP newsletter and admitted to sending secret information to Germany; the overbearing and widely disliked gas station owner Emilio Dorsam, who styled himself an enforcer of Party discipline; and Antonio Lehmann, whose print shop produced the Nazi propaganda distributed

---

* Such a claim could only be made in the period before the mass "relocation" of Japanese and Japanese Americans from the West Coast of the United States. It would, however, continue to be U.S. policy toward Germans and Italians throughout the war.

in Costa Rica.[57] Three teachers from the nazified German school were arrested as well.[58] But the deportees also included other Germans caught by the vagaries of intelligence work, such as Oskar Hering, picked up because his brother Albert was a Party member; Gerhard Wagemans, dubbed a harmless "moron" by postwar investigators, who noted that his two successive marriages to Costa Rican women earned him the scorn of racist Nazis; and Erich Ottens, a tourist from Chile who would spend the war comporting himself as an "extreme anti-Nazi" inside the U.S. internment camps.[59] Wilhelm Wiedemann, a tractor driver and naturalized Costa Rican citizen, was accused of vague pro-Nazi associations by the U.S. military attaché, Lieutenant Colonel E. Andino – himself later labeled "one of the most unreliable intelligence officers in the employ of the United States Government" by postwar investigators.[60] The Costa Rican police made their own contribution: traveling salesman Harry Julius Hermann Frey was deported at their request, despite the "little information available" about him; once in the United States, he volunteered to enlist in the U.S. Navy.[61]

In Guatemala, too, the leading Nazis were well known and easily identified because of their public activities, and with 260 Party members in the country, there were plenty of candidates for expulsion.[62] But the Guatemalan government quickly enlarged the pool of potential deportees through crude investigative techniques. The Guatemalan police chief, General Ordoñez, summoned all German males between 17 and 60 years of age in the capital to the station and interrogated them one by one in the presence of the others: "Are you a Nazi?", "Would you die for Hitler?" At least thirty-five men answered yes and were deported.[63] Harald Nehlsen, who had lived in Guatemala since 1923 and had two Guatemalan children but remained a German citizen, made a careful statement that attempted to reconcile the dilemma of divided loyalties: "I declare that I am not affiliated with the Nazi Party, and I am not a partisan of the Nazi doctrines; but I am a sympathizer and admirer of Hitler and if I were called and there were means available, I would go to defend my fatherland. . . . My first duty is to obey the laws of Guatemala."[64] Such a delicate balancing act failed to enchant the authorities of a country that had just gone to war with Hitler. Organist and piano teacher Hans Huber Peter took the risk of making a clear denial despite the fact that the AO was literally looking over his shoulder: "I declare that I am not affiliated with the Nazi Party, I am not a Nazi, nor do I sympathize with Hitler. I am Austrian, not German." Nonetheless, he was deported.[65] Father Johannes Weber, a Catholic priest serving a Spanish-speaking parish, considered himself an anti-Nazi but maintained a cautious line in his public statements for "fear of causing trouble to his relatives in Germany." Asked by Ordoñez in the presence of other Germans how he felt about the German government, he tried to avoid a direct answer by saying he was not interested in politics. Weber was deported with the others.[66]

SOUTH AMERICAN NEUTRALS

Moving from ad hoc arrangements with these three governments, Washington sought to persuade Latin American governments as a group to send their Axis nationals north for internment or repatriation. When Breckinridge Long inquired on January 15 about the legal justification for receiving deported Axis nationals from Latin American countries, State Department Legal Adviser Green H. Hackworth responded simply that "a sovereign government can take such action as its interests require" – that if a nation wished to protect itself by expelling some of its residents, self-defense, the first law of nations, made such an action acceptable.[67] The word "sovereign," though, was a reminder that the government with jurisdiction over the aliens must initiate the action; legally, as well as in accordance with the Good Neighbor policy, the request should come from the Latin American side. This problem was immediately finessed. On January 20, 1942, the State Department sent a circular telegram to its missions in eight countries in Central America and the Caribbean – Cuba, Guatemala, Nicaragua, Costa Rica, Honduras, El Salvador, the Dominican Republic, and Haiti (the countries in the Americas besides the United States and Panama that had declared war on the Axis) – instructing them to obtain the agreement of each government to send all "dangerous enemy aliens" for internment in the United States. Some were initially uninterested, but by mid-February, thanks to its lobbying, the State Department could report cooperation from all but one of them. (The exception, Cuba, interned its enemy aliens on the Isle of Pines.)[68] The degree of pressure required to gain this consent varied, but the origin of the deportation program was clear to those involved. FC chief Fletcher Warren – as coordinator of the program among FC, ARA, SD, and the War Department, he was certainly in a position to know – would state bluntly at the end of the war: "These Germans were picked up and deported on insistence from Washington."[69]

It required more persuasion to obtain the cooperation of neutral Latin American governments less beholden to the United States than the small client states of Central America and the Caribbean. In Colombia, where Ambassador Braden had begun even before the United States entered the war to urge the government to expel dangerous Axis nationals and had lobbied for the internment of SCADTA pilots and Nazi leaders in the United States, President Santos demurred on the grounds that Colombian law and national sovereignty prohibited the internment of its residents in foreign countries; moreover, Santos claimed, the Germans were all under adequate surveillance. Until November 1943, Colombia remained a neutral country, and international law frowned upon neutral nations delivering the nationals of one belligerent to the custody of the enemy.[70] Pressure from Washington continued, however. The U.S. War Department and FBI Director Hoover complained that suspect Germans were able to move freely and Colombia could not be counted upon to restrain them.[71] Braden now counseled patience. "[The] Colombian Government has leading Nazis under close surveillance and I think [the] situation is well in hand at present," he wrote, noting that the SCADTA pilots "for the most part are older men, commercial flyers, and are not likely material for combat pilots." Still, he hoped they could ultimately be deported to Germany, because their "knowledge, experience and acquaintanceship" made them more dangerous in Colombia.[72]

Santos's agreement to the plan was finally secured with the promise of military aid under the Lend-Lease program, including planes, patrol boats, and financial assistance.[73] According to his Treasury Minister, the Colombian President also decided to cooperate to ward off the expected alternative: the establishment of more U.S. bases in the Caribbean.[74] To overcome the legal obstacles to deportation, the Germans on U.S. lists were "invited to leave the country."[75] As an added incentive, the Director of Police informed the "volunteers" that they would be sent to prison or to a detention camp if they refused.[76] Others were able to stay by signing a promise to observe Colombian laws and paying a "security deposit" of an amount determined by local police chiefs – an obvious invitation to graft.[77]

It was not hard to identify the leadership of the AO; not only did the Colombian police have photographs of Party meetings, but the leaders had also signed public statements, such as *Landesgruppenleiter* Emil Prüfert's congratulatory birthday greeting on April 20, 1938, to "the Führer of Greater Germany and savior of the German people."[78] The deportees ranged from Prüfert, Nazi leaders Joachim Marggraff and Theodor Funck, and SCADTA pilots Rudolph Bethke, Helmuth Schmidt, and William Lange[79] to Ernst Strack, described by the AO as "hardworking" and "withdrawn," and having "little contact with German colony life";[80] Dietrich Theodore Becker, a possible "mental case" against whom there was no evidence of Nazi activity; Emil Wilhelm Krueger, a member of the opposition German Social Democratic Party, deported although there were "no documents in the file indicating why Krueger was removed"; and Gustav Adolph Kill, who was an avowed anti-Nazi whom the ONI judged "inimical to Axis aims." So was Carl Specht, a labor organizer for Indian rubber tappers in the Colombian interior. Postwar investigators noted that "for this reason [Specht] incurred the enmity of some of the American rubber interests. It is doubtless these persons who accused Specht to the authorities. . . . It is felt that Specht is much more likely to be extremely anti-Nazi than pro-Nazi." (Once interned, Specht volunteered for the U.S. Army to fight fascism.)[81]

Later expulsions in 1943 and 1944 would include four deportees actually accused of spying for Germany: Hermann Heinrich Rullhusen, Herbert Eskildsen Schwartau, and Max Vogel all admitted to passing on secret messages received from *Abwehr* agent Georg Nicolaus in Mexico. Paul Emil Schirrmeister was also denounced as a spy, but U.S. investigators later concluded that the denunciation – from Schirrmeister's ex-mistress – was motivated by jealousy, that there was never any evidence against him, and that he was an "imbecile" too stupid to be an agent.[82] Since the evidentiary standards were so lax, the deportation program was highly vulnerable to this kind of manipulation for private ends.

Ecuador's President Carlos Arroyo del Río proved to be more difficult. The former dean of the University of Guayaquil's School of Law, he objected to the extralegal approach the U.S. was urging upon him. He refused to consider sending Axis nationals to the United States until after the upcoming pan-American conference at Rio, saying he preferred to be part of a multilateral Latin American effort.[83] Ambassador Boaz Long and FBI agent Clarence Moore held frequent discussions with Arroyo del Río, but were unable to obtain an agreement in principle until February 9.[84] There followed two months of bickering over just which Axis nationals were dangerous. Reading down a list of proposed deportees prepared by U.S. officials, Arroyo del Río

observed with considerable spirit that there were at least 3 or 4 Italians who ought not to be on the list. He referred to one as a man he had known since he was a little boy, who had slowly built himself into a position of prominence and now after more than 40 years in Ecuador was a very old man, incapable of any activities in connection with Fascism.

In the case of another, Mr. Yannuzzelli, the President observed that the Italian was about 80, had not been back to Italy for more than 40 years, was not of sound mind, lived far removed from the centers of civilization, and in his opinion was not dangerous ... the inclusion in the list of 4 names which in his opinion should not be there had a tendency to vitiate the entire list in his mind, certainly so far as the Italians were concerned.[85]

Arroyo del Río finally consented to the deportations after learning that Colombia, Peru, and Bolivia were preparing to compel the departure of Axis nationals. All four countries insisted on a guarantee from the U.S. government that the Germans would be speedily repatriated and not interned. On April 7, forty-eight deportees boarded the *Etolin* at Guayaquil. Forty-two of them were from the U.S. list.[86] The troop ship *Acadia* took away another 125 Germans, 10 Italians, and 15 Japanese on April 21. Of the Germans, 16 were diplomatic officials, 67 were "forced to leave," and 42 "volunteers" chose to leave because of blacklisting and the likelihood of future expulsion or internment, according to the Spanish minister representing German interests in Quito.[87] One of the volunteers was Gunter Beckmann, a mechanic with the SEDTA airline, who recalled his decision this way: "We all told ourselves, 'better a camp in North America than a camp in the Amazon.'"[88] Gunter Lisken had no choice. Although he, like Beckmann, was not a Party member, Lisken was the local representative for the *Vereinigte Stahlwerke* (the precursor of the big steel firm Thyssen), and the FBI thought he was the head of the local SA, the storm troopers.[89] (Nobody interviewed for this study credited that accusation. The reaction of Roberto Hahn, a Jewish refugee and longtime resident of Guayaquil, was typical: "Can you believe that? You know what a nebbish is? If he was the top SA man here, then my name is Moritz.")[90] Others hardly constituted a menace. Ludwig Weber was fingered as a "Nazi leader in Riobamba," although he was not in the Party and could not have been much of a leader in any case, since he was the only German in that town.[91] Another deportee was a German Jew with no visible means of support, who told a fantastic story of having worked for U.S. intelligence in Colombia identifying dangerous Nazis before crossing the border to follow a woman with whom he had fallen in love. His name was Erich Rath – Ambassador Braden's favorite informant, whom the U.S. Embassy had employed as its principle source of intelligence on the Nazi threat. (See Chapter 2.) Rath's protests went unheeded: he was expelled, then interned alongside the people he had denounced.[92]

THE CROSSING

Deportees interviewed today almost never complain of mistreatment during internment – the deprivation of liberty aside – except for the sea voyage to the United States. The *Acadia*, with cabin space for 200 passengers, took on board a total of 675 Axis nationals from Peru, Ecuador, and Colombia on its northward journey, resulting in "unimaginable overcrowding," food and water shortages, and a lack of bathing facilities. The German envoy to Peru, Noebel, praised the State Department protocol official aboard for doing what he could to ameliorate the situation but credited a higher power for preventing a serious incident. "Thank God there was good weather and safety," Noebel wrote in his report to the AA. "Had we needed to go into the lifeboats, it would have been a catastrophe."[93]

The experience was not untypical of the hastily organized transports. To pick up prisoners from Central America, the Army diverted the troop carrier *Kent* first to Limón, in Costa Rica, then to Puerto Barrios, to collect the Germans from Guatemala, who had spent the night sleeping on banana leaves on the railroad platform. Reporting to the AA, Walter Olivier wrote that the Costa Rican guards seemed "not influenced by hatred; many a simple man among them expressed his regret that we were being forced to leave the country." The behavior of the Germans' new captors was another matter. "Completely undisciplined Marines searched through our luggage," Olivier wrote. "The contents of many cognac bottles found their way into the parched throats of the seamen, and a few perfume bottles met the same fate." The deportees were stowed in the hold of the *Kent* and not permitted to go above deck for five days, trapped with the stench of vomit; they sweated through the journey, lying in their underwear in triple tiers of hammocks which sometimes broke, sending their occupants crashing down on one another. On arrival at New Orleans, their suitcases were returned, Olivier noted, "several pounds lighter than they had been before."[94]

A Costa Rican colonel, Gómez Ayau, reported the drinking and pilfering by the Marine guards. The U.S. Legation rejected his charges as biased and "anti-American," but an investigation by the Army's Inspector General confirmed that some of the soldiers did become "slightly inebriated" drinking confiscated liquor and that several hundred dollars' worth of property "was removed and retained by persons unknown" aboard the *Kent*.[95] These shipboard experiences were repeated in later transports aboard the *Cuba* and the *Madison* bringing deportees from Costa Rica, Ecuador, and Peru in 1944; the deportees on these trips never complained of abuse, but they did report being overcrowded, having only a single toilet for 230 seasick passengers, having to bathe and wash diapers in seawater because fresh water was scarce, and receiving their baggage returned with locks broken and valuables missing.[96]

On arrival at the port of San Francisco or New Orleans, the deportees went through delousing showers, then stood before Immigration and Naturalization Service (INS) officials, who solemnly requested that they present their visas for entry into the United States. Some of the new arrivals thought it was a joke. "What visa – I was kidnapped!" was a typical reply.[97] But the visa matter was not a jest: it was a ruse, a key element of the contrivances orchestrated to create a fictitious legal cover for the juridically dubious deportation program. U.S. consulates had been deliberately instructed not to issue visas to the departing Axis nationals. The overwhelming majority of the deportees had broken no laws in Latin America, but this scheme transformed them into lawbreakers: since they did not hold visas, their presence in the United States was illegal, and they were subject to detention or expulsion as the U.S. government saw fit.[98] "Only in wartime could we get away with such fancy skullduggery," an INS official reminisced.[99]

The German deportees were held under a muddle of legal and diplomatic arrangements made to satisfy the requirements of Latin American governments or of national and international laws. Those from Colombia, Peru, Ecuador, and Bolivia were officially en route to Germany under a promise of safe conduct, not to be detained any longer than it took to ship them onward. Those from Panama were in temporary custody of the United States while remaining under the jurisdiction of the Panamanian government. Those from other countries were held for violation of U.S. immigration laws or putatively at the request, usually a verbal and informal one, of the government of their country of residence.

AGENTS OR IMMIGRANTS?

U.S. officials assumed at first that the deportees were as dangerous as the newspapers and intelligence reports said they were. The State Department said it was intended to clear out "as many as possible of the German agents who have been placed here at great trouble and expense by the German Government for the purpose of facilitating subversive actions in this continent."[100] In June 1942, Breckinridge Long likewise asserted that the program was designed to remove the many "agents" who "had been sent" to Latin America.[101] He wrote of five thousand to six thousand Axis "agents" successfully removed

from the territory *to which they were assigned by the services of their respective governments*.... As a result of this movement, the United States and the other American Republics as far south as Chile and Argentina will have been relieved of the presence of German agents *implanted* throughout this territory.[102]

The sincerity of the belief that the deportees were deliberately placed Nazi agents is confirmed by the surprise U.S. officials expressed upon getting a closer look at the German "agents" they brought up from Latin America. Once the Germans arrived in the United States, their custodians had trouble finding many who seemed menacing among them. In the first shipment, the U.S. government expected to intern "young Nazis of military age."[103] But one-third of the first group from Guatemala and Costa Rica was made up of men between forty and fifty years old; another third were over fifty.[104] Many had lived in Central America since the 1920s or before – far too early to have been "placed" there by Nazi intelligence.

In distant Berlin, the authorities knew that the German expatriates living in Latin America for years or decades were not agents deliberately placed there, but German Foreign Office officials relying on information from the *Auslandsorganisation* labored under the same misimpression of unity among the deportees that caused Washington to seek their expulsion. A report even reached the Foreign Office that the deportees from Costa Rica and Guatemala were "all members of the Party and its organizations."[105]

As usual, both Washington and Berlin were wrong. When an officer from the Special Division visited Camp Blanding, he reported that "there is information in the records of the Department attributing Nazi-Fascist sentiments or activities to only 11 of the 116 deportees from Guatemala." A U.S. army colonel who had served in Guatemala also visited with the internees, "many of whom were old friends of his and with whom he talked in Spanish. According to [Camp Blanding commander] Kunzig, this colonel gave as his opinion that the bulk of the people were not Nazis but merely business and professional men who had been evicted from Guatemala in order that their property might be caused to change hands." Joseph Green and Bernard Gufler, assistants to Breckinridge Long, concluded: "It appears possible that the Guatemalan authorities may either have collected the persons they sent to the United States in a haphazard manner or may actually have sent out many of them in order to obtain control of their property or businesses and that possibly persons who should have been got out of Guatemala as dangerous Nazis may have escaped being taken."[106]

In fact, cross-checking the list of all Guatemalan deportees against the membership list of the *Auslandsorganisation* reveals that of the 558 Germans brought from Guatemala from 1942 to 1945, 120 were Party members.[107] As in other countries, somewhat more than half of the local Nazis were left behind. The rest of the internees represented a broad spectrum of attitudes, ranging from flag-waving patriots who hoped for a German victory in the war, through apolitical farmers with little connection to German community life, to Jewish refugees, Social Democrats, and other prima facie opponents of Hitler's regime. They were all caught up in mass measures adopted on the assumption that German national identity was a sufficient indicator of probable dangerousness, along with the gullible acceptance of Nazi Party organizers' claims that they had been successful in arousing the transnational allegiance of all German expatriates.

GUILT BY NATIONAL IDENTITY

The dissimilarity between the kind of Nazi U.S. (and German) officials believed was being taken into custody and the people who actually filled the camps can be partly explained by the difference between, on the one hand, the sensationalist tales in circulation on the eve of the war and the misreading of Latin American conditions by both governments and, on the other hand, the relatively low percentage of Party members among the internees and the tepid enthusiasm of some of these Party members themselves.

Just as the Nazi regime in Germany expected all Germans abroad to be a part of its transnational project for the glory of the greater Reich, so the government of the United States believed that the German communities of Latin America were united, monolithic, and threatening. The existence of an investigative apparatus should not obscure the fact that the anti-German effort rested on the principle that no screening was required. This perspective guided the development of policy and greatly lowered the standards of evidence applied by U.S. intelligence agents searching for potential subversives. A key State Department policy memorandum of November 1942 summarizing the results of the deportation program to date insisted that distinguishing between dangerous and nondangerous enemy aliens was not necessary, since their national identity alone was sufficient evidence of their collective guilt:

Our experience in this matter and general observation of Axis methods lead to the conclusion that *all German nationals without exception* ... and more individuals than might be expected among the political and racial refugees from Central Europe *are all dangerous* and should be removed from their present sphere of activity as rapidly as possible.[108]

This assertion of universal German dangerousness does not stand up to scrutiny. It certainly did not reflect the United States' experience with the 300,000 German citizens living peacefully within its borders, nor was the highly selective domestic program of interning fewer than 1 percent of those Germans based upon such a principle.[109] Only a steady diet of inaccurate news and intelligence reporting, combined with an abiding belief in Latin American vulnerability and incompetence, could have produced such a claim. But while the State Department's conclusion that Latin America's Germans were "all dangerous" did not actually lead to mass deportations of entire populations comparable to the "relocation" of ethnic Japanese from the West Coast of the United States, it did provide a basis for taking action against individuals of German origin in the absence of specific derogatory evidence about them.

Nor did this document represent the idle musings of some Washington bureaucrat. The memorandum, with its explicit instructions to consider every German a menace to be eliminated from the region, was distributed to all U.S. diplomatic missions in Latin America in order to create a single standard for deportation efforts, and it was cited by U.S. officials carrying out the expulsions.[110] Six months later, the document was sent out a second time with a covering note calling for greater efforts to persuade Latin American governments to cooperate.[111]

THE COMMITTEE FOR POLITICAL DEFENSE: RETROACTIVE MULTILATERALISM

Throughout the first year of the program, the more enlightened State Department officials tried to reconcile their desire to remove Germans from Latin America with the noninterference ideal of the Good Neighbor policy. Sumner Welles repeatedly instructed U.S. diplomats in the spring of 1942 to be circumspect. "Remember that this movement must be carried out so as to avoid offending Guatemalan sensibilities and public opinion," he told U.S. officials in Guatemala City.[112] "You should not (repeat not) insist on who should or who should not be included on the list," he told the Legation in Tegucigalpa.[113]

But the recalcitrance of some Latin American leaders proved frustrating. Secretary Hull complained in November 1942 that "we are confronted by an intense national pride in sovereignty which will not permit compliance with suggestions that we be given Axis nationals."[114] U.S. officials disregarded such regional sensitivities in enforcing the Proclaimed List – and reaped a harvest of resentment at all levels of Latin American society. The

State Department now came up with the idea that a multilateral mechanism might ameliorate similar conflicts arising over the expulsion of the Axis nationals.

The Emergency Advisory Committee for Political Defense (CPD) was established at the Foreign Ministers summit held at Rio in January 1942 as the principal inter-American mechanism for responding to the Axis threat.[115] Based in Montevideo, the CPD was composed of seven representatives from Uruguay, Argentina, Chile, Mexico, Brazil, Venezuela, and the United States. The committee was responsible for coordinating inter-American policy on Axis subversion, thereby bringing into reality the Good Neighbor's promise of consultation and mutuality.

In practice, however, the United States made every effort to ensure that the CPD would function merely as a rubber stamp. It was secretly manipulated by the North American delegate, Carl B. Spaeth, and limited to retroactive approval of unilateral measures already adopted in Washington.

Spaeth, former head of the Western Hemisphere Division of the Board of Economic Warfare and a man untroubled by compunctions about interventionism, bluntly acknowledged his role in correspondence with the State Department. "The Committee will be no more than what our Government is able to make of it," he wrote, brushing off concerns about preserving the multilateral nature of the CPD. Spaeth outlined his strategy of using cooperative delegates from other countries as fronts to present his proposals, so that these would not seem to have originated with the United States – a tactic the United States had already used successfully at the summit meetings. "Unless we assume direct or indirect leadership, we are frequently going to find it necessary to reject proposals of other members," Spaeth worried. "Such an embarrassing negative position will appear to be much more 'dominating' than the affirmative approach suggested above [of making sure all proposals actually originated with the U.S. delegation]."[116] In Spaeth's view, Latin Americans could not be trusted to manage their own affairs – they could not even be permitted to make suggestions regarding them, in a forum supposedly created for that purpose.

Spaeth spent much of his first year at the CPD sidetracking proposals "strongly pressed by other governments" for equitable policies, such as an intelligence-sharing arrangement the State Department had promised at Rio but which U.S. intelligence agencies did not want. He earned plaudits from Washington officials for his successful stonewalling of Latin American proposals.[117] Instead, Spaeth pushed through measures calling for the very actions the United States already had been carrying out for some time, to provide a diplomatic figleaf. The key CPD declaration on combating Axis subversion, Resolution XX, called for the internment of dangerous Axis nationals in neighboring countries, when local facilities were inadequate. It was drafted in the State Department and presented by Spaeth himself. The timing of Resolution XX clearly made it a retroactive endorsement of U.S. policies already underway: it was officially approved by the Montevideo committee and circulated to all governments in the hemisphere in June 1943 – eighteen months after the first deported Germans arrived in the United States.

THE GOOD NEIGHBOR'S BALANCING ACT

The CPD's resolution put a multilateral label on the regional deportation efforts, but officials in Washington knew that the program was made in the United States. In a memorandum sent to all diplomatic posts in Latin America in May 1943, the State Department provided an update of the status of its efforts to remove "the nuclei of Axis infection." Since most Latin American countries were not doing enough to restrain their Axis nationals, the memo said, "this Government has continued to press for the deportation of such enemy aliens to this country for internment or, failing that, for their removal from the American Hemisphere." To overcome the difficulty presented by "the statutory regulations and/or political attitudes of a considerable number of American republics which prevented their deporting Axis nationals to the United States for internment," the State Department now placed its hopes in Resolution XX.[118] Diplomatic posts were instructed to use the resolution to pressure the governments to which they were accredited to intern more Germans.[119]

The nod toward multilateralism did not change the discrepancy in power between North and South, nor did it alter the behavior of U.S. diplomats on the ground, who continued to press for deportations according to Washington's agenda. Their actions were hardly secret. The Spanish minister representing German interests in Guatemala reported that the Guatemalan government informed him that the deportation of 141 Germans in January 1943 "was carried out at the request of and according to instructions by the government of the USA."[120]

Observing the process from the State Department's Central America desk, John Moors Cabot grew increasingly worried. He had long worked for better understanding between the United States and Latin America. In the 1930s, he used family money to endow a journalism prize, still awarded today, to encourage better reporting on Latin America in the United States media and vice versa.[121] After the January deportations, he wrote of "a danger which I have long feared, to-wit, that pressure on other Republics to deport specific individuals is likely to cause more resentment than any benefit which might accrue therefrom is worth." Cabot acknowledged that President Ubico had made the initial suggestion for a few deportations a year before. Now, however, U.S. officials were going well beyond an agreement to accept custody of those Germans Guatemala wished to expel – and were demanding the delivery of some Guatemalan citizens of German origin Ubico did not want to relinquish. "I am seriously concerned at the considerable number of cases in which we have insisted upon the deportation of citizens of the country, at times, I believe, rather against the wishes of the local authorities," Cabot wrote, noting that the practice was not limited to Guatemala:

We have been even more insistent that other Central American Republics deport their own citizens to the United States. I have no doubt that these deportations have awakened bitter resentment among the deportees' relatives and friends, who in several instances have been prominent and influential people. In later years when the Good Neighbor Policy will be judged historically in the other Republics by its acts rather than by its professions, I fear that we shall find it difficult to explain why we went so far in insisting upon these deportations.[122]

The tension between the not entirely compatible aims of demonstrating respect for Latin American sovereignty while carrying out anti-Axis strategies designed without Latin American participation persisted throughout the war, and it tended to pit the Latin Americanists of ARA against the Europe-oriented officials in Breckinridge Long's Special Division and Fletcher Warren's Division of Foreign Activity Correlation, with Adolf Berle their most powerful backer and spokesman. In June 1943, Philip Bonsal of ARA wrote to Long to urge that the deportation program be wound down. Allied victories that had pushed the Germans out of North Africa and turned the tide of the war against the Axis powers had reduced the danger to the Western Hemisphere, but despite this, continued pressure for expulsions was causing damage to inter-American relations. Bonsal credited the deportation program with precluding the possibility of spying or sabotage by ridding countries of their Nazi organizations. However, he noted, "many of the people subject to this program have resided for a great many years in the other American republics. For the governments of those republics to allow the people in question to be forcibly removed for internment in the United States produces all sorts of hardships and local resentments which should be avoided unless the objective to be obtained is truly vital to the war effort."[123]

By the time they began to raise such concerns, however, the influence of the Latin Americanists within the State Department was waning. Sumner Welles, their leader and mentor and the only one with access to the White House, was already weakening; he yielded to the temptation to apply pressure to force a defiantly independent Argentina into line with the Allied cause and, after yielding to more mundane temptations, had to resign from the Department in August 1943 under the cloud of a sex scandal.[124] His replacement, the former General Motors executive Edward R. Stettinius, Jr., with his corporate background and lack of Latin American experience, was a poor substitute. He was generally rated as ineffective: an "innocent," said his critics; a "zero," said the harsher among them.[125] Ambassador Claude Bowers wrote from Chile: "There is a general fear through South America that the passing of Welles from the Department means less interest in South America in Washington, and even a change, if not abandonment, of our 'good neighbor policy.'"[126] Such fears were not misplaced. Secretary Hull, after years of jealous rivalry with FDR's close friend Welles, now suspected the "Welles men" of disloyalty, and he began to push them – and their practices – to the far margins of policymaking.[127]

THE BOLIVIAN COUP

In early 1941, Welles had warned FDR of the danger to inter-American relations should the United States decide "to determine for itself whether or not the government of some other American republic were subservient to Nazi or Fascist influence and…intervene directly in order to correct that situation. If we adopted such a policy we would…afford exactly the opportunity which the Nazi propagandists are seeking to raise the old charge of Yankee imperialism," he wrote.[128] It proved to be a prescient insight.

The project of expelling Germans joined with the misperceptions distorting U.S. treatment of Latin America in late 1943 to create a dispute with Bolivia that had far-reaching implications. German influence in that country had long been considerable. Britain and the United States purchased the minerals – mainly oil and tin – making up most of Bolivia's exports, but German businesses dominated the country's internal market. Bolivia also invited German military instructors to serve its army in the 1930s, although they hardly lived up to their reputations. Ernst Roehm arrived in La Paz in 1929 and was immediately promoted to lieutenant colonel, but when the Bolivians refused to make him their supreme commander, he went home to Germany (where he would head the combative SA or storm troopers, until he was murdered on Hitler's orders in the 1934 "Night of the Long Knives").[129] The worst disasters of the Chaco War against Paraguay, in which 65,000 Bolivian soldiers died, occurred under the leadership of Commander-in-Chief and German import Hans Kundt.

The FBI inflated the impression of German might, printing an illustration that showed 12,000 German inhabitants of Bolivia lined up like storm troopers ready to march – although 8,500 of them were Jewish refugees. The remaining 3,500 were "men, women and children of German nationality or of German origin and Bolivian nationality."[130] Of those, 184 were Nazi Party members on the eve of the war.[131]

Germans may have been influential in Bolivia (though hardly as influential as the FBI believed), but their influence did not outweigh Bolivia's interest in maintaining good relations with its principal customers, and so when the war broke out the country readily took a number of steps directed against the Axis. The government broke relations with the Axis powers in January 1942, declared it was "advancing towards a state of war" in April 1943, and declared war on December 4, 1943.[132] Bolivian authorities placed supervisors in all important German businesses but resolved to keep them operating: the Chamber of Commerce estimated that 70 percent of the wholesale and large-scale retail business was in German hands, so closing those firms outright would have dealt a crushing blow to Bolivia's feeble economy.[133] President Enrique Peñaranda undertook these measures without objection but resisted expropriating the businesses or deporting German nationals to the United States because he refused to accept the "statements from anonymous sources" offered as incriminating evidence by U.S. intelligence.[134]

Peñaranda's government faced a challenge by two groups: the *Movimiento Nacionalista Revolucionario* (MNR), a political party whose members' convictions ranged from fascist to socialist; and *Razón de Patria* (Radepa), a military lodge formed among Bolivian officers held in Paraguayan prisoner of war camps during the Chaco War. Both organizations had vaguely defined but strongly nationalist programs whose main goal was to remove from power Peñaranda and his backers, the powerful mining companies. They believed that Bolivia's widespread poverty, 80 percent illiteracy rate, and what one scholar termed "the most inequitable land-tenure system in the world" were the consequences of Bolivia's leaders' favoring the mine owners and selling out the country's mineral wealth to the United States at below market value.[135]

Peñaranda, whose followers called him the "Bolivian Cincinnatus," was no more tolerant of public protest than was his namesake. When miners and their families demonstrated at Catavi in December 1942, soldiers fired into the crowd, killing hundreds. The Catavi massacre shocked Latin American public opinion and brought the miners into the ranks of the MNR, which continued its demonstrations. In December 1943, using his recent declaration of war as a pretext, Peñaranda adjourned the national Chamber of Deputies, banned opposition newspapers, and suspended elections. (The president of the Chamber of Deputies remarked that the decrees amounted to an inoffensive war against the Axis but an effective one against the Bolivian people.) In response, on December 20, 1943, the MNR and Radepa launched a bloodless coup that toppled Peñaranda's government.[136]

Observers predisposed to see outside manipulators at work whenever anything of importance happens in Latin America immediately labeled the junta a "Nazi-Fascist" body. Some of the army officers had been in touch with Argentine military leaders, and Argentina had been pursuing a rogue policy of neutrality that permitted German agents to operate on its territory; when Edelmiro Farrell and Juan Perón seized power in February 1944, the United States refused to recognize the new regime. (The State Department's campaign against Argentina would go well beyond pressures placed upon European neutrals such as Spain, Switzerland, Sweden, or Turkey, which took comparable positions in the war – but they were not in America's "backyard.")

But a direct link from the Bolivian junta to Germany could not be established. Some members of the MNR had social acquaintances among Bolivia's Germans – as they did with other foreigners. The German Embassy had, for a time, subsidized the MNR newspaper *La Calle*, although that did not lead to complete editorial control; for example, the paper supported the Republicans in the Spanish Civil War.[137] The FBI's chief evidence of a Nazi connection was that some in the junta were friends of Major Elias Belmonte – the Bolivian officer who had supposedly written a letter in July 1941 asking Germany for help organizing a revolt, although since December 1941 other U.S. officials had known that it was the work of a British propagandist.[138] For its new Defense Minister, the junta selected Major Celestino Pinto, who could not be accused of Nazi sympathies. He had trained at a military college in France and asked permission at the beginning of the war to serve in the French Army and fight against the Germans.[139]

The German ties to the junta were gossamer ones. Not surprisingly, given Bolivia's racial makeup, the Nazi doctrine of Aryan supremacy found little resonance there. More troubling was the MNR's unsavory deployment of anti-Semitic themes in its propaganda. Rather than indicating subservience to Berlin, the MNR's anti-Semitism was a cynical response to two developments in Bolivian society: popular discontent over the unusually high rate of Jewish refugee immigration and the convenient embodiment of "international capitalism" by Mauricio Hochschild, owner of the largest tin mine in Bolivia, who not only happened to be Jewish, but also opposed his miners' struggles for higher pay and better working conditions. As an MNR propaganda target, he proved irresistible.

Relations between Jewish refugees and urban Bolivians were tense. In hopes of repopulating the desolate border region near Paraguay devastated by the Chaco War, Bolivia had established a generous immigration policy in the late 1930s, welcoming ten thousand Jewish refugees between 1938 and 1941 on condition that they work in the agricultural sector. (In a country of only three million people, this constituted the largest number of refugees proportional to its population accepted by any American nation – one refugee for every three hundred Bolivians. The U.S. rate was about one refugee per thousand inhabitants.)[140] Several thousand of these refugees arrived with fraudulent visas purchased from a corrupt Bolivian official, creating a national scandal.[141] The arrivals from Central European cities – hardly equipped for tropical farming – settled for the most part in La Paz, supporting themselves as peddlers or opening small shops with financial assistance from the American Jewish Joint Distribution Committee in New York. By joining the scramble for scarce housing and jobs and competing with small shopkeepers, the Jewish newcomers drew hostility from the local inhabitants, the plight of refugees everywhere. The animosity came from across the political spectrum: the pro-Allied newspaper *La Razón* editorialized frequently against Jewish immigration, and no less a figure than Mauricio Hochschild himself called for a suspension of Jewish immigration – which President Peñaranda, not the MNR, duly ordered in May 1940.[142] When U.S. envoys arrived in La Paz in 1944 to investigate the alleged Nazi connections of the new government, they reported that Israel Kleinman and Guillermo Mueller, leaders of the Jewish community of La Paz, had told them that Bolivian resentment of Jews was traceable not to Nazi influence but to local circumstances.[143]

To the extent that the MNR exploited anti-Jewish sentiment, it engaged in a reprehensible practice – as reprehensible as tactics used by opponents of refugee immigration in many other countries. But the Bolivian response was not evidence of German influence. If opposing the entry of Jewish refugees was proof of Nazi sympathies, then the U.S. State Department and both houses of Congress must have been filled with Nazi sympathizers.

Whatever its slogans, the new regime's actions could not have been clearer. The Bolivian junta, led by Major Gualberto Villarroel, immediately pledged "effective cooperation with the United Nations [i.e., the Allies] and especially with the United States in their war effort against the Axis powers . . . without vacillation within the briefest periods and without the useless verbiage which has been characteristic of the deposed government."[144] They promised to deliver to the United States all the country's quinine bark (the basis of an antimalarial drug essential for jungle fighting in the Pacific), to nationalize German- and Japanese-owned businesses, and offered to expel "dangerous and influential Axis nationals" – which would seem an unlikely step for a Nazi-backed regime to take.[145]

There was one piece of unwelcome news, however: the junta sought to negotiate a higher price for Bolivia's tin in order to pay for "a plan of social assistance that will improve the living conditions of the mining laborers."[146] The price of tin was a constant source of popular complaint in Bolivia. The new regime's request for a fair price for the country's principal export was not a scheme to deprive the Allies of an essential war material but rather an attempt to remedy the abysmal lot of the Bolivian miners who produced it. (The Villarroel government would also abolish forced labor and convene the country's first National Indian Congress.)

Despite the concrete pro-Allied measures, Secretary Hull decided that the junta was the product of a Nazi-Argentine plot. He ordered the embassy to cut off discussions with the new regime. The War Department sent a message to its officers in La Paz, who had been holding informal talks with the military men in the junta, telling them to "put clamps on their lips."[147] The United States suspended all tin imports and refused to recognize the Provisional Government.

Although Adolf Berle believed the MNR was simply "the Bolivian version of the Nazi Party," the Latin Americanists in the State Department such as Duggan and Bonsal were skeptical.[148] So was a young analyst in the Research and Analysis Branch of the OSS, Arthur M. Schlesinger, Jr., who wrote at the time that the MNR would probably improve stability in Bolivia by remedying social injustices and that rumors of its fascist connections were disinformation.[149] Even Berle had to admit that "the military factors in the Bolivian situation are precisely nil."[150]

Berle and Hull placed more faith in the erroneous reports of Hoover's FBI than in information from the embassy indicating just how eager the new government was to demonstrate its solidarity with the Allied cause. They were also listening to such sources as tin baron Mauricio Hochschild, who was understandably hostile to the pro-labor junta and passed the word to the U.S. government that the "Bolivian regime is purely Nazi and utterly impossible."[151] Rewriting history, Hull now informed FDR that the deposed President Peñaranda "had distinguished himself for his pro-United States sentiments"[152] – even though Special Division officials had long been frustrated by Peñaranda's refusal to cooperate in expelling Germans.[153] There seemed to be no one in a high position interested in an accurate assessment of the local circumstances behind the Bolivian coup rather than uncritically accepting rumors of a German puppetmaster at work behind the scenes. This was unfortunate, for it precipitated a six-month confrontation that contributed greatly to the deterioration of inter-American relations and the demise of the Good Neighbor policy.

The effort to undermine the new government began in Montevideo, where the CPD passed a resolution introduced by Uruguay's delegate Alberto Guani, a favorite channel for Carl Spaeth, recommending that the other American nations consult among themselves before granting recognition to a government established by force. The United States opposed actually calling a consultative meeting of foreign ministers, which might have created a forum for the denunciation of nonrecognition as a form of intervention.[154] Instead, the State Department decided on its own to withhold recognition, and "consultation" consisted of urging other governments to follow suit. Aware that to break ranks could put them in the position of challenging the United States, no Latin American government except for Argentina recognized the new Bolivian regime. This use of the CPD would "strengthen the growing feeling in Latin America that the United States was taking advantage of nominally inter-American procedures to impose its unilateral policies on the other American governments," as a survey of the region put it a few years later.[155]

By taking this decision, Washington violated a central tenet of the Good Neighbor policy: the commitment not to use nonrecognition to enforce changes in the composition of Latin American governments. Up to that point, Welles and Hull had agreed that U.S. prestige only suffered by the withholding of recognition, what Foreign Minister Genaro Estrada of Mexico called "an insulting practice" that "offends the sovereignty of other nations [and] implies that judgment of some sort may be placed upon the internal affairs of those nations by other governments."[156] Already back in 1930, Herbert Hoover formally revoked the policy of using nonrecognition as a pressure tactic in South America, and the same acknowledgment of full sovereignty was extended to Central America in Roosevelt's first term.[157] The fear of an illusory German menace now destroyed a principle that was close to the hearts of many of our neighbors.

A QUID PRO QUO

Throughout the war, the United States expected cooperation with its anti-Axis policies in exchange for economic assistance for Latin America, and Latin American governments paid for that assistance with deliveries of raw materials and expelled German nationals. In the early months of 1944, Bolivia began to realize that a payment of the latter kind might be the only way to buy the diplomatic recognition, and resumption of tin exports, the country so desperately needed.

In April, the counselor to the Bolivian Embassy in Washington, Carlos Dorado, asked Duggan what the Bolivian government could do to obtain recognition. Duggan replied that a "clear and convincing demonstration" of a pro-Allied stance, such as the deportation of the Germans wanted by the United States, might help assuage the doubts of his colleagues. Dorado replied that such a move would be difficult, since "some of these persons were important cogs in the economic life of the country, whatever else they might be in addition. Unless they could be replaced by others with capital and technical knowledge the economic life of the country would be badly affected. Nevertheless, he would transmit the idea to his government as coming from him."[158]

Meanwhile Duggan continued to try to persuade Hull to see the Bolivian government for what it was. The regime's cooperation with the Allied war effort had been a distinct improvement over Peñaranda's, Duggan argued: the military officers of Radepa had recently expelled the MNR from government, as the United States desired; deliveries of quinine and rubber were exceeding levels reached before the coup; and Villarroel's government had taken a step Peñaranda would not, by expropriating major Axis-owned businesses. The U.S. Embassy in La Paz acknowledged that "No definite proof was ever available, even at the time of the 'Nazi-Putsch,' to establish direct connection between the MNR and the Nazi party. At the present time it seems doubtful that the party was anything but a completely national one."[159] Duggan now wrote that "far from being a probable danger to hemisphere security, Bolivia has become a probable asset to hemisphere cooperation and security and to the United Nations war effort," and urged immediate recognition.[160]

Philip Bonsal, Duggan's deputy, was then on a Latin American tour and the two corresponded privately and frequently.[161] This exchange of letters between the State Department's two most experienced remaining Latin America officers with unique access to knowledgeable sources illuminates the damage done to the Good Neighbor's commitment to noninterference in the internal affairs of Latin American countries.

Bonsal wrote to Duggan from Mexico City, his first stop, that "we are making a great mistake to delay Bolivian recognition" because the mining interests might be motivated to organize a countercoup.[162] "The Secretary is warming up slightly to recognition," Duggan could respond by April 27, although Hull still insisted upon "the deportation of Axis ringleaders and implementation of the decree expropriating Axis goods."[163] Bonsal replied on May 1 that he found the news

most depressing. To tie recognition to two piddling matters on which we failed to make much progress with our great and good friend Peñaranda seems to me very unwise and very dangerous. We are continuing on a highly mistaken path. The deportation issue, as far as Bolivia is concerned, is a complete phony, but to inject it at this time and in this connection can have very far-reaching effects. The matter is personal and sentimental and will be remembered.[164]

At this point, Secretary Hull dispatched his ambassador to Panama, Avra Warren, to La Paz on a mission that was supposed to be kept secret, officially for fact-finding purposes, but actually, as Duggan told Bonsal, in order to extract the Germans from Bolivia.[165]

"We have gone through all sorts of contortions here with regard to Bolivia," Duggan wrote to Bonsal on May 6, noting that Secretary Hull feared press criticism should he recognize a government he had publicly demonized. It was clear by mid-1944 that the Bolivian regime was not a threat to the Allies, and no one now believed that there was any German danger to the Western Hemisphere. Duggan thought "the Department should do what is right [recognize the sitting government] and take the rap," but Hull was still looking to save face. While the secretary mulled over the possibility finding a way to "insinuate . . . to the Bolivians the idea that they should deport some Axis ringleaders," Duggan recounted, a telegram arrived from U.S. Chargé d'Affaires Robert Woodward in La Paz saying the Bolivians had inquired whether delivering some of their dangerous enemy aliens might result in recognition. Duggan's earlier suggestion to Dorado had borne fruit. "This was like manna falling from heaven," Duggan told Bonsal. "The Secretary moved in very fast, egged on by Messrs. Berle, [former Ambassador Pierre] Boal, [legal advisor Green] Hackworth, and [Breckinridge] Long. Although we had previously been talking about the deportation of a few *ringleaders*, our eyes got bigger and bigger and the figure jumped first to 53, then to 93, and finally to 162."[166]

Avra Warren arrived in La Paz on Sunday, May 7, accompanied by General Ralph Wooten, Commander of the Sixth United States Army Air Force. In meetings with Major Villarroel, who was still wavering over the deportations, Warren insisted that without them there would be no recognition. General Wooten saw Villarroel the next day and spoke "as a soldier to a soldier," declaring that "he was here to transport quinine or Germans, whichever the case might be, and that, in the absence of cargo, he would be leaving on Wednesday." The Bolivian government gave its approval May 9, although Villarroel was said to be "incensed" at the pressure from Warren's delegation.[167]

The arrests took place on May 17. That day and night there was a constant stream of visitors to the U.S. delegation asking for the release of one or another of the Germans from the expulsion list for having served the country in the Chaco War, or for having a Bolivian family, or because of advanced age. W. Tapley Bennett, Jr., an aide to Warren, remembered "the talks with Bolivian officials, and the wife of the President pleading with Ambassador Warren, 'please don't send my children's tutor away.' Well, we did send him away. We had a fleet of ten planes. They were DC-3s but they looked very big as they all landed in tandem at 14,000 feet in the high Andean sun."[168] On May 18, eighty-one Axis nationals – fifty-two Germans and twenty-nine Japanese – boarded the U.S. bombers en route to the Canal Zone.[169]

To preserve appearances, the United States claimed that there was no connection between the Warren trip, the expulsions, and the question of recognition. But Latin Americans saw clearly that the United States was again acting unilaterally, dispensing with promised consultations, and reaching deeply into the internal affairs of a Latin American country to force compliance with Washington's policies. Brazil's foreign minister Oswaldo Aranha, one of the most reliable U.S. allies on the continent, who had tried to mediate in Bolivia but was cut out by the United States, "violently" denounced the Warren mission to U.S. Ambassador Jefferson Caffery. "I shall not repeat all he said for the Department would think he was either putting on an act or was about to break relations with us," Caffery wrote.[170]

From Santiago, Philip Bonsal relayed to Duggan the stinging criticism he was receiving over the deal from historically friendly Bolivian officials. The former Bolivian foreign minister, Alberto Ostria Gutiérrez, who had cooperated with U.S. proposals at inter-American summit conferences in 1936, 1939, and 1940, was "extremely disturbed," Bonsal wrote. "He told me frankly and vehemently that he thought the removal of the Germans recently carried out by air was a mistake from every point of view. He said specifically that it was a serious error for us to request it and for Bolivia to have acceded to it, particularly as part of the price for recognition."[171]

On return to Washington, Avra Warren produced a pro forma report circulated to all Latin American countries except Argentina, which had already recognized the Bolivian government. It praised Villarroel personally and his government in general for supplying essential war materials to the Allies, arresting rubber smugglers, expropriating Axis-owned firms, and, above all, for having "committed itself irrevocably to the cause of the United Nations" by deporting the Axis nationals.[172] Bonsal, now writing from Tegucigalpa, had by then had an earful of complaints. He wrote a last letter to Duggan: "We are all, of course, looking forward to Avra Warren's report. While I have no doubt that the document itself will be a very straight-forward, honest piece of work...I do not think we should have any illusions as to the real views of the neighbors regarding this type of procedure."[173]

Back in Bolivia, the Villarroel government found itself facing "a great hue and cry" by the opposition "charging that the Government had 'delivered itself' to the United States ... [and] had compromised the independence and sovereignty of Bolivia by the recent action of turning over the enemy aliens."[174] Chargé Woodward reminded the State Department that "German businessmen have not been popularly considered in Bolivia to constitute a danger but rather as accepted members of the community, and the deportation on May 18 had almost no popular support."[175]

Confirmation that the United States had erred badly came from a surprising source: the Vice President of Mauricio Hochschild's mining company, Dr. Adolf Blum, a German Jew and no friend of the new government. (Hochschild himself had been jailed by the Provisional Government after he met secretly with U.S. officials to offer his cooperation to "destroy the regime" – the mining interests' countercoup attempt predicted by Philip Bonsal.)[176] In late May, Blum met with the U.S. Commercial Attaché, Walter P. McConaughy, and offered a devastating assessment of U.S. policy in the Bolivian crisis. This critique by an impartial source highlighted not only the recent fiasco but also what was wrong with the traditional U.S. approach to Latin America in general. As McConaughy reported:

[Dr. Blum] declared that deportation of Axis nationals residing in Bolivia certainly was not a vital interest of ours and indicated that we were misguided [when] we had made an issue out of the deportation question. He said that none of the Axis nationals deported was important or dangerous and that if the universal opinion that we were responsible for the deportations was correct, we had expended most of our remaining good will and our bargaining power on an illusory and relatively worthless objective. He added that we had exposed ourselves to ridicule and discredit by the apparent emphasis we had quixotically placed on this matter and that we had alienated the sympathy of a large number of Bolivians who had no particular brief for the Axis but who naturally sympathized with helpless victims of circumstance such as the Axis nationals, and who were antagonized by arbitrary and highhanded methods of achieving insignificant objectives.... Resentment was accumulating as the significance of the affair was assimilated, and was not dying down with the passage of time. The provisional Government has suffered a loss of prestige in the eyes of most Bolivians by acceding.... The deportations of a few nonentities with harmless records could not be successfully defended.

Dr. Blum said that as he saw it there were two underlying fallacies in our policy toward Bolivia. One was the assumption that Bolivian politicians and revolutionists are motivated by ideological and philosophical considerations. We seem to assume that they all have to be on one side or the other in total war, whereas the truth is that they have no real convictions one way or the other. They are not pro-Nazi or pro-Argentine. Neither are they pro-United Nations in the abstract. They are first pro-themselves and second pro-Bolivia....

He said that the revolution of December 20 was a run-of-the-mill Latin revolution such as has been characteristic of Latin American countries for well over 100 years.[177]

Blum was not overstating the impact on the provisional government of having yielded to the U.S. demands. The internationally respected diplomat Victor Andrade, later to become Bolivia's Foreign Minister, would write in his memoirs that the whole incident was a form of intervention "which seriously harmed the Villarroel government and had drastic effects on the future of Bolivia."[178]

The dispute with Bolivia demonstrated just how far from its security-related origins the deportation program had come. It was hard to argue that a few Germans left alone in Bolivia posed a threat to the Western Hemisphere or to the Allied war effort in 1944. Instead, deporting Germans became a means for the Bolivian government to meet the standards of legitimacy established unilaterally by the United States, while for the U.S. government it was a face-saving device to allow restoration of normal relations with a regime it had publicly, and erroneously, vilified as a Nazi satellite. The cost was high in lost credibility and respect from Latin Americans who had only recently begun to hope that Washington's imperious ways might be a thing of the past.

Within a month of recognition, Duggan was forced out of government, accused by Hull of passing secrets to Welles for Welles's newspaper column – and fearful that his past service to Soviet intelligence had been exposed.[179] Bonsal left Washington and served as ambassador to Colombia, Bolivia, Morocco, and Cuba.[180] With their departure, the State Department was left firmly in the hands of the interventionist faction, who would now go on to bury what remained of the Good Neighbor policy under the debris of a hostile and fruitless crusade against the Argentine government.

As for the Germans deported from Bolivia, they came under close scrutiny only once they were interned in the United States. Postwar investigations showed that about twenty were Nazi Party members, including Felix Kuno Wintruff, local head of the Party; for eight of these there was no evidence of any pro-Nazi activity; the others' "activity" consisted of subscribing to Nazi propaganda sheets or attending Party meetings.

The remainder made up the usual cross-section of German expatriate society picked up in deportation actions across Latin America. Richard Feucht was deemed "a drunkard [of] no political importance" by postwar investigators. Leo Hamermann was a Jewish refugee deported by Bolivian officials

who were "anxious . . . to make a good showing with the American government." Friedrich Ising was a mining engineer whose name did not appear on
any agency's list of dangerous Germans, and who "never engaged in Nazi
activities." Wilhelm Schediwy was a "devout Catholic" with an "excellent
reputation" whose Jewish acquaintances testified that he had always been
anti-Nazi. Johannes August Hans Ridder was the only German residing in
the town of Yacuiba. There was no evidence of Nazi activities against him,
and more than one hundred Yacuiba residents signed a petition requesting
his release.[181]

The entire exercise predictably offended Latin American opinion, since
it showed the Colossus of the North resolutely reverting to the old ways;
and as an exercise in promoting security, it proved to be pointless. When the
deportees landed in the United States, Justice Department officials running
the internment camps reviewed the paperwork and immediately threatened
to refuse to take custody of at least a third of the group against whom there
was no evidence or even any suspicion of activity sufficient to have warranted
deportation.[182] But that was not a realistic option: they were on U.S. soil, and
something had to be done with them. The Germans from Bolivia settled in
alongside the diverse assortment of deportees from fifteen countries already
interned in U.S. camps.

5

Internment

"One couldn't complain. A nation fighting for its life has more important things
to do than to ensure thorough justice for every emigrant. We weren't tortured,
gassed, or shot, only locked up – what more could one expect?"
                                    –Erich Maria Remarque, *The Night in Lisbon*[1]

Crystal City, Texas, late 1945. The 16mm movie camera, placed high in a
tower for a bird's-eye view, pans across a small southwestern desert town. An
ice truck on delivery makes its rounds of neat wooden shacks surrounded by
flowerbeds and vegetable gardens. Like any other small town, this one has
its general store, laundry, blacksmith, garage, volunteer fire department, and
hospital; the latter, the film's narrator informs us, has announced its 250th
live birth. The large, circular community swimming pool is as crowded as one
might expect in a place where midday temperatures can reach 120 degrees.
The splashing and shouting of hundreds of children at play comes in jarring
contrast to the barbed wire fence and guard towers surrounding the town
on all sides.

We are watching an official documentary of the Crystal City Detention
Facility made by the Immigration and Naturalization Service at the end of
the war. INS Commissioner Argyle R. Mackey looks directly into the camera
and assures us that the four thousand German and Japanese inhabitants
of Crystal City "lived, worked and played under a tradition of American
standards of decent and humane treatment." The photography attests to
this: smiling detainees holding their trays in the chow line, families sitting
down to dinner in their own kitchens, Japanese gardeners performing their
meticulous work, German musicians playing in the camp orchestra, students
graduating from the camp's accredited high school.[2]

These halcyon images square with the memories of some former Crystal
City residents, particularly those who were children or resilient teenagers
at the time of internment. "The prison camp was beautiful, at least for us
kids," recalled Hans Joachim Schaer, 5 years old when interned with his

parents from Costa Rica. "In the mornings we had a bottle of milk, we had a swimming pool, we had a dispensary, they treated us nice." Werner Kappel was 19 when arrested with his father in Panama. "When you're young, nothing bothers you as much," he said. "It was harder on the older people."[3] Four years of administrative experience and steady physical improvements carried out cooperatively by the authorities and the internees themselves created, by 1945, one of the most comfortable detention facilities for civilian internees run by any country involved in the war. The unspoken contrast with newsreel footage of liberated camps in Europe and the Pacific was impossible to miss.

But behind the harmonious picture of postwar tranquility at this model camp lay a far more conflicted reality in the half-dozen major internment facilities for deportees from Latin America. A look inside the camps does more than reveal a hidden world: observing the behavior of the deportees in internment supplies yet more evidence that most were anything but dangerous, since they were unwilling to participate in the schemes cooked up by the minority of committed Nazi prisoners. It offers a unique and until now untapped documentary record for deepening our understanding of the nature of the internees and of the communities from which they were removed and shows how unsuccessful the deportation program was in its principal goal of identifying dangerous suspects. Finally, putting a human face on the objects of policy, something disregarded by many works of history, should make it easier to understand the angry criticism that came from Latin Americans.

SWASTIKAS IN U.S. CAMPS: NAZI ATTEMPTS AT CONTROL

The first German deportees to arrive were held in encampments and forts run by the U.S. Army's Provost Marshal General. Then, as their numbers increased, they were moved to specially prepared camps under the authority of the Border Patrol, a division of the Immigration and Naturalization Service, itself part of the Justice Department. The largest camps were in Texas: Camp Kenedy, for single men; Camp Seagoville, for single women and married couples without children; and Crystal City, for family groups and the overflow from other facilities. Interned civilians were not officially subject to the Geneva Convention on Prisoners of War, but the U.S. government followed the principle that "the treatment rendered alien enemies in this country will largely determine the treatment to be afforded to American citizens to be contemporaneously interned in other countries."[4] Specific camp regulations varied from place to place, and leniency was the rule. This allowed for some unusual activities to take place under the jurisdiction of the U.S. government.

When 29-year-old Gunter Lisken arrived at Crystal City from Ecuador in 1944, a burly German-American man approached him and growled, "Listen up, kid. In this camp we're all Nazis and anyone who doesn't agree, we'll break his skull." On April 20, Hitler's birthday, Lisken and some of the other deportees from Latin America were shocked to see fellow inmates, mostly longtime U.S. residents, parading through the camp in brownshirts and singing Nazi songs all the way to the assembly hall, where they held a celebration under a huge portrait of Hitler. "We couldn't believe our eyes, that there could be so much permissiveness in an internment camp," Lisken recalls.[5]

It struck many observers at the time as odd that internees should be allowed to display Nazi symbols in American camps. As part of a live-and-let-live approach favored by several camp commanders to maintain order with minimum force, those internees who so desired were permitted to observe German national holidays, publish newspapers filled with fascist and anti-Semitic content, decorate their quarters with swastikas and even wear Nazi uniforms.[6]

Under these lax conditions, and as a result of the broad spectrum of political beliefs among the German internees, the camps were riven by the same conflicts that had divided the communities from which they came. "The government takes the view that the internees are uniformly of German origin. The internees are well aware of the fact that it is the mixture of detainees of different origins and opinions that causes difficulties," wrote a Swiss inspector after visiting a U.S. internment facility.[7] Nazi Party members, the most numerous politically active group among the internees, tried as they had done in Latin America to seize control of all available community institutions, to extend the transnational reach of the Nazi state to the German microcommunities artificially created inside the camps.

Camp authorities asked the internees to select an internal leadership, with spokespersons as well as work officers, financial officers, cleanliness officers, and the like. The vote was held early, when the first wave of deportations had brought many hardcore pro-Nazis who dominated the elections, and Party members quickly captured the influential posts and used them to reward their supporters and punish their opponents. Hermann Egner, former school director in Managua and now Housing Officer at Camp Kenedy, arranged to prevent Jews and anti-Nazis from drawing on a relief fund created from the canteen's profits to support needy internees. (The YMCA's War Prisoners' Aid committee took over relief payments to those deprived of funds.) In Oklahoma, Stringtown camp spokesman Ingo Kalinowsky, one of the earliest members of the Nazi Party in Costa Rica, took delivery of Red Cross care packages sent from Germany and distributed them to his cronies. The German spokesman at Kenedy tried to organize a work stoppage, but the internees didn't support him, and he was replaced. Nazi teachers in camp schools, deported and interned to prevent them from propagandizing in schools in Latin America, now carried on their efforts literally before a captive audience.[8]

As in Latin America, Nazis used the leverage of their homeland regime's backing to induce the ambivalent into toeing the line. Every internee received three dollars a month from the U.S. government in the form of coupons to spend at the canteen for cigarettes, cold drinks, snacks, and sundries. Those with frozen U.S. bank accounts or whose cash was confiscated upon arrival at the camps were permitted to withdraw a small amount per month as well. Via the Swiss, representing German interests in the United States, the German government contributed the significant additional sum of four dollars a month – but only to those prisoners who signed an oath of loyalty to the German Reich. One socialist opponent of Hitler signed the oath, declaring aloud that he was loyal to Germany but not to its leadership. The temptation to double one's monthly spending money, rather than Führer-worship, motivated others to sign as well. U.S. officials were careful not to let the list of signers' names get back to Germany, where it might be cross-checked against internee lists to identify the disloyal nonsigners for reprisals against their families. Nazis in the camps had already used lists of those refusing repatriation to identify targets for harassment. Camp authorities cited "past experience" in refusing to ask internee spokespersons in 1944 to compile lists of volunteers for repatriation, "inasmuch as it would again furnish the Speakers with information as to who does not wish to return to Germany, which information is often used to the detriment of these people and to camp life in general."[9]

UNUSUAL SUSPECTS: DISSIDENTS AND JEWS

The irony of interning people as Nazis, then being compelled to protect them from Nazis, was nowhere more starkly clear than in the cases of physical violence against dissident internees. Otto Kugler had emigrated to Honduras in 1930 and resumed his profession, practicing dentistry. As with so many of the Germans picked up for deportation from Latin America, the accusations against him were limited to a vague assertion that he had spread Nazi propaganda. Interned at Camp Kenedy, Kugler performed dental work for the other prisoners for free. Camp commander Ivan Williams estimated that Kugler thereby saved the U.S. taxpayer $16,767 in medical costs. Williams also noted that Kugler's "anti-Nazi attitude led to active persecution from the camp Nazis. On one occasion he was saved by the guards after he had been dragged from the hospital and was being beaten. It became necessary to give him a room in the hospital and to escort him to meals under guard for a period of three months. Nevertheless his attitude did not change."[10]

Kugler's was not an isolated case.[11] Fritz Sauter, a 19-year-old Costa Rican-born son of German parents, was deported to the United States for allegedly shouting "Heil Hitler" on July 4, 1943, according to an informant. The embassy labeled him a Nazi. Postwar investigators from the Justice Department reached a different conclusion. Sauter so tenaciously defended his allegiance to Costa Rica that friction with the pro-Nazi group in Camp Kenedy "finally culminated in a fight in which a considerable number of the pro-Nazis attacked him." For his own safety, he was transferred to Camp Algiers, Louisiana, where most of the inmates were Jews or non-Nazis. "At that camp he was reported as well behaved, studious, a Catholic, with anti-Nazis as his closest friends, and not known to have engaged in political discussions." The report concluded with a telling indication of Sauter's sympathies: "He enlisted in the U.S. Army in January 1945."[12]

Even in the barbed-wire idyll of Crystal City, guards had to rescue a German couple attacked by a Nazi gang; the two were given lodging in a trailer next to the guardhouse. There are indications that the club-wielding gangs inside the camps were made up principally of sailors from the German merchant marine and Germans resident in the United States, rather than deportees from Latin America.[13] Otto Stetzelberg, a deportee from Peru, informed the Gestapo after repatriating to Germany that the sailors "without exception . . . behaved as good Germans and never denied that they joined up for Adolf Hitler's Reich."[14] Justice Department official Jerre Mangione, after an extensive tour of the camps, reported that the most difficult prisoners were the former members of the German-American Bund.[15] Edward Heims, a Jewish internee from San Francisco, was beaten up in the mess hall at Fort Lincoln, North Dakota, by a German seaman who didn't want to share a table with a Jew. Lincoln's commander I. P. "Ike" McCoy, well-liked by the 287 German sailors in camp, grumbled to the Border Patrol's Willard Kelly, supervisor of the camp system, that the six Jewish prisoners in his charge "have caused us considerable trouble playing up this persecution complex and, as a matter of fact, their entire troubles are brought on by themselves."[16]

Similar attitudes toward the Jewish internees were displayed by other U.S. officials, who complained that one of them "made a nuisance of himself for several years in an effort to get released from confinement"; officials rejected numerous appeals on behalf of the Jews as a matter of course. Rabbi S. B. Yampol of Nashville regularly made the 150-mile round-trip drive to Camp Forrest, Tennessee, to hold religious services for twenty Jewish refugees from Panama held there under the enemy alien internment program. "They are greatly embittered by the Axis powers and would give their lives for the annihilation of the cruel German regime," he wrote the State Department. "Among them is a physician, a mining engineer and a mechanic who are most eager to give of their skill and knowledge. . . . Should these men, our friends, be classified as our enemies and kept imprisoned?" The answer, from Albert E. Clattenburg of the Special Division, was that the Jewish internees had a choice: "These and other aliens have been sent to the United States by the other American Republics as dangerous or potentially dangerous to be repatriated or interned for reasons of hemispheric safety. Any such persons not desiring repatriation are, of course, subject to internment." If they did not like the U.S. camps, in other words, the Jews were free to go to Hitler's

Germany.[17] Needless to say, none of them took up the State Department's astonishing suggestion.

For the first year and a half of U.S. participation in the war, Jews languished in the same camps with their enemies. Fred Kappel, spokesperson for the Jewish internees in Camp Blanding, Florida, sent a steady stream of entreaties on their behalf to every U.S. government agency he could think of. He managed to persuade the camp commander to segregate the Jews in their own tents, where they sat and listened to Nazi internees outside singing fight songs and rehearsing victory speeches.[18] The American Jewish Joint Distribution Committee and the National Refugee Service weighed in on their behalf, asking U.S. government officials to release the Jewish internees, without success.[19]

At Stringtown, eighteen Jewish refugees seized in Latin America as suspected "dangerous enemy aliens" were relegated to a steam-filled room in the basement leading to the camp showers. Other prisoners trooped through their quarters from morning to night on their way to bathe, some taking the opportunity to call them "Jewish swine" and "dirty Jews." After Lieutenant Colonel Bertram Frankenberger, himself Jewish, took over as camp commander, they were moved to more private quarters and interviewed one by one by an officer. Their testimony is revealing, not only because of their Kafkaesque predicament but also because of the diversity it indicated among the rest of the German group.[20]

The interviews made clear that the first days at Stringtown were frightening ones for the Jewish internees. They were threatened and excluded from the only organized activities, English classes and sports, because of objections by Nazi prisoners. Wilhelm Heinemann, arrested in Panama after a U.S. military intelligence officer became suspicious of a cup of coffee in his restaurant (see Chapter 2), reported that at first "we were told by a certain rabid element that the Jews would be exterminated." The transcript of the officer's questions and Heinemann's responses ends with this note:

At this point the internee almost completely broke down due to nervousness and stated that in no way had he ever been connected with subversive activities against this country and does not understand why he has been interned.[21]

Throughout his confinement, Heinemann suffered "extreme mental anguish" at the prospect that he might be sent to his death in Germany (an option not ruled out by the State Department until late 1942) and at one point contemplated suicide.[22]

Interestingly, several of the Jewish prisoners made statements that confirm the picture of a German internee group divided between a coercive Nazi faction and a passive majority. "A lot of internees would be nice but do not associate with us because they are afraid of the Nazi element," said Erwin Klyszcz. Fred Kappel, transferred to Stringtown from Camp Blanding, stated that "the other internees rather pity us because they don't understand why we are here interned the same as the Nazis or people who are in favor of Germany." Isidore Rosenberg noted a change in the summer of 1942, after some of the most fervent Nazis went back to Germany under an initial exchange agreement and more Germans arrived from Latin America. "Since the people from Costa Rica and Guatemala are here it is better," he said. "They are more intelligent. Also, the group that was repatriated helped our situation, because the remaining internees have been much nicer."*

Emil Loewenthal's statement is especially intriguing: "I have heard them [the Nazis] say that there are not enough of them to fight us but they are hoping that more will come and then they will take care of us." Since there were only 18 Jews, mostly older men, among a total internee population of 531 German adult males at Stringtown, Loewenthal's comment is a further sign that the number of fervent Nazis was actually quite modest, that their influence inside the camps rested on intimidation and seizing key positions in the internal hierarchy rather than on numerical strength. Despite the nominal Nazi Party membership of a substantial minority of prisoners, Nazi activists could not draw on large numbers of adherents to carry out their schemes.[24]

This suggests that the microcosm of German expatriate society inside the camps reflected the communities in Latin America whence the internees came: a small number of fanatics used appeals to patriotism to get others to sign up as Party members and applied coercive measures to bring still more into line. But a readiness to take concrete action, and face the possible consequences, was quite another matter. In the internment camps of North America and in the cities below the Rio Grande, the image of a monolithic German populace ready to march in lock-step at Hitler's command proved greatly exaggerated.

Indeed, the number of the zealous willing to incur even a small risk for their beliefs may have been quite meager. When the 531 internees at Stringtown were forbidden to give the Hitler salute, Nazis organized a group defiance of the regulation and were punished with thirty days in separate quarters. The protestors numbered just fifteen.[25] Their pathetic showing illustrates just how inoffensive were most of the allegedly "dangerous enemy aliens" deported and incarcerated. "For many of the interned Germans, it is the first time they have had any direct experience with hard-core Nazis," observed Camp Kenedy's commander Williams, "and they find they have little in common with them."[26]

THE CAMPS: FRESH MILK AND RATTLESNAKES

For internees not involved in the confrontations between Nazis and anti-Nazis, camp life was generally peaceful, comfortable, and dull. "This is no

---

* This is the same group of deportees from Costa Rica and Guatemala that the German Foreign Office thought were "all members of the Party and its organizations" and the commander of Camp Blanding could not believe were dangerous. See Chapter 4.

concentration camp, this is a country club," Colonel Kunzig, commander of the U.S. Army's Camp Blanding in northern Florida, told 116 internees arriving from Guatemala. Most tended to agree with him. "We grew tan and swelled up like doughnuts from the good meals," internee Karl-Albrecht Engel reported in a letter to the German government, going on to describe the Camp Blanding menu: three hot meals a day, starting with eggs and sausages in the morning and ending with oysters or meat and potatoes for dinner. The canteen sold three kinds of beer. Windblown sand and smoke from a nearby railway were minor irritants, but complaints were rare, perhaps in part because the lenient Colonel Kunzig, after talking with his charges, concluded that they were harmless.[27]

Deportees in the first wave in early 1942 not fortunate enough to land in Kunzig's country club went instead to Stringtown, the worst civilian detention station in the United States. A former state penitentiary in southern Oklahoma, Stringtown was set in a swampy hollow with hot breezeless summers and cold wintry winds. Prison Warden Fred Hunt, on his own initiative, wrote to the State Department requesting a copy of the Geneva Convention on prisoners of war, because he had no idea what standards to offer the deportees placed in his care. The first commander sent by the Army to supervise the prisoners, Colonel A. Noble Ladd, announced to the assembled internees that there was a cemetery nearby, and it would be easy to get there, because anyone who broke the rules would be shot. Roll call could take up to three hours. Six hundred men, most over fifty years old, were crowded into buildings designed for far fewer; locked in their barracks for most of the day (or all day when the weather was bad), the internees had to lie on their vermin-infested beds or stand up in the corners, because there was no room for chairs. Some of them slept in barred prison cells. The sick were not cared for. The stench from the toilets drifted into the dormitories, and there was no potable water outside of mealtimes. In the heat of June, Ladd kept them locked inside for two weeks straight "by mistake."[28] By October, a new commander had made improvements, reduced the overcrowding through transfers to other camps, built a library and an assembly hall with a movie screen, and offered food comparable to U.S. Army field rations. Stringtown's undistinguished service as an internment camp ended in May 1943.[29]

Camp Blanding's internees had already been transferred a year earlier, most of them going to Camp Kenedy, the largest facility for male deportees from Latin America. A former Civilian Conservation Corps (CCC) camp 35 miles southeast of San Antonio, Camp Kenedy was hurriedly expanded in April to handle over seven hundred internees, but it was not finished when they arrived. The dismayed internees were herded into the stockade by mounted Texas police handling lassos and found a disordered site still under construction. There were no books in the library, no organized activities; "the main physical exercise consists of walking around the camp inside barbed wire," reported Swiss inspectors, who found the place in an "uproar."[30]

The first summer at Kenedy was the worst. Border Patrol officials in charge of the camp believed that the Germans would soon be repatriated, so making improvements would be "a waste of both time and money." The so-called "Victory Huts" were second-hand castoffs; they didn't weather well, cracking and leaking badly. (Camp authorities followed the Geneva Convention standard of segregating nationalities, and applied their customary view of racial hierarchies. That meant that the smaller number of Japanese internees had it even worse, living en masse in old CCC dormitories instead of the four-man huts.)[31]

After a year of operation, Kenedy got a "new face" as the infrastructure was completed and the internees and camp authorities realized they were in for the long haul and started planting gardens and decorating their huts, and sports facilities were provided. Father Johannes Weber, deported from Guatemala, painted a mural depicting scenes from the life of Jesus on the camp's chapel walls. Commander Williams found Weber indispensable for maintaining the morale of the prisoners – "and for mine,"

22. German deportees from Latin America arrive by train at Camp Kenedy. Credit: Photo by Ivan Williams, Commander, Camp Kenedy. RG59-RAG-6-4, National Archives.

23. A German internee stands in the entrance to his prefabricated "Victory Hut," standard issue at Kenedy. Credit: Band 1, E2200 W/15, Schweizerisches Bundesarchiv, Bern.

he told a visiting Justice Department official. (Asked why Weber was interned, Williams replied that Weber's dossier indicated that "he is supposed to be a Nazi." In Williams' opinion, though, "He's no more of a Nazi than I am.")[32]

The camp never reached the level of comfort at Crystal City, and the thin walls and feeble heating units couldn't keep out the winter cold. Still, even the German government acknowledged, in response to inquiries from internees' relatives, that conditions in the U.S. camps were acceptable. Internees in letters at the time and interviews conducted years later had only positive things to say about their treatment by the guards. Gerardo Bohnenberger from Guatemala, who spent two years in Kenedy, expressed a typical sentiment. "*Muy correctos*," he said. "I have no complaints against them."[33] Nosy neighbors in town wrote to the local paper to protest the "pampering" of Axis internees. Commander Williams replied to the *San Antonio Express* and the *San Antonio Light* that he followed the principle of the Geneva Convention, namely "to treat them as humanely as we want our boys to be treated by the enemy."[34]

In fact, what little publicity the deportation program received produced opposition from unexpected quarters. At its national convention in September 1943, the American Legion resolved: "That we condemn the practice of importing into the United States aliens from other countries for detention in enemy alien relocation centers and request its discontinuance at once."

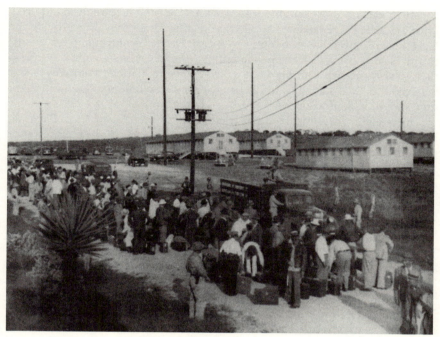

24. Internees lining up to be checked out of main gate for repatriation to Germany. Credit: Photo by Ivan Williams, Commander, Camp Kenedy. RG59-RAG-6-13, National Archives.

That was not a rare expression of civil libertarianism from the vocal patriotic organization, but a typical instance of the Legion's antiimmigrant attitude. While James H. Keeley in the Special Division imaginatively speculated that the resolution might be the work of a "fifth columnist...fighting to keep us from further upsetting the Nazi machinery south of the border," the State Department reassured the Legion that "no aliens are brought here for detention except in the national interest."[35]

Inside the camps, Nazi internees did their best to throw their weight around. Karl Gieseler, who had been a close aide of *Landesgruppenleiter* Hentschke in the Nazi local in Guatemala, was one of the chief troublemakers. On one occasion he stormed into the kitchen backed by five toughs, declared the cooks incompetent, and announced that he could run the kitchen better himself. After losing that skirmish, Gieseler led a group of ten prisoners into a huddle near the fence. Guards in the nearest tower, who couldn't tell what they were doing, ordered them away from the wire "and were invited by the group to make them do it. After some argument back and forth the guards finally settled the matter by dropping tear gas bombs into the group."[36]

There was no more trouble from Gieseler, but the factionalism endured. Otto Stetzelberg, repatriated to Germany, offered on arrival to provide the Gestapo with the names of twenty-three *Freie Deutsche*, outspoken opponents of the Nazi regime, at Kenedy. He granted that they had a right to express themselves – clearly the mark of a newcomer to Hitler's Germany – but believed they had served as informers for the camp command, and thought they should be kept track of.[37]

Thirty-eight Germans from Nicaragua, Honduras, Costa Rica, Panama, Ecuador, and the Dominican Republic signed, at some risk to themselves, a petition to the U.S. government. "The signers have been sent here from Latin American Countries without investigation – as far as we know – and trial of any kind," the internees wrote.

We are legitimate immigrants to Latin American Countries, have lived there for from 25 to 5 years approximately, some of us are naturalized, are married to natives and have children born and registered in these Latin American Countries, have partly worked for American companies, direct- or indirectly, and have therefore all our interests in this hemisphere. . . . We furthermore at no time participated in any political activities against our local Government and [have] shown no adversity for the policies of the USA before or during the war.

They offered testimonials to their good conduct from camp authorities, and requested hearings to "obtain thus the same advantages and considerations as given to resident aliens in the USA." Albert Clattenburg, assistant chief of the Special Division, rejected the request out of hand, as he had rejected the appeals of the Jews: their two options were repatriation or internment for the duration. For this group, the hearings would come only after the war, in 1946, when every signer for whom records exist was found to be not dangerous.[38]

Until the completion of Crystal City, families and single women* were held at Seagoville, south of Dallas, in a former women's prison designed to resemble a college campus, under the command of Joseph O'Rourke. German internees slept on maple beds in brick buildings, one room per family, while the Japanese were relegated to wooden Victory Huts. There was a two-thousand-book library, movies, language lessons, a music teacher, elementary school and weekly story hour in English and Spanish for the children. Photography buffs had a darkroom at their disposal, while dancers enjoyed the Victrola. Seagoville internees were aware of their privilege. Karl Wecker wrote to a relative, "I am rather pampered than persecuted. And while I profoundly detest being deprived of my freedom, I am treated in

---

* Single women were generally not targeted for deportation. Those interned at Seagoville included Latin Americans married to German men already repatriated; they did not join their husbands because they wished to avoid the war in Europe or were apprehensive about life under Nazism. Others had served as maids in German homes in Latin America. They agreed to internment after losing their jobs when the households were broken up by the deportations.

a correct and humane fashion by the detaining authorities." Internee Alicia Klemm made her approval even more obvious. Pregnant on arrival at Seagoville, she gave birth to a boy on 19 May 1942, and named the baby Joseph O'Rourke Klemm after the camp commander.[39]

Seagoville was too small to accommodate all the families brought from Latin America plus the U.S. internees, so Crystal City was opened for business in January 1943, in a dry region 110 miles south of San Antonio. Families with school-age children were moved there, and only childless couples, a few with infants, and single women remained at Seagoville. Crystal City was originally a migrant labor camp surrounded by spinach fields; a statue of Popeye in the middle of the town attested to the importance of the local cash crop. Like Camp Kenedy, Crystal City welcomed its first arrivals before construction was complete. The camp had a rather grim aspect at first, but detainees were allowed to use their personal funds for "morale boosters," a concept which soon broadened to include cultivating flowers, building screened porches, landscaping their gardens, and ordering clothing from Montgomery Ward catalogs. The largest families had their own cottages, one-story frame buildings with kitchens, bathrooms, showers, and hot water. Even the Victory Huts here had running water and iceboxes. The screens couldn't keep out the desert critters – Black Widow spiders, millipedes, cockroaches, biting ants, even rattlesnakes and moccasin snakes – that came through the cracks in the walls. Summer temperatures inside the huts hovered between 100 and 120 degrees from morning to night, and the heat sometimes led to "breakdowns." But there were few other complaints.[40]

At Crystal City, every child received a liter of milk a day, and so did every couple. Arturo Contag, a Nazi Party member from Quito, and his wife had eight kids, so every morning there were nine bottles of milk lined up on their porch. "I never had it this good in Ecuador," he liked to tell the other internees.[41] The camp was divided between German and Japanese sections, and labor was also divided. Every man had to participate in camp chores, such as delivering ice and milk or doing laundry for four thousand people; additional work was available for eighty cents a day. Japanese gardeners beautified the public areas around the hospital and the schools. Germans produced nearly all the camp furniture and repaired vehicles in their machine shop. Japanese tailors from Peru did alterations for a small fee in camp scrip. Japanese truck farmers from the West Coast grew 50 percent of the fresh vegetables consumed in the camp. With 1,600 minor children in detention at the camp's peak size, schooling was an important activity. Elementary classes were conducted in four languages (English, German, Japanese, and Spanish for the Latin American children); an English-language high school sent many of its graduates on to college after the war. The kids spent most of their free time at the huge swimming pool, converted from a refurbished irrigation tank with $2,500 in materials furnished by the government and labor supplied by the internees.[42]

Despite the impressive level of organization, Crystal City was not immune to the political conflict taking place in other camps. Kurt P. Biederbeck, "Chancellor" of the German internees, informed the German Foreign Office that the *Freie Deutsche* at Crystal City were declaring their loyalty to the Reich, but one "with a social democratic government at the helm," in order to obtain benefits restricted to "loyal" Germans.[43] At the other end of the spectrum, the Nazi presence was conspicuous. Some internees wrote to their wives in Latin America that the Nazis in camp were allowed to hold Party meetings and that "the party chiefs browbeat the non-Nazis into line."[44] When a train left Crystal City carrying repatriating Germans to New York for embarkation, a crowd of internees gathered for the sendoff singing *Deutschland über Alles,* some giving the Hitler salute, children marching in *Pfadfinder* uniforms.[45]

LATIN AMERICAN CAMPS: LIFE IN "THE ANTHILL"

Political tension notwithstanding, the physical conditions of internment in the United States (except at Stringtown) came as a relief to those deportees who had been transferred from Latin American camps and jails, including U.S.-administered Camp Empire at Balboa in the Panama Canal Zone. This was a transit camp for deportees from all over Latin America. Run by military men responsible for defending the primary target in the Western Hemisphere, it was no country club. The first arrivals went two weeks without bathing and saw their Red Cross care packages plundered by U.S. soldiers. Many of the internees were mature or older men from the white-collar professions, unaccustomed to hard physical labor, who were ordered to clear thick brush with machetes in the intense midday heat. Working in their underwear, they swallowed salt tablets every half hour under the gaze of occasionally brutal guards. Sickness, exhaustion, and ringworm were common. One internee suffered a heart attack; another lost fifty pounds. Roaming police dogs attacked Alfredo Brauer and forced him up against the barbed-wire fence, lacerating him so badly he spent a week in the hospital.[46]

In Cuba, U.S. officials persuaded the government to intern German nationals at a prison on the Isle of Pines, offering to fund the project as well. Sanitary conditions were acceptable in the six-story stone building, but the prisoners were locked inside for a month or more at a time without being able to go out for sunshine or exercise. Family visits were restricted to five minutes a month. U.S. ambassador Spruille Braden claimed in his memoirs that he arranged for a special women's facility to be built for Axis nationals because the matron of the Cuban women's prison was renting out her charges as prostitutes.[47]

Nicaraguan dictator Anastasio Somoza, after consulting with U.S. Ambassador Boaz Long, ordered the roundup of all German citizens and several Italians and Japanese. Some 120 of them were sent to the notorious

Managua prison known as *El Hormiguero*, The Anthill, where they stood or squatted on the bare floor of a large roofless cell enclosed with wire. There were no washing facilities and so little food that the inmates had to rely on meals brought by their families. Most of the prisoners grew ill, but German doctors were not allowed to visit them. Some of the elderly Germans and those who were married to Nicaraguans – more than half of the total – were moved to a confiscated German farm, "Quinta Eitzen," where conditions were somewhat better. But there was not much room for debate in Somoza's Nicaragua. When the Spanish Vice-Consul offered to represent the Germans on internment and exchange issues, he was charged with spying and jailed for a year. The Germans were left for much of the war without a diplomatic representative. The local head of the Red Cross was not inclined to lobby for better treatment – he happened to be Somoza's private secretary.[48]

Costa Rica placed Germans awaiting deportation in the San José penitentiary and, when that filled up, built an internment camp in the warehouse district. On their own initiative, the prisoners replaced the bedbug-ridden mattresses with new ones, sprayed DDT in their cells, whitewashed the building, and asked their families to bring them meals. Prison authorities firmly upheld the Calderón Guardia administration's tradition of graft. Family members could obtain access by bribing the guards with bottles of whiskey; renting a room inside the prison for conjugal visits cost twenty *colones* an hour. The director of the secret police, Undersecretary of Public Security Colonel Rodríguez, summoned Germans to his office for private interrogations, demanding cash from the men and sex from the women in exchange for leniency. In an indication of who really controlled the internment program, however, Costa Rican officials did not release anyone from the camp without first getting approval from the U.S. minister.[49]

Not all Latin American internment facilities were so debased. Conditions were relaxed at the Hotel Sabaneta in Fusagasugá, Colombia, fenced off as an internment camp for those Germans well-connected enough to avoid deportation to the United States. The hotel was home to some one hundred Germans by 1944. Walter Held, interned at "Fusa" for three months, was then released to live on a nearby farm he owned. While in camp, he said, "most of us spent the whole day playing cards." Meals were "simple, not bad, but simple." Other Germans got out merely by renting rooms in town and checking in regularly with the guards. Götz Pfeil-Schneider claims he often left the hotel to go drinking in Bogotá with friends on the police force. "It was a very good life we had there in Fusa," he remembers.[50]

Ecuador ordered some of its German residents who were not deported to the United States to abandon the busy port of Guayaquil for the third-largest city, Cuenca, located well inland on the high Andean plain. They were free to move about within city limits.[51] Venezuela, where Nazi activity was never taken as a serious threat, was even more forbearing, sending only diplomats and their families to the United States for repatriation and interning only German sailors at various sites under comfortable conditions. Ordinary German residents were left alone – to the consternation of U.S. officials seeking a crackdown. (The Venezuelan government nonetheless somehow remained secure from the putative Nazi menace.)[52] Mexico restricted 550 German sailors to Guadalajara, where they reported twice daily to the migration office but were encouraged to seek work rather than be interned because Governor Barba González found it hard to finance their living expenses. In February 1942, they were moved to a camp at Perote, where they joined a number of German civilians.[53]

SEPARATION OF FAMILIES

Until the establishment of Crystal City, deportees were separated from their families and often unable to communicate with them. Mail service for internees was plagued by long delays, an inevitable result of wartime conditions and the censorship process. Delays of months were routine. The families of some deportees heard nothing from their men for a year and a half, greatly increasing the mental anguish on both sides. Camp Kenedy authorities dealt with the shortage of Spanish-speaking censors at first by prohibiting the writing of letters in Spanish, which meant many internees could not communicate with their Latin American families.[54]

That some letters home never made it out of the United States at all is evident; the undelivered originals are still sitting in the dusty file boxes of the Special War Problems Division today. These letters and the copies in the censors' files testify to the distress caused by the separation of families. Heinrich Meendsen-Bohlken, a farmer residing in Guatemala for twenty-three years, petitioned the U.S. government from internment not to be repatriated to Germany because "I love my wife and she cannot and will not go to Germany. I love Guatemala, where I passed all my manhood and I would feel a stranger in my country of birth, where I have no family and friends." To his Guatemalan wife, Lucía de la Cruz, the internee wrote:

You are suffering the bitternesses of life, alone, solely because I am a German. You, who never liked my countrymen, said that I was an exception. . . . Now, what injustice! I am here as a criminal prisoner and [the Nazis] are laughing at us because they are free with their German wives, although they were founders of the party. I, on the contrary, a friend of the Americans, am here imprisoned, for the one great crime of having been born in Germany.

Meendsen-Bohlken reminded his wife to collect "the affidavits for Mr. Edward F. Ennis of the Department of Justice in Washington" and ended with few words of encouragement. (Postwar investigators found no evidence of any kind against Meendsen-Bohlken, and characterized his political sentiments as "violently anti-Nazi.")[55]

Ernst Blumenthal, interned at Kenedy, wrote to the Swiss Legation to ask that his wife Anneliese be reunited with him. "My wife literally vegetates in a most sub-altern position as a woman-servant. Her physical state is as low as possible," Ernst wrote. With a salary of $10 a month and in poor health, Anneliese was "on the point of starving in a disastrously hot, tropical climate," and being "the wife of me, a JEW, does not get one cent of relief from the German Representative in Colombia." Anneliese wrote to her husband in December 1942, after having had no word from him for ten months:

Dear Mucki,

It is so long since I have heard from you; the reason is a mystery to me. Every day I wait for mail, which might bring me news regarding our reunion. I hope you are not sick, or that nothing has happened to you. . . . I have such a longing to be no longer alone; I would like to be with my *Hase* [rabbit] and to rest. How long will it last until mankind is freed from the leprosy in human form?* Write soon, my love, don't keep me waiting long for mail, it is all I have here, except my work from early morning to late evening. My life is so unhappy and bitter, and I often feel so unlucky. . . . One must have great strength to endure everything. Continue to care for me as I do for you. Receive in thought my love and kisses.

Your Anneliese.

Both Blumenthals had been held in a German concentration camp before fleeing to Latin America. Ernst would spend the entire war in a series of U.S. camps, joined by Anneliese in mid-1943.[56]

DESTITUTION AND DANGEROUS WOMEN

Beyond such psychological strain, family members left behind faced endless difficulties. The most obvious was the need to find a source of income. Wives and children who might have wanted to continue a business or look for work found their companies blacklisted or ruined by the war, their savings frozen, real property confiscated, and potential employers unwilling to hire Germans for fear of landing on the Proclaimed List themselves. For the same reason, landlords evicted their German tenants and hotels would not rent them rooms. A few foresighted individuals had cash hidden away; others sold eggs or garden vegetables in the markets. The rest relied on relief funds provided by the German government via the Spanish or Swiss Embassy.[57]

Those women whose marriages were not official, who were not German citizens or who had been expatriated by Nazi anti-Jewish law, were ineligible for German relief payments. They were left to fend for themselves, sometimes doubly blacklisted by the remnant pro-Nazi German community, which charged them with racial impurity, and by the U.S. Embassy and local government, which charged them with political unreliability. Ostracized

---

* That is, Nazism. "Mucki" and "Hase" are terms of endearment in German.

at every turn, at least one Latin American wife was forced to sell herself. Twenty-one-year-old Rosa Grothe watched her husband Kurt bundled off to internment in the United States from their home in rural Honduras; he was repatriated to Germany in July 1942. Rosa was unable to keep their little store open on her own, and she knew as a *mulatta* she would be unwelcome in a Germany ruled by racial laws. The way out of her predicament is made dismally clear by an FBI report that Rosa was "in contact with American sailors from vessels touching at La Ceiba while working in a local cantina of unsavory reputation." After about a year of that life, Rosa volunteered to be interned in the United States.[58]

German men were almost without exception the principal targets of deportation. The State Department considered German women to be "inherently non-dangerous" by virtue of their gender.[59]* The only case found in the files where a woman was directly targeted for deportation was Theolinde Zillmer-Zosel, and it is indeed an oddity. Zillmer-Zosel, who called herself "Tabú," came to Guatemala in 1935 and was deported in 1942. In between, she claimed to have worked as a secret agent for Goebbels, directed President Ubíco's counterespionage organization, and served the U.S. embassy in some secret capacity. German authorities refused to accept her for repatriation, declaring that she had been stripped of her citizenship for treasonous acts and would be tried and imprisoned if returned to Germany. U.S. officials determined that she was delusional. Fletcher Warren solved the dilemma of what to do with Tabú with the observation, "I believe she has been sent to Seagoville. Can't we forget her?" She was interned until the end of the war.[60]

Once deported, the men were of necessity largely idle during the period of their internment. They had to keep up their own morale and overcome boredom in the camps through sports and hobbies. ("Most of us studied English," recalled Gerardo Bohnenberger. "The pessimists studied Russian.")[61] But it was the women left behind who struggled actively to cope with daunting circumstances. Along with the principal task of feeding themselves and their children, many deportees' wives tried to defend their property from confiscation, usually caught up in a hopelessly corrupt process. They collected affidavits, character references, and other documents on behalf of their husbands. Those who had contacts among the local elite or government officials lobbied for the return of their men. Those without connections sometimes agitated in public.

From San Salvador, a group of "twelve forlorn and unhappy women" repeatedly petitioned the U.S. State Department after "waiting for more than a year for the reunion with our husbands."[62] One of the twelve, Carmela Groskorth, wrote to her husband that there was still no response as of

---

* Art would later imitate life in Alfred Hitchcock's 1946 film *Notorious*, when Ingrid Bergman, infiltrating a ring of German-Brazilian agents, received instructions from her FBI handler to memorize the names and statements of "everyone you meet – I mean the men, of course."

July 1943: "It is so aggravating to find ourselves before a most cruel indifference. We are now ready to write to the Society for the Prevention of Cruelty to Animals. Perhaps this Society will take an interest in us."[63]

In Costa Rica, hundreds of women signed a petition by the wives of German deportees demanding the return of their husbands. They obtained the backing of the influential and progressive-minded Archbishop Víctor Sanabria Martínez, and one of them, Ester Pinto de Amrhein, sued successfully in the Costa Rican Supreme Court on behalf of her husband Franz, a thirty-one-year resident of Costa Rica. Two Costa Rican presidents supported her appeal. But apparently Costa Rican sovereignty mattered little in the eyes of U.S. officials running the internment program: despite the highly dubious nature of the charges against him, Amrhein was released only in March 1946. Although never involved with the Nazis, he had been seized because of his important commercial position.[64] (See Chapter 7.)

In Panama, Lydia Albert de Brauchle wrote in August 1943 to the Minister of Government and Justice, Camilo de la Guardia, Jr., asking him to intercede with U.S. authorities for the release of her husband Alfred and son Erwin:

They were interned on the 11th of December 1941 for I don't know what reason. We immigrated as farmers with the permission of the Panamanian government in 1929 and since then we have been living in the mountains. My conscience tells me our conduct has always been good, always according to the laws of the country. I heard several people say that the internment of my husband and my son was caused by a mistake or a calumny. I am 60 years old and incapable of working, since I am often sick. Therefore I implore your Excellency to investigate this affair again to see if it is possible for them to free both or at least my son Erwin. He was only 17 years old when he came to Panama, so he has spent nearly all of his life here, never involving himself in politics, because this is not his character.[65]

A postwar U.S. government investigation found no accusations against either Brauchle and no indication of any reason for their arrest. Erwin Brauchle returned home in 1947; his father Alfred never did. He died in Crystal City.[66]

Although their protests did not achieve their immediate goal of getting their husbands back, the women did compel a change in U.S. practices, showing that the objects of foreign policy can also influence its evolution. At first, the deportation program was intended to prevent potentially subversive Germans from making trouble in Latin America. But soon after the deportations began, it was clear even to the State Department that the plan had backfired. "In our hurried effort last winter to remove from Central America as many as possible dangerous subversive males," Secretary Hull wrote to Attorney General Biddle in November 1942, "we left behind for eventual repatriation their inherently non-dangerous wives and minor children. Our representatives in those countries now report that these women and children who were left behind constitute a most dangerous focus of anti-American propaganda and that they should be removed at the earliest possible opportunity."[67] In other words, in an effort to rid Latin America of pro-Axis propagandists, the United States had handed Axis propaganda a most effective argument: the Colossus of the North was splitting up families and leaving women and children to starve.

Now the wives, driven to political activism by adverse circumstances, suddenly lost their gender's "inherently non-dangerous" status and became threatening in U.S. eyes. The policy shift their activities brought about can be read in the passenger manifests of U.S. transports. Beginning in 1943, the ships formerly reserved for men started ferrying volunteer women and children to New Orleans, and Crystal City was established as a family internment camp.[68]

Family reunification was not an altruistic policy, and the State Department readily exploited the desire of families to stay together in order to achieve its goals. When the U.S. Embassy was at an impasse in its efforts to persuade the Costa Rican government to hand over another batch of German male suspects, some of them socially well-connected, Chargé d'Affaires Edward G. Trueblood blocked the transportation of the wives and children of men already interned in the United States until the Costa Rican government agreed to "at least an equal number of dangerous male enemy aliens to be deported simultaneously" – thereby turning popular pressure for family reunification into pressure on the Costa Rican government to approve additional new deportations it opposed.[69]

Some of the men deported from Guatemala urged their families not to join them in internment but instead to try to endure the separation where they were, in the hopes of regaining their confiscated property or at least permission for the men to return home after the war was over. However, the Spanish Embassy was running out of relief funds, and other German assets in Guatemala were frozen by the Banco Central, under unofficial U.S. tutelage. Here, too, the families' destitution provided a leverage point for more deportations. "If we do not concur in the proposal to release frozen German funds, pressure probably will be forthcoming to induce us to remove to the United States for internment most or all of the German nationals now receiving relief funds," warned Ambassador Boaz Long. "Very good," responded the Special Division's Sidney Lafoon. "Let's not unfreeze."[70]

This order, coming near the end of 1943, showed the State Department's determination to expand, rather than wind down, the deportation–internment program, even as it was receiving strong indications that most of the people already seized were anything but spearheads of Hitlerian conquest. This look at life in the microcosm of the camps has revealed the range of coercion, acquiescence, and resistance to the attempt by the minority of active Nazis to control the camp community, to extend the transnational reach of the Nazi state into these artificial enclaves of expatriate life just as they had tried in the German "colonies" of Latin America before removal to the United States. The evidence shows that support for national socialism among the internees did not run deep enough for most of them to be willing to incur any degree of personal risk in the pursuit of Nazi goals. Yet while the intelligence agents drawing up deportation lists and the diplomats pushing them through may have been indifferent to matters of culpability or innocence, the Justice Department officials running the camps were not; as their surprise turned to dismay over the harmlessness of their captives, they began to insist that the program be altered.

6

Justice

"The whole operation, if once in a great while it caught someone who was actually, potentially involved, I just couldn't find it, I never did."
                        –Justice Department investigator Raymond W. Ickes, 1997[1]

Laurel, Maryland, 1942. Gasoline rationing or no, Assistant Secretary of State Breckinridge Long makes the long drive after work to his colonial estate, Montpelier Manor, although, he grumbles, "the war has already taken its toll of comforts and conveniences . . . no more assistant butlers, housemen, kitchen helpers, footmen, etc." For years, Long has used his office to skillfully manipulate the visa system to prevent all but a trickle of Jewish refugees from entering the United States. "They are lawless, scheming, defiant – and in many ways unassimilable," he confides to his diary. "Some are certainly German agents." As head of the Special Division, Long also oversees the deportation and repatriation of Germans from Latin America, and from this position, he repeatedly blocks the reinvestigation of the Jewish internees among them. After all, if the supposedly dangerous German Jews were to be released for lack of evidence, he warns his colleagues in the State Department, "we might be considerably embarrassed."[2]

The Jews from Latin America locked up at Camp Forrest in Tennessee ask for hearings, on the grounds that they hate the Axis and are not even German nationals anymore, since they were expatriated by Nazi decree. "I do not see that we have to be concerned about the *citizenship* of these people," Long writes in an exasperated memo denying the request. As a result of his order, eighty Jews will spend at least another winter behind barbed wire; some will be released only after the end of the war.[3]

Late at night in his vast, empty mansion, his beloved thoroughbreds asleep in their stables, the Assistant Secretary nurses his resentment at his growing number of critics. "I have incurred the enmity of various powerful and vengeful elements," he scribbles. "The Communists, extreme radicals, Jewish professional agitators, refugee enthusiasts who blindly seek the admission of persons under the guise of refugees, and their sympathetic agents in the Government . . . they all hate me."[4]

Breckinridge Long's notorious role in the failure to rescue more Jewish refugees from Nazism stands as an egregious illustration of the influence of personal values and individual actions on the shaping of government policy.[5] At the same time, he reflected beliefs widespread within the bureaucracy and U.S. society at large that linked Jews to Bolshevism, disloyalty, and dishonesty. This helps explain why people who counted themselves among the sworn enemies of Nazism found themselves targets of a U.S. policy designed to thwart Nazi aims.

Long's impact on the internees from Latin America has been as little-known as the deportation program itself, but here, too, it was of crucial importance. He and his like-minded subordinates in the Special Division helped bring Jews and other non-Nazis into the camps and ensured that they would not receive hearings or be otherwise enabled to argue their case. With security concerns and diplomatic appearances paramount in their minds and their judgment clouded by prejudice, Long and his coterie discounted the

25. Assistant Secretary of State Breckinridge Long was the most senior U.S. official closely involved in the internment program. He resisted investigation of Jewish internees on the grounds that, should they be proved innocent and released, "we might be considerably embarrassed." Credit: Myron H. Davis/TimePix.

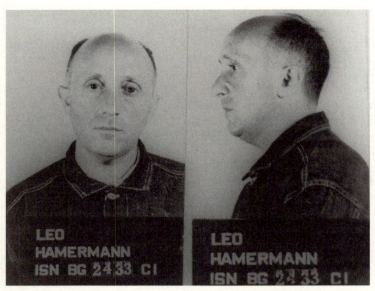

26. One such internee was Leo Hamermann, a Jewish refugee from Nazi Germany deported by Bolivian officials who had no evidence against him but who were "anxious . . . to make a good showing with the American government." Credit: Name Files of Enemy Aliens, Special War Problems Division, RG59, National Archives.

possible innocence of some internees and worried instead about the possibility of scandal that might arise from their release.

Fortunately for some of the internees, the State Department was not in charge of the camps – by late 1942, the Justice Department was, and it was directed by several people whose values were quite different from Long's. Camp administrators and inspectors from the Justice Department grew increasingly uncomfortable over the treatment of the internees, and their concerns would lead to a confrontation between Justice and State officials whose outcome was a change in internment policy: the attempt, for the first time, to discriminate between dangerous and nondangerous Germans. This policy shift would not have happened without the combination of tenacious protests by internees and their relatives, objections raised by Latin American officials and private citizens, and the presence of a few receptive, civil rights-minded individuals in key positions in the bureaucracy.[6]

The man directing the internment of dangerous enemy aliens residing in the United States was Edward Ennis, head of the Justice Department's Alien Enemy Control Unit (AECU). Like his boss, Attorney General Francis Biddle, Ennis was a liberal, whose commitment to civil rights later led him into a long career with the American Civil Liberties Union; he became its president in 1969. His job at the AECU placed him in a paradoxical position: he opposed mass internment on principle and objected to the incarceration of more than 110,000 Japanese and Japanese Americans who were placed in camps on the basis of their ethnicity alone – even while he supervised the process that produced more internments. In the months after Pearl Harbor, his office received mail from U.S. citizens demanding that all Japanese, Germans, and Italians be sent to camps. The communications were so numerous that the AECU prepared a form letter assuring the complainant that aliens were excluded from sensitive military areas and that "every precaution has been taken and will be taken to protect the peace and safety of the United States." In the midst of this outcry, and ever mindful of his own responsibility for ensuring U.S. security, Ennis helped guide Biddle toward a relatively fair process – for German and Italian residents – of interning only those individuals against whom there was some evidence of subversive potential, and only after they were given the chance to defend themselves at a hearing. With Biddle's backing, Ennis prevented J. Edgar Hoover's FBI from making arrests and house searches without proper warrants when approaching Germans and Italians. Some of the U.S. internees were wrongly accused, and the evidence used against them was not always the kind that would have held up in court, but AECU procedures were respectable by wartime standards – especially in comparison to what happened in other Allied countries, not to mention in those controlled by the Axis powers.[7]

In March 1942, with the number of civilian internees exceeding the capacity of the U.S. Army facilities, the State Department asked the Justice Department to assume responsibility for holding the deportees from Latin America. At Biddle's insistence, Breckinridge Long promised that families would not be separated – although a memo to the Attorney General from his Special Assistant, Lemuel B. Schofield, saying that a transport would soon arrive with seven hundred unaccompanied males from South America should have tipped him off that this condition would not be fulfilled.[8]

FIRST REVIEW

The inclusion of the Justice Department gave Ennis some influence in the Latin American deportation program, and he used it to press for more fairness. His camp commanders had been letting him know that they did not believe most of their charges were dangerous. Camp Kenedy commander Ivan Williams was of the opinion that "those heads of governments in Latin America arrested anybody not born in their country and sent them to us as alien enemies. A lot of them don't know what they're doing here. I can't say I do either."[9] Jerre Mangione, a special assistant in Ennis' Alien Enemy Control Unit, toured the U.S. camps for two months and reported that "many of their occupants represented no threat to the national security; had they been accorded due process of law, they would probably never have been interned."[10] Ennis was also hearing from such quarters as the American

Jewish Joint Distribution Committee and the National Refugee Service's Joseph Chamberlain, who lobbied Biddle, Secretary of War Henry Stimson, and the Provost Marshal General to release the Jewish prisoners.[11]

Meeting with State Department officials in September 1942, Ennis protested against the insubstantial accusations used to justify the internment of innocuous Germans, at one point declaring that some of them were no more enemy aliens "than I am." He cited in particular the cases of the Jewish refugees and threatened to begin unilaterally releasing internees brought to the United States if State did not furnish proof of their dangerousness.[12]

One case Ennis took up with the State Department was that of Roger Jean Jacques Van den Vaero, a French national deported as a Nazi sympathizer from Costa Rica. Ennis noted that Van den Vaero was a member of the pro-Allied Comité de Gaulle and that there were no allegations against him. When the U.S. Legation in San José investigated, it was able to provide the information that Van den Vaero was known as a "millionaire beachcomber," a "remittance man" who lived off a family trust fund and who liked to lounge around his house wearing only earrings and a loincloth – but admitted that there was no evidence that he was a Nazi. The legal attaché reported that "Van den Vaero was crazy, but neither a spy nor a Fifth Columnist, and probably would still be here if he had paid Don Paco and Rodriguez the 5,000 *colones* that they asked for to save him from arrest." (Rodríguez was Costa Rica's police chief, mentioned earlier in connection with corruption at the San José prison. Don Paco was Francisco Calderón Guardia, Secretary of Public Security and brother of the Costa Rican president. His nickname was *Paco a medias*, "One-Half Paco," because of his reputation for taking a 50 percent cut on government contracts.) Nonetheless, the State Department continued to oppose Van den Vaero's release.[13]

Ennis found a sympathetic listener in James H. Keeley, Jr., the acting chief of the State Department's Special Division, who was beginning to have some qualms of his own. Keeley had noted that enemy aliens in the United States received hearings, but those the State Department brought up from Latin America did not. "I don't like it," Keeley wrote in November 1942:

It isn't in keeping with the principles of justice for which we are fighting. No one wants to be soft as regards a dangerous alien enemy, but we need not copy the methods of our enemies by refusing to permit a man who claims to be innocent somehow to arrange for a hearing of his case on its merits.... To give such aliens a hearing, or a rehearing in those cases where the semblance of a hearing may have been given in the Republic that sent them here, should not endanger the safety of the United States.

Keeley tried to persuade his boss, Breckinridge Long, to agree to the Justice Department's proposal, because "whether they be innocent or guilty of subversive activities inimical to the safety of this hemisphere, it seems to me that they are entitled to have their cases reviewed somehow, somewhere." Long rebuffed the request.[14]

By early 1943, with another big wave of deportations approaching, Ennis realized he could not rely on the State Department to free innocent internees or to furnish reliable testimony against those deported in the future. He had already been unsuccessful in promoting the idea of more Cuba-like schemes where dollars would subsidize local internment instead of deportation to the United States.[15] Now, with Biddle's support, Ennis initiated two key changes in the internment process. For the first time, hearings were organized for some of the deportees from Latin America who could present evidence that they were wrongly interned. This applied to them the same standards for internment that the Justice Department used for U.S. residents: "An enemy alien, if at liberty, must constitute a threat to the internal security of the United States before his internment is ordered."[16] Meanwhile Ennis recruited a Justice Department lawyer to travel to Latin America to review the charges against internees already in U.S. custody and, more urgently, revise the lists of candidates for imminent deportation with a critical eye.

Ennis could not have made a better choice for this task than Raymond Ickes. The son of Interior Secretary Harold Ickes, Raymond was raised in New Mexico and spoke fluent Spanish. When the war began he had already had extensive trial experience as a 29-year-old assistant U.S. attorney in the criminal division of the Southern District of New York. Ennis got him on the phone and asked him to come to Washington to join the AECU as the head of Central and South American affairs.

When Ennis explained the program to intern alien enemies from Latin America, Ickes recalled, the AECU director expressed the concern "that lots of them were being railroaded up here not because they were dangerous Axis nationals but because they owned a *finca* [farm] next to someone else's property and the most convenient way to get the *finca* was to get them interned in the United States," Ickes remembered. "My duty was not only to get the dangerous Axis nationals deported, but to see that innocent farmers weren't taken." Ickes had already enlisted in the Marine Corps, so Ennis arranged a deferment, introduced him to James Bell, a Spanish-speaking lawyer from New Mexico who would be Ickes's assistant, and sent the two men on their way.[17]

THE ICKES MISSIONS

The first step was a brief trip in mid-February 1943 to Central America, to reinvestigate some cases involving internees already in the United States, followed by two longer trips throughout the region in the spring and summer to review new lists of proposed deportees. Ickes was appalled at what he found. "Most of these people had no more business being in detention in the United States than I had," he said. The typical FBI agent posted to an embassy in Latin America as "legal attaché," responsible for drawing up the deportation lists, was a new recruit put to work after a crash course amounting to two weeks of lectures. Even so, the FBI agents' preparation "was far better than what the ONI and G-2 people got. They weren't of top-notch raw material to begin with." Asked whether he remembered Lieutenant Jules DuBois's denunciation and the subsequent deportation of Wilhelm Heinemann for serving a cup of coffee with a twisted straw in the bottom (see Chapter 2), Ickes chuckled, recounted the story, and said, "In a lot of incidents the credibility was about the same as in the Heinemann case." Were other intelligence agents as credulous and inventive as "the ubiquitous DuBois"? "Some yes, some no. More yes than no, unfortunately."[18]

Ickes and Bell faced a daunting challenge. Two young men without important job titles, flying in for a few days to tell the embassies how to run their affairs, "went over like a lead balloon in most cases."[19] But Ickes impressed the ambassadors who met him. "He knows his job," Ambassador Henry Norweb in Lima wrote to a colleague. "He speaks good Spanish, made a favorable impression on Peruvian officials, and, while sticking to his own instructions as he understands them, he is reasonable and entirely willing to give every consideration to the other fellow's point of view."[20] Ickes and Bell were supported by Attorney General Biddle, who had sent letters to the heads of all U.S. missions in Latin America asking for their cooperation, and more importantly, by a memo circulated to the missions by Breckinridge Long, who tacitly acknowledged defeat. Long noted Ennis and Biddle's determination to free internees in their custody against whom there was no credible evidence on record – even if, in the view of the State Department, that meant having removed dangerous persons from Latin America only to turn them loose inside the United States. "Consequently, if there is any difference of opinion between the Ambassador and the representative of the Attorney General, who will be Mr. Raymond Ickes, persons about whom there is doubt should not be sent. In other words the Ambassador should adopt the point of view of Mr. Ickes. . . . Should Mr. Ickes not agree with the Ambassador and a hearing on that person should develop, it is quite possible that the person whom we consider to be dangerous might be released."[21]

Ickes and Bell went to work, cutting most deportation lists by more than half, eliminating the names of persons against whom there were absolutely no charges or whose accuser was unknown. Documentation of subversive potential was, of course, almost nonexistent, so they still had to accept oral statements by informants who seemed trustworthy. Describing the process years later, Ickes said there was mostly "hearsay evidence: 'so and so has a reputation of being very active in social affairs and has traveled back and forth to Germany' – that sort of evidence which is hardly sufficient in ordinary times, and shouldn't have been sufficient even then, although it was because we were so concerned.

"I was open-minded, and I wanted to err on the side of keeping these people out of circulation," Ickes said. "But when I got into it a little deeper and I saw how flimsy the pretext for interning an individual was, I got more upset by the numbers in this category." Next to police and government officials, the prime source of denunciations was "local influential citizens, people who had access to the right cocktail parties... big landowners, prosperous merchants, and so on." Since the typical FBI agent did not speak Spanish and rarely bothered trying to corroborate information, "the local people could get away with almost anything."[22] His memoranda at the time confirm his recollection. In a typical reproach to the embassy in San José, Ickes wrote that some Latin American leaders were demanding that their selected deportees be taken before they would agree to the expulsion of suspects chosen by U.S. intelligence. "Experience has indicated that in too many instances we have had to accept for internment *an inordinately large number* of apparently harmless individuals disliked for one reason or another by the local governments, in order to get *a very few* persons who can properly be considered dangerous subjects."[23] The outcome, Ickes believed, was harmful to the war effort and to U.S. standing in Latin America, because it "tends to create a feeling in the Central and South American Republics that the United States Government is bungling its share of the internment program and that it is doing exactly what it condemns in its enemies by interning those inconsequential individuals who have no influence, while the rest escape."[24]

The FBI's claims withered under the scrutiny of the Justice Department investigators. On a return trip in December 1943, Bell combed through files from all offices in the San José Embassy and compared them to FBI data used to deport and intern 143 of Costa Rica's Germans. He found the FBI reports riddled with mistakes. Thirty-five of the men were labeled "one of the most dangerous" Germans in Costa Rica. Although such categorization was always said to come from a reliable source, Bell determined that of the thirty-five cases, in fourteen there was "no evidence whatsoever of any activities which might be considered detrimental to the cause of the United Nations [the Allies]." In fifteen cases there were one or two allegations of such activities. In a further twenty-two cases, the Bureau in Washington had added its own incorrect allegations while summarizing the reports from the field; half of those inventions bore the sanctifying classification of "confidential and reliable." Bell's conclusion: "In only six cases was the evidence on these 'most dangerous individuals' sufficient to classify them as a genuine threat."[25]

Summing up the program a half-century later on the basis of his wartime investigations in eighteen countries over two years, Ickes concluded that the deportation program did not contribute to U.S. or hemispheric security. "When I got down there, I saw that this was not accomplishing anything," he said. "It was wheel-spinning, and a complete abrogation of human rights.... The whole operation, if once in a great while it caught someone who was actually, potentially involved, I just couldn't find it, I never did."[26]

This is a damning critique by a U.S. official with unique insider access to the most intimate details of the deportation program in every participating

Latin American country.[27] It must be taken very seriously. There is no need to be troubled by the usual caveats about relying on oral history[28] – not only because Ickes's memory and lawyer's precision were still impressive when interviewed in 1997, but also because his recall of the events is thoroughly confirmed by memoranda he wrote at the time and by extensive postwar investigations carried out separately of hundreds of individual internees.[29]

Archival research supports Ickes's characterization of the deportation program as unimportant from a security point of view. However, it did result in the internment of a small number of leading Nazi organizers, such as Hentschke of Guatemala and Prüfert of Colombia, along with a somewhat larger number of fervent Party members and a handful of confessed spies.[30] Ickes himself acknowledges having shared in some of the wartime "group hysteria," approving the internment of some individuals on the basis of hearsay because the fear of Nazi subversion was so great – a context that made the deportation program, in his words, "understandable, not justifiable."[31] If these caveats make it harder to paint the program in black and white, they should not obscure the overall picture. Ickes's condemnation of the operation as a violation of human rights reflects the same thinking that led to a presidential apology and compensation for the Japanese and Japanese-American internees from the West Coast in 1988, and ten years later, for the Japanese deported from Peru: the recognition that exaggerated security concerns combined with prejudice produce widespread injustice and inefficiency.

Before he left the Justice Department to serve in the Marine Corps (winning a Silver Star for bravery in the Pacific campaign), Ickes's activity undoubtedly helped save many innocent people from internment.[32]* Ironically, his work pruning the deportation lists also persuaded Edward Ennis that the program's deficiencies had been corrected and made the AECU director a convert. In September 1943, after Ickes returned from South America, Ennis wrote an enthusiastic note to the State Department saying that "now that only individuals against whom there is available credible evidence indicating that they are in fact dangerous are being interned," the deportations should be extended to Chile, Uruguay, Paraguay, and Venezuela.[33] Ickes and Bell dutifully traveled to Chile to compile a list of 283 acceptable candidates for deportation.[34] Chile, far less beholden to U.S. demands than were the smaller countries of the circum-Caribbean, eventually agreed to send five of them.

---

* However, his instructions were occasionally evaded after his departure from the embassy. Some of the people he placed on the "insufficient" list (i.e., insufficient evidence to warrant deportation) wound up in U.S. camps anyway. See, for example, the postwar reports on Werner Kuhne, Alexander Petsche, and Emil Rinck, in "Name Files of Interned Enemy Aliens from Latin America," alphabetical, Boxes 31–50, SWP, RG59, NA, and Ennis to Special Division, 12 Oct 1943, 740.00115EW1939/7456 1/2, RG59, NA.

PAROLE

In part, Ennis may have been trying to mend his fragile relationship with the State Department. Disputes with Breckinridge Long's office had continued throughout 1943 over a second key reform instituted at the insistence of the AECU. In late 1942, the Justice Department began to review the cases of internees from Latin America who protested their internment on the grounds that they were Jewish refugees or active anti-Nazis. All Jewish internees and a number of non-Jews who faced harassment from Nazis inside the camps were transferred to Camp Algiers, a new facility near the port of New Orleans. By April 1943, Biddle and Ennis were determined to grant them parole status, letting them out of the camps to take up residence in Midwestern cities, where they could work and would report regularly to an immigration officer.[35] At one point, Biddle engaged in classic bureaucratic warfare, using the excuse of departmental budget cuts to declare that Camp Algiers would have to be closed and its inmates dispersed. Long's office fought back, claiming that some of the Latin American governments had consented to the deportation program only on condition that they retain jurisdiction over the Germans they provided to the United States; therefore, oral and written agreements prevented the US government from taking any steps that would result in the release of the internees. This was deliberately disingenuous. An attached internal memorandum outlining this argument for Long's use, written by a subordinate, acknowledged that "the request to have these enemy aliens in the Republic of Panama detained and interned was made by the United States Government," as it was in the other countries.[36]

Biddle won the argument because his department controlled the camps: "the Department of Justice is at liberty to fix the terms and kind of detention according to its own standards."[37] By June, Ickes's assistant Jim Bell was back in Central America reviewing cases, and nearly sixty Jews were released on parole from Camp Algiers that summer. The development created consternation in the U.S. embassies that had pushed hard to get such people deported on security grounds. For some officials, avoiding "embarrassment," as Breckinridge Long so revealingly put it, was more compelling than the possibility that innocent people might be spending years of their lives in unwarranted detention.[38] The status of those let out of the camps was unclear, and this fact complicated the problem. U.S. diplomats said they were placed on "relaxed internment," a casual-sounding term that made some Latin American officials wonder why they had agreed under pressure to deport them as "dangerous" in the first place if the U.S. government now felt "relaxed" about them. (The internees themselves seemed to think they had been freed, and wrote letters to their relatives in Latin America saying they were working and earning good wages. INS officials ordered them to refrain from making any "reference to release or parole of any nature.") The Departments of Justice and State agreed that in discussing internees released on parole, "the phrase 'internment at large' be used in preference to such terms as 'relaxed internment' and 'relaxed detention' so as to avoid the undesirable connotations of the word 'relaxed.'"[39]

The terminology mattered little to the internees now on the outside. The Norwegian Arne Minden Aas, having spent nearly two years as one of the few citizens of an Allied country interned in camps intended for Nazis, was able to take up residence in Chicago in October 1943.[40] Leon Fuerst, a Jew who had been in a German concentration camp in 1933, fled to Honduras in 1936, and was deported to the United States even though "there is absolutely no adverse evidence in the file," was paroled in 1944. (Justice Department investigators after the war would characterize his case as "shocking.")[41]

The internees released on "at-large" status confirmed by their conduct the improbability of the original charges against them, if any existed. Otto Kugler, the dentist beaten by Nazi thugs at Kenedy, was paroled and "behaved unimpeachably, practicing dentistry."[42] Sixteen parolees served in the U.S. Army before the war was over. Fred Kappel's son Werner, 19 years old when picked up in Panama for internment, was released on parole and then drafted, and was gravely wounded fighting in the Philippines, receiving a Purple Heart and a Combat Infantryman Badge.[43]

Emmanuel Gordon was another Jew sent to Buchenwald by the Nazis after *Kristallnacht*, the Nazis' organized anti-Semitic pogrom of November 1938. He spent months as a refugee in France and Switzerland before finding asylum at the Sosua agricultural colony in the Dominican Republic. In 1942, he was deported at the insistence of the U.S. Embassy, although it later "in effect admitted that there was never anything against him, and suggested that his arrest was instigated by [Sosua director] Schweitzer, with whom Gordon had had a dispute." After more than a year and a half in the U.S. camps, Gordon was placed on at-large status in August 1943, the postwar investigation reported, "and since then has tried to enlist six times, has given blood nine times, and has bought more than $1000 worth of war bonds."[44]

That Breckinridge Long and his division at the State Department sought to keep people like Gordon and Kappel behind barbed wire for the duration of the war speaks to the influence of individuals in the chain of command, to the role of personal values and prejudices in the making of policy. Gordon and others like him were released thanks to the incessant protests of their fellows, like the indefatigable Fred Kappel and the rabbis and representatives of American Jewish organizations, along with the receptivity of a few Justice Department officials, such as Ickes, Bell, Ennis, and Biddle, who believed that civil and human rights are not a peacetime luxury to be discarded in times of crisis but can be compatible with defending a democracy.

Yet even while camp commanders and Justice Department officials were discovering the harmless nature of many of their charges and beginning to release some of those who posed no conceivable threat to national security, the U.S. and Latin American governments moved ahead with a campaign to seize or destroy what the deportees had left behind.

7

Expropriation

> "I think it is undesirable for the written record to show that the initiative came from us.... If we really must take the initiative and exert pressure in connection with deportations, it should at least be done with great discretion."
> –State Department Central America Division Chief John Moors Cabot[1]

Guatemala City, November 1945. Hitler is dead and the war is over, but Washington authorities have not yet decided how to dispose of a thousand Germans from Latin America still held in U.S. camps. The embassies make their recommendations. U.S. diplomats in the Guatemalan capital, who have worked assiduously for four years to expel as many Germans as possible, now choose their targets with care. "In the Embassy's opinion the following five persons are the most important internees in the United States," reads a dispatch to the State Department, listing men who have "represented major Axis commercial and/or agricultural interests in this country." The five are Karl Heinz Nottebohm and Kurt Nottebohm, leaders in banking and commerce; their general manager Martin Knoetzsch; Helmuth Sapper, owner of the largest block of coffee plantations in Alta Verapaz; and the chemical, paint, and hardware importer Hermann Kaltwasser. These were no newcomers to Guatemala: Kaltwasser arrived in 1914, Knoetzsch in 1910; the Nottebohms and Sapper were born there. The embassy is candid: "there is no evidence to show that any of these persons were Nazi Party members or that they collaborated with the Nazi Party and its inimical activities. In some instances, evidence has been produced to show that the persons concerned were at least personally or passively *anti-Nazi*." Nevertheless, it urges Washington to ensure that the five men never return to Guatemala.[2]

Why deport and intern anti-Nazis at all and then prevent them from returning after the war is over? "The Embassy is fully impressed with the weakness of these three cases," the memo continues, referring to Knoetzsch and the Nottebohms.[3] Weak cases, indeed. Guatemalans readily testify to Knoetzsch's reputation as a staunch antifascist who signed a public notice protesting the nazification of the German School, and the U.S. government knows it was he who obtained the local Nazi Party membership list and secretly delivered it to the Guatemalan Foreign Ministry as an act of patriotism toward his adopted homeland.[4] Kurt Nottebohm considers himself a "pure Guatemalan" with no interest in German affairs, and no one can link him or Karl Heinz to the Nazis.[5] There is no evidence against Sapper either; he did not vote in the 1938 offshore plebiscite organized by the German government, and at the beginning of the war, while a roomful of German expatriates were announcing their readiness to fight for Germany, Sapper declared that he was "not a supporter of the doctrines of Hitler."[6] As for the last of the five, "the Kaltwasser case is one of the most difficult of all," the embassy acknowledges. "There is no evidence against him to show that he was either a Nazi sympathizer or even indirectly engaged in Nazi Party affairs. Nevertheless, he was one of the main outlets of German products in Guatemala." The return of any of the five "should be resisted on grounds of their economic importance, although reliable evidence of undesirable political activities is lacking."[7]

This remarkable instance of postwar honesty about the unthreatening nature of "the five most important internees in the United States," coupled with the embassy's dogged determination to keep them out of Guatemala, vividly illustrates the way the deportation program had evolved during the war from an undertaking primarily motivated by the need to ensure security against subversion into a long-term project of permanently weakening German economic competition in a region long claimed as "America's backyard."

There was no conceivable rationale for deporting, interning, and banning these men on the basis of subversive activities, and the Embassy knew it. The postwar admission that economic factors were paramount sheds light on a key aspect of the deportation program as it was practiced throughout the region while the war was still under way.

ECONOMIC WARFARE: A DIFFERENT GAME IN THE BACKYARD

"Economic warfare" is a broad term encompassing numerous policies, many of them highly effective in weakening the Axis. The Allies engaged in preemptive buying of strategic materials on the world market, thereby denying essential supplies to the German and Japanese war machines. Massive commodity purchases helped ensure that wavering countries lined up squarely on the side of those nations that were buying their products. Especially successful was the Inter-American Coffee Agreement in effect after April 1941, which provided generous access to the U.S. market, the only important remaining market after the war cut off trade with Europe. This agreement saved the Central American countries from economic collapse – even as it gave the United States added leverage over them.[8]

Within the United States, economic warfare meant cutting off the flow of capital and exports to Germany, and seizing and expropriating large firms owned by German cartels such as General Aniline and Film Company (GAF) and General Dyestuffs Corporation (GDC), subsidiaries of the notorious IG Farben. But what did *not* happen in the United States is just as important for understanding economic warfare as applied to Latin America – and thus perceiving the continuity of U.S. interference in Latin American affairs even in the era of the Good Neighbor policy.

The United States did not embark upon a program of liquidating or transferring businesses owned by individuals among the 300,000 German citizens living within its borders. Although these enemy aliens were prevented by Treasury controls from engaging in trade with Germany, they were free to continue their businesses unmolested. In the United States, "aliens of enemy nationality ... [were] generally not restricted in their financial and commercial transactions," explained a study written near the end of the war. Alien enemies who were U.S. residents since February 23, 1942, were "so-called generally licensed nationals of a foreign (blocked) country who are subject to practically no financial restrictions."⁹ Whatever their private sentiments regarding the country of their birth, these enemy aliens' economic activity was a boon to the U.S. economy, and U.S. officials saw no reason to tamper with it.

In much of Latin America, on the contrary, precisely such people were driven out of business, their property and companies seized or destroyed. This expropriation took place under intense pressure from Washington, often against the wishes of the Latin American governments concerned, and it followed the unilateral blacklisting of businesses in the region – but not in the United States – through the Proclaimed List. (See Chapter 3.) Latin American leaders resented and protested against the Proclaimed List, and they initially resisted more extensive measures for the same reason that the United States did not destroy its own domestic German-owned businesses: they were an asset to the national economy. In the smaller countries of Central America and the Caribbean basin, German-owned businesses were far more important as employers and producers of wealth than they were in the United States, so the cost of their destruction was high.

The sharp difference between the policies pursued by Washington inside the United States and those it demanded for Latin America can be explained by two interrelated reasons. First, since U.S. officials viewed Latin America as a vulnerable, dependent region where the real actors were great power rivals, Germans living there were taken much more seriously as a threat than were Germans living in the United States. The second reason reveals how security and economic interests can be closely linked in the making of foreign policy. While production and commerce carried out by German nationals inside the United States contributed to the U.S. gross national product, German production and commerce in Latin America represented competition in markets the United States hoped to reserve for itself. Economic warfare thus offered the perfect opportunity to attack the German presence in Latin America on the basis of protecting security while devastating a major economic rival.

In principle, this was no contradiction: total war meant hurting the enemy wherever possible. Subsidiaries of large companies based in Germany were known to subsidize pro-Nazi propaganda, and sometimes provided cover or payments for espionage agents in South America.[10] Late in the war, the United States became concerned about preventing looted assets from being smuggled *into* German businesses abroad to keep them away from Allied occupation authorities in Europe.[11] But the level of economic controls imposed on German enemy aliens in the United States seemed sufficient to prevent them from aiding Germany in any of these ways. A similar level of controls could also have neutralized Germans running their own businesses in Latin America, as Latin American officials repeatedly reminded Washington. Why go so much further, and pursue their "commercial and financial annihilation"?[12]

Latin American officials understood the answer better, if anything, than did their U.S. counterparts, who usually spoke in the language of national security. Latin American leaders were not eager to increase their nations' already high degree of reliance upon U.S. capital by losing the German alternative – especially given the sordid record of U.S. interventionism on behalf of corporate interests. Germans who did not interfere in foreign policy or domestic politics were welcome as unusually productive members of societies in need of economic development. Thus Washington's effort to impose stringent economic warfare policies upon reluctant Latin American governments produced substantial friction over broken promises of noninterference and conflicting visions of Latin America's place in the world economy.

In the course of the war, these differences were usually resolved in favor of the United States. This was perhaps inevitable, because of the imbalance of power in inter-American relationships. But the degree and manner of the expropriation of German property that finally took place was not exclusively imposed from outside. Indeed, once the Latin American expropriations got under way, some U.S. officials began to express regrets over the process they had begun. Faced with irresistible demands from Washington, the least-democratic Latin American leaders made necessity first a virtue – and then a vice – by discovering an opportunity to balance national budgets and enrich the ruling clique in the U.S. pressure to expropriate German property.

The link between the expropriation policies and the deportation program emerges clearly in two ways: first, when U.S. officials selected for internment Germans whose only offense was successful entrepreneurship; and second, when Latin American leaders offered for deportation the owners of property that was easier to seize when there was no one left behind to defend it. The process that turned economic controls into a tool for plunder and changed a security program into the internment of innocent businessmen was initiated by deliberate U.S. policy but then adapted by Latin American leaders to suit their own purposes.

THE COSTA RICAN MODEL

Costa Rica was one of the first Latin American countries to institute strict economic controls over its Axis citizens, and other Central American countries subsequently based their policies on the Costa Rican example. The country was not high on the list of U.S. officials' security concerns on the eve of the war. Local Germans did not seem to present such a threat as did the larger and more politically organized German communities of Colombia and Guatemala, for example; the FBI, an agency not given to understating Nazi influence, reported, "It is generally conceded that though the activities of the Germans in Costa Rica were patterned after those in other Latin American countries, they were not so extensive in nature nor were they so well developed."[13] Germans grew only a fraction of the national coffee crop, but they ran important processing stations both for roasting coffee and for refining sugar, and owned large wholesale stores. Together, the country's six hundred Germans owned property valued at $23 million.[14]

Germans were somewhat more integrated into the Costa Rican elite than were their compatriots in neighboring countries. Nearly every Costa Rican president in the first half of the twentieth century had a German relative who had married into his family. That included both wartime presidents, Rafael Calderón Guardia (1940–4) and Teodoro Picado (1944–8), both of the National Republican Party.[15] However, it was Calderón's predecessor, León Cortés of the rival Democratic Party, who was overtly sympathetic to Germans. Cortés's father and son had studied in Germany, and his brother Claudio visited the front with German troops after the invasion of Poland. President Cortés appointed the director of the German Club, Max Efinger, to be his Director of Public Works.[16]

Since most Germans supported Cortés, his successors had a political incentive to cooperate with U.S. anti-German policies, even if they were not always persuaded that the German residents posed a threat to national security. Likewise, Calderón was quick to label as Nazi fifth columnists any Costa Rican opponents who criticized his policies. Chief among these was José Figueres, the dominant figure in Costa Rican politics during the three decades following the war. Figueres fearlessly denounced Calderón's corruption and the abuses of power involved in the execution of the anti-German policies. In July 1942, after a German submarine torpedoed a ship in the port of Limón, killing twenty-four dockworkers below decks, the Communist Party, Calderón's coalition allies, organized a protest in San José that led to six hours of rioting and looting "interrupted briefly by speeches by Calderón and [Communist Party head Manuel] Mora, neither of whom did anything to calm the crowd. In fact, they may have encouraged it."[17] The rioters sacked German and Italian businesses indiscriminately, including the book-store of Karl Federspiel, who had previously suffered a boycott by local Nazis for his sale of anti-Hitler publications.[18] Seventy-six people were injured and 123 buildings damaged. One hundred Germans were impris-oned, and the remainder of those living in San José were confined under house arrest.[19] Figueres then bought radio time to denounce the riot and related government excesses. Midway through his speech, police burst into the radio station, seized him, and sent him into exile, labeling him a Nazi sympathizer.[20]

Thus Calderón was not averse to using charges of pro-Nazism as a weapon against his political opponents, much as later generations of politicians would wield the accusation "Communist" during the Cold War. However, that did not lead him automatically to comply with all of Washington's plans. There were disputes between Calderón and the United States as U.S. demands broadened to include the deportation of Germans with influen-tial Costa Rican family connections and for the liquidation of productive German enterprises deemed essential to the Costa Rican economy. As in neighboring countries, Costa Rican government officials gradually came to realize that the U.S. pressure for more far-reaching measures against the Germans could not be resisted – but could be converted into an opportunity for financial gain.

The first steps taken in Costa Rica carefully balanced the need to su-pervise the German community without causing unnecessary hardship or economic losses to the nation. Anticipating wartime economic controls in October 1941, the Costa Rican government created the Coordination Of-fice, the *Oficina de Coordinación*, with representatives from the ministries of Commerce and the Treasury, to keep German-owned farms and businesses operating while diverting the profits to blocked accounts and installing Costa Rican inspectors to ensure compliance with economic restrictions. It was a model operation for achieving economic warfare goals while avoiding harm to the economy, and it was quickly imitated by other Central American coun-tries. Since the coffee and sugar produced in these German-owned facilities was destined for the U.S. market, the approval of U.S. officials was essential for the arrangement to work.[21]

They, however, were not satisfied. Arthur Bliss Lane, minister to Costa Rica in early 1942, complained that the *Oficina de Coordinación* was over-paying German managers, and that its staff was inadequate to the task ahead. Confidentially, Lane and his First Secretary, Leslie E. Reed, were sending memos to Treasury Minister Carlos M. Escalante suggesting that a new board be created to expropriate all enemy aliens and send them out of the country. In February 1942, Reed suggested placing a U.S. citizen in charge of administering alien property in Costa Rica and argued that the deporta-tion program should be widened. "The big coffee planters should be moved off their properties," he wrote. "The same is true in the sugar mills, stores and other offices. They simply should not be allowed to be physically present in any of their former properties. . . . The Germans dismissed from their properties and employment should be detained and deported, as they would constitute a constant menace if left at large in Costa Rica."²²

The menace that Reed was invoking was not the possibility of sabotage or espionage, but rather the danger that Germans whose property was taken over by government administrators would constantly seek to have the property returned – creating pressure on the government to reverse its policies.

In March, the Legation forced the issue by notifying Minister Escalante that it would terminate the agreement providing for the *Oficina de Coordinación*. The Costa Rican government duly replaced it with a larger organization for alien enemy property control, with the unwieldy name of *Junta de Custodia de la Propiedad de los Nacionales de los Países en Guerra con Costa Rica* or simply *Junta de Custodia*, Custodial Board, for short.²³

The *Junta de Custodia* was the subject of intense controversy during the war. Its work, closely monitored by U.S. diplomats with de facto veto power over its decisions (since the U.S. licensed its products for import), led to accusations of corruption against both wartime Costa Rican presidents and contributed to a polarization of Costa Rican politics that would ultimately erupt in civil war. Its impact on the German community was to devastate the holdings both of pro-Nazis and of those who seem to have had no interest in supporting the Nazi cause. And it demonstrated how a policy begun for security reasons was transformed by both sides of the U.S.-Costa Rican relationship into an effort to weaken the German economic presence to the short-term advantage of both American nations – and the long-term advantage only of the more powerful one.

CONFLICT OVER COFFEE

The three board members of the *Junta de Custodia* were former Finance Minister Tomás Soley Güell, who served as director, and two Costa Rican businessmen, Juan Trejos Quirós and Hernán Sáenz Huete.²⁴ They assumed the duties of the defunct *Oficina de Coordinación*, overseeing German-owned businesses, and immediately came into conflict with U.S. officials. Director Soley wrote to the U.S. Legation seeking approval for a plan to export the coffee produced by German farms to the only possible buyer, the United States. He explained that the profits from any such sales would be frozen, and that government administrators would oversee the transaction to ensure that the money would support the Costa Rican economy and not be used to subsidize pro-Axis propaganda or enrich Axis nationals.²⁵ Coffee produced by Germans represented 4 percent of Costa Rica's annual crop, an amount worth fighting for in the opinion of a government facing serious deficits, especially since it was mostly high-grade export-quality coffee that brought in foreign exchange. The State Department, however, refused to approve the purchase of this "German" coffee.[26] There was only one way the Costa Ricans could sell it, Secretary Hull instructed the U.S. Legation: "If detriment to local economy and labor is to be avoided, the urgent necessity of effecting the transfer of such coffee-producing properties to desirable local interests should be brought to the attention of the appropriate authorities.... The Junta de Custodia should be in a position to compel reluctant owners to effect the sale."[27]

Harvest season was approaching, and Soley was under time pressure. He appealed to the new U.S. Minister, Robert Scotten, saying that if the coffee was not harvested, not only would Costa Rican workers lose their livelihoods, but banks would lose the loans they had extended for planting, and the properties themselves would diminish in value because the fields would not be prepared for future planting. It was not merely a question of whether the United States would choose to buy 4 percent of Costa Rica's coffee; the U.S. Legation was essentially withholding permission for the entire national harvest to proceed, because if the coffee from German farms were mixed with non-German coffee at the *beneficios* (processing plants), the United States would consider it all to be tainted and refuse to purchase any coffee from Costa Rica.[28]

Losing 4 percent of the coffee crop was undesirable; forfeiting the entire crop was unthinkable. *Junta de Custodia* officials moved to expropriate the German coffee farms. By September, the *Junta* had sold some of the confiscated Axis property for $500,000 to a few well-connected buyers including Alfredo Echandi, brother of Calderón's foreign minister Alberto Echandi.[29]

CONFLICT OVER SUGAR

A parallel dispute arose over the second most important Costa Rican crop, and it had a similar outcome. In July 1942, the *Junta de Custodia* proposed exporting three million kilos of sugar, of which up to 25 percent was produced by the German firm Niehaus & Co. The manager of commercial and agricultural affairs for the custodial board, Andrés van der Laat, carefully explained that the Niehaus company was controlled and administered by *Junta de Custodia* officials, and that any funds obtained from the sale of the sugar would be frozen rather than turned over to the German owner.[30] The United States refused to buy that shipment or any other sugar from German-owned farms, which produced most of the national crop.[31] By the end of the year, Soley presented the bad news to President Calderón: the fact that the German sugar plantations and sugar refineries were under Costa Rican government management was not enough for the United States, which demanded outright expropriation. The *Junta* had been processing sugar from Costa Rican-owned plantations through the refineries, but there was so little of it that the refineries were running just one day a week. With the cane beginning to rot in the fields, Soley said, the government had only one option: expropriate the German properties as the U.S. demanded, or face losing the crop. If they failed to expropriate the German plantations and processed the German sugar anyway, Soley warned, the United States would blacklist the entire Costa Rican harvest, not only the German sugar but that produced on Costa Rican-owned farms as well.[32]

The message was clear, and the response was inevitable. Over the coming months the *Junta de Custodia* expropriated $3 million worth of "the richest and most important agricultural and industrial properties" belonging to persons on the U.S. blacklist. Some of the firms were forced to liquidate, and others were sold to Costa Ricans at bargain prices.[33] U.S. officials closely monitored, revised, and in some cases simply dictated the terms of sale.[34] The expropriations were not uncompensated seizures – at least, not on the surface. The proceeds from the forced sales went into the government treasury, and the government then paid the German owners for the properties by depositing Costa Rican Defense Bonds into blocked accounts in an amount equaling the appraised value of the farms, real estate, and businesses seized. The property changed hands, the government received the purchase price from the new buyer, and the former German owners received war bonds.[35]

In truth, however, paying in war bonds meant not paying at all. The blocked funds were drained by a capital tax of 18 percent per year, while at the same time the bonds were rapidly losing their value – down 40 percent by early 1944, then cancelled outright in 1945.[36] The defense bond scheme gave President Teodoro Picado's government a short-term fix for an acute fiscal crisis. In 1945 total government revenue from all sources was sixty million *colones* (about $10 million). Fully twenty million *colones*, one-third of the national budget, came from expropriated German and some Italian property paid for with the worthless defense bonds.[37]

There were private benefits as well. Both Costa Rican wartime presidents, Calderón and his anointed successor Picado, under pressure from the United States to seize German property, turned that challenge into an opportunity, appointing their friends to administer the German farms – positions from which the administrators could sell off stock and equipment and enrich themselves in other ways.[38]

In the first six months of 1945, the opposition Democratic Party, outraged at the uncompensated expropriations authorized solely by the executive, tried to introduce legislation preventing the President from using frozen alien assets for general budgetary purposes, but was blocked by the governing party. Other opponents of Calderón and Picado protested the auctioning off of confiscated properties at low prices to relatives of high government officials. The expulsion and expropriation of Germans was a primary factor in alienating Costa Rican elites from Calderón and Picado, helping to fuel a conflict that would culminate, three years later, in civil war.[39]* Even the State Department was uncomfortable with the level of expropriations ordered by Picado and sought to avoid "the onus for the expropriation of properties of relatively innocuous firms and individuals under the guise of economic warfare, but for the real purpose of increasing the revenue."[40] (Ultimately, of 728 properties administered by the *Junta de Custodia*, all but 47 were returned to their owners after the war.)[41]

These actions did not further the Allied war effort. Without the expropriations, had the system of German ownership and Costa Rican management remained in place, none of the blocked assets of the German plantations could have made their way to support the Axis – even supposing the German owners were inclined to offer such support. Germans with no reported connections to Nazi activities were expropriated under pressure from Washington for the same reasons that helped broaden the deportation program to include unthreatening individuals: a combination of Nazi claims to transnational unity and U.S. assumptions that Latin Americans were easily manipulated made all Germans there seem dangerous. Germans had been successful at integrating themselves and their business operations into Latin American societies; they had become a serious rival to the United States in these regional markets. And some Latin American leaders were prepared to turn difficulty, in the form of U.S. pressure, into opportunity, by converting German assets into personal or national wealth.

In the long run, however, the big loser, besides the German owners who watched property representing years of toil taken away, was the Costa Rican economy. Many a successful agricultural enterprise fell victim to mismanagement or plundering by the new owners, who had invested so little of their own capital or effort to buy properties at cut-rate prices. Costa Ricans who worked on the plantations that were liquidated lost their jobs. Once the Germans were gone, it proved difficult to find sufficient substitute capital and expertise to run the big refineries. The U.S. Legation acknowledged that "there are very few people in Costa Rica who know the sugar business and who are willing to risk their investments in an enterprise of such magnitude."[42] The closing or degradation of the German sugar plantations and refineries led to severe sugar shortages countrywide in 1944.[43]

CONFLICT OVER DEPORTATIONS

To be sure, some of the German owners who lost their property in this manner were staunchly pro-German in outlook. Ernst Ludwig Lohrengel,

---

* Wealthy Costa Ricans were not enamored of Calderón's social policies and pro-labor laws, or of his alliance with the Communist Party, either. But the legacy of corruption drove many to join a revolt led by Figueres after Calderón's party stole the election of 1948.

born in Costa Rica to German parents in 1909, owned one of the largest coffee farms in the country. Ordered to sell his property to a Costa Rican national, he found one willing to sign a secret proviso promising to sell it back to him after the war. Had he renounced his German citizenship and becoming solely a Costa Rican national himself, that might have helped Lohrengel avoid expropriation, but, as he told German officials after being deported and repatriated to Germany, his allegiance to the country of his parents' birth was too strong: "I never considered such a step, because the defense of Germandom abroad has always been the highest endeavor of my family for generations," Lohrengel wrote, closing his letter with the standard Nazi salutation, "Heil Hitler!"[44]

Although he was not a Party member, Lohrengel's declaration reminds us that some German property owners, even second-generation immigrants, did subscribe to ideas that helped Nazi organizers make inroads into the expatriate community. As with deportation and internment, the expropriation of the Germans of Latin America cannot be described simply as an assault on innocent victims. The embrace of Nazi ideology by some of them helped to create the stigma that attached itself to all German residents in the region.

But the expropriation and deportation policies did not target German owners because of their political views. If they had, these policies would have been more discriminating, as they were in the United States. In Costa Rica as elsewhere in Latin America, after the initial wave of deportations removed the leading Nazis in early 1942, the criteria shifted to economic ones, and U.S. officials continued to push for more far-reaching measures against the Germans.

The most valuable single company in Costa Rica was Niehaus & Co., a collection of plantations, real estate, and a wholesale and retail outlet in Limón; most of the company's wealth came from the production and processing of sugar and coffee. The value of the Niehaus sugar mill "Victoria" alone was conservatively estimated at $500,000. In 1941, the various Niehaus enterprises employed 1,132 persons year-round and 2,528 during the harvest. Of the four principal owners in the Niehaus family, three were naturalized Costa Rican citizens.[45] None joined the Nazi Party.[46] Willi Niehaus actually quit the German Club when the AO took it over in 1935, and there was no evidence of subversive activities against any of the owners. Postwar investigators characterized the family's political orientation as "pro-Niehaus."[47] The *Junta de Custodia* at first froze the company's assets and took over its management, hoping to satisfy the U.S. desire for control of German capital while respecting private property laws and maintaining operations in a business so crucial to the nation's economy, but the U.S. Legation lobbied for outright expropriation.[48] After the United States threatened to stop buying all Costa Rican coffee and sugar in 1943 if German firms were not expropriated, the Niehaus holdings were among the first on the list to be seized.[49]

Franz Amrhein, a widely respected businessman who had lived in Costa Rica since 1913, was a similar case. He engaged in no activities that could be considered political, with the possible exception of his fourteen-year service as Royal Vice Consul and Consul for Sweden before the war, and his unpaid work helping the Goodyear Rubber Plantation Company establish rubber tree groves in Costa Rica to aid the Allied war effort. Calderón refused to send him out of the country, but the *Junta de Custodia* did take over his businesses: a hardware and electric motor store, a car dealership representing the Ford Motor Co., and sugar and cattle operations. Costa Rican stockholders were pleased with his performance, reelecting him as manager of the auto dealership in 1943, to the great annoyance of U.S. Embassy officials.[50]

But despite repeated efforts, for years the embassy was unsuccessful in securing the deportation of Amrhein and the Niehaus brothers. To satisfy the unrelenting U.S. demands for German deportees, Calderón sent up a number of other "Germans," some of whom surprised even U.S. officials.[51] Answering a State Department request for details on the recent arrivals, the U.S. Legation reported that among those deported on October 23, 1942, were the following persons:

Behrens, Emil. He wrote to the President of Costa Rica when Costa Rica declared war, and expressed his solidarity with the Costa Rican Government. He continued to be employed by a Proclaimed List firm until that firm went out of business. His parents are living in Germany. He is not believed to be a Nazi. He was deported at the request of the Costa Rican Government.

Behrenz, Jorge. Danish. Deported at the request of the Costa Rican Government.

Cantero, Juana Sonntag. Hotel frequented by Nazi sympathizers. Pro-Nazi.

Ceska, Hardy. Czechoslovakian, known Nazi sympathizer with no apparent means of support.

Gruenwedl, Eugenio. Born in Germany November 21, 1873. Father of Hans Gruenwedl, former German aviator, now at Stringtown Internment Camp, Oklahoma. As far as known, a harmless old man. Costa Rican Government requested deportation.

Etc.[52]*

In December, Calderón sent up another "pernicious foreigner": Ernesto Gerothwohl, a Jewish refugee suffering from a serious respiratory ailment who, along with his wife, had fled Germany during *Kristallnacht* in 1938 with four dollars and a few clothes. Gerothwohl's main offense seems to have been that he pestered the Costa Rican government to take stronger action *against* local Nazi Party members. Postwar investigators found "no allegations whatsoever of pro-Nazi activity or sympathy on the part of either Gerothwol [sic]."[53]

---

* One of the group, Emil Behrens, does appear in *Nazi Party Membership Records*. However, if he was a Nazi, he was not a very reliable one. Paroled from internment in the United States, he enlisted in the U.S. Army to serve in the fight against Germany.

In the fall of 1943, the U.S. ambassador to Costa Rica was Fay Allen Des Portes, a political appointee "not particularly effective as a diplomat," according to Central America Division chief John Moors Cabot, who had served under him in his previous post in Guatemala.[54] Despite having lived for ten years in Latin America, Des Portes spoke no Spanish. During his earlier tenure in Guatemala, an aide noted that his "vanity ... makes him very susceptible to flattery," that he was careless with secret documents and discussed confidential matters in public.[55] The same aide reported that President Jorge Ubico once erupted that he was "'fed up' [with] so much pressure and interference in Guatemalan affairs on the part of [the U.S.] Legation."[56]

It was with similar levels of diplomatic tact that Des Portes approached the government of President Calderón Guardia. On August 4, Des Portes handed Calderón a list of thirty-three Axis nationals, mostly Germans and a few Italians, whom the embassy considered dangerous, and asked for their deportation to the United States. Calderón balked.[57] By September 13, the President had agreed to the deportation of only three Germans and stated that "the remainder of the enemy aliens are not dangerous."[58] He resisted the deportation even of the Nazi leader Herbert Knöhr and the well-known sympathizer Ricardo Steinvorth, the former of whom was of Costa Rican birth, and who were both married to cousins of his. Instead, he argued, since they were under house arrest, they could pose no further danger. Calderón also refused the U.S. demand for the deportation of Hans Bansbach, a pipe organ repairman who kept the organs of the principal Costa Rican cathedrals and churches in working order, stating that Bansbach was "indispensable and useful," held an affidavit from the Metropolitan Diocese, and was "harmless and no [subversive] activity on his part is known."[59] Instead, Calderón made a counteroffer of five individuals for whom neither his own government nor the embassy had any evidence of involvement in pro-Nazi activity – an example of the "trading" denounced by Justice Department investigator Raymond Ickes. It seemed obvious that Calderón was offering inoffensive, unknown Axis nationals simply to placate U.S. officials.[60]

The negotiations dragged on. On October 22, Foreign Minister Alberto Echandi informed Chargé d'Affaires Edward G. Trueblood that "frankly he saw no reason for [the Germans] being sent out of the country, adding that he thought we must have enough up there as it is by now. ... He then spoke of the case of Willi Steinvorth, an elderly man and a life-long friend of don Alberto, whose son [Eberhard] has been selected for deportation. The Foreign Minster expressed the hope that it might be possible to avoid breaking up this family."[61] After meeting with Calderón, Trueblood reported "that every one of the persons on the list had connections of one kind or another, which they were utilizing to the utmost, with the result that pressure on him was unremitting and intense."[62] Des Portes, complaining about Echandi's "antagonistic attitude toward our efforts," thought he could break the impasse by handing Calderón another list of enemy aliens "considered dangerous by my Government . . . approved by the Enemy Alien Control Unit of the United States Department of Justice for internment in the United States."[63]

Following the negotiations from his State Department office, Central America desk officer John Moors Cabot was appalled to read the latest cables from San José. "Herewith the kind of thing which . . . may well rise to damn us when the recent crisis is over," Cabot wrote to Philip Bonsal.[64]

I think it is undesirable for the written record to show that the initiative came from us . . . we certainly do not have the right to tell another sovereign government which of its citizens it should deport, or to what country they should be deported. . . .

I fear that in the post-war period, unfriendly leaders in the other republics may use incidents such as this to demonstrate that behind the façade of Good Neighborship the United States was really interfering in the internal affairs of the other republics. I see no reason why we should give them written evidence to bolster such an assertion. If we really must take the initiative and exert pressure in connection with deportations, it should at least be done with great discretion.[65]

Discretion and the Good Neighbor's promise not to interfere in Latin American internal affairs now clearly carried less weight than the campaign against the Germans. Cabot's warning was shuffled around the Department, but it did not alter the conduct of the embassy. Throughout Calderón's term, Amrhein, the Steinvorths, and the Niehaus brothers were able to avoid deportation. Naturally, while they were still in Costa Rica, they did what they could to lobby for the return of their properties. Officials at the *Junta de Custodia*, by now fully converted to the cause of widespread expropriation, tried to make use of the deportation program to remove the men who were defending their property. *Junta* manager Andrés van der Laat wrote to his contacts in the U.S. embassy in October 1943 asking them to expand the deportation list agreed to by the Costa Rican government so that Amrhein, Hans and Willie Niehaus, and other leading businessmen could "go enjoy the beauty of Crystal City." "Their absence would greatly benefit the country and the cause," he added.[66]

Here was an ally within the Costa Rican government pressing for more deportations, but it took a change of administration to complete the task of expelling the leading German producers. President Teodoro Picado, although handpicked by Calderón, was less beholden to German interests; as a weaker politician than his predecessor, he may have felt the need to shore up his position by meeting U.S. demands, a stance that probably felt natural to the new president, who had spent years as a lawyer for the United Fruit Company. At any rate, Picado moved more aggressively against the Germans Calderón had protected. In July 1944 he issued a decree summarily canceling the Costa Rican citizenship of Hans, Walter, and Willie Niehaus and then invited them and Amrhein to a meeting, where he had them seized and delivered to the U.S. Army – which whisked them to

Texas by plane without giving them the time to pack a suitcase.[67] What was the decree's legal basis for denationalizing Costa Rican-born citizens? "The fact that a citizen has been included in the Proclaimed Lists of those countries allied with Costa Rica [i.e., the United States] is an indication of culpability."[68]

Costa Rica also turned over three male members of the Steinvorth family to U.S. authorities in 1944. The first Steinvorths had arrived in Costa Rica in the late nineteenth century. Gerardo Steinvorth, who came to Costa Rica in 1920 and married a Costa Rican, served as German Consul in San José from 1929 to 1935, when he resigned after quarreling with Nazi leaders who wanted him to fly the swastika flag from his consulate. The FBI thought he was "anti-Hitler." The U.S. Legation, however, concluded that he "no doubt became a Party member" because he was able to visit Germany and retained German citizenship – "singularly unsound" reasoning, in the opinion of postwar investigators, who did not think that retention of German citizenship was proof of Party membership. Gerardo's brother Willi Steinvorth also married a Costa Rican and had been resident in the country since before the First World War. There was an active pro-Nazi in the family: their cousin Ricardo, married to a cousin of President Calderón, and confused with Gerardo by British intelligence.[69] None of the Steinvorths joined the Party.[70]

Disputing the U.S. demand to have Gerardo Steinvorth deported, Calderón's government had argued that he had "lived in the country for many years with outstanding uprightness and no dangerous activity on his part can be discovered; on the contrary, he is of a quiet and tranquil character."[71] But during Picado's term in office, Ricardo, Gerardo, and Eberhard Steinvorth were deported, despite the lack of evidence against the latter two, and despite the fact that by 1944 a German threat to Costa Rica was not a danger taken seriously by anyone.

Perhaps for good measure, Picado also deported the organ tuner Hans Bansbach, who was interned in Camp Kenedy. His wife and children remained behind in Costa Rica and lived off the charity of the parishes whose organs he had formerly kept in good repair. (When Bansbach returned to Costa Rica after the war, he told his children that he had been treated leniently in camp, where the guards would open the gates and tell him, "Go to my house and tune my piano.")[72]

From internment in Camp Kenedy, 18-year-old Eberhard Steinvorth sent a letter to his father Willi, still living in Costa Rica. (Eberhard wrote in Spanish, his first language; although he was born in Germany, he was brought to Costa Rica when he was a few months old):

I have had many troubles here because, since it cannot be kept secret that I do not desire to go to Germany but rather wish to return to Costa Rica, the militant Nazis criticize my attitude in the grossest fashion and even begin talking badly in my presence about Costa Rica and the Steinvorth family in general, which they attack for its pro-Costa Rican tendency, all nonsense and attacks that I will in no way be able to stand forever with my mouth shut.... It is simply a disgrace that we did not arrange the matter of our naturalization as Costa Ricans in a timely fashion, because the result is that one's heart is on one side and one's papers on the other, thus one sits well neither with God nor with the devil. In Costa Rica we were able to avoid the company of these radicals; here there is nothing to be done but put up with them.[73]

Had he known that Picado had cancelled the naturalized citizenship of the Niehaus brothers, Eberhard Steinvorth might have had less faith in the safety ensured by putting one's papers on the side of one's heart.

NICARAGUA: SOMOZA'S RULES

Elsewhere in Central America, the pattern was much the same. In Nicaragua, Anastasio Somoza at first resisted the requests by Chargé d'Affaires William P. Cochran, Jr., to deport twenty-one Axis nationals on a list prepared by the U.S. Legation in March 1942. Cochran reported to Washington that Somoza was wary of antagonizing elite Nicaraguan families related by marriage to the Germans on the list. Other proposed deportees were Nicaraguan citizens by naturalization or birth. Explaining Somoza's reluctance, Cochran engaged in analysis typical of U.S. officials who tended to depict Latin Americans as irrational and motivated by their emotions rather than their interests. "This reasoning is of course not Anglo-Saxon; it is nevertheless a normal Latin American psychological reaction," Cochran wrote.[74]

The Nicaraguan dictator objected especially strongly to the proposed deportation of Julio Bahlke. When Somoza had been a fugitive in 1926, he hid for some time on the German's farm, and Bahlke personally brought him his meals every day. "This is a type of personal debt which, as a Latin American, Somoza could hardly repay by ordering Bahlke's deportation," Cochran concluded.[75]

Whether irrational loyalty is a particularly Latin American psychological characteristic or not, Somoza evidently got over his inhibitions, aided by continuing U.S. pressure and the realization that Bahlke's property could bring him more rewards than could his own fidelity. In late 1942, the Nicaraguan government jailed Julio Bahlke and put his vast coffee estate, "Alemania," up for auction. Somoza sent his chief of staff, Colonel Camilo González, at the head of a unit of soldiers armed with machine guns to prevent rival bidders from entering the site. Somoza submitted the only bid and took away property worth $5 million for a suitcase filled with 380,000 córdobas taken that morning from the National Bank of Nicaragua – a sum then delivered to the Bank of London (which held the Bahlke property as collateral on a prewar loan he could not repay).[76] Bahlke was deported to the United States the following year. Smaller farms were sold at an even greater discount; one coffee farm with annual profits of $5,000 was acquired for $100.[77] As in Costa Rica, the government liquidated confiscated German property of lesser value and converted the proceeds into defense bonds. Unlike Costa Rica, Nicaragua paid these bonds to the original German owners after the war – at 60 percent of their face value.[78]

HONDURAS: BLESSED PROFITS

Fortune smiled on the friends of Tiburcio Carías, strongman and bringer of "blessed peace" to Honduras. After using the U.S. deportation program as a means to expel his political opponents, he then transformed economic warfare measures into a get-rich-quick scheme. In November 1942, Carías issued Decree No. 57, ordering the forced sale of German-owned property. State-appointed administrators arranged to sell off the property at prices as low as five cents on the dollar to members of Carías' circle of cronies, known as *la argolla*, "the ring."[79] Decree No. 71 of May 19, 1944, allowed the forced transfer by auction of any property belonging to any person of any nationality deemed to have engaged in activities favorable in any way to the Axis.[80] Numerous sales of land, farms, houses, cattle, and other property followed, often for far less than the appraised value (which the owners had often deliberately underestimated for tax purposes). At one such "auction" of coffee plantations belonging to Francisco Siercke in September 1944, Samuel Inestroza Gómez snapped up property appraised at a quarter million dollars for the bargain price of $50,000. There were no other bidders.[81] Some of the extensive remaining properties of the Siercke family were bought by a friend of Carías named Miguel Brooks.[82] The procedure became common practice. Reporting on forty-one such sales at the end of the war, the U.S. Embassy noted that "graft on the part of Honduran interventors [administrators] has been widespread."[83]

A postwar summary prepared by the War Department describing participation in anti-Axis efforts by Latin American countries praised the Honduran government for having "cooperated wholeheartedly.... It has been alleged that close friends and strong supporters of the government seized the opportunity to make large profits on these sales, and that low evaluations are being made for their benefit. Regardless, German property in Honduras is being rapidly transferred to the hands of Hondurans."[84]

Because of these confiscations, diplomatic relations between Honduras and the Federal Republic of Germany were not normalized until 1960. In 1978, Honduras agreed to compensate the surviving German owners and their descendants with the equivalent of two million marks.[85]

GUATEMALA: UNINTENDED CONSEQUENCES

Using standard economic controls, President Jorge Ubico placed restrictions on German property, especially the vast German coffee estates and import-export houses that produced 40 percent and exported 70 percent of Guatemala's coffee crop. Ubico's decrees and freezing orders affecting persons and businesses on the Proclaimed List effectively prevented German capital from leaving the country, and his administrators took over supervision of operations on the plantations.

Once comfortably ensconced in their sinecures, the new bosses comported themselves much as their counterparts did in Honduras and Costa Rica. Corruption and mismanagement led to a steep decline in productivity. The vast plantation "El Porvenir," which had produced over 24,000 quintals (5.3 million pounds) of coffee under German ownership in 1940, dropped to 13,000 quintals after the Guatemalan administrators took over. They had not risked their own investments of time, capital, or labor in the estates, nor had they been chosen for their expertise. Their director was "inept and surrounded by corrupt aides. His one qualification was his birthright: he was the president's brother."[86] Elsewhere among the largest German plantation complexes, production fell to half of prewar levels. On the thirteen largest German properties, coffee production dropped by five million kilos from 1940 to 1943.[87]

However, Ubico was unwilling to take the further step from control to expropriation. In November 1942, the Spanish envoy representing German interests in Guatemala was still "under the impression that the USA is making an effort to destroy the economic and commercial influence of Germany, but that the Guatemalan government is resisting the North American pressure to sharpen the measures taken thus far."[88] He was right.

As much as a year earlier, the State Department's Board of Economic Operations, chaired by Dean Acheson, met to consider how to handle the Guatemalan government, given its apparent unwillingness to root out the German producers. The State Department's Adviser on International Economic Affairs, Herbert Feis, argued that the Guatemalan plan to permit continued sale of German-produced coffee, with profits diverted to blocked accounts, was inadequate. Although it would prevent the funds from being used for subversive purposes, "Dr. Feis thought that individuals on the [Proclaimed] List should be *completely eliminated* from the social and economic life of Guatemala and, as he pointed out, this plan permitted them to continue operations." The only discussion of Feis's proposal was how best to achieve it. Conditions in Guatemala might not be ripe for a thoroughgoing expropriation, noted some Board members, and its economy could surely not survive such a blow. But the shift from preventing subversion to carrying out the long-range destruction of the German economic presence went unremarked and unquestioned.[89]

After difficult negotiations, the United States and Guatemala worked out a system of quotas under which the principal blacklisted coffee plantations could export just enough to fund their continued operation, rather than

drive them into the ground through a total embargo.[90] Naturally, this led
to reduced employment and lower national income in Guatemala, with pre-
dictable effects on public opinion. In February 1942, the U.S. commercial
attaché in Guatemala reported a wave of anti-American feeling prompted
by the impact of the Proclaimed Lists and especially by restrictions on coffee
imports.[91]

Ubico argued that the United States should give him authority to sell
100 percent of the German coffee production and freeze the proceeds in special accounts in the Central Bank for government purposes. He declared that
he was willing to take over German properties after the war, providing fair
compensation to the owners, but that in the meantime, these fine plantations
were deteriorating from underproduction. When U.S. Minister Des Portes
suggested that the government should simply seize the *fincas*, Ubico replied
that if he did so, since he was "a man of God," he should have to pay a just
price to the owners.[92] The Guatemalan government did not have the capital
to do that, nor the political will to so thoroughly alienate an important sector
of Guatemalan society, so Ubico stood his ground.

U.S. diplomats seemed unable to comprehend such impudence, and they
raised the pitch of their demands accordingly. In May, commercial attaché
William E. Dunn strode into the Guatemalan Finance Ministry and, referring
to local economic controls "with sarcasm," ordered the Minister to toughen
Guatemala's laws, "letting it be understood that some veiled threat was behind his demand." Ubico's patience ran out. He had Dunn and Legation First
Secretary Harold L. Williamson, who had been leaking tales of Guatemalan-
German collaboration to the Associated Press, declared personae non gratae
and expelled from the country.[93]

The necessary leverage to force the issue ultimately came, as usual, from
Washington. In 1944, Secretary Hull told his ambassador in Guatemala City,
Boaz Long, that the U.S. government would suspend the purchases of coffee
from the German farms unless the Guatemalan government nationalized
the properties. That meant that 40 percent of the country's only important
export crop would be lost.[94]

Guatemala's foreign minister expressed "the shock his country had received upon learning of our desire in this connection," Boaz Long reported.
"He reviewed Guatemala's entire program of [wartime] collaboration, de-
plored our position taken with respect to nationalization, but said that if
we demanded immediate action in the case of certain *fincas* the Guatemalan
Government would reluctantly go through with it although considering such
a demand as an unwarranted expression of lack of confidence."[95]

Ubico had no choice. Popular protest had recently ousted his fellow dictator Maximiliano Hernández Martínez from power in El Salvador, and unrest
was growing in the streets of Guatemala City. Ubico needed U.S. support
more than he needed the goodwill of the German community. On June 24, he

signed the expropriation order. A leading economic historian of Guatemala explained the implications of Ubico's decree:

By one act, Ubico eliminated the country's most efficient and productive *finqueros* [plantation owners] and made the state the largest landowner in the country. Although Guatemalan planters became the leading coffee producers by default, they could not have been entirely pleased with the expropriations. The Germans had been innovative, efficient producers, through whom many Guatemalan planters gained access to foreign markets and capital. Moreover, the expropriations set a dangerous precedent, for the state became the owner and administrator of highly productive *fincas*.... The expropriation of German property sent the oligarchy an ominous warning that the state had the right and obligation to nationalize private property. If it could confiscate German properties, it could also expropriate Guatemalan *fincas*.[96]

This same fear explains why elite opinion throughout Central America, even where unsympathetic to the German targets of expropriation, was aghast at the seizures carried out under U.S. pressure.

A veteran of the German coffee business in Guatemala observed that the value of the confiscated Axis property and assets "ought to be higher than Guatemala's national debt."[97] But Ubico did not remain in power long enough to reap the fruits of his decision. Instead, in an unexpected twist, U.S. pressure to eliminate Germans from Guatemala's economy was transformed into an agrarian reform program that Washington observed with growing horror.

Within days of signing the expropriation order, the dictator was overthrown by a popular movement of students and the urban middle class, allied with young army officers. They were not concerned with the fate of the German community; they sought an end to decades of autocratic rule. Ubico fled to New Orleans. The new government turned Ubico's decree into law, ordering the expropriation of all German property in Guatemala including real estate, buildings, stocks, bonds, and plantations.[98] When the self-described "spiritual socialist" Juan José Arévalo was elected president in late 1944, the Guatemalan government controlled about 130 large coffee estates, the *fincas nacionales*, confiscated from the German community and from Ubico and his generals worth tens of millions of dollars.[99] Seeking to redress the highly inequitable land-tenure patterns in the country, Arévalo rented out part of the lands to peasants and cooperatives. He began a national literacy program, instituted social security for workers, and devoted a third of the national budget to social welfare, education, and housing.[100] He also began talking about nationalizing the vast uncultivated lands held by the U.S.-based United Fruit Company.

This was not what the United States had in mind when it pressed for the expropriation of the Germans. In May 1945, the State Department expressed its desire "to avoid being a party to any agrarian expropriation program," adding its strong belief that "any expropriation based wholly or in part upon the Proclaimed List should be determined solely in the light of legitimate economic warfare objectives."[101] One of the principal Guatemalan informants who had helped the United States draw up its blacklists, Alfredo Schlesinger, went public to denounce the property seizures and urge that they be returned to their owners rather than be used for "vengeance."[102]

Arévalo's successor, Jacobo Arbenz, took land reform a step further. In June 1952, an agrarian reform law redistributed much of the *fincas nacionales* to landless peasants, and called for the expropriation, with compensation, of uncultivated lands. Since the United Fruit Company, the largest landowner in Guatemala, cultivated only 15 percent of its massive holdings, it was an obvious target.[103] Two years later, Arbenz was overthrown by a CIA-orchestrated coup.[104]

Some of the expropriated Germans in Guatemala received their properties back from the right-wing administrations that followed. General Miguel Ydígoras Fuentes, president in the late fifties, had befriended some of them while serving as Guatemala's ambassador to Great Britain in the 1940s. In that capacity, he had visited a number of Guatemala's deported Germans held in displaced persons' camps in occupied Germany after the war and promised to do what he could to help them.[105] Taking power in 1958, Ydígoras declared the confiscation of German properties to have been a "national shame," and he returned some of the properties to their original owners; the Nottebohm family received sixteen of its *fincas* in 1962. However, Ydígoras's administration was both corrupt and inconsistent. Twelve of the *fincas nacionales* were used for land reform redistribution of a peculiar sort, under which some of the first new "buyers" were two hundred military officers who snapped up the lots at five cents per square meter.[106] Thus ended the expropriation process put into motion by the U.S. campaign to eliminate German expatriates from Guatemala's economy.

A CONSISTENT PATTERN

Although there was substantial variation among the countries involved in the deportation program, there are also a number of indications that the pattern described was widespread. The United States increasingly sought to intern Germans not because they were deemed politically dangerous but because they ran successful businesses; it pressured Latin American governments to deport those persons and to expropriate their property; and Latin American leaders eventually yielded to and exceeded U.S. demands, turning them to their own private or national purposes.

Expropriations were most extensive in the countries that most readily supplied Germans for internment in the United States. In Panama, the seizure of German property was complete by 1945, when U.S. officials could report that "there is not a single known Axis enterprise in operation in Panama."[107]

Haiti was the first country to order the forced liquidation of all property owned by Axis nationals (chiefly Germans) on the Proclaimed List. The Haitian National Bank confiscated all German assets and disposed of them in the following manner: 5 percent went for administrative costs; 10 percent, for the costs of internment of Axis nationals; and the remaining 85 percent, to pay rents, taxes, and debts owed by the businesses seized along with a monthly stipend for living expenses for their owners – consuming 100 percent of the funds.[108] By February 1944, all German property had been made "an integral part of the property of the Haitian state"[109] – and thus, in time-honored fashion, the personal property of the authoritarian president, Elie Lescot, who routinely helped himself to government funds through his vest-pocket control of the Haitian budget.[110]

In El Salvador, exceptionally among Central American countries, although German property was controlled and administered by the government, there was no expropriation. Despite strong pressures from the U.S. Embassy, President Martínez resisted taking such a step for the same length of time that Ubico held out in Guatemala. He argued that the Salvadoran constitution's guarantee of the inviolability of property forbade forced sales, and the Salvadoran oligarchy was not eager to see a precedent established for the expropriation of large plantations. In 1944, when the Martínez government began to consider new laws to get around the constitutional protection of private property, it was overthrown by a popular uprising and the matter was dropped.[111]

The countries that did not participate in the deportation program because they were less susceptible to U.S. pressure were also better able to resist the demands for far-reaching expropriation policies. Mexico took a number of practical steps to control Axis capital, freezing German assets, prohibiting trade with the Axis countries, taking administrative control of fifty-six German coffee plantations and transferring assets from German-owned banks and commercial houses to blocked accounts in the Bank of Mexico. A regional survey of German economic interests conducted for the Foreign Trade Office of the *Auslandsorganisation* in November 1942 reported that in contrast to Central American and Caribbean countries, government control and administration of German properties in Mexico "has partly worked as a protection against North American attacks; meanwhile the German managers continue to work in reduced capacities under the administrators."[112] Allowing for a certain amount of hyperbole in the term "attacks," this was an accurate assessment.

Looking beyond the individual countries to broader U.S. policy, it is clear that by mid-1943, U.S. economic warfare in Latin America had taken on a decidedly long-term character. Under the "Axis Replacement Program," Washington now encouraged all Latin American governments to expropriate the most important German firms and put them up for sale. Officially, the goal was to replace German ownership with local ownership, "to deny to

Germany the economic bases of future aggression."[113] This was not an idle fear, of course; Germany had started two world wars and might be expected to try to draw on overseas assets to start a third. As one of the few studies of U.S. economic warfare in Latin America put it, "U.S. economic interests converged with national security concerns to dictate the elimination of a strong rival in hemispheric markets."[114]

In practice, U.S. officials acknowledged that the only adequate source of capital, technical skill, and specialized supplies to replace German sources was the United States. In a directive to U.S. embassies, Acheson urged the "avoidance of the participation in the ownership (as distinguished from financing) by United States private capital. This policy," he wrote, "is, of course, based upon the theory that extensive participation by United States private capital will expose this Government to the charge that wartime controls are being utilized to foster economic penetration in the other American republics." He continued:

It is recognized, however, that this policy cannot be applied rigidly and that participation by United States private capital may in many instances be necessary and desirable in order that managerial and technical assistance may be obtained . . . the Department's policy will necessarily be flexible and will be applied on a case by case basis.[115]

In a similarly worded document, Acheson noted that "implementation of economic warfare measures at the present time requires, to a large extent, the use of United States companies."[116] Acheson sent a questionnaire to U.S. missions in the region seeking information on potential takeover targets that made it clear U.S. companies would participate, at least in a managerial role, in the new firms.[117] U.S. officials directly involved in seeking corporate participation in the Replacement Program were less concerned with keeping a low profile; they believed the program was "designed to replace German economic interests in these republics with qualified American industries."[118] They hastened to seek air travel priorities for U.S. corporate leaders to fly to Latin America to assist in the replacement effort. In a further gesture of extraterritorial reach, U.S. diplomats reviewed and authorized – or rejected – applications from Latin American nationals to purchase properties ostensibly in the custody of Latin American governments.[119]

Many Latin Americans were wary of this undertaking. The British Foreign Office, observing the process with some distaste and with concern over its own diminishing role in the region, noted in May 1944 that Latin American governments had been reluctant participants in U.S. anti-German strategy all along because of the "economic and political preponderance of the United States" which created "a feeling of apprehension and a desire to seek reassurance elsewhere" against domination by the "Colossus of the North."[120] The new U.S. ambassador to Colombia, John Wiley, confirmed these misgivings at the end of the war, when he called for "honest-to-God Americans" to represent U.S. firms in Colombia and wrote, "Now that we are eliminating Axis influences, chiefly German, in Colombia, we should not leave a vacuum. We should replace Axis penetration with American penetration."[121]

U.S. companies were already the natural beneficiaries of economic warfare in the region in several ways. Blacklisting had ruined many of their German competitors through the Proclaimed List. When IG Farben's U.S. subsidiaries, General Aniline and Film Company and General Dyestuffs Corporation, were taken over by the Alien Property Custodian, U.S. chemical companies quickly replaced them in Latin America by marketing virtually the same products. This new effort to replace German firms throughout the region with "American" firms, while theoretically based on local ownership, was executed in such a fashion as to benefit U.S. manufacturers rather than the development of Latin American economies. Representatives of U.S. corporations tapped as experts and managers refused to consider creating or increasing local manufacturing operations but sought instead to increase sales opportunities for their own products. The result in one key sector in which German firms had been dominant was an "unprecedented expansion" by U.S. chemical companies throughout the hemisphere after the war. One study of the Axis Replacement Program judged it to have been "hastily designed, poorly organized, and ultimately disastrous" because of the "blatantly self-interested attitudes of the business elements" recruited to carry it out. Acheson's concerns over negative publicity were confirmed, as the U.S. businesspeople put in charge of the expropriated companies sought profits for their own firms instead of investment for local development and thereby "quickly managed to arouse nationalist resentment in the countries purportedly benefiting from this aid."[122]

To precisely what extent the desire to diminish the German economic presence in Latin America led directly to cases of individuals deported and interned in the United States is impossible to quantify. Nor can we easily divide the deportees into those selected by U.S. officials to eliminate trade rivals and those expelled at the initiative of Latin American governments eager to seize their assets. Despite the inter-American conflict surrounding the deportation program, sometimes the two converged. Nonetheless it is clear that such factors were important, probably even more important in the later years of the war, than were security concerns about potential subversives.

This was the assessment of Justice Department investigator Raymond Ickes, who saw the inner workings of the deportation program in every country that sent Germans to the United States. Ickes concluded that aside from a very few security-related cases, the most common reason behind the deportations was that the individual deportees had "property – real property, land – that was attractive. This was the easiest way to get it."[123]

This seemed to be true as well in the only Latin American country that turned the anti-Axis measures into a broad-based attack on its Japanese community. From his vantage point in the U.S. Embassy in Peru, John Emmerson, the only Japanese speaker on the diplomatic staff, participated as an often conscience-stricken accomplice to Peru's expulsion of nearly two thousand members of the Japanese community, who were interned in the United States during the war. Emmerson wrote in his memoirs that he never found any evidence of subversive activity by the Japanese Peru was so eager to deport.[124] Instead, he wrote,

To the Peruvians, the war was a faraway fire. Not directly involved, although pro-Allies in sentiment, they set about to enjoy the advantages, and these included war on the Axis economic stake. The measures taken against Axis nationals . . . were welcomed for their destruction of unwanted competition.[125]

The shift from fears of subversion to economic concerns as the grounds for internment was an open secret among officials at higher levels of government. After the Justice Department began releasing on parole some of the internees from Latin America against whom there was no evidence of dangerousness, the State Department protested that such releases were damaging its ability to persuade Latin American governments to continue to pursue Germans who were not Nazis but were of commercial importance. After discussions between the Justice Department and Treasury and State Department officials, and under pressure from Dean Acheson, Attorney General Francis Biddle told Acheson in February 1944 that the State Department view would prevail:

I am advised that those internees who enjoyed the most important financial and commercial positions in Latin America, and who are on your Proclaimed List, have been continued in internment or ordered interned pursuant to the representations made by your Department and members of the [inter-Departmental] Committee [on the Proclaimed List] pointing out the adverse effect of their internment at large upon our economic policies in Latin America.[126]

Indeed, none of the important German property owners mentioned in this chapter – no matter how weak or utterly absent the evidence against them – was released from internment until after the war was over.[127] Instead, they remained in the camps, alongside a thousand other Germans from Latin America who had refused during the war to be repatriated to the Third Reich.

8

Repatriation

"We prevailed upon some of the other American republics to stop it, to prevent its recurrence, and to take steps to invalidate documents already issued."
–State Department summary of its efforts to block the influx of Jewish refugees bearing Latin American passports[1]

"Patience."
–Special Division Assistant Chief Albert E. Clattenburg in May 1944, answering appeals to revive prisoner exchanges that could free Jews from Bergen-Belsen[2]

Göppingen, Germany, April 1945. Gerardo Arturo Bohnenberger, born in Guatemala to German immigrants and now back in the land of his ancestors, takes a leave from his office job in a Stuttgart ironworks to go bury his father. Otto Retting Bohnenberger had been seized along with his son and deported from their home in Quetzaltenango to internment in the United States. From Camp Kenedy, they were repatriated to Göppingen, the town of Otto's youth. While 22-year-old Gerardo was away at the factory, Otto was killed in an Allied air raid.

Thus ended the life of one German expatriate who responded from distant residence in Latin America to the Nazis' call for transnational allegiance to the Fatherland. Although Gerardo will not acknowledge it today, his father joined the Party in 1937, and apparently used his position as president of the board of directors of the German school in Quetzaltenango to push for thorough nazification of the curriculum.[3] This kind of act never threatened the security of the Western Hemisphere. But it did suggest that the elder Bohnenberger's primary loyalty lay with the old country, and it did contribute to the fears of U.S. and Guatemalan officials that Germans were not to be trusted. Those fears produced the deportation program that ultimately put the repatriates in harm's way.

When the war was over, Gerardo found work at an uncle's hardware store in Hamburg, but he longed to return to his real home. "Life there was horrible for a Guatemalan.... One remains a stranger. They treat you like this," he says today, pushing out his palms to indicate standoffishness. "I could never warm up to anyone in Germany, never.... I was there for twelve years, and they never accepted me, the Germans."[4] Returning to Guatemala in the 1950s and finding nothing left of his family's business, he made a career selling Sherwin-Williams paints. *"Ya pasó todo,"* he sighs. All that's in the past.

TOWARD REPATRIATION

The repatriation program undertaken by the United States, like those of deportation, internment, and expropriation, began as a routine wartime measure that was flawed by an inaccurate reading of the threatening nature of the Germans from Latin America. Most of those involved were not subversives, but U.S. policy was made as if they were. This led, as it did in the other operations, to inter-American disputes in which the United States placed a higher priority upon combating an apparent external challenge to the Western Hemisphere than upon respecting agreements made with its less powerful neighbors. The exaggeration of the Nazi menace in the region also contributed, in a bitter irony, to the failed opportunity to rescue victims of Nazi crimes in Europe.

The U.S. government began the roundup of Germans in Latin America in the first months of 1942 under the assumption that they would be quickly repatriated to Germany, where they could no longer pose a threat to the Western Hemisphere. There was a much smaller, routine repatriation under way to send home the German diplomats and their families, known as "officials," from countries that had broken relations with the Axis, in exchange for their counterparts from shuttered diplomatic posts in German-held Europe. The most obvious course of action was to include the "nonofficial" Germans aboard the ship that was taking the diplomats home.

FIRST PRESIDENTIAL AUTHORIZATION

Breckinridge Long's Special Division was in charge of the repatriation arrangements, and his subordinates set to work seeking transportation to send the first batch of seven hundred Germans to Lisbon and bring back U.S. citizens trapped in Europe. The first in a series of obstacles arose when the War Department refused to part with any ships urgently needed for conducting the war. This forced Long, for the first time, to seek the approval of President Roosevelt for the deportation-repatriation effort.

The State Department had not troubled the president before about the routine matter of repatriating diplomats, nor about the expulsion of dangerous Axis nationals from Latin America. Roosevelt had enough on his mind. But to break the impasse over shipping, on January 28, 1942, Long spoke with FDR about the need for vessels that could effect the repatriation voyage. "I explained the whole situation," Long wrote afterward, noting that he had described not only the necessity of shipping out Axis diplomats but of "the bringing to the United States of undesirable, untrustworthy aliens in those countries for internment in the United States." After listening to Long's presentation, Roosevelt authorized him to present a request for shipping to the "appropriate authorities" in the president's name.[5]

The State Department eventually chartered the neutral Swedish passenger liner *Drottningholm* and organized two exchange voyages, the first departing New York for Lisbon on May 7, 1942, and the second departing New York on June 3.[6] It carried 932 Germans to Europe and returned with six hundred citizens of the Americas.[7]

In the German Foreign Ministry (*Auswärtiges Amt* or AA), officials involved in the exchange arrangements realized that they were confronted with a problem. They, too, wished to send American citizens home, at least those judged to be "predominantly enemies of Germany, and who are conducting espionage or anti-German propaganda here."[8] But even more than the U.S. government, Germany placed special importance on bringing home German citizens from abroad, because of an ideological commitment to reuniting members of the *Volk*, and because of an acute labor shortage. As AA officials watched reports come in showing steadily increasing numbers of Germans from Latin America going into internment camps in the United States, they knew they would need bargaining chips to get them out, so they considered the option of the mass internment of Americans in response. But the numbers were not in Germany's favor. Reports came back from the territories under Nazi occupation saying that there were no Americans to arrest.[9] As Erich Albrecht of the AA's Legal Department pointed out to Foreign Minister Joachim von Ribbentrop, since there were 300,000 German citizens in the United States and only 9,000 U.S. citizens in Germany and territories occupied by Germany, the United States would win any hostage-taking contest.[10]

Determined to round up more bodies for exchange, the foreign ministry asked the Gestapo to arrest all available citizens of the Latin American countries that had cooperated with the U.S. deportation program.[11] But the imbalance was so great, the AA began to cast about for alternative ways of bringing home German internees from abroad. That search would lead to the initiative to trade Jews for German expatriates – a project that should have been feasible but was doomed to failure by misplaced U.S. security concerns.

BRITANNIA RULES THE WAVES

Just as British propaganda had stoked fears of the German presence in Latin America before the war, now prodding from British intelligence slowed down the exchange process and encouraged U.S. intelligence agencies to take a hard line against the repatriation of many of the Germans who wished to return.

The British Embassy had been consulted on repatriation as a matter of course, since repatriation vessels would have to pass through war zones patrolled by the Royal Navy. The British immediately raised objections to several categories of German repatriates. Why were the Americans preparing to send trained seamen, mechanics, radio operators, machinists, and engineers where they could aid the German war effort? The British, on the front lines in the European war, argued vehemently that the Germans should be held in the United States for the duration.[12]

Foreign Minister Anthony Eden claimed that the British objected only to Germans and Italians who had "technical qualifications which would render them of particular service to the enemy war effort or were espionage or sabotage agents of a key character." Then came the catch-22: if any Axis nationals were willing to return to Europe and their governments were interested in receiving them, that was de facto evidence that they were secret agents. "His Majesty's Government could not, therefore, but conclude that such Germans and Italians as were proposed for repatriation were in almost all cases persons whom the Axis governments desired to see at home," Eden told the United States.[13] Such a broad definition of who might render "particular service to the enemy war effort" threatened to remove any possibility of an exchange, since it meant the only permissible candidates for repatriation were those who did not wish to return. This made the problem of selecting Germans for repatriation "almost insoluble," complained a Special Division official.[14]

By the summer of 1942, the dispute was resolved in favor of the British position, but with somewhat narrower criteria for eliminating candidates for repatriation that did permit an exchange to go forward. U.S. officials agreed to institute a complex screening process of their own, in which all interested agencies – the FBI, Office of Naval Intelligence, Military Intelligence Division, and the Justice Department's Alien Enemy Control Unit, in addition to British intelligence – were given the opportunity to vet each list of potential repatriates before they were shipped out. Both British and U.S. intelligence objections focused on the potential military usefulness of the deportees, and they erred on the side of caution. The British still pushed for a broader interpretation of dangerousness, which was fully consistent with their own approach at home. Since 1940, the British government had interned thousands of Jewish refugees who had entered the country with German or Austrian passports.[15]

Sharing the attitude of the British, the U.S. intelligence agencies raised objections to between 30 percent and 40 percent of all persons proposed by the State Department for repatriation. Breckinridge Long thought some of the reasons to be "very valid, but a good many of them are indefinite reasons such as 'pro-Nazi,' 'suspected of espionage,' etc."[16] Entire occupational categories were ineligible, not only trained sailors and engineers, but farmers and those about whom the intelligence agencies felt they had insufficient information.[17] Nevertheless, those not cleared by the intelligence agencies were interned.

WASHINGTON WAIVES THE RULES

Deciding to intern many of the Germans who thought that their stay in the United States was merely a stopover presented a new problem: U.S. officials had signed agreements with several South American countries promising not to delay the return of Germans delivered under a repatriation arrangement. The State Department promised that Germans brought from Colombia would be "maintained here in protective custody . . . pending negotiations looking to an ultimate general exchange with the Axis powers."[18] Its minister in Quito, Boaz Long, signed an agreement stating that the Germans "will not be examined or detained by American or British authorities, but will be transported immediately on the exchange vessels from New York to Lisbon."[19] But the agreement that the Germans would be held only temporarily, made to satisfy Colombian and Ecuadorian law asserting sovereignty over their residents, was discarded when Washington joined the British in preventing Germans allegedly possessing war-related skills from returning to Europe. Summarizing the problem in mid-1942, Long's assistant Joseph C. Green acknowledged that the Germans had been brought "on the express assurance to the Colombian Government that they would be repatriated," and that "we violated our commitment to the Colombian Government" by detaining them. Likewise, "[w]e are pledged to effect the repatriation of all the Axis nationals from Ecuador without any exception." Green suggested asking the Colombians for their understanding that pilots and other skilled Germans should not be allowed to rejoin the war, but the Division of American Republics argued against sending such a message, "so long as the Colombians do not put up a howl to have something done about these people."[20]

Ecuador did protest, not only because the violation of the agreement was another example of old-fashioned unilateralism on the part of the United States, but also because Germany was retaliating by withholding Ecuadorian citizens from any exchange. Thus Ecuadorian civilians paid the price of a decision made in Washington.[21] The United States explained that "military exigencies" had superceded its agreement and asked for Ecuador's understanding.[22] Breckinridge Long noted that the neutral nations of South America "sent us Axis nationals only on the basis of our solemn promise to repatriate them. Their legal position in sending to an enemy belligerent country for internment aliens legally residing within their borders would be uncomfortable" and, moreover, their own citizens interned in retaliation by Germany were mostly members of prominent families.[23] Other countries, too, found that Germany was interning their nationals in retaliation for the deportation of Germans to the United States. They comprised a small number – five from Costa Rica, twenty-one from Guatemala, twelve from El Salvador, two from Haiti, and so on.[24] Still, reports from Europe said that some of them "were being given exceptionally bad treatment in internment camps."[25] The Special Division's Albert Clattenburg worried that a breakdown in the exchanges could spell the end of Latin American cooperation with U.S. security measures, as countries from Guatemala to Peru began to protest the fate of their nationals.[26]

With pressure from the Latin American governments on one side, and the British and the intelligence agencies pushing from the other, Long found the situation to be "like a pitchfork with me on the sharp end." Conceding the relative insignificance of the internees, he argued that most of the Axis nationals should be sent home: "[T]hey are much less dangerous to us in Germany than they are south of the Rio Grande," he believed.[27]

UNWANTED AMERICANS

After the initial two voyages of the *Drottningholm*, the State Department estimated that there were still three thousand U.S. nationals in Europe who wanted to come home.[28] Two more exchanges that summer brought the total to two thousand repatriated Germans and twelve hundred repatriated Americans.[29] The *Serpa Pinto* sailed from New York to Lisbon on July 3, and the *Drottningholm* returned to Sweden with a load of Germans on July 24.[30] But as U.S. and Latin American citizens began arriving, U.S. officials did not like what they saw. "The Americans have let it be known that they are not very satisfied with the quality of the human material they have received from Germany up to now," wrote an AA official.[31] Many were of German or Polish descent, and some could not speak English well. Attorney General Biddle found that the ship brought back "many undesirable people."[32] Other U.S. officials were disappointed that the Americans returning from Europe did not measure up to those held in China, who were "substantial persons who have represented important American business and commercial interests and a large number of missionaries."[33] Breckinridge Long agreed. "They are not quite the persons we thought would return to the United States," he wrote, noting that some of them were "destitute." He suggested, "considering the type of Americans we were receiving," that the exchanges be terminated.[34]

Nazi Germany provided the perfect excuse when it revoked the safe conduct for the third voyage of the *Drottningholm*, demanding that the ship sail not from New York but from New Orleans, in order to gain recognition for its expanded area of submarine warfare in the north Atlantic. Although this was a negotiable demand that was ultimately withdrawn, U.S. officials seized upon it to announce that Germany had violated the exchange agreement and was wholly to blame for a breakdown in the exchanges. "The original agreement was terminated by us after two shiploads had been exchanged," Secretary Hull told FDR in a message drafted by Long. "It was very apparent that the persons we were receiving were not such as to benefit our war effort. Consequently, the arrangement was terminated. Germany had broken the agreement by refusing safe conduct for the vessel to run between New York and Lisbon and we denounced the agreement on that basis."[35] In other words, the safe conduct issue was a convenient cover Washington used to halt the exchanges.

Back in Europe, U.S. citizens continued to try to find a way to come home. Jean Duras and her daughter in Krakow had been trying unsuccessfully to return to the United States since 1940 but were stymied by their expired passports; she wrote to the AA to beg to be included in the next exchange.[36] The widowed Herbert Gompertz, having landed places for himself and his children on the *Drottningholm* list, sold off their household possessions and packed up to leave, only to be left sitting on their suitcases. "My present condition is intolerable both for myself and for my children," Gompertz wrote. "Moreover I feel myself to be an American, *absolutely* wish to return to the USA and to raise my children in America."[37] Else Schulz appealed directly to Hitler in childlike German prose, writing in the third person, saying that her family members had all been taken back to America in the previous exchange and Else was left alone in Berlin "because of a mistake in spelling her name." She, too, asked to be permitted to join the next exchange. "She yearns very much for her homeland and asks you from deep in her heart for help. *Bitte, bitte.*"[38] To each writer, AA officials responded that they must await the outcome of the stalled negotiations with Washington.

SECOND PRESIDENTIAL AUTHORIZATION

The State Department had not completely abandoned repatriation efforts, however, and continued to negotiate with Germany via the Swiss with an eye to future exchanges. On August 15, Roosevelt sent this letter to his Secretary of State:

Dear Cordell:
    Are negotiations under way for the repatriation of further enemy aliens, particularly Germans, who are not members of the Diplomatic Corps?
    I believe that we should be very careful in repatriating any enemy aliens to Germany other than the Diplomatic Corps. My reason for saying this is that *all* German aliens in America are potential, if not actual, spies and the Americans in Germany are not. While I think it is tough on the Americans who must remain in

Germany throughout the war, I nevertheless think that Germany gets the best of the exchange.

> Very sincerely yours,
> Franklin D. Roosevelt[39]

FDR sent a carbon copy to J. Edgar Hoover, which suggests that it was the FBI director's complaints that had moved the president to raise the issue. Long took twelve days to compose a detailed response, which went to the president over Cordell Hull's signature.

Long's memo explained the dilemma. Nobody was interested in bringing back more impoverished Americans from Europe. However, if the United States violated the agreements with Latin American governments by ending all repatriations, it would become difficult, if not impossible, to get them to continue to cooperate by expelling more Germans. And that was unacceptable from a security standpoint. The Germans were "roaming more or less at liberty throughout areas in which they can do serious damage and from which they can send information detrimental to our cause," Long warned, but the Latin American governments would not send them to the United States without a guarantee that they would be repatriated. He proposed that the deportation and internment of Axis nationals from Latin America be continued, and that the Germans be repatriated only "if no other way remains of removing them from those countries." The president scrawled his approval: "OK – FDR."[40]

The president's order kept the deportation-internment program going, but the repatriations ceased. By that time, dissatisfaction with the returning Americans and the intelligence agencies' vigilance over potential German repatriates had effectively shut down the exchanges; there would be no more repatriations for a year and a half, until the two voyages of the *Gripsholm* in February and May 1944.[41]

REPATRIATING THE "INHERENTLY HARMLESS"

With the vetting process organized and accepted by all parties, in November 1942 the State Department circulated a memorandum to its posts throughout Latin America summarizing the changes in policy to date. The memo made clear that by the time the ships sailed, U.S. policy had come full circle, from its original intention of repatriating "dangerous" Germans to repatriating the innocent. In order to deny useful persons to the enemy, "It is particularly desirable that the repatriation of *inherently harmless* Axis nationals may be used to the greatest possible extent," the memo read.[42] Why "inherently harmless" Germans should be seized and interned in the first place was a question left unasked.

From the relative luxury of internment at the Greenbrier Hotel in White Sulfur Springs, West Virginia, Emil Prüfert could sense the change was taking place. The former *Landesgruppenleiter* of Colombia's Nazi Party had joined a group of German diplomats departing Buenaventura on the *Santa Lucia* in January 1942, expecting to return to the Fatherland to make himself useful in the struggle against the Allies. He was one of the first persons to whom the British raised objections.

While interned at the Greenbrier, Prüfert wrote several confidential letters and entrusted them to the former German chargé d'affaires in Washington, Hans Thomsen, before Thomsen sailed on the *Drottningholm*. Thomsen delivered them to the German Foreign Ministry, where they are held today in the archives. These candid reports by one of the leading Nazis in Latin America reveal no sign of distress at the loss of any mythical fifth column organization. Moreover, it was clear to the Nazis from the beginning, just as it became apparent to Justice Department officials over time, that the Germans being thrown out of Latin America included a broad range of people, many of them in no way connected to Nazism. In his letters, Prüfert complained that Germany would soon be receiving a shipment of unworthies:

Thus our border officials will have the pleasure of seeing a nice exhibition of native peoples from the jungles of Ecuador! It is regrettable, on what extraordinarily remarkable criteria the people from Ecuador, for example, were selected to be sent away. Among them can be found pure Indian women, each with her own bastards, who here in the hotel have from the beginning comported themselves à la jungle, and certainly have not done credit to the appearance of Germandom. A man with a long series of criminal convictions was sent back to Germany with his Indian woman, in spite of the fact that the man had only been let out of Germany on condition that he never come back! It would be a start if at least the attempt were made not to repatriate such elements.[43]

Without overdrawing the comparison, Prüfert's complaint calls to mind U.S. officials' distaste at the "quality" of the Americans brought back on the *Drottningholm*. In both cases, legal citizenship was but one criterion by which officials determined who qualified as a true German or a true American. The Nazis' racial criteria for membership in the national community were more explicit, but for both groups of repatriates, it was clear that, in the eyes of some, a passport was an insufficient claim to national membership for those who failed to meet quality standards.

THE VOLUNTEERS LEFT BEHIND

When the intelligence agencies presented their lists of unacceptable candidates for repatriation, since the rejected men usually had family members with them, the net result of the vetting process was to eliminate a large number of potential repatriates. These internees and their families were left sitting out the war in U.S. camps when they wished to return to Germany – although their usefulness to the German war effort had been greatly overstated.

They made up one part of an unused pool of candidates for an exchange. The other part consisted of a large number of German volunteers who asked to be repatriated from their residences in Latin America but were left behind.

When word spread that U.S. ships were coming to Latin American ports to take Germans to the United States en route to Germany, some expatriates approached the Spanish or Swiss diplomats representing German interests in Latin American countries that had broken relations with the Axis and asked to be included.

Who were these volunteers? While no dedicated anti-Nazi would have been willing to resettle in the Third Reich, voluntary repatriation was not necessarily a sign of fervent political commitment to Nazism, or of a desire to fight in the war. Many expatriates simply weighed the alternatives, finding themselves broke and unemployed, blacklisted or with businesses seized or ruined by the breakdown in international trade, while they would be welcome in Germany where there was a serious labor shortage. Although some spoke of a desire to fight for their country, one is often left guessing about the motivation for individual actions. Alfredo Behrens, a 17-year-old Guatemalan whose German father had died in 1936, volunteered for "repatriation" to a Germany he had never seen. Interned instead in the United States, he was released on parole in 1944, joined the U.S. Army, and fought in the Pacific. This series of events suggests a youthful search for direction rather than any strong commitment to Nazism – especially since Behrens belonged to no political organizations in Guatemala except the German sports club.[44]

Whether because of material difficulties, personal considerations, or ideological fervor, many Germans wanted to return home, despite the absence of an organized effort to recruit them. It is not possible to produce a precise number of these volunteers, because lists were not compiled in every country or, if they were, some no longer exist. But the surviving records indicate substantial numbers. Of 165 German men who requested repatriation from Guatemala in August 1942, only 50 were taken in the course of the war. Counting family members, the 115 left behind probably represented close to 400 volunteers who could have been used in an exchange.[45] State Department officials came up with a figure of 777 Germans in Guatemala not brought to the United States who wished to be repatriated that summer.[46] Six hundred Germans in Colombia, not included in the deportations arranged by the United States, unsuccessfully asked the German government in March 1942 to organize their transportation back to Europe "quickly, in view of the increase every moment of present economic difficulties."[47] Four hundred to six hundred Germans in Venezuela volunteered to return because they were out of work.[48] But none of the volunteers were a priority for the State Department, which was orchestrating the expulsion of Germans on its list of "dangerous alien enemies" instead.[49]

These figures alone suggest that the total unused pool of voluntary repatriates from the fifteen Latin American countries participating in the U.S. deportation program easily ran into the thousands. To that total we may add the first-mentioned unused pool of potential volunteers: those taken willingly or otherwise from Latin America and held in U.S. internment, although they were prepared to return to Germany. After the last repatriation voyage of summer 1942, they numbered 561 persons; that number was swelled by subsequent shipments of Germans from Latin America who joined them in the U.S. camps.[50] Both pools together represent a vast, unused resource for a potential exchange involving the rescue of Jews from Nazi concentration camps that, as we shall see, was blocked by the United States.

THE VOLUNTEERS IN INTERNMENT

U.S. officials determined in late 1942 not to send anyone to Germany who did not wish to go.[51] Internees were given a form to sign, or sometimes asked by their camp commander, whether they agreed to be repatriated to Germany. If they agreed, they were considered to have volunteered for repatriation.

Some of them, like Emil Prüfert, were eager and impatient to go. Others made the decision after realizing that the bleak alternative was an indefinite stay behind barbed wire. "I said yes," recalled Juan Niemann, deported from Guatemala to Texas, "because liberty is better than prison.... We didn't know what state Germany would be in – we thought the war would be over soon."[52] Walter Sommer, expelled from Colombia, considered staying in the camp, but then thought "why shouldn't I go visit my old mother?"[53] Gotthold Busch-Beckemeyer, an employee of Standard Oil who had been a resident of Chile since 1914 and a Chilean citizen since 1920, was picked up while on business in Haiti and deported for internment in the United States. When Camp Kenedy authorities asked him whether he would volunteer for repatriation to Germany, the following exchange ensued:

Q: Do you desire that you be repatriated to Germany?
A: I thought not to go back. I do not know why I go back, and I like to go back to Chile. [...]
Q: If you are unable to return to Chile or some other South American country, had you rather remain in detention, or be repatriated to Germany?
A: Then I had better go back to Germany before I would stay in the camp. If I can't get freedom in the United States, then I would go.
Q: You understand, do you not, that you have made a statement that if you are unable to return to a country in Central or South America, that you prefer to be repatriated to Germany than remain in detention in the United States. Is that right?
A: No. I didn't understand it properly what it meant. You see, my idea is if I could go back to Chile, if I could get it worked through the Minister or any Chilean business, so suddenly if I can get freedom in the United States, I look out for work. If I can't get it here, then suddenly I go back to Germany, because I get freedom. My opinion is

always I want to get freedom, never mind where. At the last I would go to Germany, but if I could get freedom here or at Chile or somewhere else – if I could get freedom here, I go to work here and do something. I am Chilean. I like Chile. That's the reason the last time I stayed there. I like to get freedom. That's the most important for me.[54]

Busch-Beckmeyer was sent to Germany in January 1945.[55] His statement, although hardly that of a fervent admirer of fascism, was clearly taken as consent to be repatriated, and such consent was required – at least in principle – before any internee would be placed aboard an exchange vessel. This policy was worked out in the fall of 1942; as late as September 1942, Breckinridge Long was still hedging on whether or not Jews and other internees unwilling to go to the Third Reich could be sent there against their wishes. When a subordinate prepared a stack of memos promising not to deport certain Jewish internees, Long had them cancelled.[56] Edward Ennis of the Justice Department spoke out strongly against repatriating the "very considerable number" of political and religious refugees brought from Latin America. "It would be rather shocking to send them back to the Nazis," Ennis argued, adding, "I should be surprised if every one of those refugees were a Nazi agent."[57] The records suggest that Justice prevailed, and none of the Jewish internees were repatriated against their will.[58]

THE OATH NOT TO SERVE

One concern U.S. officials could set aside was the possibility that repatriated Germans might add significantly to the armed strength of the enemy. Since their numbers were small, as Breckinridge Long put it, "they would not muster a corporals guard for the army or a great deal of intelligence for the governments' cause."[59] Furthermore, the German and U.S. governments both required all male candidates for repatriation between 16 and 50 years of age to sign the following statement:

I solemnly bind myself under obligation of oath not to bear arms for the duration of the present war.[60]

Gunter Beckmann, deported from Ecuador, remembered someone telling him that if he signed the oath and was then caught in uniform, he would be shot – the same reason U.S. officials gave for not permitting repatriated Americans to join the armed forces.[61] American citizens embarking aboard the *Gripsholm* in Lisbon to return home under the exchange read a posted NOTICE TO ALL MALE REPATRIATES reminding them of the seriousness of the pledge and telling them to inform their draft boards "since capture by the enemy of such persons as combatants may result in most serious penalties."[62] (When the State Department learned that one of the repatriated U.S. citizens did wind up in the army and was stationed overseas, it quickly got him reassigned to a noncombatant unit in New Jersey.)[63]

Perhaps surprisingly, given Nazi Germany's routine violations of national and international laws and the rules of war, Hitler's government also respected the oath. The German Foreign Ministry informed military authorities that repatriates who took the oath could not be inducted.[64] Wilhelm Canaris, head of the *Abwehr* (military intelligence), agreed that "because of the large number of German internees in enemy hands, the overwhelming interest lies in a strict observance of the exchange agreement by the German side.[65] When the SS requested that exceptions be made so that some volunteers from the United States could join units fighting in the East, the foreign ministry's response was adamant: "This oath includes every front and every enemy." At most, volunteers might be directed to the postal system or the railways, or other civil service.[66] A pilot who had flown for SEDTA in Ecuador was denied permission to serve in the *Luftwaffe*, although he was allowed to work as a civilian flight instructor.[67]

In interviews, repatriates Hans Kolter, Hugo Droege, Carlos Gehlert, and Walter Maul all said that this policy was carried out in practice, at least when officials knew they had signed. "The Germans respected it one hundred percent – if you wanted them to," recalled Maul, 18 years old when deported from Guatemala to the United States and of ideal fighting age when repatriated to Germany. "I had friends who joined the army despite having signed the oath. Think of it: I arrive as a nineteen-year-old man to a town in Germany, surrounded by women and children, everyone else is at the front or dead. Of course, as a man, I felt bad. Many decided to go. I also volunteered, but I was rejected. The army official knew about my oath and respected it."[68] Walter Sommer of Colombia put up with the social pressure but never found it easy. "Nobody could understand it. I was a black sheep. They couldn't tell whom I was for, Germany or what, since I had to remain out of the conflict."[69] Franz Spillman of Ecuador asked the foreign ministry for a waiver, but the AA's response, again, was firm: having signed an oath not to bear arms, he could not serve in uniform.[70] It appears that any repatriates who did join the army could do so only by concealing their oaths from military authorities.

Some of the repatriates were pleased to be back in Germany and found ways to serve what they never stopped considering as their country. Two dozen of the repatriates from Guatemala, mostly Party members, kept in touch after repatriation by sending notes to Georg Brückner, who circulated their messages in a newsletter. Some of the items reveal a clear ideological stance, at least on the part of the editor, as in these extracts from an issue in May 1944: "Willy Rossbach...reports that he is moving to the sunny South in the service of the Reich, near Milan. We congratulate him and hope that the USA-Bolsheviks don't give him a hard time with their bombs....Kurt Müller was killed, he was decorated with the Iron Cross...Klaus Brückner [the editor's son] is preparing to celebrate his first birthday tomorrow. He's come a little too late for the Western front. Maybe he'll go to the front in the next war."[71]

For some deportees, it was only once they were repatriated that they got their first true picture of Nazi Germany. Hans Kolter, who had joined the Party and especially enjoyed demonstrating his athletic prowess at the German sports club in Guatemala City, remembered the shock of arriving in Berlin and seeing how much the war and the secret police had ground down the city's spirits. Gunter Beckmann got a job translating foreign newspaper articles for the Gestapo about the construction of new airfields and war-related production in the Allied countries. He could soon tell from his access to foreign news coverage that the war would be lost.[72]

Walter Maul recalled a similar revelation upon seeing firsthand what Hitler's dreams had wrought in Germany. Opting for repatriation in February 1944, he was taken from Texas to New York by train. From his compartment window he watched "America working at full speed – factories going day and night producing armaments." From the deck of the *Gripsholm*, he saw a convoy of three hundred ships bound for Africa. The contrast with Germany was staggering. He arrived in Saarbrücken to be greeted by air raid sirens signaling the daily bombing raid; the city was already 60 percent destroyed. His train ride along the Rhine passed through ruined cities, and he grew more grim seeing the devastated industrial zone of the Ruhr valley: "I told myself there was no way this country could win the war." After a couple of months in Bochum, he was summoned for an interrogation by the German security police, and was struck by how different it was from his interview at Camp Kenedy. "The Americans said 'Sit down, Walter, let's have a chat, you want a coffee? You want a highball?' and I compared that to the treatment I got from the *Sicherheitspolizei*: waiting in a cold, lugubrious room for an hour, then this man asking me all kinds of questions. I had the imprudence to speak my mind – 'You know, Germany is in a very difficult situation because America is so strong.' I don't know if his answer was a threat or a favor, but he said 'You should be careful with what you say because here in Germany you can't speak so openly.'"[73]

Otto Stetzelberg of Peru also did not conceal his views from the Gestapo when he provided them with a written account of his time in internment in the United States. He described the conditions at Camp Kenedy as "excellent" and noted that "the American people are not yet weary of war, since the average man there absolutely does not suffer under war conditions." Stetzelberg also described his captors as courteous and fair. When he was embarking on the exchange ship in February 1944, he reported, an FBI officer gave him these parting words: "'Please tell them over there how it went for you here. Don't make it worse or better. Tell the truth, and we hope that when this war is over we can become old friends again. Have a nice trip.'"[74]

Even expatriates who had joined the AO sometimes sounded disappointed when their visions of the New Germany were replaced by the reality of life in the Third Reich. Returning to Germany after 21 years in Guatemala, Werner Robert Asmus found that whatever enthusiasm he might have had for a transnational German *Volksgemeinschaft* in the heady days of the 1930s could no longer sustain him in 1944. "I stand here completely alone, and feel as if in a foreign country," he wrote to the *Lateinamerikanischer Verein*, asking for financial assistance.[75]

But the dominant experience for the repatriates was simple survival in a country at war. Like civilians around the world, they were faced with a series of challenges, from food shortages to the aerial attacks that did not discriminate among them. Karl Heinrich Linde, a Party member from Guatemala, was killed with his whole family in the firebombing of Hamburg.[76] Enrique Ascoli, deported from Nicaragua, also died in an Allied air raid, as did Otto Bohnenberger, mentioned in the opening of this chapter.[77]

Even those who survived were not immune from its effects. In Hanover, where Hans Joachim Schaer of Costa Rica remembered that "the last years of the war in Germany were hell ... the bombardments were just day and night, day and night."[78] George Schonberger and his wife Dora Rosero Aguirre de Schonberger were repatriated after deportation from Ecuador along with their two small children. They spent the last year of the war in Jena under constant bombardment. "We had to spend long hours taking refuge in the basements to be free of the antiaircraft fire," Dora told the editors of an Ecuadorian newspaper after the war. "When the attacking forces dropped incendiary bombs, we had to leave the basements quickly, as their atmosphere became hellishly hot. More than once my clothing caught fire." Their house was destroyed in an intense bombardment ten minutes after they fled for safety.[79] Hugo Droege wound up tending a hundred dairy cows on an estate in Mecklenburg in the eastern part of Germany that came under Soviet occupation. Retreating German troops spent the night on the property and told him, "For God's sake, everyone get out before the Russians come." But Droege stayed behind to look after the cows. He buried the silverware and the hunting rifles and went about his business. "I said to myself, nothing can happen to me, I have my papers in order, I don't know how to shoot, and somebody has to stay here." There were three weeks of anarchy after the first Russian troops arrived: "I would not like to live through those three weeks again."[80]

INVOLUNTARY REPATRIATES?

Some of the Germans from Latin America who wound up in Germany as part of the exchanges later claimed that they were sent against their will. "They didn't ask," said Gerardo Bohnenberger. "They grabbed us and sent us to Germany."[81] Hugo Droege said that he refused to be repatriated and was shipped out anyway. "There were some real Nazis who did want to go to Germany, but I didn't," Droege recounted. "There were eighteen of

27. February, 1944. German families, wearing identification tags, prepare to board the *Gripsholm* for repatriation to Germany. Credit: RG59-RAG-5-3, National Archives.

us from Guatemala who didn't want to go to Germany but were forced to. We all said 'not to Germany, not to Germany,' and we were taken on the *Gripsholm* to Lisbon."[82]

It is possible, of course, that these remembered accounts have been carefully or unconsciously altered, that these men now wish to show that they so abhorred Nazi Germany they would never have consented to go there. No antifascist would have gone willingly to the Third Reich in 1942 or 1944. U.S. officials carefully tried to ensure that only voluntary repatriates were included in the exchanges. Can we dismiss these recollections as convenient fictions?

Not so easily. Droege, at least, never denied his sentiments in favor of Germany during the war. "Our sympathies were naturally with Germany, it's where we came from," he said. "It's the worst ones who tell you today 'I

28. Embarking on the *Gripsholm*. Credit: RG59-RAG-5-4, National Archives.

never had anything to do with it, I was always against it and fought against it.' Those are the worst of all."[83] One need not have been a fervent Nazi to be willing to choose relocation to Germany instead of internment in a camp for the indefinite future.

Moreover, documentary evidence supports Droege's claim that he and several other internees were sent to Germany against their will. Twelve Germans whose names are on a list of Camp Kenedy inmates refusing repatriation are also on the master list of those repatriated; one of them was Hugo Droege.[84] In light of the contradictory lists, Droege's story becomes plausible.

AN UNUSED RESOURCE

While a few internees who did not wish to go back to Germany thus may have been involuntarily repatriated, a far larger number of Germans who stated their willingness to be repatriated were left in the camps because U.S. intelligence agencies or the British government objected to their return.

29. Credit: Official U.S. Navy Photograph. RG59-RAG-1-42935, National Archives.

In two ways, then, the dazzling image of the fifth column threat in Latin America helped ensure that thousands of Germans who were willing to be repatriated were left in Latin America or held back in internment. First, a misplaced focus on rooting out supposedly "dangerous enemy aliens" made U.S. and Latin American authorities seize the diverse collection of Germans on their lists rather than those who were willing to return. Second, many of those seized who were willing to be repatriated were not permitted to because the U.S. government judged them to be dangerous, usually on specious grounds.

If this was something more than an inconvenience to those Germans who remained in the camps or mired in poverty in Latin America for the duration of the war, it was arduous for the U.S. and Latin American citizens interned in Europe awaiting their release from much harsher circumstances. And it was to prove fatal for thousands of Jewish holders of Latin American documents, who were kept in special camps in Germany pending an unconsummated trade for the very German volunteers the United States refused to deliver.

BERGEN-BELSEN: MISSED OPPORTUNITY FOR RESCUE

The Nazi regime in Germany, driven by a messianic anti-Semitic ideology that was further radicalized in the crucible of war, had by the end of 1941 set itself the task of murdering all the Jews of Europe. Without ever losing sight of this ultimate goal, Nazi leaders did permit tactical variations in policy, sometimes slowing down the machinery of mass murder where important advantages might be gained. Jews in German-occupied Poland were sometimes kept alive – if only temporarily – to perform labor.[85] To keep the peace at home in response to angry protest, in 1943 the SS freed several hundred German Jews married to non-Jews after their spouses held a rare public demonstration in the Rosenstrasse in the heart of Berlin.[86]

Such events were exceptional. So, too, were the sporadic feelers from Nazi leaders interested in trading the lives of small numbers of Jews for some kind of benefit to themselves. Jewish organizations sought to arrange the ransom of groups of Jews through difficult, often indirect negotiations with their Nazi captors. SS leader Heinrich Himmler believed it might be possible to obtain foreign exchange or useful equipment, such as trucks, in exchange for releasing some Jews to the West; since he was convinced that Jews wielded an inordinate amount of influence over Western governments, he also hoped that negotiating with Jewish organizations might lead to a separate peace or some form of diplomatic advantage with the western Allies.[87]

In December 1942, after receiving permission from Hitler, Himmler ordered the SS to collect Jews with citizenship or family connections in the Americas "in a special camp. There they should work, to be sure, but under conditions such that they remain healthy and alive. These kinds of Jews are valuable hostages for us. I imagine a total of about 10,000 of them."[88] Over the next two months, partly at the instigation of foreign ministry officials involved in exchange negotiations to bring German internees from U.S. camps back to Germany, Himmler's idea was broadened into a proposal to trade these Jews for Germans held in Palestine and the United States. At the beginning of March 1943, with exchange negotiations stalled and no readily available source of large numbers of U.S. or Latin American nationals to trade for the Germans held by the United States, the AA asked the *Reichssicherheitshauptamt* (Reich Security Main Office or RSHA, of which the Gestapo and the Criminal Police were divisions) to set aside not 10,000 but 30,000 Jews with dual nationality for a possible exchange. The AA's instructions made clear that these people were only conditionally exempt from the killing process: "If the said exchange arrangement should not be realized, then the expulsion of these Jews [to death camps in the East] may still be carried out."[89]

The AA officials – Yvo Theiss, Gustav Sethe, Herbert Ruoff, and Erich Albrecht – working on the exchanges were in the *Rechtsabteilung* or Legal Department of the foreign ministry. In their efforts to use as many Jews as possible to exchange for Germans held abroad, AA officials sometimes worked for the exemption of specific individuals, lobbying an array of security agencies to prevent potential "exchange Jews" with documents indicating they held Latin American citizenship from being transported to ghettos or death camps.[90] They also directed that relatives of persons with claims to foreign citizenship should also be spared, to increase the exchange pool.[91] In this task they encountered both cooperation and obstructionism from different departments of the RSHA.[92] The division for "foreigners police" (Referat II B 4, later Referat IV F 4, *Ausländerpolizei*) was fairly receptive; its head, Rudolf Kröning, routinely authorized the setting aside of "exchange Jews" and objected only to the inclusion of individuals who had been involved in resistance activities.[93] But Adolf Eichmann's Referat IV B 4, responsible for Jewish affairs and home to the administrators of the Holocaust, was reluctant to let any Jews escape its grasp. Eichmann pushed for a strict interpretation of citizenship that would exclude all Jews with dubious papers from any special treatment. On several occasions, his department sabotaged or ignored Kröning's lists of approved participants, sending large numbers of potential exchange candidates to Auschwitz.[94] The contradiction in Nazi policy was not merely a function of rival departments but was contained within the person of Himmler himself, whose appointment as *Reichskommissar für die Festigung deutschen Volkstums* (Commissar for the Strengthening of the German People) explicitly made him responsible for promoting the return of Germans to the Reich, while his position as head of the SS and the German Police placed him in charge of the concentration camp system designed to exterminate the very people who might be used to bring Germans back home.[95]

Still, Eichmann could not single-handedly derail the entire exchange attempt backed by higher authorities, and thousands of Jews with connections to the West, most of them Polish or Dutch, were exempted from the transports to the killing centers and set aside for a future exchange in 1943 and 1944. Most of the persons thus collected were not bona fide citizens of Latin American countries but held documents indicating a promise of future permission to immigrate, so-called *promesas* issued by humane or bribe-seeking Latin American consuls. One AA list of thirty-nine "Nicaraguan" Jews collected for a possible exchange, for example, shows that they all had German or Polish surnames, all listed home addresses in Lemberg (Lvov), and each received a Nicaraguan passport from the Nicaraguan Consul General in New York between September 1940 and April 1941.[96] Thousands of such documents were smuggled into Poland by Jewish relief organizations.[97]

All sides knew that these documents were not genuine. The consuls who issued them knew that they were false. The people who bought them from the consuls or on the black market knew it as well. So did the Gestapo, which had a special name for the *promesas: Gefälligkeitspässe* – courtesy passes.[98] Nevertheless, Himmler and the AA persuaded Kröning's department to wink at the false documents in order to build up a pool of candidates for an exchange. The Gestapo even trafficked in *promesas* itself; when papers arrived for Jews who were already dead, Gestapo agents confiscated and resold them at a profit to other Jews, who then came under their protection.[99]

To house these Jews, the German government designated a section of Bergen-Belsen a "Residence Camp" (*Aufenthaltslager*), rather than a "Civilian Internment Camp," because the latter would have been subject to international inspection under the Geneva Convention. Even without such inspection, living conditions there were comparatively tolerable – at first. When British troops liberated the camp at the end of the war, they were shocked by the ghastly scenes of starvation and epidemic, and the name "Bergen-Belsen" came to symbolize the inferno of suffering and mass death in the concentration camps. But these circumstances were relatively new, the product of a change in policy and camp administration in the fall and winter of 1944–5. Until then, the Aufenthaltslager at Bergen-Belsen was an exception within the murderous camp system: a holding facility with far less mistreatment than the typical concentration camp.

Survivors later recounted their surprise when, in July 1943, after they were selected as privileged "exchange-worthy" Jews because of their Latin American papers, they were accorded a very different treatment from that to which they had grown accustomed. In Warsaw, SS officers addressing them with the polite form *Sie* helped them load their suitcases aboard trains bound for Bergen-Belsen. "The SS murderers were very courteous," remembered Simcha Korngold. "We saw a train with elegant passenger cars, surrounded by representatives of the Red Cross." Rather than being jammed into filthy, crowded boxcars, "everyone had his own upholstered seat."[100] The importance of the Latin American papers could not have been clearer: those Jews without such documents were taken aside and shot.[101] Before the backdrop of a ravaged city, the departure scene must have been almost surreal:

[The candidates for exchange] were dressed beautifully: everyone put on the best that he or she had, thinking that [foreigners] should look very chic. Some women wore overcoats with foxes, or minks, and large velvet hats in the fashionable manner of the Aryan side, with gauze stockings and special travelling shoes. They carried pigskin handbags and English plaid blankets thrown across the shoulder.[102]

Upon arrival, the prisoners were permitted to retain their possessions, leading to a lively trade in goods among the Bergen-Belsen inmates, some of whom continued to wear silk clothing. They were required to perform labor for the upkeep of the camp, but they also had time to sunbathe on blankets and read novels or take English courses. "Much of what was publicized only for propaganda purposes about Theresienstadt [the model camp in Czechoslovakia designed to fool the Red Cross] was actually possible for the inmates of the 'Special Camp' in Bergen-Belsen," notes a painstaking recent study, recounting the lectures in literature and architecture, the painting classes, dance performances, regular religious services and celebrations of Jewish holidays – for which the authorities provided extra rations.[103] It remained a grim and harsh existence, but was intentionally less deadly than the standard treatment in the camp system. All of this served to underscore just how seriously their jailers took the special status of those Jews destined to be exchanged to the West.

There were two windows of opportunity when thousands of Jews holding Latin American papers were waiting in Bergen-Belsen. In the summer of 1943, 2,500 Polish Jews with *promesas* from Honduras, Paraguay, Chile, Nicaragua, Guatemala, Ecuador, Mexico, and Haiti arrived in the camp and remained until late October. When negotiations for an exchange brought no results, most of them were sent to die at Auschwitz.[104] In early 1944, some 3,700 Dutch Jews, most holding Latin American documents, were brought to Bergen-Belsen and held there for more than half a year.[105] Still others were held at Vittel in France and elsewhere.[106]

Tragically for those awaiting rescue, on both occasions the U.S. and Latin American governments refused to recognize these Jews as their citizens and rejected an exchange until, for the vast majority, it was too late. The total number of Jews with Latin American papers actually saved by the single exchange finally carried out in February 1945 was 136 people.[107] By that time, Bergen-Belsen had deteriorated into a death camp, the special privileges supplanted by horrifying sanitary conditions and starvation rations that killed many of the remaining inmates.

If thousands spent months waiting in the special holding facility at Bergen-Belsen and German authorities envisioned an exchange of between 10,000 (Himmler's estimate) and 30,000 (the AA's request), why were so few saved in this manner? Some of the blame for the failed negotiations – and all of the blame for the killing – lies with the Nazis, who were not unified and who generally sought to extract maximum advantage from their dealings with the Allies.[108] However, given the commitment on the German side to carrying out an exchange and the considerable trouble taken to make it possible, the response of the American nations was crucial. And instead of moving heaven and earth to bring about such an exchange, the United States urged Latin American governments to reject the Jews, basing its policy on the fear that the refugees would pose a security threat to the Western Hemisphere. It was a familiar argument – and a deadly one.

FEAR OF A REFUGEE THREAT

Jews had long been associated with radicalism in the American mind. The widely distributed *Protocols of the Elders of Zion*, fabricated in 1905 by the Czar's secret police, had warned of an international Jewish conspiracy to promote world revolution. Henry Ford's *The International Jew*, cited approvingly by Hitler and read by millions in the United States, echoed the same theme.[109] More than one hundred anti-Semitic organizations were active in the decade before the war, a period when the presence of Jews in high-profile positions among Roosevelt's advisers – Felix Frankfurter, Samuel Rosenman, Bernard Baruch, David Niles, Henry Morgenthau – gave rise to persistent rumors that Jews were running the government, were behind the "Jew Deal."[110] Polls taken at the outset of the war showed that one-third to one-half of the American population thought Jews had "too much power" in the United States.[111] Asked in 1938 if large numbers of Jewish exiles should be given sanctuary in the United States, 82 percent of Americans said no.[112]

It was against this background that individual State Department bureaucrats decided to interpret narrowly immigration law to ensure that even the small annual quotas for immigration from Germany established under U.S. law went unfilled in nearly every year from 1933 to 1945. After 1939, they were following an order given by Breckinridge Long to U.S. consulates abroad to all but terminate the granting of visas even within allowable limits. Long based his decision on his conviction that there were many radicals and subversives among Jewish refugees.

Breckinridge Long was not the only policymaker who linked Jewish refugees to the danger of subversion. The State Department cooperated in preparing a *Saturday Evening Post* article warning the public that "disguised as refugees, Nazi agents have penetrated all over the world, as spies, fifth columnists, propagandists or secret commercial agents"; they were already "undermining United States' influence in South America."[113] Undersecretary Sumner Welles characterized the possibility that the Germans would release a large flow of refugees as an "attack on the Western Hemisphere," and Roosevelt agreed.[114] At a press conference on June 5, 1940, FDR himself warned that "among the refugees there are some spies, as has been found in other countries," explaining that "especially Jewish refugees" could be coerced to report to German agents under the threat that if they did not do so, "we are frightfully sorry, but your old father and mother will be taken out and shot." Roosevelt said this applied to "a very, very small percentage of refugees coming out of Germany," but that "it is something we have got to watch."[115]

Three weeks later, Secretary Hull ordered U.S. diplomatic posts in Europe to use "extreme care" in examining visa applications, anticipating "a drastic reduction in the number of quota and nonquota immigration visas."[116] Breckinridge Long recorded the true impact of the new procedure in his diary: "The cables practically stopping immigration went!"[117] To his colleagues, he explained that without changing any laws, the consuls could simply "put every obstacle in the way" using bureaucratic devices to "postpone and postpone and postpone the granting of the visas."[118]

Long's bold declaration often has been cited as evidence of his desire to exclude Jewish immigrants and use security concerns merely as a pretense. But Long's private thoughts at the time seem to bear out his genuine worries over infiltration. "The refugee problem is a thorny one – and there is plenty of criticism either way the decision lies," Long confided to his diary. "One side is dissatisfied in any case. But I weather that – and try to play it safe against any possible Fifth Column."[119]

Was the threat real? For all the concern about alien subversives, fewer than one-half of one percent of all refugees arriving from Nazi or Soviet territory in 1940 were ever taken into custody for questioning. Only a fraction were ever indicted on any charge, and most of those were for violations of immigration regulations rather than espionage.[120] When Ambassador Spruille Braden, not one to play down the Nazi threat, looked into the matter, he found "no case where Gestapo agents had been included amongst the refugees" nor any example of refugees forced to spy by pressure placed on their relatives.[121] The undeniable presence of anti-Semitic ideas in the bureaucracy helped convince the officials guarding the security of the nation that Jews were especially untrustworthy. But although State Department officials did not cite it, there does seem to have been at least one case of an *Abwehr* agent, Heinz Luening, who posed as a Jewish refugee en route to Cuba; he was the only spy executed in Latin America during the war.[122] If the talk of keeping out spies was a mere subterfuge, it was an elaborate one, given the paper trail of discussion of security concerns stretching from junior State Department officials to the Oval Office. At any rate, the policy of the United States, rather than sparing no effort to rescue Jews from Europe while examining them for infiltrators, was dedicated to keeping them out.

WARNINGS TO LATIN AMERICA

Defending the United States against refugees meant extending the restrictive policy to the entire Western Hemisphere, so the State Department worked to persuade Latin America to go along. In the dark early days of the American war effort, even officials who were usually better attuned to the true circumstances of Latin American affairs were convinced of the danger. In a cable originating with Laurence Duggan and initialed by Welles, the State Department told its representatives to press Latin American governments to clamp down even on the return of their own citizens, since the Axis would use exchange vessels "to slip in agents under the guise of nationals of these other countries. Such fake nationals would, of course, be fully provided with fraudulent passports, birth certificates, and the like.[123] In April 1942, the State Department repeated its warnings to be wary of issuing visas to refugees because "many" of them were "secret agents or sympathizers of the totalitarian countries."[124]

Several years of this approach helped prepare the ground for some rather bizarre notions to take root in the U.S. bureaucracy. In response to a State Department inquiry of December 1941, U.S. consulates in France hastened to reassure Washington that HICEM, the European affiliate of the Hebrew Immigrant Aid Society, was not a front for the Gestapo.[125] Even more striking is an exchange of messages in spring 1941 between the U.S. Embassy in London and James Dunn, State Department Political Adviser. The British at the time were routinely interning Jewish refugees on the presumption that some of them might be spies. "If your people do get information that Germans or Austrians who have posed as refugees from Nazi oppression have proved to be Nazi agents I should be very glad to know of it," a British official asked the embassy. "We have been somewhat surprised in this country at the slightness of the evidence we have found of such penetration among our own refugees from Germany. I am not yet convinced that the evidence does not exist, if only we could find it."[126]

Forwarding the message to Dunn, the embassy noted that one of its diplomats, Robert Coe,

remembers some sort of report, when he was in the Department, of a special "school" which the Germans had set up in Prague for the purpose of "making Jews out of non-Jews." He remembers seeing that in this so-called 'school' instruction in the Hebrew language and the Talmud, and alteration of features were included in the curriculum.[127]

Dunn responded that, after a "thorough search of the records" of the State Department and the intelligence agencies, he could not offer any evidence of actual cases of bogus refugees, nor any information about the Prague school. "However," Dunn wrote, "a gentleman in the Department recalls having seen something in connection with this school about a year ago but cannot recall whether it was a newspaper or magazine article, a moving picture, or a report. He remembers, in particular, that the results of the plastic surgery practiced were remarkable."[128] One possible origin was the *Saturday Evening Post*, which had run an ominous story headline "WAR BY REFUGEE" in March 1941. The author, citing an "unofficial report," claimed that "in Prague the Gestapo operates a special school where Nazis are taught to act as Jews. They learn to speak Yiddish, to read Hebrew, to pray. They are supposed to submit to circumcision."[129] Since the story was based on State Department sources, the circle had been completed – the Department was now citing news reports of rumors it had initiated.[130]

A SUCCESSFUL DEFENSE

Throughout 1943 and into 1944, Washington continued to urge that all repatriates from Europe be "carefully scrutinized" to weed out impostors. Latin American governments responded to these messages by rejecting the efforts at "repatriation" by those whose citizenship was most in doubt: the Jews with false papers.[131] Meanwhile, the State Department rejected any exchange of the Bergen-Belsen Jews for Germans already in internment because, as Clattenburg told a Jewish delegation pleading for such a move, it would amount to "an exchange of trained, specialized personnel against individuals not having such attributes."[132]

In January 1944, under pressure from officials from the Treasury Department and the Senate who were threatening to make public details of the State

Department's obstruction of rescue efforts, President Roosevelt ordered the creation of the War Refugee Board (WRB). Jewish organizations had long called for a single body to coordinate a response to the Nazi persecution of the Jews. Now an executive order required the State Department and other government agencies to cooperate with the Board's efforts "to take all measures within its power to rescue the victims of enemy oppression who are in imminent danger of death."[133] The Board pressed the State Department to reverse itself and start encouraging Latin American governments to recognize the validity of the passports while urging Germany not to mistreat their holders. Several crucial months of resistance followed. Central America desk officer John Moors Cabot claimed in his memoirs that at a meeting in James Dunn's office to draw up a telegram urging Latin American governments to recognize the false passports, "every official called to the meeting protested vehemently against this – we did not know [sic!] that Hitler was even then liquidating millions of Jews."[134]

As of March 1944, a State Department internal report could still state that "this Government's views regarding the issuance of fraudulent documents has not changed," and claimed credit for continuing to encourage Latin American governments to reject the documents:

It is oversimplification to say that several hundreds or thousands of Jewish refugees will be killed if South American passports are not supplied to them. . . . We should not be forced, and we should not willingly accept, a proposal which is essentially fraudulent and improper. . . .

There have been instances where persons holding such passports later traveled to or though the United States and, once having arrived in this country, have remained here creating a problem for our immigration people. Furthermore, as Dr. Berle's and Mr. Gordon's offices inform us, Nazi agents have used such fraudulent documents to gain admittance to countries in this hemisphere.

As a result of this our Government took a definite stand against the practice. We prevailed upon some of the other American republics to stop it, to prevent its recurrence, and to take steps to invalidate documents already issued.[135]

The report went on to blame "heedless persons" for irresponsibly pushing the State Department into "embarrassment and misunderstandings with the other American republics" by urging the adoption of "a reprehensible practice in which we, ourselves, are not willing to engage; . . . *it would be futile* in helping individuals to escape the Nazis as the latter would know about the false documents; finally our government would become involved in illegal practices which would quickly descend to a low level of competition in fraud, deceit, bribery, counterfeiting and double-crossing, debasing the whole problem of saving refugees and placing this government in an untenable and malodorous position."[136]

Even at this late date, the priorities remained clear: avoiding "embarrassment" and "debasement," and keeping out those elusive Nazi refugee-agents.

Because of its stubborn refusal to recognize that waiving technicalities – as the Nazis were fully prepared to do – would be far from futile and could actually save lives, the stench that ultimately clung to the State Department was the smell of death.

Washington's energetic appeals to Latin American governments to restrict the entry of refugees proved effective. Carl Burckhardt of the International Committee for the Red Cross wrote in January 1944 that "Reich officials said they were prepared to exchange these people for German civilian internees in the corresponding Latin American nations, [but] the respective governments did not recognize the Latin American citizenship of the passholders. Thus the passes were taken away from these internees and they now fear that they will be deported [to the death camps in the East]."[137]

Not until early April, after a personal plea by Treasury Secretary Henry Morgenthau, did Secretary Hull finally give his support to the WRB.[138] On April 10, 1944, the United States asked the Swiss to convey a message to Berlin urging the recognition of the Latin American papers pending the next exchange of civilians.[139] The following day, Hull wrote to U.S. missions in Latin America asking them to prevail upon the governments to which they were accredited to recognize the passports on humanitarian grounds, promising that the Jews would be diverted elsewhere.[140]

But not that much had changed. Meeting with Meier Schenkolewski of Agudas Israel in late May 1944, Clattenburg explained, as he had on a similar occasion ten months before, that many Germans in U.S. camps were refusing to agree to their own repatriation, while "a number of those desiring repatriation whether from the United States or from other countries had been found non-repatriable on the grounds of security." When Schenkolewski glumly remarked that it appeared that there was therefore not much hope for the rescue of the Bergen-Belsen Jews, Clattenburg counseled "patience."[141]

At the end of May, the Committee for Political Defense in Montevideo, the inter-American security council that had spent the war issuing resolutions calling for tight restrictive measures on Axis nationals, recommended that the American nations inform Germany that Jews with Latin American documents were under their protection and authorize negotiations toward an exchange using Germans "who desire to be repatriated and who are selected in accordance with such security safeguards as the republics may mutually deem appropriate."[142] Regular and forceful reminders to the German government that the Allies considered the Jews with Latin American documents to be under their protection may have helped keep up to two thousand of them alive in the exchange camps until the end of the war.[143] But for the rest, the turnabout was too little, too late. The policy of seizing Germans suspected of potential subversion while leaving volunteers for repatriation behind had gone on for too long. By mid-1944, with Germany under constant aerial bombardment, there were few volunteers to be found. When the United States tried to organize a new collection of

German volunteers from Latin America who were "consistent with security and blockade requirements," the response was disappointing.[144] Costa Rica found only two volunteers in the entire country.[145] Venezuela located eight.[146] A pool of volunteers could have been composed a year earlier, when the Nazis were prepared to trade and more Germans were willing to go home, but U.S. policy blocked the deal on specious grounds.

In January 1945, the *Gripsholm* finally sailed for Marseille carrying the last shipment of Germans to be repatriated during the war. They were exchanged for U.S. and Latin American citizens, including 136 of the remaining survivors from Bergen-Belsen who held *promesas*. Charles Klein, a Czech Jewish lawyer who had spent the previous six months in the camp, and Felicitas Plaut, a German Jew who had been there a year, provided a description of the camp they had left, showing just how far conditions had deteriorated from the earlier scenes of stylishly dressed inmates relaxing in the sun:

Approximately 3500 persons of the Jewish race are held in a separate enclosure at Bergen Belsen. Of this number there are many persons from South America and a few persons who claim American nationality.... The camp itself was steadily becoming more crowded and at the time of the departure of Mr. Klein and Mrs. Plaut the 80 centimeter beds were being used to accommodate two persons each. Under these circumstances it was impossible for inmates to protect themselves from disease. Vermin were rampant.

Food supplied to the inmates was constantly deteriorating.... Two washrooms were available for 3500 inhabitants. There was a shortage of water and at no time was warm water available.

All male inmates at the camp were compelled to work.... If they refused to work they were beaten to compel them to work. A number of individuals died from such beatings.

Mr. Klein estimated that about 15 persons per day died in the Jewish section of the Bergen Belsen camp. He said that the bodies were disposed of by cremation.[147]

WHAT MIGHT HAVE BEEN

Nothing short of military defeat could stop the Nazi Holocaust, and the Allies were expending their blood and treasure to win the war as rapidly as possible. But within the limits of the possible, one can imagine a different fate for some of the victims had the Allies been less constrained by false estimates of the subversive potential both of German expatriates and of the Jews themselves. That there was untapped potential for rescue efforts is clear from several facts.

First, resources for housing Jews were clearly available. At a meeting in Bermuda in April 1943 to discuss the refugee problem, British and U.S. officials got off to bad start, exchanging notes that accused the other ally of claiming all credit internationally for joint efforts to care for refugees. The U.S. note defensively listed a series of measures taken on behalf of refugees in recent years, including "approximately 110,000 persons of the Japanese race ... being housed and maintained at public expense after removal from vital military areas."[148] The attempt of a government to take credit for assisting civilians, two-thirds of them U.S. citizens, uprooted by its own executive order demonstrates extraordinary chutzpah. More to the point, U.S. officials were prepared to go to considerable trouble and expense (and to violate constitutional protections) to house more than a hundred thousand Japanese-Americans when perceived military necessity made it a priority.

On separate occasions, the Allies found the resources to move some 100,000 non-Jewish refugees from Poland, Yugoslavia, and Greece to havens in the Middle East and Africa.[149] Mexico found room for 15,000 Spanish Republican refugees but only 1,850 Jewish refugees.[150]

It seems likely that a positive rather than negative response from the American governments to the Bergen-Belsen scheme would have brought more Jews to safety. This is suggested by the successful rescue of 136 of the "exchange Jews" that did take place in early 1945, as well as by an example of what could be achieved when Germany's negotiating partners responded energetically to the opportunity to save Jewish lives. In August 1943, the Spanish government persuaded the Nazis to recognize a group of 367 Sephardic Jews in Saloniki as Spanish citizens, since they claimed to trace their ancestry back to the Jews who were expelled from the Iberian peninsula in 1492. These tenuously "Spanish" Jews were sent to Bergen-Belsen, and, after further negotiations with Franco's government, every one of them was delivered to Spain.[151]

Because of incidents such as these, a comprehensive study of Bergen-Belsen concludes that "whenever nations insisted upon the delivery of their own citizens [no matter how frail the proof of citizenship], interned Jews were actually released and thereby saved."[152] The Nazis' ideological commitment to exterminating all the Jews within reach still allowed for exceptions to achieve other goals. The drive to bring Germans abroad *heim ins Reich* (home to the Reich) provided the countervailing ideological weight needed to allow a few thousand Jews to be released from the camps, and German volunteers from Latin America provided the numbers needed to carry out a trade. Had the response from the Americas been different, they might well have been saved.

Epilogue

The New Menace

"It makes us look utterly silly to insist that other countries deport Germans while we import Nazis."

> –The State Department's R. Newbegin, upon learning of the secret government operation to smuggle Nazi scientists and intelligence agents into the United States[1]

Washington, DC, September 1943. Albert Clattenburg, assistant chief of Breckinridge Long's Special Division, returns from a long tour of the U.S. internment camps where he has just received his first close-up look at the fruit of his labors. Personally meeting the internees who until then had been mere names on a page has come as something of a shock. Back in the State Department, he files a report based on his interviews with the interned Germans and with camp authorities that is a devastating indictment of the program he helped to create.

Clattenburg begins his report with a nod to the well-intentioned origins of the deportation program. "Our transfer of these enemy aliens to this country for internment is based upon our sincere desire to extirpate the carefully-prepared organizations of the Axis governments in the other American republics and thus to ensure the political security of this hemisphere." Unfortunately, Clattenburg continues, he has discovered that the program was quickly perverted by the cynicism and venality of Latin American leaders:

The motives of the other American republics in cooperating with us have only a thin veneer of concern for hemispheric security. The Governments in those countries have been concerned with the political advantage of removing individuals likely to foment internal opposition against them.... They have had (and in many instances this may have been the governing motive) an economic reason for cooperating with us in that they have been able to strengthen their internal position by seizing the business and property of deported Axis nationals....

The more intelligent of [the deportees themselves believe] that the local Government picked on them as an easy source of graft and that we, in order to break up German commercial influence, connived with the local officials to obtain their expulsion.[2]

Clattenburg seems even more disturbed by his impression that he and his colleagues have helped bring about the very problem they had hoped to solve. His report divides the internees into three groups: "Germans of position, responsibility and intelligence" in whom deportation has now sowed a "stony hatred" of the United States; the "fawning, cringing individuals" who feel an injustice has been done but wish to ingratiate themselves with U.S. authorities; and the "inoffensive individuals . . . who may be good Germans but are nevertheless so far removed from Germany in their contacts that in the normal course of events they would never have done anything to injure us." In a depressed tone, Clattenburg concludes that the deportation program has managed to transform these ordinary people into enemies of the United States. "If they did not do so before, they will certainly work against us henceforth politically and economically. They will be a constant menace to us," he writes. He concludes by recommending what he acknowledges to be "a harsh and cruel program": "We cannot afford to allow any of these people to go back to the other American republics. They will hate us as long as they live."[3]

Clattenburg's insights two years before the end of the war prefigured U.S. policy when the war was over. The State Department attempted to deport the remaining internees to occupied Germany and ban them from ever returning to the Americas, but immediately ran into trouble. Internees filed habeas corpus suits in federal court, contending that shipping people off to the ruined cities of Germany was unjustified cruelty. "They wanted to send us to Germany, but we had no relatives there any more," remembered Alfredo Brauer of Ecuador. "We had no idea where to go – we even wrote 'Foreign Ministry' on our baggage tags because we really didn't have any idea."[4] The courts ruled that there was no legal basis to treat them as illegal immigrants subject to deportation, since they had been brought to the United States involuntarily.[5] President Harry Truman signed an executive order[6] giving the Secretary of State removal powers under the Alien Enemy Act, a law dating back to 1798, but when the State Department issued deportation orders against some of the internees, "such a furore arose from the press, from letters to members of Congress, and the institution of legal proceedings" that it was forced to become more selective.[7]

The Department of State therefore formed a hearing board, the Alien Enemy Control Section (AECS), to collect and review all evidence held by any government agency or embassy post regarding those Germans from Latin America still in internment at the end of the war. There were 531 cases (plus about 500 family members). The AECS applied the same system the FBI's

Custodial Detention Index had used before the war, rating the internees "A" if they were dangerous Nazis, "B" if they were "small fry" or if the evidence against them was unclear, and "C" if they were probably harmless. All "A" Germans were to be deported to Germany. "B" internees would be deported as well, unless they had mitigating family ties in Latin America. Germans rated "C" would be released.[8]

Of the 531 individuals, 413 were summarily released without a hearing after a preliminary review of their files indicated no compelling reason to hold them. The AECS hearing board then released more than half of the remaining 118, and recommended deportation for a hard core of about 50 cases. Members of the hearing board concluded that some of the Germans it set free may have been interned legitimately as potential supporters of the German war effort, but they expressed shock and outrage at other cases of individuals detained with no apparent justification.[9]

The deportation proceedings provided yet another occasion for conflict with Latin American leaders who believed the United States had behaved in decidedly unneighborly fashion throughout its wartime campaign against the region's Germans. At the Inter-American Conference on Problems of War and Peace held in Chapultepec Castle in Mexico City in February and March 1945, all American governments had resolved to prevent the return of individuals dangerous to hemispheric security. But once again Washington seemed to be trying to impose its decisions on its neighbors.

Costa Rica's President Picado, under pressure from the country's archbishop, the press, and the public for condoning the forced repatriation to Germany of German internees with Costa Rican wives and children, told reporters that he "had no personal enmity towards these Germans and that their repatriation to Germany was not to cover up any mishandling of their properties in Costa Rica." Picado complained that "he had requested that the deportees be returned but that his request had not been granted by the American Government."[10] Victor Guardia, President of the Costa Rican Supreme Court, argued that the Act of Chapultepec made determining who could safely be permitted to return the responsibility of each government, rather than a policy to be "dictated" by Washington – especially since U.S. officials had been so wrong about so many of the Germans rounded up for internment.[11] From Puerto Limón, U.S. Vice-Consul Hilton F. Wood described critical newspaper articles as "abundant" and reported "the general opinion of the educated Costa Ricans . . . that the United States was not only reverting to a policy of imperialism but was well on the road to a new extreme. . . . It is surely felt now that the constitution and laws of a sovereign nation have been subjected to the will of another nation."[12]

Meanwhile, other Latin American governments were protesting directly and vehemently that they had never agreed to relinquish jurisdiction over their German residents, and that these economically valuable or socially well-connected people should now be returned.[13] The president of Haiti requested the return of Georges Reinbold, a Haitian citizen and the largest exporter of Haitian coffee, "the one man capable of restoring prosperity to the [Artibonite] Valley."[14] The Ecuadorian Foreign Ministry absolved nearly all German deportees of representing any menace to the security of the hemisphere, stating that the evidence against them consisted merely of accusations by the U.S. Embassy, which were unfounded or unprovable, or occasionally actual Party membership, which was provable but had been legal until 1941. With ten to fifteen Ecuadorian citizens testifying on behalf of each deportee in many cases, the government resolved to bring them all home.[15]

The United States, once again, seemed to have one set of rules for itself and a different set of rules for Latin America. Because of the brake of public opinion and Department of Justice misgivings over wholesale expulsions, the U.S. government was not carrying out the draconian measures it wished to impose upon Latin American governments when it came to its own internees.[16] Germans with U.S. citizen wives or children could be exempted from deportation even as the State Department prepared to deport internees with Latin American families – an inconsistency cited as an "act of discrimination" that violated "inalienable family rights."[17] Pressure from another quarter made it essential to wind down the internment program as rapidly as possible. Congress, itching to cut President Truman's budget, was demanding to know how long the Justice Department was going to continue to spend its funds for the support of so many aliens brought up from Latin America.[18]

By the end of 1945, the State Department judged that "our position in the matter was creating so much ill will for the United States...as seriously to jeopardize the Good Neighbor Policy." Under bilateral agreements signed during the war, the United States could not unilaterally repatriate to Germany any Germans from Peru, Ecuador, or El Salvador, and after deciding to accede to the wishes of those nations, "it was clear that the same opportunity would have to be offered to the other Governments concerned. They would in any event shortly find out about our action toward the three and would demand similar treatment."[19] By spring 1946, those Germans in U.S. camps who wished to return to their homes in Peru, Ecuador, El Salvador, or Bolivia could do so. The Jewish internees were released from the supervision of the Justice Department; of the original eighty-one, four had died, two voluntarily returned to Latin America, one went to Germany to help in reconstruction, and the rest sought to stay in the United States. By departing to Mexico or Canada and re-entering the country with legal entry visas, they were able to begin the process of acquiring citizenship. In 1954, the Refugee Relief Act of 1953 was amended so that aliens "brought to the United States from other American republics for internment" could request a change of immigration status. That law permitted the Jewish internees to join several hundred Peruvian Japanese internees in becoming U.S. citizens.[20]

It was a different story for internees who had been repatriated to Germany. Those in the eastern zone who hoped that their Latin American documents would give them some protection against the severe treatment meted out by the Soviet occupiers sometimes saw their passports "torn up before their eyes by Russian military authorities."[21] Dora Rosero Schonenberger, trapped with her husband George in Jena at the end of the war, flew an Ecuadorian flag over their house, but the soldiers laughed it away. She later told Ecuadorian journalists that "the cruelty of the Muscovites reached terrible extremes." The Schonenbergers' savings account disappeared when the Soviets destroyed the bank's archive. Her family finally bribed their way out of the Soviet zone with two bottles of cognac. In the British zone, they slept on the floor of a destroyed factory converted into a camp for Latin Americans; there she gave birth to a daughter.[22] In February 1947, they and other Germans from Latin America lost their last meager refuge when they were ruled ineligible for treatment as "displaced persons" and the occupation forces "took appropriate action to deny them DP care and to evict them from assembly centers."[23]

Endless difficulties faced those who wished to return to their homes in Latin America. Their countries of residence might be willing to accept them, but obtaining an exit visa from Allied occupation authorities was nearly impossible for anyone who had once been interned as a dangerous Nazi. U.S. embassies in Latin America forwarded information to the occupation authorities urging that certain Germans not be permitted to leave, sometimes on such frail grounds as "slight evidence of connections with Blacklisted firms."[24] The State Department forbade the granting of transit visas or space on U.S. vessels to anyone who had been repatriated during the war.[25] To prevent genuine war criminals from escaping to Latin America, the Combined Repatriation Executive and Combined Travel Board met regularly with representatives of the U.S., British, and French occupation forces to review, and usually reject, applications by Germans wishing to travel abroad. The Latin American deportees were also caught up in this system. French authorities, however, were more lenient.[26] The Schonenbergers obtained French visas and passage to Buenos Aires in the summer of 1946.[27] Hugo Droege finally got out in 1948, making the trek on foot to the French border with two Guatemalans, hitchhiking to Paris, and eventually obtaining passage on a series of steamers and small planes for a circuitous return to Guatemala and reunion with his wife and children after an absence of five years.[28]

In Washington, the crush of lawsuits, Congressional pressure, and insistence by Latin American diplomats on the right to have their residents returned gradually wore down the spirit of those U.S. officials campaigning to have the German internees sent to Germany against their will. Even the hard-charging Spruille Braden, who as Assistant Secretary for American Republic Affairs was waging a highly publicized campaign to bring down the government of Argentina whose principal effect was to rally

Argentines behind Juan Perón, could not persuade Latin American countries to deport more Germans on U.S. security lists directly to Germany. In 1946 he dispatched the transport vessel *Marine Marlin* south of the border to collect another shipload of expellees, but the voyage was a "fiasco." Uruguay provided just two of the Germans sought by the United States. Mexico and Brazil yielded a discouraging "handful." Chile, Colombia, Cuba, Ecuador, Paraguay, and Peru deported none. U.S. diplomats considered what options they had to exact better cooperation but decided that "we had already put on all the pressure our relations with these countries would stand."[29]

The State Department was losing its taste for this battle. The expulsion of Nazis was fading from the agenda, eclipsed by the struggle against a new enemy.

On December 4, 1946, the *Washington Post* published an article headlined "'Best Brains' in Germany to Help U.S.: 1000 Scientists Being Brought In by Army; Some Were Nazis; 270 Already Here." The article referred to Operation Paperclip, a once-secret program that eventually brought 765 German scientists, engineers, and technicians into the United States. Some, like Werner von Braun, were veterans of Germany's V-2 rocketry project. Between half and three-quarters were former Nazi Party members or SS men, and more than a few of them were guilty of war crimes.[30] In a parallel operation, the Army's Counterintelligence Corps (CIC) was recruiting former SS and Gestapo officers for espionage work, notably Klaus Barbie, "the butcher of Lyon," and Otto von Bolschwing, a senior aide to Adolf Eichmann.[31]

When the government's warm welcome of high-ranking Nazis was made public, a State Department official who had been fighting Latin American governments to obtain further expulsions wrote that "this would seem to pretty well cut the ground from under us in any attempt to urge action on the part of the American Republics.... It makes us look utterly silly to insist that other countries deport Germans while we import Nazis, and I have no enthusiasm in bringing further pressure to bear on them."[32]

Morale continued to drop during proceedings to deport the last remaining thirty-eight Germans considered to be hardcore cases that dragged on into late 1947. The State Department's legal adviser, who was losing every court case, questioned whether "continued residence in the Western Hemisphere of these 38 obscure individuals scattered in 10 countries is actually prejudicial to the welfare and security of the Americas; or whether, from an over-all point of view, it would not be better policy to return them to their scattered domiciles than to return them, homeless, jobless and resentful, to the Germany which is in process of de-Nazification."[33] The government prosecutor tapped to argue for the forced deportation to Germany of Ricardo Steinvorth, despite the latter's Costa Rican birth and Costa Rican citizenship, responded that he could think of no legal argument to make.[34] Federal judges were unsympathetic to the government side. District Court Judge John Bright ruled in August 1947 that the internees had the right of voluntary departure to the country of their choice. In a pretrial conference, Judge John C. Knox gave his personal opinion that "[t]o deport, for example, an Ecuadoran to another country we happen to occupy . . . that's Siberia to me. It is like selling Uncle Tom down the river. That a Government can go into another country and transport a man against his will thousands of miles across the sea . . . is repulsive. . . . If this situation were to become generally known, it would be subject to the severest criticism."35

After a court ruling that the thirty-eight aliens were not in violation of immigration law but had been *prevented from complying* with immigration law – departing to a country that would receive them – "by the actions of the State Department," Attorney General Tom Clark decided in September 1947 to release all the remaining German internees because "the time has come for the Government to do everything possible to dispose of such cases, finally and completely."36

Before the decade was out, the turnabout was complete. In 1949, at the initiative of U.S. occupation authorities in Germany facing a serious over-population problem because of the millions of ethnic Germans resettled from Eastern Europe, the State Department began exploring the possibility of encouraging the mass migration of Germans to Latin America. This was, as John C. Dreier of the Division of American Republics put it, "a rather drastic shift in policy on the part of this Government which, a few years ago, was still taking the position that Nazi emigration to Latin America was undesirable."37 In the new perspective provided by the Cold War, some State Department officials noted that such immigrants "would at least be anti-Communist."38 Others praised the vaunted industriousness of Germans and thought it "in our interest to assist emigration of non-Communist Germans to Latin American countries."39

The reappraisal of German settlers in Latin America was accompanied by a renaming of the external danger to the hemisphere. In Bolivia, the revolutionary MNR, formerly dubbed "Nazi-Fascist" by Cordell Hull, was recast by his successors as a dangerous "Communist" movement.40 The ruling dictators among the Good Neighbors quickly conformed to the new line. Tiburcio Carías of Honduras, whose cooperation with U.S. anti-Nazi policy had given him an excuse during the war to expropriate and deport his political opponents, now passed a law aimed at the latest enemy: the Ley Fernanda of 1946 promised to punish "foreigners guilty of totalitarian and antisocial activities who intervene in Honduras in order to establish a communist or totalitarian system."41

At the same time, there was a parallel shift in the role of the intelligence network created in the region during the war. The close working relation-ship established between U.S. intelligence and local security forces for the purpose of hunting Nazis continued into the new era, as the two groups, and sometimes the same individuals, now cooperated to hunt Communists –

applying equally shabby standards of evidence, and producing far more sanguinary results. The Somozas and Batistas of the region easily switched from
denouncing their rivals as "Nazis" to labeling all opposition "Communist,"
and the military and economic aid from Washington that kept them firmly in
power flowed more lavishly the more vividly they painted the red menace.

Conclusion

There Went the Neighborhood

"'Intervention' seems again to be becoming almost synonymous with 'nonintervention.'"

—Former Undersecretary of State Sumner Welles[1]

Cutting through the hyperbole about a subversive "fifth column" to identify the Nazis' limited aims and gains in Latin America in the years before World War II reveals that the overbearing attempts of the *Auslandsorganisation* to bring the expatriate German communities into the Nazi fold, and the bungled efforts of the German spies, achieved little else than to ruin the reputation of the communities they claimed to champion. The actions of the Nazis in Europe cast a long, menacing shadow; German battlefield successes in 1940 and 1941 seemed unstoppable; and to some extent, overseas Party organizers were able to draw on the expatriates' tradition of strong cultural identification with and continuing links to Germany as they pursued their schemes.

But such transnational sentiment among unassimilated immigrants does not automatically constitute a security threat to their host states. In the story described in these pages, transnational sentiment was misused (by Nazi Germany) and misread (by the United States) in disturbing ways. The expatriates' pride in being German was manipulated by the Nazis; while it did not create the legions of footsoldiers ready to seize the hemisphere in the nightmare scenarios of U.S. planners, it did seem to make more plausible the extravagant claims of Nazi leaders that German communities abroad were outposts of the Third Reich.

And yet the 300,000 Germans living in the United States were viewed with relative equanimity, while U.S. officials feared that sympathy for Germany among Germans south of the Rio Grande would lead to the toppling of governments. This alarm arose all the more easily because of the longstanding ideological posture of the United States toward Latin America. Germany's aggressive trade policy presented a challenge in markets that Washington, Wall Street, and Main Street all agreed belonged naturally to the United States. Political unrest and coup attempts were instantly attributed to Nazi intrigue, given the abiding belief among U.S. policymakers that Latin Americans were inherently inferior and incompetent, that the region was vulnerable and in need of protection, and that any unwelcome developments or signs of resistance to U.S. influence must be the work of outsiders.

When it came time to identify the Germans in the region who might pose a menace to security, the United States sent a collection of intelligence agents endowed with more enthusiasm than skill, who readily accepted anonymous or self-interested denunciations without being able to evaluate the evidence. Latin American security forces, especially the more corrupt variety serving Central American and Caribbean dictators, helpfully delivered "dangerous Nazis" who often had committed no greater crime than owning a piece of real estate coveted by a member of the local elite. Once they were deported, Germans in the U.S. internment camps confirmed through their behavior what should have been apparent in the communities whence they came: although a majority responded sympathetically to Nazi Germany from afar and some either joined the Party or opposed it, only a very few were prepared to undertake action on behalf of the Nazi cause that involved any element of personal risk.

Tellingly, the United States met with most cooperation from dictatorships and most resistance from democracies that tried to defend the rights of their residents. Dictators were eager to enrich themselves and use the system for their own personal advantage, while democratic governments, more responsive to their populations, were less keen to sacrifice their sovereignty. When Latin American governments hesitated to go along with Washington's plans for deporting or expropriating their German residents, even U.S. diplomats committed to good relations tried to force their hand. Most previous accounts have told us that the war years constitute the apogee of inter-American cooperation, and that the short-lived Good Neighbor principle of noninterference in Latin American affairs was a victim of the crusade against Communism in the 1950s. But the campaign against the region's Germans shows that overblown fears of an external threat to the hemisphere brought about the end of the Good Neighbor policy during the Second World War, not the Cold War; indeed, the policy itself now looks more and more like a decorative, fair-weather veneer that held up only as long as circumstances remained ideal and that depended on the presence of authoritarian regimes. U.S. officials seeking to extirpate the German menace resorted to traditional, pre-Rooseveltian practices: blacklists that ruined Latin American businesses, produced without consulting local governments (angering officials throughout South America); the threat of devastating economic boycott if Central American governments did not toe the line; demands for the deportation of even those Germans deemed inoffensive by local governments, including those possessing Latin American citizenship; the diplomatic nonrecognition of a Bolivian regime until it agreed to deliver; greater support for compliant dictatorships than for principled democracies. The disputes generated by these forms of intimate interference in Latin American affairs, in contravention of the signed agreements of the 1930s, went well beyond the normal frictions that routinely arise in relations among friends and allies. This kind of hardball diplomacy eroded the goodwill built up during the prewar Good Neighbor era, especially as the emergency of Pearl Harbor passed, the threat to the region receded, and Washington's continued exertions to expel the last vestiges of the German presence began to appear less defensive and more hegemonic.

If criminal Nazi aggression in Europe and the enduring transnational links of expatriate Germans supposedly turned all German emigrants into security risks, why did the U.S. government insist on the radical expropriation of German farms and businesses in Latin America, but not in the United States itself? Officially, policymakers claimed that German capital posed more of a threat in Latin America, because Germans might use their profits to pay for propaganda that could sway malleable Latin American opinion to the side of the Axis. The rapid alignment of nearly every Latin American nation on the side of the Allies revealed the poverty of this argument. Meanwhile, the measures taken against German immigrants within the United States, in the economic field as with internment policy, were far more relaxed. German-owned businesses in the United States, if properly supervised and regulated, could remain productive and add to the gross national product without contributing any capital or resources to the German war effort. German-owned businesses in Latin America, under similar controls, could safely have done the same for Latin American countries, as Latin American leaders persistently reminded Washington – but productive Germans in Latin America did not increase U.S. economic strength; instead, they maintained a position in markets the United States wanted for itself. U.S. economic warfare officials routinely looked to the postwar period in establishing "root and branch" standards for the elimination of the German economic presence from Latin America, even while admitting that such expropriation was irrelevant to the war effort and often ruined individual Germans who had no connection to, and in some cases even actively opposed, the Nazi enemy.

The emergency internment of enemy nationals was not unique to the United States. All nations involved in the war engaged in the practice.[2] But because of its exceptional relationship with Latin America, the United States took an exceptional step other major powers did not, or could not, take: removing for internment enemy aliens from foreign countries not under occupation. In carrying out this policy, U.S. officials departed from the standards set for individual internment of U.S. residents, ignoring the element of selectivity and breaking national and international laws.

The Alien Enemy Act of 1798, created to secure hostile French nationals and never invoked during the 150 years before World War II, does permit the "summary apprehension" of nationals of an enemy power in wartime.[3] However, since nothing in the statute permits the apprehension of aliens outside U.S. boundaries, the designers of the deportation program found it necessary to reach for such absurd contrivances as the charge that individuals who had been brought by force into the United States had violated immigration laws since they lacked the foresight to acquire entry visas before being snatched from their homes.

The contraventions of international law included the detention of individuals for reasons not related to their own actions, the deportation without charge of civilian noncombatants from a nonbelligerent to a belligerent country, the indefinite internment of civilians without serious inquiry or hearings, and the use of civilians for forced labor.[4] Although some of these principles were codified only after World War II in the 1949 Geneva Convention Relative to the Protection of Civilian Persons in Time of War, they reflected customary international law in place since at least the Hague Peace Conferences of 1899 and 1907.[5]

The internment program not only affected the individual deportees, their families, and their communities; other groups also felt its impact. When Berlin first learned that Latin American governments were cooperating in the U.S. roundup of German citizens, the German regime retaliated by interning innocent civilians, scouring the territory under its control for citizens of the Americas. Nazi Germany did not need any encouragement to commit outrages against civilians, but in these cases, the chain of cause and effect is clear.[6] The U.S. unwillingness to repatriate whole categories of German internees for often spurious security reasons contributed to a breakdown of the prisoner exchange program that left many Americans languishing in German camps – as President Roosevelt acknowledged, when he wrote that terminating the exchanges was "tough on the Americans who must remain in Germany throughout the war."[7]

The program was tough on the Jews as well. Under a strict application of the national principle, Jewish refugees from Germany should not have come into internment at all, since they were no longer German citizens after being stripped of their citizenship by Nazi law in 1941. Instead, they were doubly marked, both by their German language and origins that brought them into the purview of the anti-German policies, and by their Jewishness, which made them untrustworthy in the eyes of many U.S. bureaucrats. Not only did they have to endure months or years of incarceration behind barbed wire in camps designed for their enemies, but they were spared a worse fate only because officials in the State Department who considered sending the Jews to the Third Reich, such as Breckinridge Long and Albert Clattenburg, did not prevail over cooler heads at Justice.[8]

In a tragic turn, the crusade against a mythical fifth column worked to the detriment of a possible rescue of several thousand Jews holding Latin American citizenship documents in concentration camps. Set aside by the Nazis to be traded for German internees, most of them were left to die, partly because U.S. officials feared Jewish refugees might be dangerous to U.S. security and lobbied against their acceptance, and partly because anti-subversive policy thwarted the use of Germans who were willing to be traded for them.

These were high costs to pay for a program that did not meet its principal goal. Philip Bonsal, one of the most experienced State Department officers dealing with Latin America who was often critical of the methods employed, believed the roundups prevented sabotage and other subversive acts that the Germans might have performed had they not been interned.[9] Yet there was no sabotage committed even by the card-carrying members of the Nazi Party left behind by the inefficient deportation program, and the conduct of the deportees in the camps suggests that the number willing to engage in such activities would have been very small – and most hardcore Nazis were easily identifiable based on their previous actions. That there was no sabotage on the West Coast after the Japanese Americans were forcibly relocated has not been generally taken as proof that that the relocation policy was a wise one. In Latin America, a more carefully selective program, one in line with the more limited actions taken against Germans and Italians in the United States (if more professionally run), would have been sufficient to ensure security at a much lower cost.

Most of the internees from Latin America were incarcerated despite the lack of any evidence of subversive acts or intent, other than the vague "pro-German" or "pro-Nazi sentiments" attributed to some of them. This characterization of their feelings was often accurate, but it could have been made as well about many Germans in Latin America who were not interned, and it applied equally to significant numbers of the Germans in the United States who were let alone and caused no problems, or, mutatis mutandis, to some among the 110,000 West Coast Japanese and Japanese Americans who were incarcerated without charge and have been widely recognized as innocent victims of misguided government policy. That a German might nurture sympathetic feelings for Germany even in the early Hitler years is not surprising; however abhorrent we may find such sentiment today, it was not, in legal principle or in domestic U.S. practice, an internable offense.

The recovered history of the enemy alien program in Latin America suggests that using national or ethnic markers to determine who is a threat to national security will not only lead to injustice but is likely to be ineffective as well. Racial or ethnic profiling, discredited before the turn of the twenty-first century, has at this writing come back into vogue. Such practices predictably net an unsettling number of innocents while missing malefactors who do not fit the profile and alienating entire communities who could otherwise furnish valuable allies as well as enemies. Even in the presence of a real threat and a real war, as in 1941 and again today, the existence of transnational links within migrant networks and the persistence of cultural affinities instead of rapid assimilation do not in themselves add up to a menace to the national welfare. If governments were to base their security measures on evidence of *suspicious activity*, rather than on perceived *suspicious identity* determined by ethnicity, religion, or nationality, they might well be able to learn something from the past, instead of being condemned to repeat it.

To be more competent, however, one must have reliable information about regions or cultures that are not well represented or well understood in the corridors of power. Years of mistreatment and neglect had left the United States government unprepared to undertake serious investigation of Latin American conditions when crisis came. With few exceptions, its diplomatic staff and especially its intelligence agencies would have benefited from better training, more experience, and greater understanding of the locales to which they were assigned. When individuals know more about a region, they are less likely to rely on the shortcut of ideological presumption and stereotype and more apt to make a careful assessment of local conditions with some attention to local opinion and knowledge. This is particularly evident in the dissent that came from such well-informed officials as Laurence Duggan and Philip Bonsal. The actions of officials who had no such specialized knowledge, but who did have a commitment to the principles of fairness and individual rights, such as Attorney General Francis Biddle, AECU director Ennis, and his assistant Raymond Ickes, suggest that a just and successful foreign policy would benefit from a greater presence of policymakers from both categories.

But in Latin America, then as now, the rules do not apply. Policies judged adequate to ensure the safety of the United States were evidently too good for our southern neighbors. That is why a calculation of the costs associated with the program should not be limited to the damage done to ethical standards and the law, to the diversion of resources from the war effort – the funds, shipping, and personnel required for this complex operation; nor to the costs incurred by the internees, who lost homes, property, businesses, and productive years of their lives, and whose families were split apart. To that accounting must be added a significant cost in international credibility and esteem. The vehemence of Latin American protest against the Proclaimed List and other high-handed economic warfare measures, along with indignation at the treatment of Latin American residents and nationals, can have surprised only those U.S. officials who were unaware of how completely of a piece such policies seemed to be with Washington's traditional treatment of Latin America.

Perhaps the saddest irony is that respect for the rights of individuals, a feasible opportunity to save lives, and the principles of the Good Neighbor policy – mutuality, noninterference, and respect – were sacrificed to achieve a war aim of dubious value. Despite the clamor of the small local Nazi groups, Hitler's Germany never evinced much interest in Latin America in the first place, and its spies were caught thanks to time-tested investigative techniques, not civilian internment. Postwar investigations of the individual deportees only confirmed the paucity of evidence substantiating the threat that brought them into the camps. In the dogged pursuit of the destruction of the civilian German presence in Latin America well after any possibility of invasion had receded, when U.S. officials were openly admitting that persons they had interned were harmless, it became clear that the aim of ensuring wartime security had given way to other, more long-term objectives. The completion of U.S. hegemony in Latin America after World War II thus was partly the inevitable result of the outcome of the conflict, and partly the product of careful design.

During the Second World War, as later during the Cold War, misdirected security fears and poor appreciation of local conditions led the United States to intervene in Latin American affairs to combat an ostensible external threat to the region. Through the 1930s, the Good Neighbor had built up capital in the form of a wary trust that was quickly squandered by a reversion to the traditional, paternalistic approach as soon as Washington thought a rival had appeared on the scene. U.S. policymakers again assumed that they understood Latin America better than those who lived there, and that the outside world's great power adversaries were the real actors while Latin Americans were either "theirs" or "ours."

After the war, as the CIA arrived to hunt Communists, the German communities lay in ruins: farms degraded, businesses shuttered, schools and clubs defunct. Nazi hubris and Hitler's war had helped bring on this devastating backlash, and Yankee ambition completed the job. Soon the ignominious deportation program receded into the past, displaced by the crusade against the new enemy and overshadowed by far greater anguish. And as it had for more than a century, Latin America could only look on its northern neighbor with profound disillusion.

Notes

Prologue

1. Werner Kappel, telephone interviews with author, Sun City, Florida, 30 Mar 1999 and 25 Feb 2000. See also "Records of the War Department on KAPPEL, Werner Julius," in folder "Kappel, Werner. Panama," Name Files of Interned Enemy Aliens from Latin America, 1942–1948, Box 41, Special War Problems Division, RG59, National Archives, College Park, MD.

Introduction

1. Russell D. Buhite and David W. Levy, eds., *FDR's Fireside Chats* (Norman: University of Oklahoma Press, 1992), 192.
2. Spruille Braden, *Diplomats and Demagogues* (New Rochelle, NY: Arlington House, 1971), 240; Braden to Welles, 24 Nov 1941, folder 12, Box 67, Sumner Welles Papers, FDR Library, Hyde Park, NY; Hull, "Reference to Air Field in Colombia," 17 Sep 1941, reel 28, Cordell Hull Papers (microfilm), Manuscript Division, Library of Congress, Washington, DC (hereafter LC). See also David Bushnell, *Eduardo Santos and the Good Neighbor, 1938–1942* (Gainesville: University of Florida Press, 1967), 60–1.
3. Alberto Vargas to Ministerio de Relaciones Exteriores (hereafter MRE), 17 Sep 1940, "Actividades Nazis 1940," Actividades Nazis 1940–2, Archivo del Ministerio de Relaciones Exteriores, Bogotá, Colombia (hereafter AMRE); Turbay to MRE, 25 Jul 1941, Embajada de Colombia en Washington, AMRE.
4. Deportee numbers by nationality in White to Bingham, 28 Jan 1946, "Statistics," Subject Files 1939–54, Box 70, Special War Problems Division (hereafter SWP), RG59, National Archives, College Park, MD (hereafter NA).
5. Mola quotation in Congressional Record, Senate, vol. 86, pt. 6, 76th Congress, 3rd sess., 6773.
6. Ernest May, "The Alliance for Progress in Historical Perspective," *Foreign Affairs* 41 (July 1963): 759–60, cited in Walter LaFeber, *Inevitable Revolutions: The United States in Central America* (New York: Norton, 1983), 82.
7. Josephus Daniels Diary, 14 Jan 1939, reel 7, Daniels Papers, Manuscript Division, LC.

8. Department of State, *Policy of the United States Government in removing dangerous Axis nationals from the other American republics*, 28 May 1943, "711.5," Costa Rica: San José Embassy Confidential File, Box 26, RG84, NA.

9. See Lars Schoultz, *Beneath the United States: A History of U.S. Policy toward Latin America* (Cambridge, MA: Harvard University Press, 1998); John J. Johnson, *A Hemisphere Apart: The Foundations of United States Policy toward Latin America* (Baltimore: Johns Hopkins University Press, 1990).

10. For statistics on German internments in the United States, see Chapter 4. The rounded figures for the other countries named are approximate, since we do not have consistent German population figures for them.

11. For figures as of June 1937, see Hans-Adolf Jacobsen, *Nationalsozialistische Außenpolitik, 1933–1938* (Frankfurt: Alfred Metzner Verlag, 1968), 662–3, and compare to Michael Naumann, "Ausgewählte Daten zur Auslandsorganisation der NSDAP, Stand am 30.6.1939," based on Bundesarchiv document NSD 8/43 (Auslandsorganisation der NSDAP. Statistik, 30.6.1939, Geheim). Courtesy Michael Naumann, Institut für Zeitgeschichte, Aussenstelle Berlin-Lichterfelde.

12. The higher estimate is from Francis MacDonnell, *Insidious Foes: The Axis Fifth Column and the American Home Front* (New York: Oxford University Press, 1995), 47; the lower from Susan Canedy, *America's Nazis: A History of the German American Bund* (Menlo Park, CA: Markgraf, 1990), 86.

13. "22,000 Nazis Hold Rally In Garden," *New York Times,* 21 Feb 1939.

14. Hans-Jürgen Schröder, "Die Vereinigten Staaten und die nazionalsozialistische Handelspolitik gegenüber Lateinamerika," *Jahrbuch für Geschichte von Staat, Wirtschaft und Gesellschaft Lateinamerikas* 7 (1970): 309–71; Lloyd C. Gardner, *Economic Aspects of New Deal Diplomacy* (Madison: University of Wisconsin Press, 1964), 52.

15. Adolf A. Berle to Chiefs of the Diplomatic Missions in the Other American Republics, *The Pattern of Nazi Organizations and Their Activities in the Other American Republics*, 6 Feb 1941, p. 26, 862.20210/414A, RG59, NA. Stimson in Senate Committee on Foreign Relations, *Hearings on S. 275*, 77th Congress, 1st sess. (Washington, 1941), pt. 1, 131; Bernard Baruch, *My Own Story: The Public Years* (New York, 1960), 275. Both quoted in Gardner, *Economic Aspects*, 122–4.

16. *Minutes of the first meeting of the Latin America Conference on 12 June 1939 in the Auswärtiges Amt,* 12 Jun 1939, R67412, Rückwanderung aus Südamerika – Allgemeines, Kulturabteilung, Politisches Archiv des Auswärtigen Amtes, Bonn (hereafter PAAA).

17. JRT, "German Kulturpolitik in the Other American Republics," 5 Oct 1942, in folder "Reports Prepared by the Special Section," Office of Intelligence Research, Division of Research for the American Republics, Box 13, Division of American Republics (ARA), RG59, NA.

18. Hull to Biddle, 9 Nov 1942, 740.00115EW1939/4570, RG59, NA.

19. Nearly two thousand were from Peru, which offered to send *all* of its Japanese to the United States – estimated at 30,000 people – a suggestion not unwelcome in principle at the State Department, but declined because of a lack of available shipping. Keeley to Long, doc. 740.00115EW1939/5670, RG59, NA, College Park, MD. See also C. Harvey Gardiner's *Pawns in a Triangle of Hate: The Peruvian Japanese and the United States* (Seattle: University of Washington Press, 1981) and P. Scott Corbett, *Quiet Passages: The Exchange of Civilians between the United States*

and Japan during the Second World War (Kent, OH: Kent State University Press, 1987).

20. Francis Biddle, *In Brief Authority* (Garden City, NY: Doubleday & Co., 1962), 207. See also Rockefeller to Welles, *Reclassification of Italians – Repercussions in Latin America*, 26 May 1942, 740.00115EW1939/3520 3/5, RG59, NA; Luigi Rossi, "L'etnia italiana nelle Americhe: la strategia statunitense durante la seconda guerra mondiale," *Nuova Rivista Storica* 79: 1 (1995): 115–142; Orazio A. Ciccarelli, "Fascist Propaganda and the Italian Community in Peru during the Benavides Regime, 1933–1939," *Journal of Latin American Studies* 20 (1988): 361–88.

21. Venezuela also ran its own internment facility and declined U.S. overtures to deport its German residents to the United States.

22. See Leslie B. Rout, Jr., and John F. Bratzel, *The Shadow War: German Espionage and United States Counterespionage in Latin America during World War II* (Frederick, MD: University Publications of America, 1986); Stanley E. Hilton, *Hitler's Secret War in South America 1939–1945: German Military Espionage and Allied Counterespionage in Brazil* (Baton Rouge: Louisiana State University Press, 1981); and Maria Emilia Paz, *Strategy, Security, and Spies: Mexico and the U.S. as Allies in World War II* (University Park: Pennsylvania State University Press, 1997).

23. FBI, *German Espionage in Latin America*, June 1946, 862.20210/6-1746, RG59, NA, pp. 38, 105–6; Hoover to Neal, 14 Oct 1946, 862.20210/10-1446, RG59, NA. The eight are named in Chapter 2.

24. The phrase is from William Roseberry, "Social Fields and Cultural Encounters," in Gilbert M. Joseph, Catherine C. LeGrand, and Ricardo D. Salvatore, eds., *Close Encounters of Empire: Writing the Cultural History of U.S.-Latin American Relations* (Durham, NC: Duke University Press, 1998), 517.

Chapter 1 Contamination

1. Krause, Danckers, Hentschke, and Gieseler, *An alle deutschen Landsleute in Guatemala Stadt und Land!* 13 Dec 1933, special file, German deportees collection, German Embassy, Guatemala City; Hermann Kaltwasser, *Petition for non-repatriation*, 22 Dec 1943, "K," Name Files of Interned Enemy Aliens from Latin America, 1942–8, Box 33, Special War Problems Division (hereafter SWP), RG59, National Archives, College Park, MD (hereafter NA); Edgar A. Heinemann, *Lilric* (Guatemala City: Afanes, S.A., 1993), 189; Stefan Karlen, *"Paz, progreso, justicia y honradez": das Ubico-Regime in Guatemala, 1931–1944* (Stuttgart: Franz Steiner Verlag, 1991), 36, 215; Anonymous leading member of Jewish community, interview by author, Guatemala City, 29 May 1996.

2. Erich Kraske to Reinebeck, 20 Jun 1937, "Kopie eines Briefes Kraskes an seinen Nachfolger Reinebeck vom 20 Juni 1936," NL 139/39, and Erich Kraske, 7 Aug 1936, "Bericht von Kraske vom 7. Aug. 1936 über die Lage in Guatemala und Costa Rica," NL 139/12, Nachlasse Kraske, Bundesarchiv, Koblenz (hereafter BA-K); Piero Gleijeses, *Shattered Hope: The Guatemalan Revolution and the United States, 1944–1954* (Princeton, NJ: Princeton University Press, 1991), 18.

3. Erich Kraske, 7 Aug 1936, as above; on school conflict see also *Denkschrift*, 28 Dec 1935, special file, German deportees collection, German Embassy,

Guatemala City; Ernesto Schaeffer, *Memoiren* (Guatemala City: n.p., n.d.),
71–3; Regina Wagner, *Los Alemanes en Guatemala, 1828–1944* (Guatemala:
Afanes, 1996), 360–2; Kenneth J. Grieb, *Guatemalan Caudillo: The Regime
of Jorge Ubico, Guatemala 1931–1944* (Athens: Ohio University Press, 1979),
15–17.

4. Hartmut Fröschle, ed., *Die Deutschen in Lateinamerika: Schicksal und Leistung*
   (Tübingen: Horst Erdmann Verlag, 1979), 849; Gunter Kahle, *Simón Bolívar
   und die Deutschen* (Berlin: Dietrich Reimer Verlag, 1980); Alberto San Román,
   Contribución de los alemanes en la conquista de Sudamérica: siglo XVI (Buenos
   Aires: Ediciones Dunken, 1996).

5. Jean-Pierre Blancpain, "Des visées pangermanistes au noyautage hitlérien: Le
   nationalisme allemand et l'Amérique latine (1890–1945)," in *Revue historique*
   281: 2 (1990): 437.

6. Blancpain, "Des visées pangermanistes," 434.

7. 1821 letter from Bolívar to von Humboldt quoted in Mary Louise Pratt, *Imperial
   Eyes: Travel Writing and Transculturation* (New York: Routledge, 1992), 112.

8. Jean-Pierre Blancpain, *Migrations et mémoires germaniques en Amérique
   latine* (Strasbourg: Presses Universitaires de Strasbourg, 1994), 70–2; Thomas
   Schoonover, *Germany in Central America: Competitive Imperialism, 1821–1929*
   (Tuscaloosa: University of Alabama Press, 1998), 149; Horst Nitschack, "La
   Recepción de la Cultura de Habla Alemana en Amauta," in *Encuentros y Desen-
   cuentros: Estudios sobre la recepción de la cultura alemana en América Latina* (Lima:
   Pontificia Universidad Católica del Perú, 1993).

9. Blancpain, *Migrations et mémoires*, 207–9, 225.

10. See Conrad Koch, *La Colonia Tovar: Geschichte und Kultur einer alemannis-
    chen Siedlung in Venezuela* (Geneva: Internationales Kulturinstitut, 1970); Ben
    MacIntyre, *Forgotten Fatherland: The Search for Elizabeth Nietzsche* (New York:
    Farrar Straus Giroux, 1992).

11. Aside from Germany, later Israel, and a handful of other countries, most na-
    tions of the world base their citizenship laws principally on *jus soli*, the right of
    soil – conferring citizenship on people born in the national territory regardless
    of ancestry.

12. Fritz Gaedicke, *Familien-Aufzeichnungen*, unpublished, 1910, in Blancpain, "Des
    visées pangermanistes," 452–3; FBI, *German Espionage in Latin America*, June
    1946, p. 3, 862.20210/6-1746, RG59, NA. For an exploration of the significance
    of club life for creating a sense of solidarity and belonging among Germans in
    a different context, see Vernon L. Lidtke, *The Alternative Culture: Socialist Labor
    in Imperial Germany* (New York: Oxford University Press, 1985), esp. chapter
    3, "Club Life," 50–74.

13. Jean Roche, *La colonisation allemande et le Rio Grande do Sul* (Paris: Institut
    des hautes études de l'Amérique latine, 1959), 4, 542–50; Walther L. Bernecker
    and Thomas Fischer, "Deutschland und Lateinamerika im Zeitalter des Impe-
    rialismus, 1871–1914," *Ibero-Amerikanisches Archiv* 21:3–4 (1995): 273–302;
    Blancpain, "Des visées pangermanistes," 468–71.

14. Nelson A. Rockefeller, Typescript of conversation with Mr. & Mrs. Monahan,
    pp. 1–5, 7 Feb–14 Mar 1949, "The US and the World," Box 18, RG III 4 A,
    Nelson A. Rockefeller Personal Papers, Rockefeller Family Archives, Rockefeller
    Archive, North Tarrytown, NY (hereafter RAC).

15. FBI, "Colombia Today," March 1942, p. 22, in folder "FBI Reports – Colombia," Box 141, Harry Hopkins Papers, FDR Library, Hyde Park, NY.

16. Nancy Mitchell argues that Germany never sought to challenge the United States in this period, that U.S. alarm was the result of taking vocal pan-Germanists at their word rather than perceiving how minor was their influence over the German government; see Nancy Mitchell, *The Danger of Dreams. German and American Imperialism in Latin America* (Chapel Hill: University of North Carolina Press, 1999). Fiebig-von Hase credits a more substantial German threat in *Lateinamerika als Konflktherd*, 507, 512, 742, 753, 843–6, 1087; See also Thomas Baecker, "Deutschland im karibischen Raum im Spiegel amerikanischer Akten (1898–1914)," *Jahrbuch für Geschichte von Staat, Wirtschaft und Gesellschaft Lateinamerikas* 11 (1974): 167–237; Melvin Small, "The United States and the German 'Threat' to the Hemisphere, 1905–1914," *Americas* 28:3 (1972): 252–70.

17. Anne Saint Saveur-Henn, "Die deutsche Einwanderung in Argentinien (1870–1933): zur Wirkung der politischen Entwicklung in Deutschland auf die Deutschen in Argentinien," in *Nationalsozialismus und Argentinien: Beziehungen, Einflüsse und Nachwirkungen*, Holger M. Meding, ed. (Frankfurt: Lang, 1995), 23.

18. Schoonover, *Germany in Central America*, 158–66; Blancpain, *Migrations et mémoires*, 272; Frederick C. Luebke, *Germans in Brazil: A Comparative History of Cultural Conflict During World War I* (Baton Rouge: Louisiana State University Press, 1987), 119–46, 162–74, 220–3; Emily S. Rosenberg, *World War I and the Growth of United States Predominance in Latin America* (New York: Garland, 1987), 153–65.

19. State Department policies on economic warfare would make much of the distinction between the World War I blacklist, based on "nationality," and the World War II blacklist, based on "ideology." However, the standards for inclusion were again quite broad the second time around. Dean Acheson, *Action Taken by the United States Government in the Economic Field to Eliminate Axis Influence from the Other American Republics*, 2 Jun 1942, "711 1942," Colombia: Bogota Embassy, Security-Segregated General Records, 1938–49, Box 23, RG84, NA. See Chapters 3 and 7 in this volume.

20. Hermann Kellenbenz and Jürgen Schneider, "La emigración alemana a América Latina desde 1821 hasta 1930," *Jahrbuch für Geschichte von Staat, Wirtschaft und Gesellschaft Lateinamerikas* 13 (1976): 386–403; Stefan Rinke, *"Der letzte freie Kontinent": Deutsche Lateinamerikapolitik im Zeichen transnationaler Beziehungen, 1918–1933* (Stuttgart: Hans-Dieter Heinz, 1996), vol. 1, 294–5.

21. Blancpain, "Des visées pangermanistes," 468; Rinke, *"Der letzte freie Kontinent,"* vol. 1, 402.

22. Ursula Schlenther, "Rassenideologie der Nazis in der ethnographischen Literatur über Lateinamerika," in *Der deutsche Faschismus in Lateinamerika, 1933–1943*, Heinz Sanke, ed. (Berlin: Humboldt-Universität zu Berlin, 1966), 75. For a bibliography of German travel writing on Latin America of the first quarter of the twentieth century, see Jürgen Kloosterhuis, *'Friedliche Imperialisten.' Deutsche Auslandsvereine und auswärtige Kulturpolitik, 1906–1918* (Frankfurt: Lang, 1994), vol. 2, 908–912.

23. The quotation is from Arnold Ebel, *Das Dritte Reich und Argentinien: Die diplomatischen Beziehungen unter besonderer Berücksichtigung der Handelspolitik, 1933–1939* (Köln: Böhlau, 1971), 25. See also Walther L. Bernecker and Thomas Fischer, "Deutsche in Lateinamerika," in *Deutsche im Ausland – Fremde in Deutschland: Migration in Geschichte und Gegenwart*, Klaus J. Bade, ed. (Munich: C. H. Beck, 1992), 213–14; Matthias Schönwald, "Nationalsozialismus im Aufwind? Das politische Leben der deutschen Gemeinschaft Argentiniens in den frühen zwanziger Jahren des 20. Jahrhunderts," in *Nationalsozialismus und Argentinien: Beziehungen, Einflüsse und Nachwirkungen*, Holger M. Meding, ed. (Frankfurt: Lang, 1995), 52–6; Saint Saveur-Henn, "Die deutsche Einwanderung," 26; Ronald C. Newton, *German Buenos Aires, 1900–1933: Social Change and Cultural Crisis* (Austin: University of Texas Press, 1977), 63; Rinke, *"Der letzte freie Kontinent,"* vol. 1, 379.

24. Rinke, *"Der letzte freie Kontinent,"* vol. 1, 402–3.

25. Hans-Adolf Jacobsen, *Nationalsozialistische Außenpolitik 1933–1938* (Frankfurt: Alfred Metzner Verlag, 1968), 90ff; Olag Gaudig and Peter Veit, "El Partido Alemán Nacionalsocialista en Argentina, Brasil y Chile frente a las comunidades alemanas: 1933–1939," *Estudios Interdisciplinarios de América Latina y el Caribe (Tel Aviv)* 6: 1 (1995): 71–87.

26. Donald M. McKale, *The Swastika Outside Germany* (Kent, OH: Kent State University Press, 1977), 19–39.

27. McKale, *The Swastika*, 45–9; "Biographie Ernst Wilhelm Bohles," *NS 9: Auslandsorganisation der NSDAP* (Koblenz: Bundesarchiv, 1992), 11–12; Rudolf Hess, *Anordnung Nr. 66/35 des Stellvertreters des Führers*, 1 Apr 1935, p. 13, Appendix 2, NS 9 Findbuch, Auslandsorganisation der NSDAP, BA-K.

28. Bohle admitted as much in a postwar interrogation. See McKale, *The Swastika*, 58. See also Hans-Adolf Jacobsen, "Zur Struktur der NS-Außenpolitik 1933–1945," in *Hitler, Deutschland und die Mächte. Materialien zur Außenpolitik des Dritten Reiches*, Manfred Funke, ed. (Düsseldorf: Droste Verlag, 1978), 137–85.

29. Blancpain, "Des visées pangermanistes," 476–7.

30. Reiner Pommerin, *Das Dritte Reich und Lateinamerika: Die deutsche Politik gegenüber Süd- und Mittelamerika 1939–1942* (Düsseldorf: Droste Verlag, 1977), 41–2.

31. Gaudig and Veit, "El Partido Alemán," 76–9.

32. Jürgen Müller, *Nationalsozialismus in Lateinamerika: Die Auslandsorganisation der NSDAP in Argentinien, Brasilien, Chile und Mexico, 1931–1945* (Stuttgart: Verlag Hans-Dieter Heinz, 1997), 209.

33. *Karibischer Beobachter* 5: 8 (15 April 1938).

34. Dawid Bartelt, "'Fünfte Kolonne' ohne Plan. Die Auslandsorganisation der NSDAP in Brasilien, 1931–1939," *Ibero-Amerikanisches Archiv* 19: 1–2 (1993): 3–35.

35. See Roche, *La colonisation allemande*, 542; Wolfgang Kießling, *Exil in Lateinamerika* (Frankfurt am Main: Verlag Philipp Reclam, 1984), 62; Olaf Gaudig and Peter Veit, *Der Widerschein des Nazismus: Das Bild des Nationalsozialismus in der deutschsprachigen Presse Argentiniens, Brasiliens und Chiles 1932–1945* (Berlin: Wissenschaftlicher Verlag, 1997), 484; Jürgen Müller, "El NSDAP en México: historia y percepciones, 1931–1940," *Estudios Interdisciplinarios de*

América Latina y el Caribe (Tel Aviv) 6: 2 (1995): 92; Russell B. Porter, "'Cold' Nazi Terror in Mexico Holds German Community to Party Line," *New York Times,* 30 Aug 1940; *First Phase – Axis Penetration in Latin America,* 1944, p. 9, folder 85, CIAA Report Drafts, Box 11, Record Group III 40, Nelson A. Rockefeller Personal Files, Washington, DC, Files, Rockefeller Family Archives, RAC; FBI, *Bolivia Today,* June 1942, p. 33, "FBI Reports – Bolivia," Box 141, Hopkins Papers, FDR Library; FBI, *German Espionage in Latin America,* p. 10, June 1946, 862.20210/6-1746, RG59, NA.

36. Gunter Beckmann, interview by author, Quito, 21 Jan 1998; Hans Griesbach, interview by author, Quito, 8 Feb 1998; Fernando Tinajero, *Itinerario de un acercamiento: Colegio Alemán, 1917–1992* (Quito: Asociación Ecuatoriana-Alemana de Cultura y Educación, 1992), 82–93.

37. For one example, see Wilhelm Lothes to Gestapo, 30 Oct 1942, p. 3, "Lothes, Wilhelm," 3601000203, Rückwandereramt der AO, Bundesarchiv, Lichterfelde (hereafter BA-L).

38. *Uschla* stood for *Untersuchungs- und Schlichtungsausschuß,* investigating and adjustment committee. It was the disciplinary body that punished dissidents within the Party and adjudicated disputes among Party members.

39. Carlos Heymann Albán, interview by author, Guayaquil, 18 Feb 1998. See also Friedrich Katz, "Einige Grundzüge der Politik des deutschen Imperialismus in Lateinamerika von 1898 bis 1941," in *Der deutsche Faschismus in Lateinamerika, 1933–1943,* Heinz Sanke, ed. (Berlin: Humboldt-Universität zu Berlin, 1966), 22–3; Blancpain, *Migrations et mémoires,* 282.

40. Wolfgang Kießling, *Alemania Libre en Mexiko,* 2 vols. (Berlin: Akademie-Verlag, 1974), vol. 1, 58–66, 151; Kießling, *Exil in Lateinamerika,* 107–20, 310–54; Patrik von zur Mühlen, *Fluchtziel Lateinamerika: Die deutsche Emigration 1933–1945: politische Aktivitäten und soziokulturelle Integration* (Bonn: Verlag Neue Gesellschaft, 1988), 110–18.

41. Von zur Mühlen, *Fluchtziel Lateinamerika,* 118–19; Kießling, *Alemania Libre,* 441–586.

42. Kießling, *Exil in Lateinamerika,* 422; von zur Mühlen, *Fluchtziel Lateinamerika,* 119. The most reliable estimate of Party membership for all Latin America is 7,602 as of 30 Jun 1937, from AO records, in Jacobsen, *Nationalsozialistische Außenpolitik,* 662–3. Since the Party was banned throughout Latin America the following year, membership did not increase significantly between 1937 and 1939. See Michael Naumann, "Ausgewählte Daten zur Auslandsorganisation der NSDAP, Stand am 30.6.1939," based on Bundesarchiv document NSD 8/43 (Auslandsorganisation der NSDAP), Statistik, 30.6.1939, Geheim. Courtesy Michael Naumann, Institut für Zeitgeschichte, Aussenstelle Berlin-Lichterfelde.

43. Jacobsen, *Nationalsozialistische Außenpolitik,* 602; Katz, "Einige Grundzüge," 57.

44. Statistics on Nazi membership in Latin American countries vary, partly according to sources used; the most reliable are Senate Committee on Military Affairs, *Nazi Party Membership Records,* Senate Committee Prints 79/2/46, Part 2, March 1946, and Part 3, September 1946, S1535-S1538 (Washington, DC: U.S. Government Printing Office, 1946), and Jacobsen, *Nationalsozialistische Außenpolitik,* 662–3.

45. Roche, *La colonisation allemande.*

46. See Naumann, "Ausgewählte Daten." Note: The population figures for *Reichsdeutsche* in this document are lower than most other estimates and should be considered together with other sources; I have adjusted the figures (and made them approximate) to allow for the AO's undercount.

47. Ronald C. Newton, "The United States, the German-Argentines, and the Myth of the Fourth Reich, 1943–47," *Hispanic American Historical Review* 64: 1 (1984): 81–103.

48. Jürgen Müller, "Entwicklung und Aktivitäten der NSDAP in Argentinien, 1931–1945," in *Nationalsozialismus und Argentinien: Beziehungen, Einflüsse und Nachwirkungen*, Holger M. Meding, ed. (Frankfurt: Lang, 1995), 70.

49. Werner Ascoli, interview by author, Guatemala City, 24 May 1996.

50. Otto Luis Schwarz, interview by author, Guayaquil, 16 Feb 1998.

51. *Wir wandern und singen: Liederbuch der NS-Gemeinschaft 'Kraft durch Freude',* 1935, in folder "Freitag, Guenther Herman Otto, Costa Rica," Name Files of Interned Enemy Aliens from Latin America, 1942–8, Box 39, SWP, RG59, NA. Author's translation.

52. Hebe Clementi, "El negro en América Latina," in *Discriminación y racismo en América Latina*, Ignacio Klich and Mario Rapoport, eds. (Buenos Aires: Grupo Editor Latinoamericano, 1997), 46; Werner Aron and Gert Aron, *The Halo of the Jungle* (Quito: unpublished memoir, 1967, rev. 1996), 6; Arthur P. Whitaker, *The United States and South America: The Northern Republics* (Cambridge, MA: Harvard University Press, 1948), 55; Richard Graham, ed., *The Idea of Race in Latin America, 1870–1940* (Austin: University of Texas Press, 1990).

53. Marionilde Brepohl de Magalhães, *Pangermanismo e Nazismo: A trajetória alemã rumo ao Brasil* (Campinas, Brazil: Editora da UNICAMP/FAPESP, 1998), 158.

54. See Detlev J. K. Peukert, *Inside Nazi Germany: Conformity, Opposition, and Racism in Everyday Life*, trans. Richard Deveson (New Haven, CT: Yale University Press, 1982), 41, 70. Quotation from JRT, "German Kulturpolitik in the Other American Republics," pp. 1–6, in folder "Reports Prepared by the Special Section," Office of Intelligence Research, Division of Research for the American Republics, Box 13, ARA, RG59, NA.

55. Interview, Hugo Droege, 22 May 1996, Guatemala City; Christel K. Converse, "The Rise and Fall of Nazi Influence among the German-Chileans" (Ph.D. diss., Georgetown University, 1990), 120; Jürgen Buchenau, "Not Quite Mexican and Not Quite German: The Boker Family in Mexico, 1865–1995" (unpublished ms., 1996), 9; Müller, *Nationalsozialismus in Lateinamerika*, 278.

56. Wagner, *Los Alemanes en Guatemala*, 348–9.

57. Claus Bussmann, *Treu Deutsch und Evangelisch: Die Geschichte der Deutschen Evangelischen Gemeinde zu Asunción/Paraguay von 1893–1963* (Stuttgart: Franz Steiner Verlag Wiesbaden GMBH, 1989).

58. Hans-Jürgen Prien, "Die 'Deutsch-Evangelische Kirche' in Brasilien im Spannungsbogen von nationaler Wende (1933) und Kirchenkampf," *Jahrbuch für Geschichte von Staat, Wirtschaft und Gesellschaft Lateinamerikas* 25 (1988): 511–34.

59. Von zur Mühlen, *Fluchtziel Lateinamerika*, 60.

60. "*Das Judentum trifft sich selbst!!*" in *Karibischer Beobachter*, 15 Dec 1938, pp. 5–6. There are copies of several years of the *Karibischer Beobachter* at the Ibero-Amerikanisches Institut at the Neue Staatsbibliothek, Preussischer Kulturbesitz zu Berlin. See also Kießling, *Exil in Lateinamerika*, p. 420.

61. Federico de Urrutia, *La Paz que quiere Hitler,* 1939, Actividades Nazis 1939–1940, Archivo del Ministerio de Relaciones Exteriores, Bogotá (AMRE). See also Müller, *Nationalsozialismus in Lateinamerika,* 276–8; von zur Mühlen, *Fluchtziel Lateinamerika,* 61; Alicia Gojman de Backal, "Deutsche Beteiligung an der Bewegung der 'Goldhemden' im Mexiko der 30er Jahre," in *Europaische Juden in Lateinamerika,* Achim Schrader and Karl Heinrich Rengstorf, eds. (St. Ingbert: Werner J. Rohrig Verlag, 1989), 425–34.

62. Von zur Mühlen, *Fluchtziel Lateinamerika,* 60.

63. Edgar A. Heinemann, *Lilric* (Guatemala City: Afanes, S.A., 1993), 189.

64. Anonymous leading member of Jewish community, interview by author, Guatemala City, 29 May 1996.

65. A. Schmidt to German chambers of commerce in Latin America, 2 Jul 1940, and Fiuhl to Lateinamerikanischer Verein, 3 Oct 1940, "Richtlinien der Wirtschaftsgruppe Groß-, Ein- und Ausfuhrhandel für die Ausfuhr nach Süd- und Mittelamerika," R 64 III/2, Lateinamerikanischer Verein, BA-K. See also McKale, *The Swastika,* 126.

66. Dr. Ilse Grossman, interview by author, Quito, 30 Jan 1998; Roberto Hahn, interview by author, Guayaquil, 16 Feb 1998; Hans Ungar, interview by author, Bogotá, 16 Mar 1998. See also Benno Weise Varon, *Professions of a Lucky Jew* (New York: Cornwall Books, 1992), 99.

67. For an alphabetical list of overseas Party members, see *Auslandsorganisation* membership list, on microfilm in the Manuscript Division of the Library of Congress as "Germany (territory under allied occupation, 1945–1955: U.S. Zone), Office of Military Government," Shelf no. Mss. 18,049, 3 reels. For a listing by country, see Senate Committee on Military Affairs, *Nazi Party Membership Records,* Senate Committee Prints 79/2/46, Part 2, March 1946, and Part 3, September 1946, S1535–8 (Washington, DC: U.S. Government Printing Office, 1946).

68. Leslie B. Rout, Jr., and John F. Bratzel, *The Shadow War: German Espionage and United States Counterespionage in Latin America during World War II* (Frederick, MD: University Publications of America, 1986), 44.

69. Hans Kolter, interview by author, Guatemala City, 27 May 1996.

70. Walter Held, interview by author, Bogotá, 9 Mar 1998.

71. Carlos Gehlert, interview by author, Guatemala City, 30 May 1996.

72. Alfredo Brauer, interview by author, Quito, 5 Feb 1998.

73. Ian Kershaw, *The Nazi Dictatorship: Problems and Perspectives of Interpretation* (London: Edward Arnold, 1989), 126.

74. Knöhr circular letter, 11 Nov 1934; Kriebel to Knöhr, 15 Nov 1934; Kraske to Kriebel, 23 Jan 1935; Kriebel to Kraske, 24 Apr 1935. All courtesy Dr. Ricardo Kriebel *fils,* San José.

75. FBI, *Costa Rica Today,* Sep 1943, p. 71, "FBI Reports – Costa Rica," Box 142, Hopkins Papers, FDR Library; Jackson to Gordon, 25 July 1941, 164.12/4539 1/2, RG59, NA. The North American members did not resign until 1941, further indicating that the Club can hardly have been a bastion of Nazi subversion.

76. *Documents on German Foreign Policy* 5: 821–85.

77. Dieckhoff to AA, 11 Apr 1938, "Volksabstimmung vom 10. April 1938," German Consul in Bahia to AA, 14 Apr 1938, "Volksabstimmung vom 10.

April 1938," Reinebeck (Guatemala) to Chef AO, 19 Mar 1938, "Volksabstimmung vom 10. April 1938" (emphasis added), R46292, Rechtsabteilung, PAAA; Arnold J. Toynbee, *Survey of International Affairs* 1 (1938): 234.

78. Bohle report to Hitler, 3 May 1938, R46292, in folder "Volksabstimmung vom 10. April 1938," Rechtsabteilung, PAAA, Bonn; 8mm b&w silent film of vote in Ecuador, courtesy Hardy de von Campe, Guayaquil, 1938; photos of vote in Guatemala, courtesy Hans Kolter, Guatemala City, 1938; interviews with Kolter, Guatemala City, 27 May 1996; Hugo Droege, Guatemala City, 22 May 1996; Inge von Schröter, San José, 26 Mar 1998; Hardy de von Campe, Guayaquil, 16 Feb 1998. A postwar report on one German from Guatemala indicates he went "for the beer": Livingston, *Summary of Justice Files,* 4 Jan 1946, in folder "Beyer, Pablo," Name Files of Interned Enemy Aliens from Latin America, 1942–48, Box 36, SWP, RG59, NA.

79. See also E. W. Bohle, *Aufruf zur Wahl,* 21 Mar 1938, reprinted in Marionilde Brepohl de Magalhães, *Pangermanismo e Nazismo: A trajetória alemã rumo ao Brasil* (Campinas, Brazil: Editora da UNICAMP/FAPESP, 1998), 254; E. Andino, *Military Attaché Report,* 25 Jun 1942, in folder "Ehrenberg, Paul Engineer German Costa Rica," Naval Attache – Guatemala City Personality Files, 1940–6, Box 34, Office of Naval Intelligence (hereafter ONI), RG38, NA; Hallett Johnson to SecState, 7 Dec 1945, in folder "711.5," Costa Rica: San José Embassy, Confidential File, Box 39, RG84, NA; Hardy de von Campe, interview with author, Guayaquil, 16 Feb 1998.

80. Siedler circular telegram, 26 Mar 1938, "Volksabstimmung vom 10. April 1938," R46292, Rechtsabteilung, Politisches Archiv des Auswärtigen Amtes (hereafter PAAA), Bonn.

81. Figures in Bohle report to Hitler, 3 May 1938, R46292, in folder "Volksabstimmung vom 10. April 1938," Rechtsabteilung, PAAA, Bonn.

82. *Strictly Confidential Memorandum,* 29 Jan 1943, in folder "A8–5(1-Costa Rica) Germans," Naval Attaché – Guatemala City, Personality Files 1940–6, Box 45, ONI, RG38, NA; Victor Heck, in folder "A," Name Files of Enemy Aliens, 1942–8, Box 31, SWP, RG59, NA; Lafoon, *Schreiber, Karl,* 6 Dec 1945, in folder "Schreiber, Wilhelm Karl," Name Files of Interned Enemy Aliens from Latin America, 1942–8, Box 47, SWP, RG59, NA.

83. Gaudig and Veit, "El Partido Alemán," 82; Pommerin, *Das Dritte Reich,* 40–1; Alton Frye, *Nazi Germany and the American Hemisphere* (New Haven, CT: Yale University Press, 1967), 113; Jobst-H. Floto, *Die Beziehungen Deutschlands zu Venezuela 1933 bis 1958* (Frankfurt: Peter Lang, 1991), 135.

84. Pommerin, *Das Dritte Reich,* 45–9.

85. Paul Schmidt, *Statist auf diplomatischer Bühne: 1923–45* (Bonn: Anthenäum Verlag, 1949), 311, cited in Paul Seabury, *The Wilhelmstrasse: A Study of German Diplomats Under the Nazi Regime* (Berkeley: University of California Press, 1954), 25.

86. Copy of minutes, 12 Jun 1939, "Rückwanderung aus Südamerika – Allgemeines," R67412, Kulturabteilung, PAAA.

87. AO total membership in Latin America went from about 7,600 members to about 8,000 members over the two-year period. For figures as of June 1937, see Jacobsen, *Nationalsozialistische Außenpolitik,* 662–3, and compare to Naumann, "Ausgewählte Daten."

88. Copy of minutes, 12 Jun 1939, "Rückwanderung aus Südamerika – Allgemeines," R67412, Kulturabteilung, PAAA. Also reprinted in Akten zur deutschen Auswärtigen Politik (ADAP), Serie D., Bd. VI, Dok 509, 583–9.

89. Wise, *Summarization of steps which have been taken in various of the other American Republics to prohibit the dissemination of propaganda of belligerent Countries,* 9 Aug 1941, 800.20210/883, RG59, NA.

90. Pommerin, *Das Dritte Reich,* 78, 195.

91. Norman J. W. Goda, *Tomorrow the World: Hitler, Northwest Africa, and the Path toward America* (College Station: Texas A&M University Press, 1998), 112, 170.

92. Jürgen Müller, "Hitler, Lateinamerika und die Weltherrschaft," *Ibero-Amerikanisches Archiv* 18: 1/2 (1992), 89–90.

93. Pommerin, *Das Dritte Reich,* 340.

94. Hitler's remarks in Jochen Thies, *Architekt der Weltherrschaft: Die "Endziele" Hitlers* (Düsseldorf: Droste Verlag, 1976), 166–7.

95. Rauschning's book was first published in France with the title *Hitler m'a dit: confidences du Führer sur son plan de conquête du monde,* trans. Albert Lehman (Paris: Coopération, 1939). The quotation is my translation of the phrase "armes...d'un maniement plus délicat" from page 80. The line is usually rendered in English as "more difficult weapons," a poor translation of the 1940 German version "diffizilere Waffen." The book was published in the United States as *The Voice of Destruction* (New York: G. P. Putnam's Sons, 1940).

96. See Müller, "Hitler," 74–8; Klaus Volland, *Das Dritte Reich und Mexiko: Studien zur Entwicklung des deutsch-mexikanischen Verhältnisses 1933–1942 unter besonderer Berücksichtigung der Ölpolitik* (Frankfurt: Peter Lang, 1976), 29–42; Wolfgang Hänel, *Hermann Rauschnings "Gespräche mit Hitler": eine Geschichtsfälschung* (Ingolstadt: Zeitgeschichtliche Forschungsstelle, 1984); Fritz Tobias, "Auch Fälschungen haben lange Beine. Des Senatspräsidenten Rauschnings 'Gespräche mit Hitler,'" in Karl Corino, ed., *Gefälscht! Betrug in Politik, Literatur, Wissenschaft, Kunst und Musik* (Nördlingen: Greno, 1988), 91–105. Another former Nazi, Otto Strasser, published even more sensational, and even more dubious, "quotations" from Hitler in *The Gangsters around Hitler – with a Tropical Postcript: Nazi Gangsters in South America* (London: W. H. Allen & Co., 1942). But Strasser is rarely taken seriously as a reliable source.

97. Müller, "Hitler," 67–101; Pommerin, *Das Dritte Reich,* 289, 340.

98. Bohle interrogation, State Department Special Interrogation Mission, 5–8 Sep 1945, pp. 12 and 20–1, 862.20210/3-446, RG59, NA.

99. Pommerin, "Überlegungen," 365–77. How many expatriates would have answered the call is another question.

100. Canaris order banning sabotage in Louis De Jong, *The German Fifth Column in the Second World War* (Chicago: University of Chicago Press, 1956), 225. Bohle order to avoid "foreign policy complications" in Pommerin, *Das Dritte Reich,* 35. The FBI's postwar summary found incidents of sabotage to be "nil." See FBI, *German Espionage in Latin America,* June 1946, 862.20210/6-1746, RG59, NA.

Chapter 2 Assessment

1. FDR discussing Western Hemisphere security in *Complete Presidential Press Conferences of Franklin D. Roosevelt* (New York: Da Capo, 1972), 13: 313. The spelling error was the transcriber's, not Roosevelt's.
2. Jules Dubois, *Danger over Panama* (Indianapolis: Bobbs-Merrill, 1964), 53.
3. For warnings on refugees, see Chapter 8.
4. *Summary of Justice Files,* [Jan–Feb] 1946, "Merz, Karl Franz, Panama," Name Files of Interned Enemy Aliens from Latin America, 1942–48, Box 44, Special War Problems Division (hereafter SWP), RG59, National Archives (hereafter NA).
5. Dubois, *Danger over Panama,* 57.
6. For Heinemann and Dubois, see Bryan to Green, 21 May 1942, 740.00115 EW1939/3200, RG59, NA; *Confidential: Wilhelm Heinemann (Panama),* 14 Jan 1946, "Heinemann, Wilhelm, Panama," Name Files of Interned Enemy Aliens from Latin America, 1942–48, Box 40, SWP, RG59, NA; *Summary of Justice Files,* Jan–Feb [?] 1946, "Merz, Karl Franz, Panama," Name Files of Interned Enemy Aliens from Latin America, 1942–48, Box 44, SWP, RG59, NA. On Canal preparations, see Stetson Conn, Rose C. Engleman, and Byron Fairchild, *Guarding the United States and Its Outposts* (Washington, DC: Office of the Chief of Military History, Department of the Army, 1964), 310; Lester D. Langley, "The United States and Panama, 1933–1941: A Study in Strategy and Diplomacy" (Ph.D. diss., University of Kansas, 1965), 175–80. On refugees as spies, see Chapter 8.
7. David Haglund, *Latin America and the Transformation of U.S. Strategic Thought* (Albuquerque: University of New Mexico Press, 1984), 69, 74–5, 99, 178, 182, 187–8; Braden to Welles, 9 Aug 1941, folder 12, Box 67, Welles Papers, FDR Library.
8. See Dawid Bartelt, "'Fünfte Kolonne' ohne Plan. Die Auslandsorganisation der NSDAP in Brasilien, 1931–1939," *Ibero-Amerikanisches Archiv* 19: 1–2 (1993): 3–35; Stanley E. Hilton, "Acção Integralista Brasileira: Fascism in Brazil, 1932–1938," *Luso-Brazilian Review* 9 (1972): 3–29.
9. Simone Schwarz, *Chile im Schatten faschistischer Bewegungen: der Einfluß europäischer und chilenischer Strömungen in den 30er und 70er Jahren* (Frankfurt: Verlag für Akademische Schriften, 1997), 18–19.
10. George F. W. Young, "Jorge González von Marées – Chief of Chilean Nacism," *Jahrbuch für Geschichte von Staat, Wirtschaft und Gesellschaft Lateinamerikas* 11 (1974): 309–33, quote at 317. See also Sandra McGee Deutsch, *Las Derechas: The Extreme Right in Argentina, Brazil, and Chile, 1890–1939* (Stanford: Stanford University Press, 1999).
11. Ronald C. Newton, *The 'Nazi Menace' in Argentina, 1931–1947* (Stanford, CA: Stanford University Press, 1992), 191.
12. Louis De Jong, *The German Fifth Column in the Second World War* (Chicago: University of Chicago Press, 1956), 222–3; Haglund, *Latin America,* 175–6.
13. See Silvia Galvis, "Peripecias de los Nazis Criollos," *Credencial Historia* 67 (Jul 1995): 12–15; "40 to 200 Are Seized in Colombia Drive on Subversive Elements," *Washington Star,* 5 Aug 1941.

14. Cole Blasier, *The Hovering Giant: U.S. Responses to Revolutionary Change in Latin America, 1910–1985* (Pittsburgh: University of Pittsburgh Press, 1985), 47.

15. 11 Sep 1941, in Russell D. Buhite and David W. Levy, eds., *FDR's Fireside Chats* (Norman: University of Oklahoma Press, 1992), 192.

16. Richard Breitman and Alan M. Kraut, *American Refugee Policy and European Jewry, 1933–1945* (Bloomington: Indiana University Press, 1987), 121.

17. Francis MacDonnell, *Insidious Foes: The Axis Fifth Column and the American Home Front* (New York: Oxford University Press, 1995), 119.

18. Adolf A. Berle, *Navigating the Rapids, 1918–1971* (New York: Harcourt Brace Jovanovich, 1973), 326.

19. A typical contemporary report is by the Counter-Subversion Section of ONI, *Activities of the Fifth Column,* 13 Jan 1942, 862.20200/52, LM195, reel 8, RG59, NA. Louis De Jong was the first to debunk thoroughly the myths in *The German Fifth Column.* Donald M. McKale is also skeptical; see his *The Swastika Outside Germany* (Kent, OH: Kent State University Press, 1977), 168–75. Francis MacDonnell succinctly reviews the issue in *Insidious Foes,* chapter 6.

20. The phrase is De Jong's in *The German Fifth Column,* page v.

21. *Congressional Record – Senate,* vol. 86, pt. 1, 76th Congress, 3rd sess., 680, pt. 6, 6773, 6775.

22. MacDonnell, *Insidious Foes,* 7, 133–6.

23. Claude G. Bowers, *Chile through Embassy Windows, 1939–1953* (New York: Simon & Schuster, 1958), 60.

24. FDR to Secretary of State, 9 Jan 1941, in folder "Diplomatic Correspondence – South & Central America," PSF 50, FDR Library.

25. Percy Bidwell, *Economic Defense of Latin America* (Boston: World Peace Foundation, 1941), 24; H. Montgomery Hyde, *The Quiet Canadian: The Secret Service Story of Sir William Stephenson* (London: Hamish Hamilton, 1962), 134.

26. *The Coming Struggle for Latin America* (Philadelphia: Lippincott, 1938); "Totalitarian Inroads in Latin America," *Foreign Affairs* 17 (1938): 78–89; "Swastika Over the Andes: German Penetration in Latin America," *Harper's Magazine* 177 (1938): 176–86; *Dawn over the Amazon* (New York: Duell, Sloan and Pearce, 1943). For the widespread popularity of these accounts, see Frederick B. Pike, *FDR's Good Neighbor Policy: Sixty Years of Generally Gentle Chaos* (Austin: University of Texas Press, 1995), 232.

27. Beals, *The Coming Struggle,* 66, 85.

28. Lawrence Martin and Sylvia Martin, "Nazi Intrigues in Central America," *The American Mercury* 53: 211 (July 1941): 66–73.

29. *Hitler Over Latin America: Why the Embargo Against Spain Must Be Lifted Now!* (New York: Lawyers Committee on American Relations with Spain, 1939), 14.

30. John Gunther, *Inside Latin America* (New York: Harper & Row, 1941), 6, 160.

31. "No hay tales 'agentes' en el Canal de Panamá," *La Prensa* (New York), 3 Aug 1940.

32. Henry L. Stimson and McGeorge Bundy, *On Active Service in Peace and War* (New York: Harper & Brothers, 1947), 319.

33. *Trabajo* 25 Apr 1942, described in Charles D. Ameringer, *Don Pepe: A Political Biography of José Figueres of Costa Rica* (Albuquerque: University of New Mexico Press, 1978), 12, n. 31.

34. Hugo Fernández Artucio, *The Nazi Underground in South America* (New York: Farrar & Rinehart, 1942), 12.

35. Ernesto Giudici, *Hitler conquista América* (Buenos Aires: Editorial Acento, 1938), and see James A. Cane, "'Unity for the Defense of Culture': AIAPE and the Cultural Politics of Argentine Anti-Fascism, 1935–1943," *Hispanic American Historical Review,* 77: 3 (Aug 1997): 443–82.

36. Waldo Heinrichs, *Threshold of War: Franklin D. Roosevelt and the American Entry into World War II* (New York: Oxford University Press, 1988), 21.

37. Russell B. Porter, "Colombia's Nazis Armed for Attack," *New York Times,* 18 Aug 1940, 16. Actual Nazi Party membership figures are discussed later.

38. Russell B. Porter, "Germans Maintain Losing Airline Inside Panama Canal Defense Zone," *New York Times,* 10 Aug 1940; William Burden, *The Struggle for Airways in Latin America* (New York: Arno Press, 1977), 67.

39. FDR to Welles, 21 Jan 1941, and Welles to president, 22 Jan 1941, "State: Welles, Sumner: Jan–May 1941," PSF 77, FDR Library.

40. Devon Francis, "Nazi Planes in Ecuador: Appraisal of Threat," *Washington Post,* 6 Mar 1941; Burden, *The Struggle for Airways,* 67.

41. Richard Watts, Jr., "Colombia Imperils Democracy by Closing Eyes to Nazi Threat," *New York Herald-Tribune,* 16 Sep 1940.

42. Because of Latin American sensitivities, the Department's Latin American Division tried to discourage Brown and other journalists from doing such stories. But there was no shortage of government officials working at cross-purposes to the division. Briggs, *Proposed March of Time Film on Fifth Column Activities in Brazil, Uruguay and Argentina,* 4 Jun 1940, "General Memoranda Jan–June 1940," Memoranda Relating to General Latin American Affairs, Box 3, Division of American Republics (ARA), RG59, NA.

43. Cornelius Vanderbilt, Jr., "Can Hitler Take Central America?" *Liberty Magazine,* 14 Nov 1940, 58.

44. Colombia's population was approximately nine million. Some 300 of the 4,000 resident Germans were Nazi Party members. Costa Rica's population was about 800,000. From a German population estimated between 850 and 1,000, fewer than 60 joined the Party. Senate Committee on Military Affairs, *Nazi Party Membership Records,* Senate Committee Prints 79/2/46, Part 2, March 1946, and Part 3, September 1946, S1535–8 (Washington, DC: U.S. Government Printing Office, 1946); Robert H. Davis, *Historical Dictionary of Colombia,* 2nd ed. (London: Scarecrow Press, 1993), 404; Jacobo Schifter Sikora, *El Judío en Costa Rica* (San José: Editorial Universidad Estatal a Distancia, 1979), 82; [Duggan], *Latin America – Totalitarian Activities,* 1941, reel 45, Hull Papers (microfilm), Manuscript Division, Library of Congress, Washington, DC (hereafter LC); FBI, *German Espionage in Latin America,* p. 2, June 1946, 862.20210/6-1746, RG59, NA.

45. Alberto Vargas to MRE, 17 Sep 1940, in folder "Actividades Nazis 1940," Actividades Nazis 1940–2, Archivo del Ministerio de Relaciones Exteriores, Bogotá (AMRE); Turbay to MRE, 25 Jul 1941, Embajada de Colombia en Washington, AMRE.

46. Haglund, *Latin America,* 182.

47. On BSC see H. Montgomery Hyde, *Room 3603: The Story of the British Intelligence Center in New York During World War II* (New York: Farrar and Straus,

1962); Hyde, *The Quiet Canadian*; William Stevenson, *A Man Called Intrepid: The Secret War* (New York: Harcourt, Brace, Jovanovich, 1976); Thomas E. Mahl, *Desperate Deception: British Covert Operations in the United States 1939–44* (Washington and London: Brassey's, 1998); William S. Stephenson, ed., *British Security Coordination: The Secret History of British Intelligence in the Americas 1940–1945* (New York: Fromm International Publishing, 1998). The Hyde and Stevenson books and the Stephenson secret history should all be treated with caution; they contain so many misstatements, some deliberate, that the publisher of *A Man Called Intrepid* recently reclassified the book as fiction. For insight into the publishing history of BSC, see Charles C. Kolb's review for H-DIPLO at http://www.h-net.msu.edu/reviews/showrev.cgi?path=3330945077241.

48. The best disinformation is wrapped around a core of truth. Belmonte certainly sympathized with the Nazis; while he was in exile in Germany in 1943, the *Sicherheitsdienst* proposed smuggling him to Argentina aboard a submarine to stir up pro-German sentiment there. Reinebeck, 30 Sep 1943, "Südamerika: Tätigkeit des SD, d- Abwehr, d- Agenten und Polizeiattachés," Fiche 2007, Inland IIg, Politisches Archiv des Auswärtigen Amtes, Bonn (hereafter PAAA).

49. Braden to Welles, 9 Aug 1941, folder 12, Box 67, Sumner Welles Papers, FDR Library; Adolf Berle Diary, 4 Sep 1941, 7 May 1942, Adolf Berle Papers, FDR Library; Philip W. Bonsal to Gerald Keith, 19 Apr 1942, Box 19, Arthur Bliss Lane Papers, Manuscripts and Archives, Yale University Library; Lane to Bonsal, 28 Apr 1942, Box 67, Lane Papers. For the FBI's continued citation of the Belmonte letter, see FBI, *Bolivia Today,* June 1942, and Hoover to Hopkins, 21 Dec 1943, "FBI Reports – Bolivia," Box 141, Hopkins Papers, FDR Library. On the Belmonte affair, see especially Cole Blasier, "The United States, Germany, and the Bolivian Revolutionaries (1941–1946)," *Hispanic American Historical Review* 52: 1 (February 1972): 26–54; for a sign that the old legend lives on, see Kolb's review of the Stephenson secret history, cited earlier.

50. The most extensive examinations suggest that the BSC altered, if it did not invent, the map in question. See Nicholas John Cull, *Selling War: The British Propaganda Campaign Against American "Neutrality" in World War II* (New York: Oxford University Press, 1995), 170–5. Francis MacDonnell, "The Search for a Second Zimmerman Telegram: FDR, BSC, and the Latin American Front," *International Journal of Intelligence and Counterintelligence* 4: 4 (Winter 1990): 487–505. The map was so rudimentary that Hitler responded to Roosevelt's charge: "I'm not a schoolchild who draws maps in a school atlas. South America is as far away as the moon as far as I'm concerned. Those are the dumbest claims." Max Domarus, *Hitler: Reden und Proklamationen 1932–1945: Kommentiert von einem deutschen Zeitgenossen, Band II: Untergang (1939–1945)* (Würzburg: Schmidt, 1963), 1778, quoted in Reiner Pommerin, *Das Dritte Reich und Lateinamerika: Die deutsche Politik gegenüber Süd- und Mittelamerika, 1939–1942* (Düsseldorf: Droste Verlag, 1977), 275. See also Sterling to James, "Map on German Expansion," 3 Nov 1941, in folder "Diplomatic Correspondence – Germany: 1940–41," PSF 31, FDR Library; Drew Pearson, "Secret Nazi Map," *Times-Herald,* 4 Nov 1941.

51. Donovan to Welles, *Memorandum on South America,* undated, Nov 1941?, folder 12, Box 77, Welles Papers, FDR Library. Donovan forwarded the British memorandum to Welles at FDR's request.

52. Cull, *Selling War,* 173. The BSC repaid Berle by leaking derogatory information about him.

53. There were a few other dissenting voices. William Borchard, a Yale professor who joined the State Department delegation at a summit meeting in Lima in 1938, and J. Fred Rippy, a leading Latin American historian at Chicago, did not believe that German influence was growing. But their views did not carry much weight. Irwin F. Gellman, *Good Neighbor Diplomacy: United States Policies in Latin America, 1933–1945* (Baltimore, MD: The Johns Hopkins University Press, 1979), 78, 109; Leslie B. Rout, Jr., and John F. Bratzel, *The Shadow War: German Espionage and United States Counterespionage in Latin America during World War II* (Frederick, MD: University Publications of America, 1986), 30.

54. On Tetens's role, see Ronald C. Newton, "'Graue Eminenzen und schiefe Existenzen': Die deutschsprachigen Berater der Alliierten in Argentinien während des Zweiten Weltkrieges," in *Alternative Lateinamerika: Das deutsche Exil in der Zeit des Nationalsozialismus*, Karl Kohut and Patrik von zur Mühlen, eds. (Frankfurt: Vervuert Verlag, 1994), 182–200.

55. Both quotations from Dean Acheson, *Present at the Creation: My Years in the State Department* (New York: W. W. Norton & Co., 1969), 157.

56. Gellman, *Good Neighbor Diplomacy,* 129.

57. Spruille Braden, 1952–1953, Oral History Collection, Columbia University, 1169–70, 1180, 1183, 1191; Spruille Braden, *Diplomats and Demagogues* (New Rochelle, NY: Arlington House, 1971), 255–6; Strong's demand also contained in his cable of 14 Dec 1941 in 740.00115 Pacific War/22, RG59, NA.

58. Michel Fortmann and David G. Haglund, "Public Diplomacy and Dirty Tricks: Two Faces of United States 'Informal Penetration' of Latin America on the Eve of World War II," *Diplomacy and Statecraft* 6: 2 (1995): 566. Strong presumably was thinking of the Natal province of Brazil.

59. Duggan to Secretary of State, *Proposed Appointment by War Department of Colonel Carl H. Strong as Military Attaché to Central America,* 31 Aug 1943, in folder "General Memoranda July–Aug 1943," Memoranda Relating to General Latin American Affairs, Box 8, Division of American Republics Affairs (hereafter ARA), RG59, NA.

60. Cabot to SecState, 3 Jul 1940, *Foreign Relations of the United States (FRUS) 1940,* V: 113–15.

61. Lieutenant Colonel F. M. June, *Confidential Intelligence Report,* 23 Oct 1942, "Schlesinger, Alfredo," Naval Attaché – Guatemala City, Personality Files, 1940–6, Box 40, ONI, RG38, NA.

62. Jeffrey M. Dorwart, *Conflict of Duty: The U.S. Navy's Intelligence Dilemma, 1919–1945* (Annapolis: Naval Institute Press, 1983), 106–8.

63. Naval Attaché memorandum, 20 Mar 1940, 810.00N/691, RG59, NA.

64. Wilson to Welles, 18 Nov 1941, folder 7, Box 75, Welles Papers, FDR Library.

65. Russell (World Trade Intelligence) to Warren (Foreign Activity Correlation), 26 Mar 1942, 800.20210/5-1442, RG59, NA.

66. John Moors Cabot, *First Line of Defense: Forty Years' Experiences of a Career Diplomat* (Washington, DC: School of Foreign Service, Georgetown University, 1980[?]), 18.

67. Berle to G-2 ONI and Hoover, 24 Jun 1940, "SIS (General) 1940," SIS: General File 1940-2, Box 1, ONI, RG38, NA.

68. Strong, Train, and Hoover, *Agreement between MID, ONI and FBI for Coordinating Special Intelligence Operations in the Western Hemisphere*, 30 Apr 1943, 102.31/475, RG59, NA.

69. Richard Gid Powers, *Secrecy and Power: The Life of J. Edgar Hoover* (New York: Free Press, 1987), 252; Rout and Bratzel, *The Shadow War*, 40.

70. Rout and Bratzel, *The Shadow War*, 42. The FBI had decided as early as February 1941 to increase training in Spanish and Portuguese, but the results were disappointing. Harley Notter to Finley and Bonsal, 24 Feb 1941, "General Memoranda Jan–Feb 1941," Memoranda Relating to General Latin American Affairs, Box 4, ARA, RG59, NA.

71. The FBI agent in Colombia at this time, William C. Spears, could not speak Spanish. Braden to SecState, 6 Aug 1941, folder 12, Box 67, Welles Papers; German Legation Bogotá, *Boletín Alemán*, 1940, various dates, in folder "Propaganda Totalitaria – 1940," Actividades nazis – 1940–2, AMRE; FBI, "Colombia Today," 97–100; Duggan to Lane, 20 May 1942, Box 19, and Lane to Duggan, 10 Jun 1942, Box 67, Lane Papers.

72. Hoover to Biddle, 18 Feb 1942, "J. Edgar Hoover/Memos 1942," folder 33, Box 2, Biddle Papers, Georgetown University Library, Special Collections Division.

73. FBI, *Colombia Today*, p. 83, March 1942, "FBI Reports – Colombia," Box 141, Hopkins Papers, FDR Library.

74. FBI, *Bolivia Today*, pp. 3, 32, 42, June 1942, "FBI Reports – Bolivia," Box 141, Hopkins Papers, FDR Library.

75. Duggan to Gordon and Berle, 29 Oct 1941, "General Memoranda Oct.–Nov. 1941," Memoranda Relating to General Latin American Affairs, Box 6, ARA, RG59, NA.

76. Duggan to Braden, 18 Nov 1941, 800.20210/1043A, RG59, NA.

77. Warren to Long, 8 Aug 1942, "Warren, A.M. 1942," General Correspondence 1942 Q–Z, Box 144, Long Papers, Manuscript Division, LC.

78. Keith to Lane, 18 Jul 1942, and Hoover to Lane, 30 Sep 1942, Box 19, and Lane to Hoover, 13 Oct 1942, Box 67, Lane Papers.

79. Chapin to Welles, *Axis Aspirations in South America*, 17 Apr 1942, "General Memoranda Mar 19–April 1942," Memoranda Relating to General Latin American Affairs, Box 7, ARA, RG59, NA. Chapin also noted that Bill Donovan's Office of the Coordinator of Information and Nelson Rockefeller's Office of the Coordinator of Inter-American Affairs had submitted reports of "similar" quality.

80. FBI, *Ecuador Today*, p. 39, June 1942, "FBI Reports – Ecuador," Box 142, Hopkins Papers, FDR Library.

81. On the frailty of the Spanish Falange in Latin America, see Rosa María Pardo Sanz, *¡Con Franco hacia el Imperio! La política exterior española en América Latina, 1939–1945* (Madrid: Universidad Nacional de Educación a Distancia, 1995), and Stanley G. Payne, *Fascism in Spain, 1923–1977* (Madison: University of Wisconsin Press, 1999), 342–4, 538 n. 96.

82. Stanley E. Hilton, *Hitler's Secret War in South America 1939–1945: German Military Espionage and Allied Counterespionage in Brazil* (Baton Rouge: Louisiana State University Press, 1981) 14–17.

83. Rout and Bratzel, *The Shadow War*, 9.

84. Rout and Bratzel believe the Allies' radio intercepts prevented any such sink-ings; they were informed by the FBI in 1982 that there was never any "con-clusive evidence" of a Latin American connection to torpedoings. See *The Shadow War,* 347. David Kahn, in *Hitler's Spies: German Military Intelligence in World War II* (New York: Da Capo Press, 1978), concluded that the Ger-man reports from Latin America "sank not a single vessel...the enormous efforts of Germany's Latin American spies had, in general, gone for naught" (p. 327). Hilton, on the other hand, links the sinking of two ships off the Brazilian coast to spotting by German spies. See Hilton, *Hitler's Secret War,* 78.

85. Ladislas Farago, *The Game of the Foxes: The Untold Story of German Espionage in the United States and Great Britain during World War II* (New York: David McKay, 1971), 51–4 on Canal, quote at xiv.

86. FBI, *German Espionage in Latin America,* June 1946, 862.20210/6-1746, RG59, NA; Hilton, *Hitler's Secret War,* 216–29, 290–1.

87. Maria Emilia Paz, *Strategy, Security, and Spies: Mexico and the U.S. as Allies in World War II* (University Park: Pennsylvania State University Press, 1997), 170–1.

88. Rout and Bratzel, *The Shadow War,* 454.

89. Donald F. Whitehead's admiring *The FBI Story* (New York: Random House, 1956), 273–6, says that Germany was able to meet only 2 percent of its plat-inum needs because of the crackdown. Stephen J. Randall, in *Colombia and the United States: Hegemony and Interdependence* (Athens: University of Georgia Press, 1992), 176, says that 30 percent of Colombian production continued to reach the Axis. Smugglers' nationalities in Dorsz to Alexander, 5 Sep 1944, in folder "Removal of Enemy Aliens, Aug–Sept 1944," Subject Files, 1939–54, Special War Problems (SWP), RG59, NA.

90. FBI, *German Espionage in Latin America,* 38, 105–6; Hoover to Neal, 14 Oct 1946, 862.20210/10-1446, RG59, NA; and see Kalinowsky and Nicolaus in "Name Files of Enemy Aliens," alphabetical folders in SWP Boxes 31–50, RG59, NA.

91. Munro to Henderson, 29 Jun 1944, Bolivia: Cochabamba Consulte, Records of the Legal Attaché, 1944–6, Box 1, RG84, NA. See also Gasque to Woodward, 8 Feb 1944, Bolivia: Cochabamba Consulate, Records of the Legal Attaché, 1944–6, Box 1, RG84, NA.

92. Henderson to Munro, 5 Jul 1944, Bolivia: Cochabamba Consulte, Records of the Legal Attaché, 1944–6, Box 1, RG84, NA.

93. Hubbard to Henderson, 26 Oct 1944, Bolivia: Cochabamba Consulte, Records of the Legal Attaché, 1944–6, Box 1, RG84, NA.

94. Nichols to Henderson, 18 Jan 1945, Bolivia: Cochabamba Consulte, Records of the Legal Attaché, 1944–6, Box 1, RG84, NA.

95. Scotten to SecState, 9 Mar 1944, "711," Ecuador: Quito Embassy Confidential File, Box 17, RG84, NA.

96. Vallejo Sánchez to MRE, 29 Nov 1940, Informes Confidenciales – Nazis 1939–40, AMRE; Gómez Picón to Santos, 26 Jul 1940, Informes Confidenciales – Nazis 1939–40, AMRE.

97. Santos to López de Mesa, 22 Nov 1940, in folder "Informaciones Confiden-ciales – Listas," Informaciones Confidenciales – Nazis – 1939–40, AMRE.

98. Raymond Ickes, interview by author, Berkeley, CA, 18 Sep 1997. See Chapter 6 for more on the Ickes mission.
99. Eva Bloch, interview by author, Guayaquil, 18 Feb 1998; Gunter Lisken, interview by author, Guayaquil, 17 Feb 1998.
100. Nester to SecState, *Request for Allotment of $180.00 for Intelligence Information,* 4 Dec 1941, and Nester memo, 21 May 1942, in "Ultra-Confidential for Consul General Use Only," Ecuador: Guayaquil Consulate General, Records Re Payment of Funds for Intelligence Information, 1941–3, Box 1, RG84, NA; United States Senate Committee on Military Affairs, *Nazi Party Membership Records, Part 2* (Washington, DC: U.S. GPO, 1946–8), 114, 212; Spanish Minister in Quito to Spanish Foreign Minster, 22 Apr 1942, R41557, Zivilgefangenen-Austausch-Vereinigten Staaten von Amerika, Rechtsabteilung, PAAA; AmLegQuito to MRE, 16 Mar 1942, Serie B, Embajada de Estados Unidos, Ministerio de Relaciones Exteriores, Archivo Histórico de Quito (hereafter AHQ).
101. Nester to Guarderas, 5 Jan 1943, Serie B, Embajada de Estados Unidos, MRE, AHQ.
102. Ickes to Nester, 18 Mar 1943, "711," Ecuador: Quito Embassy Confidential File, Box 10, RG84, NA.
103. J. M. Schelling, *Intelligence Report,* 4 Jun 1940, "US-Guatemalan Relations C-9-b/18685," Intelligence Division Confidential Reports of Naval Attaches 1940–6, Box 428, ONI, RG38, NA; Phillips to Shipley, 19 Aug 1941, and Riheldaffer to Phillips, 26 Aug 1941, "SIS (Administration, Policy, Finance) 1940–10 October 1941," SIS: General File 1940–2, Box 1, ONI, RG38, NA.
104. Josephus Daniels, "Diaries," 7 Apr 1941, reel 7, Daniels Papers, Manuscript Division, LC.
105. Braden oral history, 1195.
106. Braden, *Diplomats and Demagogues,* 281.
107. Robert P. Joyce, *Intelligence Work in Cuba,* 20 May 1943, 800.20210/5–2043, RG59, NA; Adolf Berle Diary, 28 Apr 1943, Adolf Berle Papers, FDR Library.
108. Braden oral history, 1216; Braden, *Diplomats and Demagogues,* 283.
109. For exile informants in Argentina, see Newton, "'Graue Eminenzen,'" and Leslie B. Rout, Jr., and John F. Bratzel, "Heinrich Jürges and the Cult of Disinformation," *International History Review* 6 (1984): 611–23.
110. Cabot to Toop, 20 Feb 1942, "General Memoranda Feb. 10–March 19, 1941," Memoranda Relating to General Latin American Affairs, Box 6, ARA, RG59, NA.
111. Alfredo Schlesinger, *Locura racial* (Guatemala City: n.p., 1938), and *El arma secreta: la quinta columna* (Guatemala City: n.p., 1940); *Subject: Alfredo Schlesinger,* 18 Mar 1943, "Schlesinger, Alfredo," Naval Attaché – Guatemala City, Personality Files, 1940–6, Box 40, ONI, RG38, NA; Cabot to Toop, 20 Feb 1942, "General Memoranda Feb. 10–March 19, 1941," Memoranda Relating to General Latin American Affairs, Box 6, ARA, RG59, NA; Lt. Col. F. M. June, *Confidential Intelligence Report,* 23 Oct 1942, "Schlesinger, Alfredo," Naval Attaché – Guatemala City, Personality Files, 1940–6, Box 40, ONI, RG38, NA; Livingston, *Summary of Justice Files,* 4 Jan 1946, "Beyer, Pablo," Name Files of Interned Enemy Aliens from Latin America, 1942–8, Box 36, SWP, RG59, NA.

112. FBI to Lafoon, *Heinrich Friedrich Wilhelm Hoelscher, Bolivia,* 8 Feb 1946, "Hoelscher, Heinrich, Bolivia," Name Files of Interned Enemy Aliens from Latin America, 1942–6, Box 41, SWP, RG59, NA.

113. Dawson to SecState, 7 May 1942, 740.00115EW1939/3092, RG59, NA; Patrik von zur Mühlen, *Fluchtziel Lateinamerika: Die deutsche Emigration 1933–1945: politische Aktivitäten und soziokulturelle Integration* (Bonn: Verlag Neue Gesellschaft, 1988), 222–5.

114. Boal (La Paz) to Secretary of State, 16 Oct 1943, 740.00115EW1939/7493, RG59, NA.

115. Copy in Olson to Trujillo, 10 Apr 1946, in folder "711.5," Ecuador: Quito Embassy Confidential File – Classified General Records, Box 35, RG84, NA.

116. Arthur Weilbauer, *Ein Weiter Weg* (Quito: n.p., 1982), 51; María-Luise Kreuter, *¿Dónde queda el Ecuador? Exilio en un país desconocido desde 1938 hasta fines de los años cincuenta* (Quito: Abya-Yala, 1997), 235.

117. Drew to SecState, 1 Apr 1942, 740.00115EW1939/2607, RG59, NA.

118. Fletcher Warren to SecState, *Erich RATH and the A.N.F.B.,* 8 Apr 1943, 862.20210 Rath Erich/8, RG59, NA.

119. Wolfgang Kießling, *Exil in Lateinamerika* (Frankfurt am Main: Verlag Philipp Reclam, 1984), 422–7.

120. AmEmbBogota to SecState, 8 Apr 1943, 862.20210 Rath Erich/13, RG59, NA; Braden oral history, p. 2490; Braden, *Diplomats and Demagogues,* 243.

121. Directorate of the ANFB, *Vom Informationswesen unserer Bewegung,* in folder "Informes Secretos – Quinta Columna," Informes Confidenciales Sobre Entidades Nazis Años 1942–3, AMRE.

122. Hans Ungar, interview with author, Bogotá, 16 Mar 1998.

123. *Suspected Germans Etc., Addendum No. 18,* 19 Mar 1941, in folder "Informes Confidenciales – Listas – 1941 – Quinta Columna," Informes Confidenciales Sobre Actividades Nazis – 1941, AMRE.

124. FBI, *German Espionage in Latin America,* 20.

125. Keith to Lane, 18 Jul 1942, Box 19, Lane Papers.

126. The chart accompanies Braden to SecState, 15 Dec 1941, 862.20221/428, RG59, NA; Rath's authorship is confirmed by Castillo to Jefe de Seguridad Nacional, *Erick [sic] Rath,* 15 Oct 1942, "Informes Secretos – Quinta Columna," Informes Confidenciales Sobre Entidades Nazis Años 1942–3, AMRE. The strike force myth regularly appeared as the most sensational charge in these widely distributed and influential summaries of Nazi activity: Adolf Berle to Chiefs of the Diplomatic Missions in the Other American Republics, *The Pattern of Nazi Organizations and Their Activities in the Other American Republics,* p. 25, 6 Feb 1941, 862.20210/414A, RG59, NA; [Laurence Duggan], *Latin America – Totalitarian Activities,* 1940, reel 45, Hull Papers (microfilm), Manuscript Division, LC; FBI, *Colombia Today,* March 1942, "FBI Reports – Colombia," Box 141, Hopkins Papers, FDR Library; *First Phase – Axis Penetration in Latin America,* 1944, folder 85, CIAA Report Drafts, Box 11, Record Group III 40, Nelson A. Rockefeller Personal Files, Washington, DC Files, Rockefeller Family Archives, RAC. The credulous Russell B. Porter also repeated the story in "Colombia's Nazis Armed for Attack," *New York Times,* 18 Aug 1940, 16.

127. Thousands of expatriate Germans were brought home by Hitler's regime for labor and military service. See McKale, *The Swastika,* 111; Reiner Pommerin,

"Überlegungen des 'Dritten Reiches' zur Rückholung deutscher Auswanderer aus Lateinamerika," *Jahrbuch für Geschichte von Staat, Wirtschaft und Gesellschaft Lateinamerikas* 16 (1979): 370.

128. Ickes interview.

129. Vallejo Sánchez to MRE, 29 Nov 1940, Informes Confidenciales – Nazis 1939–40, AMRE; FBI, *German Espionage in Latin America,* June 1946, 862.20210/6-1746, RG59, NA; Hoover to Lyon, 17 Jul 1946, 862.20210/7-1746, RG59, NA.

Chapter 3   Blacklisting

1. Bonsal to Welles, *The Proclaimed List,* 2 Jan 1942, "General Memoranda Jan–Feb 1942," Memoranda Relating to General Latin American Affairs, Box 6, Division of American Republics (ARA), RG59, National Archives, College Park, Maryland (hereafter NA).

2. Héctor Pérez-Brignoli, *Breve historia de Centroamérica* (Madrid: Alianza Editorial, 1985), 98. See also David F. Schmitz, *Thank God They're on Our Side. The United States and Right-Wing Dictatorships, 1921–1965* (Chapel Hill: University of North Carolina Press, 1999), 46–84.

3. Richard Millett and Marvin A. Soloman, "Trujillo violó una mujer en una iglesia," *Ahora* 492 (16 Apr 1973): 2–10; Rayford W. Logan, *Haiti and the Dominican Republic* (London: Oxford University Press, 1968), 69.

4. Quotation from Jesús de Galíndez, *The Era of Trujillo: Dominican Dictator* (Tucson: University of Arizona Press, 1973), 26. See also Robert D. Crassweller, *Trujillo: The Life and Times of a Caribbean Dictator* (New York: Macmillan, 1966), 79–82, 434; Graham H. Stuart and James L. Tigner, *Latin America and the United States* (Englewood Cliffs, NJ: Prentice-Hall, 1975), 435–6; William Krehm, *Democracies and Tyrannies of the Caribbean* (Westport, CT: Lawrence Hill, 1984), 169.

5. Crassweller, *Trujillo,* 215; Spruille Braden, *Diplomats and Demagogues* (New Rochelle, NY: Arlington House, 1971), 279. Eric Paul Roorda has masterfully demonstrated Trujillo's careful cultivation of U.S. military officials while snubbing the more troublesome diplomats who sometimes asked difficult questions. See *The Dictator Next Door: The Good Neighbor Policy and the Trujillo Regime in the Dominican Republic, 1930–1945* (Durham, NC: Duke University Press, 1998).

6. "Washington Pomp Welcomes Somoza," *New York Times,* 6 May 1939, 1.

7. Laurence Duggan, *The Americas: The Search for Hemisphere Security* (New York: Henry Holt and Company, 1949), 102; Bryce Wood, *The Making of the Good Neighbor Policy* (New York: Columbia University Press, 1961), 340.

8. Wood, *The Making,* 145–7.

9. Gordon Connell-Smith, *The United States and Latin America: An Historical Analysis of Inter-American Relations* (New York: John Wiley and Sons, 1974), 163; Robert N. Burr and Roland D. Hussey, eds., *Documents on Inter-American Co-operation, 1881–1948,* vol. 2 (Philadelphia: University of Pennsylvania Press, 1955), 112–14.

10. David Haglund, *Latin America and the Transformation of U.S. Strategic Thought* (Albuquerque: University of New Maxico Press, 1984), 45.

11. Frederick B. Pike, *FDR's Good Neighbor Policy: Sixty Years of Generally Gentle Chaos* (Austin: University of Texas Press, 1995), 137–49; Haglund, *Latin America,* 57; Irwin F. Gellman, *Secret Affairs: Franklin Roosevelt, Cordell Hull, and Sumner Welles* (Baltimore, MD: Johns Hopkins University Press, 1995), 320, 335.

12. Burr and Hussey, *Documents,* 118; Alton Frye, *Nazi Germany and the American Hemisphere* (New Haven, CT: Yale University Press, 1967), 110–13.

13. Burr and Hussey, *Documents,* 130–4.

14. Jacobo Schifter Sikora, *Las alianzas conflictivas: las relaciones de Estados Unidos y Costa Rica desde la Segunda Guerra Mundial a la guerra fría* (San José: Libro Libre, 1986), 70–9; Adolf A. Berle, *Navigating the Rapids, 1918–1971* (New York: Harcourt Brace Jovanovich, 1973), 329.

15. Burr and Hussey, *Documents,* 141–4.

16. Randall Bennett Woods, *The Roosevelt Foreign-Policy Establishment and the 'Good Neighbor': The United States and Argentina, 1941–1945* (Lawrence: Regents Press of Kansas, 1979), 23.

17. Gellman, *Secret Affairs,* 335.

18. Carlos Lleras Restrepo, *Crónica de mi propia vida,* vol. II (Bogotá: Stamato Editores, 1983), 291.

19. Irwin F. Gellman, *Good Neighbor Diplomacy: United States Policies in Latin America, 1933–1945* (Baltimore: Johns Hopkins University Press, 1979), 15, 143–4.

20. Allen Weinstein and Alexander Vassiliev, *The Haunted Wood: Soviet Espionage in America – the Stalin Era* (New York: Random House, 1999), 10–21.

21. See Martin Weil, *A Pretty Good Club: The Founding Fathers of the U.S. Foreign Service* (New York: W. W. Norton, 1978), esp. chapters 2–3.

22. Robert E. Quirk, *An Affair of Honor: Woodrow Wilson and the Occupation of Vera Cruz* (Lexington: University of Kentucky Press, 1962), 77.

23. Gellman, *Secret Affairs,* 50.

24. Sumner Welles, *Seven Decisions That Shaped History* (New York: Harper, 1951), 119.

25. Ernest Gruening, *Many Battles: The Autobiography of Ernest Gruening* (New York: Liveright, 1973), 162.

26. Merwin L. Bohan oral history, p. 9, 15 Jan 1974, Harry S. Truman Library, Independence, MO. Later, as Assistant Secretary for Latin American Affairs, Spruille Braden would delve so deeply into internal Argentine politics that it was said he believed himself "elected by Providence to bring down the government of Argentina." Albert P. Vannucci, "Elected by Providence: Spruille Braden in Argentina in 1945," in *Ambassadors in Foreign Policy: The Influence of Individuals on U.S.-Latin American Policy,* C. Neale Ronning and Albert P. Vannucci, eds. (New York: Praeger, 1987).

27. Acheson's remark in Gaddis Smith, *The Last Years of the Monroe Doctrine, 1945–1993* (New York: Hill and Wang, 1994), 57.

28. Spruille Braden, 1952–3, Oral History Collection, Columbia University, 924, 3186.

29. Thomas Miller Klubock, "From Welfare Capitalism to the Free Market in Chile: Gender, Culture, and Politics in the Copper Mines," in *Close Encounters of Empire: Writing the Cultural History of U.S.-Latin American Relations,* Gilbert M.

Joseph, Catherine C. LeGrande, and Ricardo D. Salvatore, eds. (Durham, NC: Duke University Press, 1998), 369–99.

30. Braden to Secretary of State, 14 Apr 1939, 711.21/934, RG59, cited in Shirley N. Rawls, "Spruille Braden: A Political Biography" (Ph.D. diss., University of New Mexico, 1976), 106–7.

31. Braden to Welles, 20 Jun 1941, folder 12, Box 67, Welles Papers, FDR Library.

32. Press conference 614-A, 12 Jan 1940, Press Confs, XV, 78, FDR Library, cited in Wood, *The Making,* 359.

33. Braden, *Diplomats and Demagogues,* 255.

34. Braden oral history, 3186.

35. Braden, *Diplomats and Demagogues,* 203; Bohan oral history, 44.

36. Braden to Secretary of State, 31 Dec 1941, 740.00115EW1939/1661, RG59, NA.

37. Quoted in Jordan A. Schwarz, *Liberal: Adolf A. Berle and the Vision of an American Era* (New York: The Free Press, 1987), 20–2.

38. Schwarz, *Liberal,* 22.

39. Stimson quoted in Lars Schoultz, *Beneath the United States: A History of U.S. Policy toward Latin America* (Cambridge, MA: Harvard University Press, 1998), 311. Some U.S. diplomats in Panama reported that Panamanian opposition figures were crying "Nazi" to gain U.S. sympathy; see Juan Manuel Pérez, "Panamá: The rise and fall of Arnulfo Arias, 1931–1941," Ph.D. diss., Georgetown University, 1993, 304. See also Lester D. Langley, "The United States and Panama, 1933–1941: A Study in Strategy and Diplomacy" (Ph.D. diss., University of Kansas, 1965), 182–240; Langley, *The United States and the Caribbean in the 20th Century* (Athens: University of Georgia Press, 1982), 173–6; Michael L. Conniff, *Panama and the United States: The Forced Alliance* (Athens: University of Georgia Press, 1992), 93–7.

40. The discussion of Ubico draws on Stefan Karlen, *"Paz, progreso, justicia y honradez": das Ubico-Regime in Guatemala 1931–1944* (Stuttgart: Franz Steiner Verlag, 1991), 212–17; Kenneth J. Grieb, *Guatemalan Caudillo: The Regime of Jorge Ubico, Guatemala 1931–1944* (Athens: Ohio University Press, 1979), 248–51; Sharon Y. Clifford, "The Germans in Guatemala during World War II" (Master's thesis, Florida Atlantic University, Boca Raton, 1974), 33–47; and the excellent study by Regina Wagner, *Los Alemanes en Guatemala, 1828–1944* (Guatemala: Afanes, 1996).

41. Hugo Droege, interview by author, Guatemala City, 22 May 1996.

42. Kenneth J. Grieb, "Guatemala and the Second World War," *Ibero-Amerikanisches Archiv* 3: 4 (1977): 377–94; Thomas M. Leonard, *Central America and the United States: The Search for Stability* (Athens: University of Georgia Press, 1991), 115.

43. See Woods, *The Roosevelt Foreign-Policy Establishment,* 23–6.

44. Haglund, *Latin America,* 135–6; Dye to Berle, *German Competition in Ecuador,* 1939[?], "Latin American Republics: General," Box 60, Berle Papers, FDR Library.

45. Haglund, *Latin America,* 136.

46. Stanley E. Hilton, *Brazil and the Great Powers, 1930–1939: The Politics of Trade Rivalry* (Austin: University of Texas Press, 1975), xx; Hans-Jürgen Schröder, "Die Vereinigten Staaten und die nationalsozialistische Handelspolitik gegenüber Lateinamerika," *Jahrbuch für Geschichte von Staat, Wirtschaft und Gesellschaft Lateinamerikas* 7 (1970): 309, 312, 320.

47. Lloyd C. Gardner, *Economic Aspects of New Deal Diplomacy* (Madison: University of Wisconsin Press, 1964), 52.

48. Hans-Jürgen Schröder, *Deutschland und die Vereinigten Staaten, 1933–1939. Wirtschaft und Politik in der Entwicklung des deutsch-amerikanischen Gegensatzes* (Wiesbaden: Franz Steiner Verlag, 1970), 234, 246.

49. Schröder, "Die Vereinigten Staaten," 313.

50. R. A. Humphreys, *Latin America and the Second World War*, 2 vols., vol. 1 (London: Athlone, 1981), 6.

51. Dana G. Munro, *The Latin American Republics* (New York: Appleton-Century Co., 1942); Samuel Flagg Bemis, *The Latin American Policy of the United States* (New York: Harcourt, Brace & Co., 1943); J. Lloyd Mecham, *The United States and Inter-American Security, 1889–1960* (Austin: University of Texas Press, 1962).

52. William Appleman Williams, *The Tragedy of American Diplomacy*, 2nd rev. ed. (New York: Dell Publishing Co., 1972); Gardner, *Economic Aspects*; David Green, *The Containment of Latin America: a History of the Myths and Realities of the Good Neighbor Policy* (Chicago: Quadrangle Books, 1971).

53. Gardner, *Economic Aspects*, 122, citing Special Conference with the Senate Military Affairs Committee, 31 Jan 1939, PPF-1P, Roosevelt Papers, FDR Library.

54. Georg-Alexander Höbbel, "Das 'Dritte Reich' und die Good Neighbor Policy: die nationalsozialistische Beurteilung der Lateinamerikapolitik Franklin D Roosevelts, 1933–1941" (Ph.D. diss., Hamburg, 1997), 286–96.

55. Berle to Chiefs of the Diplomatic Missions in the Other American Republics, *The Pattern of Nazi Organizations and Their Activities in the Other American Republics*, pp. 36–7, 6 Feb 1941, 862.20210/414A, RG59, NA.

56. "Weekly Progress Report No. 16," 13 Jan 1941, 5, Box 68, Welles Papers.

57. "Council of National Defense: Coordinator of Commercial and Cultural Relations between the American Republics," n.d. 1941, Box 57, Berle Papers.

58. Harley Notter, 6 Sep 1940, in folder "General Memoranda July 1940–Sept 1940," Memoranda Relating to General Latin American Affairs, Box 3, and Harley Notter to John Dickey, 14 Feb 1941, in folder "General Memoranda Jan–Feb 1941," Memoranda Relating to General Latin American Affairs, Box 4, ARA, RG59, NA.

59. Dean Acheson, *Action Taken by the United States Government in the Economic Field to Eliminate Axis Influence from the Other American Republics*, 2 Jun 1942, in folder "711 1942," Colombia: Bogotá Embassy, Security-Segregated General Records, 1938–49, Box 23, RG84, NA.

60. Daniels Diary, March 4, 1941, cited in Gardner, *Economic Aspects*, 126.

61. Braden to Welles, 28 Jan 1941, folder 12, Box 67, Welles Papers.

62. "Press Release Issued by the Department of State," 17 Jul 1941, *Foreign Relations of the United States (FRUS) 1941*, VI: 268–9; Welles, "Procedures and Policies on Maintenance of the Proclaimed List of Certain Blocked Nationals," 28 Aug 1941, *FRUS 1941*, VI: 271–83.

63. Collado to Board of Economic Operations, "Report by the Proclaimed List Clearance Committee," 9 Dec 1941, in folder "Board of Economic Operations – Oct.–Dec. 1941," Box 56, Berle Papers.

64. Welles, "Procedures and Policies," 271–83.
65. Acheson, *Action Taken*. Within days of initial publication, the complaints starting coming in. Sumner Welles noted "a great deal of confusion" within the foreign service over the operation of the Proclaimed List and told Dean Acheson of numerous errors, among them "the inclusion in the blacklist of a reputable American citizen doing business in São Paulo, who is stated to be a Yale graduate. I should think this would hurt your feelings particularly." (Acheson graduated from Yale in 1915.) Welles to Acheson, 20 Jul 1941, and Welles to Acheson, 19 Aug 1941, Folder 8, Box 73, Welles Papers.
66. Welles to Bowers, 1 Oct 1941, *FRUS 1941,* VI: 294–5.
67. Caffery (Rio) to Secretary of State, 21 Oct 1941, *FRUS 1941,* VI: 301, and Caffery (Rio) to Secretary of State, 19 Dec 1941, *FRUS 1941,* VI: 319.
68. "Con las personas incluidas en las listas negras pueden mantener relaciones comerciales los habitantes de Costa Rica," *La Tribuna,* 29 Nov 1941, 1.
69. Silvia Galvis and Alberto Donadio, *Colombia Nazi 1939–1945: Espionaje alemán, la cacería del FBI, Santos, López y los pactos secretos* (Bogotá: Planeta Colombiana Editorial S.A., 1986), 110; "Colombiano dice que la confección de las listas negras no pueda hacerse sin la intervención directa de las autoridades colombianas," *La Tribuna* (San José), 22 Nov 1941, 1.
70. David L. Gordon and Royden Dangerfield, *The Hidden Weapon: The Story of Economic Warfare* (New York: Harper, 1947), 146–7.
71. Melby, "Memorandum of Conversation," 5 Aug 1941, *FRUS 1941,* VI: 270.
72. Ortiz to Tewksbury, 26 Nov 1941, Serie N; Ortiz to Tewksbury, 28 Nov 1941, Serie N; and Tewksbury to Ortiz, 1 Dec 1941, Serie B, Embajada de Estados Unidos, Ministerio de Relaciones Exteriores (MRE), Archivo Histórico de Quito (hereafter AHQ). Dickey to Welles, 9 Jul 1942, folder 11, Box 177, Welles Papers.
73. Bonsal to Welles, 8 Oct 1941, *FRUS 1941,* VI: 295–6.
74. López de Mesa to President of Colombian Senate, 20 Jan 1942, in folder "Listas Negras – Varios – 1941," Listas Negras – 1941, Archivo del Ministerio de Relaciones Exteriores, Bogotá.
75. Stanley Hilton, *Oswaldo Aranha: uma biografia* (Rio de Janeiro: Editorial Objetiva, 1994), 370–2.
76. Adams to Acheson, "Recommendation that Aspirin Powder and its Ingredients Be Made Subject to Export License," 3 Nov 1941, in folder "General Memoranda Oct–Nov 1941," Memoranda Relating to General Latin American Affairs, Box 6, ARA, RG59, NA.
77. Military Intelligence Division, *Axis Espionage and Propaganda in Latin America* (Washington, DC: War Department, 1946), 21–2.
78. Boal to Welles, 22 Dec 1941, 740.00112AEW1939/6329, RG59, NA.
79. Braden to Welles, 24 Nov 1941, folder 12, Box 67, Welles Papers; Acheson, *Action Taken*.
80. Spaeth to Acting Secretary of State, 8 Apr 1942, folder 14, Box 83, Welles Papers.
81. Acheson, *Action Taken*. Emphasis added.
82. Bonsal to Welles, *The Proclaimed List*.

83. Martin Domke, "Western Hemisphere Control Over Enemy Property: A Comparative Survey," *Law and Contemporary Problems* 11: 1 (Winter-Spring 1945): 3–16; Gordon and Dangerfield, *The Hidden Weapon,* 145–8.
84. Buenos Aires Protocol, in Burr and Hussey, *Documents,* 113–14. Emphasis added.
85. Max Brill to MRE, 20 Sep 1942, Serie N, Embajada de Estados Unidos, MRE, AHQ.
86. "Name Files of Enemy Aliens" for Antonio Lehmann, alphabetical, Special War Problems Division (hereafter SWP), Boxes 31–50, RG59, NA.
87. "Name Files of Enemy Aliens" for Heinrich Schulte, alphabetical, SWP Boxes 31–50, RG59, NA.
88. U.S. Senate, *Nazi Party Membership Records.*
89. Acheson, *Action Taken,* and Galvis and Donadio, *Colombia Nazi,* 114. See also documents on Laboratorios Román in folder "Listas Negras 1943," Informes Confidenciales Sobre Actividades Nazis 1942 – 1943 – 1944, AMRE, and Bustillo Franco to MRE, 2 Oct 1941, in Listas Negras 1941, AMRE, Bogotá.
90. Lane to Bonsal, 27 May 1942, Box 67, Arthur Bliss Lane Papers, Manuscripts and Archives, Yale University Library.
91. Caicedo Castilla to MRE, 6 Nov 1941, Listas Negras-1941, AMRE.
92. Trueblood to Secretary of State, 27 Sep 1943, "711.2," Costa Rica: San José Embassy Confidential File, Box 25, RG84, NA.
93. Hull, 28 Jan 1942, *FRUS 1942,* V: 285–6.
94. SecState to AmEmbBogota, 31 Mar 1943, 740.00112AEW1939/23233, RG59, NA.
95. SecState to AmEmbBogota, 31 Mar 1943, 740.00112AEW1939/23233, RG59, NA.
96. *Comité de Consulta,* 5 Jun 1943, "Listas Negras – Varios," Informes Confidenciales Sobre Actividades Nazis – 1942 – 1943 – 1944, AMRE.
97. Welles, "Procedures and Policies," 271–83.
98. USEmbBogotá, form letter in Spanish (author's translation), n.d., "Listas Negras – Varios," Informes Confidenciales Sobre Actividades Nazis – 1942 – 1943 – 1944, AMRE.
99. Acheson, 4 Aug 1942, *FRUS 1942,* V: 58–73.
100. Lane to Welles, forwarding Derby memo, 31 Mar 1943, Box 67, Lane Papers.
101. Lane to Keith, 19 Dec 1942, Box 67, Lane Papers.
102. Lane to Welles, 19 Dec 1942, Box 67, Lane Papers.
103. John E. Findling, *Close Neighbors, Distant Friends: United States-Central American Relations* (New York: Greenwood Press, 1987), 97. See also Gellman, *Good Neighbor Diplomacy,* 31, and George Black, *The Good Neighbor: How the United States Wrote the History of Central America and the Caribbean* (New York: Pantheon Books, 1988), 62.
104. Lane to Welles, 27 Oct 1941, and Lane to Welles, 26 Nov 1941, Box 66, Lane Papers.
105. Lane to Welles, 17 Mar 1943, Box 67, Lane Papers.
106. Lane to Welles, 17 Mar 1943, Box 67, Lane Papers. Lane also sent a copy to Henry Wallace. Lane to Wallace, 22 Apr 1943, Box 67, Lane Papers.

107. Alfonso López Michelsen, *Los Elegidos* (Bogotá: Tercer Mundo, 1967, first published in Mexico by Editorial Guarania, 1953), 168.
108. López Michelsen, *Los Elegidos,* 87–8.
109. López Michelsen, *Los Elegidos,* 215. The U.S. commercial attaché originally tasked with drawing up the Proclaimed List for Colombia was certainly not a shiftless drunkard. Merwin Bohan was "extremely able and hard-working," his ambassador recalled. Bohan remembered that he and five secretaries were overwhelmed with work in the first months of compiling the blacklist, putting in fourteen to sixteen hours a day. Braden, *Diplomats and Demagogues,* 203; Bohan oral history, 44. On Handel Industrie Maatschattij, see Gustavo Humberto Rodríguez, "Segunda administración de López Pumarejo," in Alvaro Tirado Mejía, ed., *Nueva Historia de Colombia* (Bogotá: Planeta Colombiana Editorial, 1989), I: 373–96; Lleras Restrepo, *Crónica,* V: 333; Alvaro Tirado Mejía, "Colombia: Siglo y medio de bipartidismo," in Mario Arrubla, ed., *Colombia Hoy* (Bogotá: Siglo Veintiuno Editores, 1978), 167.

Chapter 4   Deportation

1. DoS Swiss to Legation Washington, 16 Jun 1943, Band 5, Noten von und an Staatsdepartement, April–Juni 1943, E2200 Washington/15, Schweizerisches Bundesarchiv (hereafter SBA), Bern.
2. *Memorandum regarding activities of the United States Government in removing from the other American Republics dangerous subversive aliens,* November 3, 1942, p. 2, Subject Files 1939–54, Box 180, Special War Problems Division (hereafter SWP), RG59, National Archives, College Park, Maryland (hereafter NA).
3. Ralph N. Clough, 16 Apr 1990, Foreign Affairs Oral History Program, Georgetown University Library.
4. Steve Lewontin, "'A Blessed Peace': Honduras under Carías," in *Honduras: Portrait of a Captive Nation,* Nancy Peckenham and Annie Street, eds. (New York: Praeger, 1985), 85–8; Comité Liberal Demócrata de Honduras en México, *Homenaje a las Víctimas de San Pedro Sula* (México, D.F.: Otras Publicaciones, 1945), 107.
5. Mario Argueta, *Tiburcio Carías: anatomía de una época, 1923–1948* (Tegucigalpa: Editorial Guaymuras, 1989), 173–7.
6. OSS, "Situation Report: Latin America," 6 Sep 1944, R&A 1306.49, Latin America Division Bi-weekly Situation Reports 1944–5, Box 1, RG226, NA. For heartrending details of this and other massacres, see Comité Liberal Demócrata, *Homenaje.*
7. William Krehm, *Democracies and Tyrannies of the Caribbean* (Westport, CT: Lawrence Hill, 1984), 99.
8. Acheson, *Action Taken by the United States Government in the Economic Field to Eliminate Axis Influence from the Other American Republics,* 2 Jun 1942, "711 1942," Colombia: Bogota Embassy, Security-Segregated General Records, 1938–49, Box 23, RG84, NA.

9. Christian Zinsser, "Diplomatische Mission in Honduras," *Jahrbuch für Geschichte von Staat, Wirtschaft und Gesellschaft Lateinamerikas* 12 (1975): 434–55. Zinsser was accused of being a Gestapo agent and expelled from Central America before the U.S. entry into the war. This article presents his denial. Evidence supporting or refuting the accusation is lacking, but Zinsser's article provides some insights into the Honduran German community. Party membership figures are 41 in Hans-Adolf Jacobsen, *Nationalsozialistische Außenpolitik 1933–1938* (Frankfurt: Alfred Metzner Verlag, 1968), 662–3, and Michael Naumann, "Ausgewählte Daten zur Auslandsorganisation der NSDAP, Stand am 30.6.1939," based on Bundesarchiv document NSD 8/43 (Auslandorganisation der NSDAP. Statistik, 30.6.1939, Geheim). There are 47 names for Honduras in Senate Committee on Military Affairs, *Nazi Party Membership Records,* Senate Committee Prints 79/2/46, Part 2, March 1946, and Part 3, September 1946, S1535–S1538 (Washington, DC: U.S. Government Printing Office, 1946), four of whom joined after June 1939.

10. Thomas M. Leonard, *Central America and the United States: The Search for Stability* (Athens: University of Georgia Press, 1991), 114.

11. Erwin to SecState, 24 Apr 1942, 740.00115EW1939/2864, RG59, NA.

12. Clough oral history. For Erwin's initiative in suggesting the names of Germans to deport, see Erwin to SecState, 7 Apr 1942, and Welles to AmLegTegucigalpa, 8 Apr 1942, 740.00115EW1939/2613, RG59, NA.

13. All information in this paragraph to this point from individual postwar reports, listed alphabetically, in Name Files of Enemy Aliens, SWP Boxes 31–50, RG59, NA; totals of Nazi Party members taken from the same records, plus crosschecking *Nazi Party Membership Records,* as in note 9, against names of deportees from Honduras, in *German Nationals Deported by the Other American Republics Who Were Deported by the United States,* in folder of same name, Subject Files 1939–54, Box 121, SWP, RG59, NA.

14. The six deportees explicitly named as political opponents of Carías are Franz Jeffre, Fred Karl Berger, Heinrich F. W. Faasch, Paul Feldman, Johannes Richard Heyer, and Johann Wilhelm Maier. See the individual postwar reports in Name Files of Enemy Aliens, SWP Boxes 31–50, RG59, NA. The quotation is from Jeffre's file.

15. Erwin to SecState, 24 Nov 1942, 740.00115EW1939/5343, RG59, NA.

16. Stetson Conn and Byron Fairchild, *The Framework of Hemisphere Defense* (Washington, DC: Office of the Chief of Military History, Department of the Army, 1960) 9–12; War Department reports Dec 1941–Jan 1942, folder 15 & 16, Map Room Files (hereafter MR) 36, FDR Library, Hyde Park, NY; Boaz Long to SecState, 19 Dec 1941, "Diplomatic Correspondence – Ecuador," PSF 28, FDR Library; series of MID reports in 740.00115 PW/48, RG59, NA.

17. Hoover to Berle, 15 Jan 1942, 740.00115PW/93, RG59, NA; *Laxity in Enforcement of Surveillance Measures by the Dominican Government,* 5 Mar 1942, R&A 251, M1221, OSS Intelligence Reports, RG59, NA; Hoover to Berle, August 21, 1942, 740.00115EW1939/4403, RG59, NA.

18. See Chapter 7, "Expropriation."

19. Hull to Diplomatic Representatives in the American Republics, 13 Dec 1941, *FRUS 1942,* I: 289–90.

20. Michel Fortmann and David G. Haglund, "Public Diplomacy and Dirty Tricks: Two Faces of United States 'Informal Penetration' of Latin America on the Eve of World War II," *Diplomacy and Statecraft* 6: 2 (1995): 536–77.

21. David Bushnell, *Eduardo Santos and the Good Neighbor 1938–1942* (Gainesville: University of Florida Press, 1967), 18; Arthur P. Whitaker, *The United States and South America: The Northern Republics* (Cambridge, MA: Harvard University Press, 1948), 48; George Grant Mason, Jr., *Can the United States Retain Latin American Trade and Cultural Relations against German, Italian and Japanese Competition?* (Washington, DC: The George Washington University Press, 1939), 5. See also Matthew Josephson, *Empire of the Air: Juan Trippe and the Struggle for World Airways* (New York: Arno Press, 1972).

22. Braden to Secretary of State, 31 Dec 1941, 740.00115EW1939/1661, RG59, NA; Carlos Lleras Restrepo, *Crónica de mi propia vida*, vol. IV (Bogotá: Stamato Editores, 1983), 170; Stephen J. Randall, *Colombia and the United States: Hegemony and Interdependence* (Athens: University of Georgia Press, 1992), 175.

23. David G. Haglund, "'De-lousing' SCADTA: the Role of Pan American Airways in US Aviation Diplomacy in Colombia, 1939–1940," *Aerospace Historian* 30:3 (Sep 1983): 177–90.

24. Spruille Braden, *Diplomats and Demagogues* (New Rochelle, NY: Arlington House, 1971), 230–40, and Spruille Braden, 1952–53, Oral History Collection, Columbia University, 2682–2700.

25. Thomas Schoonover, *Germany in Central America: Competitive Imperialism, 1821–1929* (Tuscaloosa: University of Alabama Press, 1998), 192.

26. William Burden, *The Struggle for Airways in Latin America* (New York: Arno Press, 1977), 72–8.

27. Adolf Berle Diary, 12 Oct 1940, Adolf Berle Papers, FDR Library.

28. Hull to AmLegGuatemala, 12 Dec 1941, 740.0011EW1939/17332, reel 89 M982, RG59, NA; Jacobo Schifter Sikora, *Las alianzas conflictivas: las relaciones de Estados Unidos y Costa Rica desde la Segunda Guerra Mundial a la guerra fría* (San José: Libro Libre, 1986), 125–32.

29. Airgram and enclosures from Edwin C. Wilson to Secretary of State, No. 300, October 20, 1941, Panama. 740.00115PW/1, RG59, NA.

30. Wilson to Secretary of State, No. 406, October 31, 1941, 740.00115PW/2, RG59, NA.

31. William L. Langer and S. Everett Gleason, *The Challenge to Isolation, 1937–1940* (New York: Harper and Brothers, 1952), 611–13. After the war, a scholar investigating the event wrote to both Wilson and Fernández Artucio, but neither could supply any evidence of Nazi intrigues beyond a handrawn map made by a lone, "slightly pathological" latecomer to the NSDAP. Louis De Jong, *The German Fifth Column in the Second World War* (Chicago: University of Chicago Press, 1956), 222–3.

32. Cited in Long to Biddle, 6 Apr 1943, 740.00115PW/1392, RG59, NA.

33. Wilson to SecState, 7 Dec 1941, 740.0011PW/697, reel 226 M982, RG59, NA; Lane to Secretary of State, No. 375, December 8, 1941, 740.00112A EW1939/4471, RG59, NA; Wilson to Secretary of State, 10 Dec 1941, 740.00115EW1939/1593, RG59, NA; Cockrell to War Dept., 15 Dec 1941, 740.00115EW1939/1655, RG59, NA; Letter to War Dept., December 11, 1941, 740.00115EW1939/1653 and 1654, RG59, NA; Ecklauer, 2 Feb 1942,

"Deutsche Zivilgefangene in Nicaragua," R41839, Rechtsabteilung, Politisches Archiv des Auswärtigen Amtes, Bonn (hereafter PAAA).

34. Adolf Berle Diary, 10 Dec 1941, Berle Papers. Dates of declarations of war in Joyce, 16 Dec 1941, "General Memoranda Oct–Nov 1941," Memoranda Relating to General Latin American Affairs, Box 6, ARA, RG59, NA.

35. Dwyre to SecState, 11 Dec 1941, Hull to AmLegGuatemala, 12 Dec 1941, and Dwyre to SecState, 16 Dec 1941, 740.0011EW1939/17564, reel 89 M982, RG59, NA; Dwyre to Secretary of State, 19 Dec 1941, 740/0011EW1939/17707, RG59, NA.

36. Hull to AmLegGuatemala, 12 Dec 1941, 740.0011EW1939/17332, reel 89 M982, RG59, NA.

37. Cabot to Bonsal, 16 Dec 1941, 740.00115EW1939/1599, RG59, NA. Italics in original.

38. Edwin C. Wilson to Secretary of State, No. 503, January 14, 1942, 740.00115PW/78, RG59, NA.

39. Wilson to SecState, 21 Jan 1942, 740.00115PW/90, RG59, NA. During the First World War, the United States had asked the Panamanian government to arrest all German men and deliver them to Canal Zone authorities for internment. In April 1918, the Germans were shipped to New York, officially remaining under Panamanian authority but in the custody of the United States. Attorney General Thomas W. Gregory and Secretary of State Robert Lansing agreed that there was no precedent in international law for the transfer of civilian internees from one ally to another. See U.S. Department of State, *Papers Relating to the Foreign Relations of the United States,* 1918, Suppl. 2, 232–44.

40. Postwar investigation in Herbert Jabs folder in alphabetical Name Files of Enemy Aliens, SWP Boxes 31–50, RG59, NA. See Chapter 5 for more on factional struggles inside the camps.

41. See Westermeier folder in alphabetical Name Files of Enemy Aliens, SWP Boxes 31–50, RG59, NA, and Panama list in *Nazi Party Membership Records.*

42. See individual files on Panamanian internees alphabetical Name Files of Enemy Aliens, SWP Boxes 31–50, RG59, NA.

43. "Fragebogen für Auslandsdeutsche Flüchtlinge" and accompanying documents, in Rückwandereramt der AO, Ursprung file, Panama group, Bundesarchiv Berlin-Lichterfelde (hereafter BA-L).

44. "Fragebogen für Auslandsdeutsche Flüchtlinge" and accompanying documents, in Rückwandereramt der AO, Karlinger file, Panama group, BA-L; Party membership listed under Guatemala group in *Nazi Party Membership Records.*

45. Kaufmann folder in alphabetical Name Files of Enemy Aliens, SWP Boxes 31–50, RG59, NA.

46. *Confidential: Carl Bald, Panama,* 4 Feb 1946, "Bald, Carl, Panama," Name Files of Interned Enemy Aliens from Latin America, 1942–8, Box 36, SWP, RG59, NA.

47. *Confidential: Hans Bartsch (Panama),* 4 Feb 1946, "Bartsch, Hans, Panama," Name Files of Interned Enemy Aliens from Latin America, 1942–8, Box 36, SWP, RG59, NA.

48. Karliner folder in alphabetical Name Files of Enemy Aliens, SWP Boxes 31–50, RG59, NA.

49. Wolff folder in alphabetical Name Files of Enemy Aliens, SWP Boxes 31–50, RG59, NA.

50. For Panama totals, see White to Lafoon, 30 Jan 1946, in folder "Statistics," Subject Files 1939–54, Box 70, SWP, RG59, NA; *German Nationals Deported By The Other American Republics Who Were Deported By The United States,* in folder of same name, Subject Files 1939–54, Box 121, SWP, RG59, NA; and author analysis of Panamanian cases in Name Files of Enemy Aliens, SWP Boxes 31–50, RG59, NA.

51. These data are from author's analysis of 531 postwar investigations in Name Files of Enemy Aliens, SWP Boxes 31–50, RG59, NA. The nine known repatriate cases are from "Fragebogen für Auslandsdeutsche Flüchtlinge" and accompanying documents, in Rückwandereramt der AO, alphabetical name files grouped by country, BA-L.

52. Their names appear in *Nazi Party Membership Records* but not in any of the deportation records.

53. Manuel Oñós de Plandolit to Spanish Foreign Ministry, 3 Aug 1943, "Deutsche Zivilgefangene in Panama, 1941–1944," R41856, Rechtsabteilung, PAAA.

54. Hull to AmLegManagua, 30 Dec 1941, 740.00115EW1939/1641, RG59, NA.

55. Ennis to Special Division, 12 Oct 1943, 740.00115EW1939/7456 1/2, RG59, NA.

56. This estimate comes from cross-checking two master lists of deportees against the two overseas NSDAP membership lists compiled from captured German records. *Nazi Party Membership Records* lists members by country. There is a second alphabetical list available at the Bundesarchiv-Lichterfelde and on microfilm in the Manuscript Division of the Library of Congress as "Germany (territory under allied occupation, 1945–1955: U.S. Zone). Office of Military Government," Shelf no. Mss. 18,049, 3 reels. The master list of deportees repatriated to Germany is *German Nationals Deported by the Other American Republics Who Were Deported Via the United States,* in folder of same name, Subject Files 1939–54, Box 121, SWP, RG59, NA. For those not returned to Germany, I have used my tabulation of 531 postwar reports by the Alien Enemy Control Section of the State Department; see the Note on Sources in the Bibliography.

57. List of deportees in Costa Rica MID report of 6 Jan 1942, in folder A8-5(3CR) Free Germans, in Naval Attaché – Guatemala City, Personality Files 1940–6, Box 45, ONI, RG38, NA. Krogmann referred to as *Ortsgruppenleiter* for Costa Rica in Albrecht to St.S & RAM, *Treatment of Reichsdeutsche in America and German countermeasures,* 6 Feb 1942, "Deutsche Zivilgefangene in den Verein. Staaten. v. Amerika 1941–1942," R41876, Rechtsabteilung, PAAA. See postwar investigations of individual cases in alphabetical Name Files of Enemy Aliens, SWP Boxes 31–50, RG59, NA.

58. Costa Rica MID report of 6 Jan 1942, in folder A8-5(3CR) Free Germans, in Naval Attaché – Guatemala City, Personality Files 1940–6, Box 45, ONI, RG38, NA.

59. See individual cases of postwar investigations in alphabetical Name Files of Enemy Aliens, SWP Boxes 31–50, RG59, NA.

60. Tenney, *Case of Wilhelm Wiedemann,* 13 Mar 1946, "Wiedemann, Wilhelm, Costa Rica," Name Files of Interned Enemy Aliens from Latin America, 1942–8,

Box 50, SWP, RG59, NA. Wiedemann does not appear on the Nazi Party list for Costa Rica.

61. Compare Costa Rica MID report of 6 Jan 1942, in folder A8–5(3CR) Free Germans, in Naval Attaché – Guatemala City, Personality Files 1940–6, Box 45, ONI, RG38, NA, to Frey's file in postwar investigation reports in alphabetical Name Files of Enemy Aliens, SWP Boxes 31–50, RG59, NA.

62. The numbers were stable: 259 in Jacobsen, *Nationalsozialistische Außenpolitik,* 662–3; 260 in Naumann, "Ausgewählte Daten."

63. Guatemalan Police Department, *Datos Personales,* various dates, "Guatemala Photos of Deported Germans, 1936–47," Boxes 17–18, Naval Attaché, General Correspondence, ONI, RG38, NA.

64. Guatemalan Police Department, *Datos Personales,* 19 Dec 1941, "Guatemala Photos of Deported Germans, 1936–47," Box 18, Naval Attaché, General Correspondence, ONI, RG38, NA.

65. Guatemalan Police Department, *Datos Personales,* 28 Jan 1942, "Guatemala Photos of Deported Germans, 1936–47," Box 17, Naval Attaché, General Correspondence, ONI, RG38, NA.

66. Green to FC, 14 Apr 1942, 740.0011EW/4–1442, reel 194 M982, RG59, NA. See Chapter 5 for a U.S. camp commander's praise of Weber in internment.

67. Green to Hackworth, 15 Jan 1942, 310.6215/12 1/2, RG59, NA.

68. Memorandum (J. D. Neal), Department of State Office of Foreign Activity Correlation, 16 Feb 1942, 740.00115EW1939/2133, RG59, NA.

69. Warren to SecState, 17 Nov 1945, *FRUS 1945,* IX: 289–90.

70. Long to Fahy, 10 Jul 1942, 740.00115EW1939/4307, RG59, NA. For a useful analysis, see Natsu Taylor Saito, "Justice Held Hostage: U.S. Disregard for International Law in the World War II Internment of Japanese Peruvians – A Case Study," *Boston College Law Review* 40: 1 (Dec 1998): 275–348.

71. Hoover to Berle, 15 Jan 1942, 740.00115PW/93, RG59, NA.

72. Braden to SecState, 3 Jan 1942, 740.00115PW/55, RG59, NA.

73. Stimson to Hull, 29 Dec 1941, 740.00115EW1939/1646, RG59, NA; Braden to Secretary of State, 31 Dec 1941, 740.00115EW1939/1661, RG59, NA; Hull to AmEmbBogota, 30 Dec 1941, 740.00115EW1939/1661A, RG59, NA; Braden to Secretary of State, 15 Jan 1942, 740.00115EW1939/1718, RG59, NA; Walmsley to Duggan, 15 Jan 1942, 740.00115EW1939/1838, RG59, NA.

74. Lleras Restrepo, *Crónica,* VI, 170.

75. Walter Held remembered the message as *invitado a abandonar el país,* a phrase that also appears frequently in AMRE documents. Held, interview by author, Bogotá, 9 Mar 1998.

76. AmLegQuito to Ministerio de Relaciones Exteriores, 10 Mar 1942, in Serie B, Embajada de Estados Unidos, MRE, Archivo Histórico de Quito (hereafter AHQ), Ecuador; Walter Held, interview with author, Bogotá, 9 Mar 1998.

77. Skowronski to *Auswärtiges Amt,* 29 May 1942, R41557, Zivilgefangenen-Austausch-Vereinigten Staaten von Amerika, Rechtsabteilung, PAAA; MRE, *Lista de los alemanes a quienes el Ministerio de Relaciones Exteriores autorizó para dirigirse a la Policía Nacional a fin de que otorgaran las garantías necesarias para permanecer en el país,* in folder "Actividades Nazis 1941," Actividades Nazis – 1940–2, AMRE.

78. *Karibischer Beobachter* 5:8, 15 April 1938.

79. Bendetson to Warren, 24 Jan 1942, 740.00115EW1939/1967 3/7, RG59, NA; Hellermann to Sethe, 9 Jun 1942 and 24 Jun 1942, "Zivilgefangenen-Austausch-Vereinigten Staaten von Amerika," R41558, Rechtsabteilung, PAAA; Swiss Legation Washington to Special Division DoS, 20 Feb 1942, "Noten von und an Staatsdepartement, Dez.1941–Juni 1942," Band 3, E2200 Washington/15, SBA.

80. "Fragebogen für Auslandsdeutsche Flüchtlinge" and accompanying documents, in Rückwanderamt der AO, Strack file, Colombia group, BA-L.

81. See individual postwar reports on Becker, Kill, and Krueger in alphabetical Name Files of Enemy Aliens, SWP Boxes 31–50, RG59, NA. See also FBI, *German Espionage in Latin America,* p. 38, June 1946, 862.20210/6–1746, RG59, NA; Galvis and Donadio, *Colombia Nazi,* 23–35.

82. See individual postwar reports on Rullhusen, Schwartau, Vogel, and Schirrmeister in alphabetical Name Files of Enemy Aliens, SWP Boxes 31–50, RG59, NA.

83. Long to SecState, 24 Jan 1942, 740.00115EW1939/1767, RG59, NA.

84. Long to SecState, 10 Feb 1942, 740.00115EW1939/1985, RG59, NA.

85. Drew to SecState, 1 Apr 1942, 740.00115EW1939/2607, RG59, NA. See also Long to SecState, 14 Mar 1942, 740.00115EW1939/2311, RG59, NA.

86. Boaz Long to SecState, 9 Apr 1942, 740.00115EW1939/2710, RG59, NA.

87. Spanish Minister in Quito to Spanish Foreign Minster, 22 Apr 1942, "Zivilgefangenen-Austausch-Vereinigten Staaten von Amerika," R41557, Rechtsabteilung, PAAA.

88. Gunter Beckmann, interview by author, Quito, 21 Jan 1998.

89. Gunter Lisken, interview by author, Guayaquil, 17 Feb 1998; Lisken file in alphabetical Name Files of Enemy Aliens, SWP Boxes 31–50, RG59, NA.

90. Roberto Hahn, interview by author, Guayaquil, 16 Feb 1998.

91. MRE, *Documentos Sobre Juicios de Expulsión del Ecuador a Súbditos del Eje, 1946,* 3 Oct 1946, Serie F, Documentos sobre Subditos de las Naciones del Eje, 1941 a 1946, Box 669 [38], MRE, AHQ; *Nazi Party Membership Records.*

92. Hanley to Coleman, 12 Oct 1943, 862.20210 Rath Erich/23 1/2, RG59, NA; Davis to Spaeth, "Confidential: Eric Rath," 9 Nov 1945, in folder "Rath, Eric, Ecuador," Name Files of Interned Enemy Aliens from Latin America, 1942–8, Box 45, SWP, RG59, NA; AmEmbBogota to SecState, 8 Apr 1943, 862.20210 Rath Erich/13, RG59, NA.

93. Noebel, Apr 1942 (?), "Zivilinternierten-Austausch. Peru.," R41538, Rechts-abteilung, PAAA.

94. Walter Olivier to AA, October 1942, "Zivilgefangenen-Austausch-Vereinigten Staaten von Amerika," R41564, Rechtsabteilung, PAAA. See also Rudolf Lindgens to Swiss Embassy, 21 May 1942, "Deutsche Zivilgefangene in den Ver.St.v.Amerika – Lager, 1942–1944," R42003, Rechtsabteilung, PAAA; Hans Kolter, interview with author, Guatemala City, 27 May 1996.

95. Hull to AmEmbMadrid, 16 Jan 1942, 740.00115EW1939/2241, RG59, NA; Provost Marshal General Gullion, 16 Jan 1942, 740.00115EW1939/1723, RG59, NA.

96. Swiss Legation Washington to DoS, 5 Apr 1944, "Noten an Staatsdepartement, Jan.–Juni 1944," Band 10, E2200 Washington/15, SBA.

97. Alfredo Brauer, interview by author, Quito, 5 Feb 1998; Otto Schwarz Wilde, *Memorias de la Guerra* (Guayaquil: n.p., 1960), 38.

98. C. Harvey Gardiner, *Pawns in a Triangle of Hate: The Peruvian Japanese and the United States* (Seattle: University of Washington Press, 1981), 29. See also Welles to AmLegManagua, 2 Apr 1942, 740.00115EW1939/2482, RG59, NA, for similar order not to visa deportees.

99. Quoted in Jerre Mangione, *An Ethnic at Large* (New York: G. P. Putnam's Sons, 1978), 322. Mangione was a special assistant in the Justice Department's Alien Enemy Control Unit.

100. DoS to British Embassy, 25 Feb 1942, *FRUS 1942,* I: 316–18.

101. Long to Messersmith, 26 Jun 1942, "Messersmith, George S. Jan–Sept, 1942," Subject File, State Department 1939–44, Box 199, Long Papers, Manuscript Division, Library of Congress, Washington, DC (hereafter LC).

102. Breckinridge Long, *Extracting Axis Agents from South American Countries, 1942,* "Division of American Republics 1942," Subject File, State Department 1939–44, Box 191, Long Papers. Emphasis added.

103. Dwyre to Secretary of State, 19 Dec 1941, 740/0011EW1939/17707, RG59, NA.

104. Rudolf Lindgens to Swiss Embassy, 21 May 1942, "Deutsche Zivilgefangene in den Ver.St.v.Amerika – Lager, 1942–1944," R42003, Rechtsabteilung, PAAA.

105. Albrecht to St.S & RAM, *Behandlung den Reichsdeutschen in Amerika and Deutsche Gegenmassnahmen,* 6 Feb 1942, "Deutsche Zivilgefangene in den Verein. Staaten. v. Amerika 1941–1942," R41876, Rechtsabteilung, PAAA; Federer to AA, 24 Jan 1942, "Strafverfahren gegen deutscher Zivilgefangene in Costa Rica," R41909, Rechtsabteilung, PAAA.

106. All quotations in this paragraph from Green to FC, 14 Apr 1942, 740.0011EW/4-1442, reel 194 M982, RG59, NA.

107. Figures from crosschecking *Nazi Party Membership Records* against names of deportees from Guatemala, in *German Nationals Deported by the Other American Republics Who Were Deported by the United States,* in folder of same name, Subject Files 1939–54, Box 121, SWP, RG59, NA, in addition to individual postwar reports, listed alphabetically, in Name Files of Enemy Aliens, SWP Boxes 31–50, RG59, NA, for those not repatriated to Germany.

108. *Memorandum regarding activities of the United States Government in removing from the other American Republics dangerous subversive aliens,* 3 Nov 1942, p. 2, Subject Files 1939–54, Box 180, SWP, RG59, NA. Emphasis added. The memo is unsigned, and circulated under Hull's name; it probably originated in Long's office.

109. A history of the FBI notes that it detained 7,043 Germans, of whom 1,225 were interned, 2,449 paroled, and 2,589 released, with 42 unresolved cases and 47 deaths in detention. Donald F. Whitehead, *The FBI Story* (New York: Random House, 1956), 342–3. Jörg Nagler estimates domestic German internment at 2,300 in "Internment of German Enemy Aliens in the United States during the First and Second World Wars," in Kay Saunders and Roger Daniels, eds., *Alien Justice: Wartime Internment in Australia and North America* (St. Lucia, Queensland, Australia: University of Queensland Press, 2000), 78. Arnold Krammer states that 10,905 Germans in the United States were interned, but that includes the 4,058 from Latin America as well as a majority who were detained and then released. Krammer, *Undue Process: The Untold Story of America's German Alien Internees* (New York: Rowman and Littlefield, 1997),

ix, 34, 81; for inclusion of Latin American deportees in total German figure, see W. F. Kelly to A. Vulliet, 9 Aug 1948, reprinted in *The World War Two Experience: The Internment of German-Americans*, vol. IV, *German-Americans in the World Wars*, Arthur D. Jacobs and Joseph E. Fallon, eds. (Munich: K. G. Saur, 1996), 1513.

110. See, for example, Scotten to Secretary of State, 8 Jan 1943, "711.5," Costa Rica: San José Embassy Confidential File, Box 26, RG84, NA.

111. Department of State, *Policy of the United States Government in removing dangerous Axis nationals from the other American republics,* 28 May 1943, "711.5," Costa Rica: San José Embassy Confidential File, Box 26, RG84, NA.

112. Welles to AmLegGuatemala, 27 Mar 1942, 740.00115EW1939/2499, RG59, NA.

113. Welles to AmLegTegucigalpa, 8 Apr 1942, 740.00115EW1939/2613, RG59, NA.

114. Hull to Biddle, 9 Nov 1942, 740.00115EW1939/4570, RG59, NA.

115. Burr and Hussey, *Documents,* 147–9.

116. Spaeth to Welles, *General Observations in Response to Communications from Washington,* 8 May 1942, 710.Consultation (3)A 86 1/7, RG59, NA.

117. Knapp to Attorney General, 19 Aug 1943, "Special War Policies Unit, Latin American Section, FBI," Special War Policies Unit, Latin American Section, Previously Classified Files, Box 2, RG60, NA.

118. Department of State, *Policy of the United States Government in removing dangerous Axis nationals from the other American republics,* 28 May 1943, in folder "711.5," Costa Rica: San José Embassy Confidential File, Box 26, RG84, NA.

119. Department of State to AmEmbSan José, 12 Aug 1943, in folder "711.5," Costa Rica: San José Embassy Confidential File, Box 26, RG84, NA.

120. Sakowsky to Theiss, 10 Mar 1944, R41879, Deutsche Zivilgefangene in den V. St. v. Am., Rechtsabteilung, PAAA.

121. John Moors Cabot, *First Line of Defense: Forty Years' Experiences of a Career Diplomat* (Washington, DC: School of Foreign Service, Georgetown University, 1980[?]), 11; Irwin F. Gellman, *Good Neighbor Diplomacy: United States Policies in Latin America, 1933–1945* (Baltimore: Johns Hopkins University Press, 1979), 143–4.

122. Cabot to Bonsal, 25 Feb 1943, 740.00115EW1939/6164, RG59, NA.

123. Bonsal to Brandt and Long, *Internment of Dangerous Aliens in the United States Now at Large in the Other American Republics,* 14 Jun 1943, "General Memoranda May–June 1943," Memoranda Relating to General Latin American Affairs, Box 8, ARA, RG59, NA.

124. Randall Bennett Woods, *The Roosevelt Foreign-Policy Establishment and the 'Good Neighbor': The United States and Argentina, 1941–1945* (Lawrence: Regents Press of Kansas, 1979), 94.

125. Albert P. Vannucci, "Elected by Providence: Spruille Braden in Argentina in 1945," in *Ambassadors in Foreign Policy: The Influence of Individuals on U.S.-Latin American Policy,* C. Neale Ronning and Albert P. Vannucci, eds. (New York: Praeger, 1987), 56.

126. Gellman, *Good Neighbor Diplomacy,* 179.

127. Gellman, *Good Neighbor Diplomacy,* 181.

128. Welles to FDR, 17 March 1941, PSF Box 22, FDR Library, cited in Bryce Wood, *The Making of the Good Neighbor Policy* (New York: Columbia University Press, 1961), 350.

129. León E. Bieber, "La Política Militar Alemana en Bolivia, 1900–1935." *Latin American Research Review* 29: 1 (1994): 85–106; Herbert S. Klein, *Bolivia: The Evolution of a Multi-Ethnic Society* (New York: Oxford University Press, 1982), 188–200.

130. FBI, *Bolivia Today,* p. 32, June 1942, "FBI Reports – Bolivia," Box 141, Hopkins Papers, FDR Library.

131. Naumann, "Ausgewählte Daten."

132. Research Division Political Section, *The Other American Republics: Severances of Diplomatic Relations with, and Declarations of War against, the Axis,* Jul 1944, "CIAA Background Material," folder 19, Box 3, Record Group III 4 0, Nelson A. Rockefeller Personal Files, Washington, DC, Files, Rockefeller Family Archives, Rockefeller Archive Center, North Tarrytown, New York (hereafter RAC).

133. Quote from FBI, *Bolivia Today,* June 1942, p. 32. For economic warfare measures see Moraht to Außenhandelsamt der AO, 30 Nov 1942, "Wirtschaftliche Beziehungen zu Deutschland. Süd- und Mittelamerika," R116258, Handelspolitische Abteilung IXb, PAAA.

134. Wright to Lafoon, 24 Sep 1943, in folder "Bolivia A," Subject Files 1939–54, Box 69, SWP, RG59, NA; Boal (La Paz) to Secretary of State, 16 Oct 1943, 740.00115EW1939/7493, RG59, NA.

135. Christopher Mitchell, *The Legacy of Populism in Bolivia: From the MNR to Military Rule* (New York: Praeger, 1977), 5–22; Valentín Abecia Baldivieso, *Las relaciones internacionales en la historia de Bolivia,* 2 vols., vol. 2 (La Paz: Editorial los Amigos del Libro, 1979), 665–6; Cole Blasier, "The United States, Germany, and the Bolivian Revolutionaries (1941–1946)," *Hispanic American Historical Review* 52: 1 (Feb 1972):26–54.

136. David Green, *The Containment of Latin America: A History of the Myths and Realities of the Good Neighbor Policy* (Chicago: Quadrangle Books, 1971), 143–4; R. A. Humphreys, *Latin America and the Second World War,* 2 vols., vol. 2 (London: Athlone, 1981), 88–92; Klein, *Bolivia,* 217.

137. Cole Blasier, *The Hovering Giant: U.S. Responses to Revolutionary Change in Latin America 1910–1985* (Pittsburgh: University of Pittsburgh Press, 1985), 49; James M. Malloy, *Bolivia: The Uncompleted Revolution* (Pittsburgh: University of Pittsburgh Press, 1970), 361 n. 8.

138. FBI, *Bolivia Today,* June 1942, p. 42, "FBI Reports – Bolivia," Box 141, Hopkins Papers; Hoover to Hopkins, 21 Dec 1943, "FBI Reports – Bolivia," Box 141, Hopkins Papers. On Belmonte, see Chapter 2 in this volume.

139. Duggan, 6 Feb 1944, 824.00/1883-1/2, RG59, NA. Pinto's request for permission to serve France was denied, although it is not clear whether the French military or his Bolivian superiors made the decision.

140. Avni, "Peru y Bolivia," 345, 353; David S. Wyman, *Paper Walls: America and the Refugee Crisis, 1938–1941* (New York: Pantheon Books, 1968, 1985), 209.

141. Rockwell to Duggan, 2 Jun 1944, 824.00/3216, RG59, NA.

142. Winfried Seelisch, "Jüdische Emigration nach Bolivien Ende der 30er Jahre," in *Europaische Juden in Lateinamerika*, Achim Schrader and Karl Heinrich Rengstorf, eds. (St. Ingbert: Werner J. Rohrig Verlag, 1989), 77–101.

143. Bennett to Duggan, 16 Jun 1944, p. 16, 824.00/3298, RG59, NA.

144. Boal to SecState, 23 Dec 1943, 824.01/91, RG59, NA (U.S. Embassy translation).

145. Boal to Berle, 24 Dec 1943, 740.00115EW1939/7880, RG59, NA. The junta also permitted the establishment of a branch of the German Socialist Party in Bolivia – something a Nazi government would never have countenanced. Patrik von zur Mühlen, *Fluchtziel Lateinamerika: Die deutsche Emigration 1933– 1945: politische Aktivitäten und soziokulturelle Integration* (Bonn: Verlag Neue Gesellschaft, 1988), 226.

146. Boal to SecState, 23 Dec 1943, 824.01/91, RG59, NA.

147. Hull to AmEmbLa Paz, 27 Dec 1943, 740.00115EW1939/7880, RG59, NA, and Hull to AmEmbLa Paz, 2 Jan 1944, 740.00115EW1939/7880, RG59, NA.

148. Adolf Berle Diary, 6 Jan 1944, Berle Papers; Woods, *The Roosevelt Foreign-Policy Establishment*, 118.

149. Don S. Kirschner, *Cold War Exile: The Unclosed Case of Maurice Halperin* (Columbia: University of Missouri Press, 1995), 86–94.

150. Berle to Secretary of State, 15 Apr 1944, 824.01/840, RG59, NA.

151. Bowers to SecState, 4 Jan 1944, 824.01/180, RG59, NA.

152. Cordell Hull, *Memorandum for the President: The Bolivian Situation*, 5 Jan 1944, OF 659, FDR Library.

153. Keeley to Berle, 14 Jan 1944, "Bolivia A," Subject Files, 1939–1954, Box 69, SWP, RG59, NA.

154. Gordon Connell-Smith, *The United States and Latin America: An Historical Analysis of Inter-American Relations* (New York: John Wiley and Sons, 1974), 183.

155. Whitaker, *The United States and South America*, 141.

156. C. Neale Ronning, *Law and Politics in Inter-American Diplomacy* (New York: John Wiley & Sons, 1963), 13–14.

157. John E. Findling, *Close Neighbors, Distant Friends: United States-Central American Relations* (New York: Greenwood Press, 1987), 86–7.

158. Duggan, 10 Apr 1944, "Bolivia 1944," Subject File, State Department 1939–44, Box 189, Long Papers.

159. Blasier, *The Hovering Giant*, 49.

160. Laurence Duggan, *Bolivia*, 13 Apr 1944, "Bolivia 1944," Subject File, State Department 1939–44, Box 189, Long Papers.

161. The letters were declassified in 1998 after a Freedom of Information Act request by the author and are now available in the Bonsal Papers in the Manuscript Division, LC.

162. Bonsal to Duggan, 22 Apr 1944, "Duggan, Laurence, 1944," Box 4, Bonsal Papers.

163. Duggan to Bonsal, 27 Apr 1944, "Duggan, Laurence, 1944," Box 4, Bonsal Papers.

164. Bonsal to Duggan, 1 May 1944, "Duggan, Laurence 1944," Box 3, Bonsal Papers.

165. Duggan to Bonsal, 4 May 1944, "Duggan, Laurence, 1944," Box 4, Bonsal Papers.

166. Duggan to Bonsal, 6 May 1944, "Duggan, Laurence, 1944," Box 4, Bonsal Papers. Emphasis in original.

167. Bennett to Duggan, 16 Jun 1944, 824.00/3298, RG59, NA.

168. Ambassador W. Tapley Bennett, Jr., oral history interview, Georgetown University Library, 16 Jun 1988, p. 13.

169. Bennett to Duggan, 16 Jun 1944, 824.00/3298, RG59, NA. Tellingly, the presence of the Japanese is rarely mentioned in official correspondence, because their deportation was neither as hotly disputed by the Bolivians nor as eagerly desired by the United States. As the MID put it, "The Japanese situation in Bolivia has never constituted a serious threat from the subversive standpoint, as most Japanese are engaged in agricultural pursuits in the Beni, being in no position to damage the program of the United Nations." Military Intelligence Division, *Axis Espionage and Propaganda in Latin America* (Washington, DC: War Department, 1946), 99.

170. Caffery to SecState, 6 May 1944, 824.00/3076, RG59, NA. See also Caffery to SecState, 17 May 1944, 824.00/3128, and Caffery to SecState, 18 May 1944, 824.00/3132, RG59, NA.

171. Bonsal to Duggan, 22 May 1944, "Duggan, Laurence, 1944," Box 4, Bonsal Papers.

172. Hull to AmRepOfficers except Argentina, 2 Jun 1944, 824.00/3194B, RG59, NA.

173. Bonsal to Duggan, 5 Jun 1944, "Duggan, Laurence, 1944," Box 4, Bonsal Papers.

174. Duggan, 26 May 1944, "Bolivia 1944," Subject File, State Department 1939–44, Box 189, Long Papers.

175. Woodward to SecState, 2 Jun 1944, 824.00/3203, RG59, NA.

176. Bowers to SecState, 4 Jan 1944, 824.01/180, RG59, NA.

177. Woodward to SecState, 26 May 1944, 824.00/3197, RG59, NA.

178. Victor Andrade, *My Missions for Revolutionary Bolivia, 1944–1962* (Pittsburgh: University of Pittsburgh Press, 1976), 29.

179. Gellman, *Good Neighbor Diplomacy,* 180–1; Allen Weinstein and Alexander Vassiliev, *The Haunted Wood: Soviet Espionage in America – The Stalin Era* (New York: Random House, 1999), 295–6.

180. Philip W. Bonsal, *Cuba, Castro, and the United States* (Pittsburgh: University of Pittsburgh Press, 1971).

181. All information in this and previous paragraph comes from individual postwar reports, listed alphabetically, in Name Files of Enemy Aliens, SWP Boxes 31–50, RG59, NA, and from cross-checking *Nazi Party Membership Records* against names of deportees from Bolivia, in *German Nationals Deported by the Other American Republics Who Were Deported by the United States,* in folder of same name, Subject Files 1939–54, Box 121, SWP, RG59, NA.

182. Clattenburg, 24 May 1944, 740.00115EW1939/9922, RG59, NA.

Chapter 5   Internment

1. Erich Maria Remarque, *Die Nacht von Lissabon* (Gütersloh, Germany: Mohn & Co., n.d.), 172. Author's translation.

2. INS, *Alien Enemy Detention Facility,* 16mm color/b&w film, 1946[?], Accession Number N3-85-8-1, National Archives, College Park, Maryland (hereafter NA).
3. Hans Joachim Schaer, interview by author, San José, 26 Mar 1998; Werner J. Kappel, telephone interview by author, Sun City Center, Florida, 30 Mar 1999.
4. Long to Hull and Welles, 31 Oct 1941, 740.00115EW1939/1521, RG59, NA. By 6 Jan 1942, the U.S. government had decided to "supply as liberal a regime as possible for civilian enemy aliens detained or interned in this country and to treat them as favorably as prisoners of war." See *Department of State Bulletin,* 16 Jul 1944, 66.
5. Gunter Lisken, interview by author, Guayaquil, 17 Feb 1998. See also the exchange of letters between internee spokesmen and INS officials regarding the celebration of Hitler's birthday reproduced in *The World War Two Experience: The Internment of German-Americans,* vol. IV, *German-Americans in the World Wars,* Arthur D. Jacobs and Joseph E. Fallon, eds. (Munich: K. G. Saur, 1996), 1934–49.
6. See Rolland Welch, 11 Mar 1944, "Cuba III Arrived New Orleans – March 21 1944," Subject Files 1939–54, Box 7, SWP, RG59, NA; Friedrich Karl Kaul, *Es wird Zeit, dass Du nach Hause kommst* (Berlin: Das Neue Berlin, 1959), 262; Arnold Krammer, *Undue Process: The Untold Story of America's German Alien Internees* (New York: Rowman and Littlefield, 1997), 117; Arnold Krammer, "Feinde ohne Uniform: deutsche Zivilinternierte in den USA während des Zweiten Weltkrieges," *Vierteljahrshefte für Zeitgeschichte* 44:4 (1996): 595–7; Karen L. Riley, *Schools Behind Barbed Wire: The Untold Story of Wartime Internment and the Children of Arrested Enemy Aliens* (Lanham, MD: Rowman and Littlefield, 2002), chapter 5. For reproductions of camp newspapers often including starkly pro-Nazi themes, see part 4 of Jacobs and Fallon, *The World War Two Experience.*
7. G. E. Martin (IRC), *Camp de Stringtown,* 22 Sep 1942, "Stringtown '42," Inspection Reports on War Relocation Centers, 1942–6, Box 20, SWP, RG59, NA.
8. Kurt P. Biederbeck to Schulz, 7 Apr 1944, "Amerikanische Zivilinternierte in Deutschland," R41570, Rechtsabteilung, Politisches Archiv des Auswärtigen Amtes, Bonn (hereafter PAAA); Kurt P. Biederbeck to Schulz, 12 May 1944, R41879, Deutsche Zivilgefangene in den V. St. v. Am., Rechtsabteilung, PAAA; Hermann Egner to Swiss Legation Washington, *Camp Kenedy – Texas,* 27 Jun 1942, R41562, Zivilgefangenen-Austausch-Vereinigten Staaten von Amerika, Rechtsabteilung, PAAA; P. W. Herrick, *Supplemental Report on Civilian Detention Station Kenedy, Texas,* 13–14 Oct 1942, "Kenedy '42," and M.A. Cardinaux (IRC), *Camp Kenedy,* "Kenedy '43–'44," both in Inspection Reports on War Relocation Centers, 1942–6, Box 20, SWP, RG59, NA; Otto Luis Schwarz, interview by author, Guayaquil, 16 Feb 1998; John Karl, telephone interview by author, 15 Jun 1997.
9. Kurt P. Biederbeck to Schulz, 7 Apr 1944, "Amerikanische Zivilinternierte in Deutschland," R41570, Rechtsabteilung, PAAA; Eldon F. Nelson, *Alien Interment Camp,* 30 Oct 1944, "Kenedy '43–'44," Inspection Reports on War Relocation Centers, 1942–6, Box 20, SWP, RG59, NA; Clattenburg to Gufler, 10 Jul 1943, 740.00115EW1939/7082, RG59, NA; Swiss Legation Washington to DoS, *Memorandum,* 3 Jun 1944, Band 10, Noten an Staatsdepartement, Jan.–Juni 1944, E2200 Washington/15, SBA.

10. *Justice Department Summary,* 1946, "Kugler, Otto Berthold," Name Files of Interned Enemy Aliens from Latin America, 1942–8, Box 42, SWP, RG59, NA.

11. Friedrich Karl Kaul recounts the same thing happening to him in his novelized memoir, *Es wird Zeit, dass Du nach Hause kommst* (Berlin: Das Neue Berlin, 1959), 266, and see also Glover, *Confidential: Richard Ernst Ressel (Colombia),* 1 Feb 1946, "Ressel, Richard Ernst, Colombia," Name Files of Interned Enemy Aliens from Latin America, 1942–8, Box 46, SWP, RG59, NA; John Christgau, *Enemies: World War II Alien Internment* (Ames: Iowa State University Press, 1985), 35.

12. Tenney, "Confidential: Fritz Sauter, Jr. (Costa Rica)," 5 Feb 1946, in folder "S," Name Files of Interned Enemy Aliens from Latin America, 1942–8, Box 34, SWP, RG59, NA.

13. Gunter Lisken, interview by author, Guayaguil, 17 Feb 1998; Isidore Rosenberg statement in Colonel Bryan to Gufler, 14 Sep 1942, 740.00115EW1939/4525, RG59, NA. Arnold Krammer's otherwise sympathetic study of German-American internees reaches a similar conclusion. See Krammer, *Undue Process,* 122–3, 135–6. John Christgau carefully delineates the factions dividing even the interned seamen as well as U.S. residents in his *Enemies.*

14. Otto Stetzelberg to Gestapo, 6 Apr 1944, "Deutsche Zivilgefangene in den Ver.St.v.Amerika – Lager, 1942–1944," R42003, Rechtsabteilung, PAAA.

15. Jerre Mangione, *An Ethnic at Large* (New York: G. P. Putnam's Sons, 1978), 327.

16. Incident recounted and McCoy quoted from 1 Apr 1942 memo to Willard Kelly in Christgau, *Enemies,* 79. See also Max Habicht to Swiss Foreign Ministry, *Report on the Visit to Detention Stations for Civilian Internees in the United States of America,* 18 Aug 1942, Band 1, E2200 Washington/15, Schweizerisches Bundesarchiv, Bern (hereafter SBA).

17. *Confidential: Ernesto Blumenthal (Nicaragua),* 3 Jan 1946, "Blumenthal, Ernst, Nicaragua," Name Files of Interned Enemy Aliens from Latin America, 1942–8, Box 36, SWP, RG59, NA; Breckinridge Long memo, 4 Nov 1942, 740.00115EW1939/4442, RG59, NA; Yampol to Hull, 10 Aug 1942, and Clattenburg to Yampol, 8 Oct 1942, 740.00115EW1939/4158; Yampol to Clattenburg, 13 Oct 1942, and Clattenburg to Yampol, 24 Oct 1942, 740.00115EW1939/4823, RG59, NA.

18. Censor's report on Kappel to Spiegel, 14 Apr 1942, in folder "Kappel, Fred L. Panama," Name Files of Interned Enemy Aliens from Latin America, 1942–8, Box 41, SWP, RG59, NA.

19. Harvey Strum, "Jewish Internees in the American South, 1942–45," *American Jewish Archives* 42 (1990): 27–48.

20. Colonel Bryan to Gufler, 14 Sep 1942, 740.00115EW1939/4525, RG59, NA.

21. Colonel Bryan to Gufler, 14 Sep 1942, 740.00115EW1939/4525, RG59, NA.

22. Censor's report of Heinemann to Marchowsky, 17 May 1942, and Glover, *Confidential: Wilhelm Heinemann (Panama),* 14 Jan 1946, "Heinemann, Wilhelm, Panama," Name Files of Interned Enemy Aliens from Latin America, 1942–8, Box 40, SWP, RG59, NA. In August 1942, Jews were still included on lists of future repatriates: Long to Guardia, *German Nationals from Panama Interned in the United States Pending Repatriation,* 8 Aug 1942, 740.00115EW1939/3844,

RG59, NA. And in September 1942, Long refused to promise not to send Jewish internees to Germany against their will. Breckinridge Long to Mohler, 24 Sep 1942, in folder "W," Name Files of Interned Enemy Aliens from Latin America, 1942–8, Box 35, SWP, RG59, NA.

24. Colonel Bryan to Gufler, 14 Sep 1942, 740.00115EW1939/4525, RG59, NA; Max Habicht to Swiss Foreign Ministry, *Report on the Visit to Detention Stations for Civilian Internees in the United States of America*, 18 Aug 1942, Band 1, E2200 Washington/15, SBA.

25. G. E. Martin (IRC), *Camp de Stringtown,* 22 Sep 1942, "Stringtown '42," Inspection Reports on War Relocation Centers, 1942–6, Box 20, SWP, RG59, NA.

26. Jerre Mangione, *An Ethnic at Large* (New York: G. P. Putnam's Sons, 1978), 327.

27. Karl-Albrecht Engel, *Zusammenfassender Bericht über die Zeit von 1942–1945 (Guatemala – Internierung USA),* 18 Jun 1945, R 64 III/6, Heimkehrerberichte über Südamerika, Lateinamerikanischer Verein, Bundesarchiv Koblenz (hereafter BA-K); Herbert Droege to AA, *Berichte über die Internierungslager Camp Blanding und Stringtown,* Oct 1942, R41564, Zivilgefangenen-Austausch-Vereinigten Staaten von Amerika, Rechtsabteilung, PAAA; Green to FC, 14 Apr 1942, 740.0011EW/4–1442, reel 194 M982, RG59, NA.

28. Hunt to SecState, 6 Apr 1942, 740.00115EW1939/2639, RG59, NA; Hans Kröger to AA, *Bericht,* October 1942, and Herbert Droege to AA, *Berichte über die Internierungslager Camp Blanding und Stringtown,* Oct 1942, R41564, Zivilgefangenen-Austausch-Vereinigten Staaten von Amerika, Rechtsabteilung, PAAA; G. E. Martin (IRC), *Camp de Stringtown,* 22 Sep 1942, "Stringtown '42," Inspection Reports on War Relocation Centers, 1942–6, Box 20, SWP, RG59, NA; Max Habicht to Swiss Foreign Ministry, *Report on the Visit to Detention Stations for Civilian Internees in the United States of America,* 18 Aug 1942, Band 1, E2200 Washington/15, SBA.

29. Karl-Albrecht Engel, *Zusammenfassender Bericht über die Zeit von 1942–1945 (Guatemala – Internierung USA),* 18 Jun 1945, R 64 III/6, Heimkehrerberichte über Südamerika, Lateinamerikanischer Verein, BA-K; Müller to Johannes Nottebohm, 31 Oct 1942, R41564, Zivilgefangenen-Austausch-Vereinigten Staaten von Amerika, Rechtsabteilung, PAAA.

30. Max Habicht to Swiss Foreign Ministry, *Report on the Visit to Detention Stations for Civilian Internees in the United States of America,* 18 Aug 1942, Band 1, E2200 Washington/15, SBA; Albert Greutert, Swiss Consul at New Orleans, *Inspection of the Camps at Kenedy and Fort Sam Houston, Texas,* "Kenedy '42," Inspection Reports on War Relocation Centers, 1942–6, Box 20, SWP, RG59, NA; Skowronski to AA, 29 May 1942, R41557, Zivilgefangenen-Austausch-Vereinigten Staaten von Amerika, Rechtsabteilung, PAAA; C. Harvey Gardiner, *Pawns in a Triangle of Hate: The Peruvian Japanese and the United States* (Seattle: University of Washington Press, 1981), 30.

31. Gufler and Herrick, *Report on Civilian Detention Station, Camp Kenedy,* 22 May 1942, 740.00115EW1939/4715, RG59, NA; Swiss Legation Washington to DoS, 14 Jan 1944, Band 10, Noten an Staatsdepartement, Jan.–Juni 1944, E2200 Washington/15, SBA.

32. Mangione, *An Ethnic at Large,* 328.

33. Gerardo Bohnenberger, interview by author, Guatemala City, 18 May 1996.
34. Kelley to Gufler, 12 Feb 1943, 740.00115EW1939/6189, RG59, NA. Further on camp conditions see Karl-Albrecht Engel, *Zusammenfassender Bericht über die Zeit von 1942–1945 (Guatemala – Internierung USA)*, 18 Jun 1945, R64 III/6, Heimkehrerberichte über Südamerika, Lateinamerikanischer Verein, BA-K; Hugo Droege, interview by author, Guatemala City, 22 May 1996; AA, various 1942, "Deutsche Zivilgefangene in den Ver.St.v.Amerika – Lager, 1942–1944," R42003, Rechtsabteilung, PAAA.
35. Stettinius to Sullivan (American Legion), 30 Oct 1943, 740.00115EW1939/7518, RG59, NA.
36. Gufler, *Memorandum of Telephone Conversation*, 6 May 1942, "Special Division, German Exchange, 1941–1942," Subject File, State Department, 1939–44, Box 204, Manscript Division, LC; *Landesgruppe Guatemala der NSDAP*, 1935, "Namensliste der Funktionäre der Landesgruppe Guatemala der NSDAP," NL 139/8, Nachlasse Kraske, BA-K.
37. Otto Stetzelberg to Gestapo, 6 Apr 1944, R42003, Deutsche Zivilgefangene in den Ver. St. v. Am. – Lager, 1942–4, Rechtsabteilung, PAAA.
38. While the petition was not explicitly an anti-Nazi document, merely claiming "no adversity" toward U.S. policies "during the war" would have been seen as disloyal by the true believers. (One can hardly imagine a comparable statement made by American prisoners expressing no quarrel with Germany once the war was on.) German Nationals at Kenedy to State Department, 24 Oct 1942, and Clattenburg to Kelly, 11 Nov 1942, 740.00115EW1939/4957, RG59, NA; and postwar AECS reports for nearly all signers in alphabetical Name Files of Interned Enemy Aliens from Latin America, Boxes 31–50, SWP, RG59, NA.
39. Max Habicht to Swiss Foreign Ministry, *Report on the Visit to Detention Stations for Civilian Internees in the United States of America*, 18 Aug 1942, Band 1, E2200 Washington/15, SBA; Herrick, *Supplemental Report on Alien Detention Station*, 26 Jan 1943, "Seagoville '42–'43," and Schnyder and Zehnder report, "Seagoville, '44–'45," Inspection Reports on War Relocation Centers, 1942–6, Box 21, SWP, RG59, NA; Swiss Legation Washington to DoS, 29 Dec 1942, Band 4, Noten von und an Staatsdepartement, Nov.–Dez. 1942, E2200 Washington/15, SBA; Wecker quoted in Krammer, *Undue Process*, 104.
40. Maurice Perret (IRC), *Camp de Seagoville, Texas*, 6 May 1944, "Seagoville '44–'45," Inspection Reports on War Relocation Centers, 1942–6, Box 21, SWP, RG59, NA; Herrick, *Report on Crystal City Internment Camp*, 31 Jan 1943, "Crystal City," Inspection Reports on War Relocation Centers, 1942–6, Box 19, SWP, RG59, NA; Degetau to Schulz, 15 May 1944, R41879, Deutsche Zivilgefangene in den V. St. v. Am., Rechtsabteilung, PAAA; Biederbeck to Schulz, 12 May 1944, R41570, Amerikanische Zivilinternierte in Deutschland, Rechtsabteilung, PAAA; Mangione, *An Ethnic at Large*, 329.
41. Gunter Lisken, interview by author, Guayaquil, 17 Feb 1998.
42. Gunter Lisken, interview by author, Guayaquil, 17 Feb 1998. INS, *Alien Enemy Detention Facility.*
43. Kurt P. Biederbeck to Schulz, 12 May 1944, R41879, Deutsche Zivilgefangene in den V. St. v. Am., Rechtsabteilung, PAAA.
44. Rolland Welch, 11 Mar 1944, in folder "Cuba III Arrived New Orleans – March 21 1944," Subject Files 1939–54, Box 7, SWP, RG59, NA.

45. Krammer, "Feinde ohne Uniform," 597.
46. Swiss diplomats representing German interests told the State Department that each successive wave of German internees reported similar complaints, as did their letters to family members in Germany. Swiss Legation Washington to DoS, 5 Apr 1944, Band 10, Noten an Staatsdepartement, Jan.–Juni 1944, E2200 Washington/15, SBA. See also Rudolf Lindgens to Swiss Embassy, 21 May 1942, R42003, Deutsche Zivilgefangene in den Ver. St. v. Am. – Lager, 1942–4, Rechtsabteilung, PAAA; Josef Krapf to Geheime Staatspolizei Nürnberg, 23 Oct 1942, 3601000301, Krapf, Josef, Rückwandereramt der AO, Bundesarchiv Berlin-Lichterfelde (hereafter BA-L); Schroetter to AA, 21 Jun 1944, R41856, Deutsche Zivilgefangene in Panama, 1941–4, Rechtsabteilung, PAAA; Alfredo Brauer, interview by author, Quito, 5 Feb 1998; Otto Luis Schwarz, interview by author, Guayaquil, 16 Feb 1998.
47. Briggs to Bonsal, 15 Apr 1942, 740.00115EW1939/2825 1/2, RG59, NA; Lutkins to Braden, 13 Oct 1942, 740.00115EW1939/4858, RG59, NA; Larue R. Lutkins, 18 Oct 1990, Foreign Affairs Oral History Program, Georgetown University Library; Spruille Braden, *Diplomats and Demagogues* (New Rochelle, NY: Arlington House, 1971), 288.
48. Boaz Long to Secretary of State, 20 Jan 1942, "711.5," Costa Rica, San José Legation: Confidential File, Box 18, RG84, NA; Ecklauer [?], 2 Feb 1942, and Felicisimo Carpeña to AA, *Die Lage der Deutschen in Nicaragua,* 14 Jul 1943, R41839, Deutsche Zivilgefangene in Nicaragua, 1941–4, Rechtsabteilung, PAAA; Götz von Houwald, *Los alemanes en Nicaragua* (Managua: Editorial y Litografía San José, 1975), 148.
49. Inge Von Schröter, interview by author, San José, 26 Mar 1998; Scotten to Secretary of State, 16 Sep 1942 and 22 Sep 1942, "711.5," Costa Rica, San José Legation: Confidential File, Box 18, RG84, NA; "Campos de Concentración," *Siete Días,* 12 Jan 1998, Canal 7, San José, Costa Rica.
50. Hoover to Lyon, 17 Jul 1946, 862.20210/17–1746, RG59, NA; Walter Held, interview by author, Bogotá, 9 Mar 1998; Götz Pfeil-Schneider, interview by author, Bogotá, 15 Mar 1998; see also Alfonso López Michelsen, *Los Elegidos* (Bogotá: Tercer Mundo, 1967), 333.
51. María-Luise Kreuter, *Dónde Queda el Ecuador? Exilio en un país desconocido desde 1938 hasta fines de los años cincuenta* (Quito: Abya-Yala, 1997), 234; Gunter Lisken, interview by author, Guayaquil, 17 Feb 1998; Otto Luis Schwarz, interview by author, Guayaquil, 16 Feb 1998.
52. Jobst-H. Floto, *Die Beziehungen Deutschlands zu Venezuela 1933 bis 1958* (Frankfurt: Peter Lang, 1991), 122, 129.
53. Maria Emilia Paz, *Strategy, Security, and Spies: Mexico and the U.S. as Allies in World War II* (University Park: Pennsylvania State University Press, 1997), 125, 132, 145.
54. Hermann Egner to Swiss Legation Washington, *Camp Kenedy – Texas,* 27 Jun 1942, R41562, Zivilgefangenen-Austausch-Vereinigten Staaten von Amerika, Rechtsabteilung, PAAA; Swiss Legation Washington to DoS, 7 Jan 1943, Band 7, Swiss Legation Washington to DoS, 17 Mar 1944, Band 10, DoS to Swiss Legation Washington, 19 Mar 1945, Band 11, all in E2200 Washington/15, SBA; Eva Bloch, interview by author, Guayaquil, 18 Feb 1998; Otto Luis Schwarz, interview by author, Guayaquil, 16 Feb 1998.

55. Meendsen-Bohlken, "Petition for non-repatriation," 15 May 1943, in folder "M," Name Files of Interned Enemy Aliens from Latin America, 1942–8, Box 33, SWP, RG59, NA; Heinrich Meendsen-Bohlken to Maria de la Cruz Meendsen-Bohlken, "Postal Censorship Extract," 19 Oct 1943 (censor's translation), and postwar AECS report, in folder "Meendsen-Bohlken, Heinrich, Guatemala," Name Files of Interned Enemy Aliens from Latin America, 1942–8, Box 43, SWP, RG59, NA.

56. Ernst Blumenthal to Harrick at Swiss Legation Washington, 26 Nov 1942, and Swiss Legation Washington to Gufler at DoS, 2 Oct 1942, Band 4, Noten von und an Staatsdepartement, Sept.–Okt. 1942, E2200 Washington/15, SBA; An-neliese Blumenthal to Ernst Blumenthal, 2 Dec 1942 (censor's translation), and unsigned, *Confidential: Ernst Blumenthal,* 3 Jan 1946, in folder "Blumenthal, Ernst, Nicaragua," Name Files of Interned Enemy Aliens from Latin America, 1942–8, Box 36, SWP, RG59, NA.

57. Swiss Legation Washington to DoS, 27 May 1942, Noten von und an Staats-departement, Dez. 1941–Juni 1942, Band 3, E2200 Washington/15, SBA; Ecklauer [?], 2 Feb 1942, "Deutsche Zivilgefangene in Nicaragua," R41839, Rechtsabteilung, PAAA; Oda Droege, interview by author, Guatemala City, 22 May 1996; Ilse Schwark, interview by author, Quito, 28 Jan 1998; Otto Luis Schwarz, interview by author, Guayaquil, 16 Feb 1998.

58. I have given Rosa the pseudonym "Grothe" here. *Summary of Justice Files,* 8 Jul 1944, in folder titled with Rosa's real name, Name Files of Interned Enemy Aliens from Latin America, 1942–8, Box 40, SWP, RG59, NA.

59. Hull to Biddle, 9 Nov 1942, 740.00115EW1939/4570, RG59, NA.

60. Tannenberg, *Memorandum Concerning Mrs. Theolinda Zillmer-Zosel,* 14 Apr 1942, Band 3, Noten von und an Staatsdepartement, Dez. 1941–Juni 1942, E2200 Washington/15, SBA; Hellmann to AA, 26 Jan 1943, R42003, Deutsche Zivilgefangene in den Ver. St. v. Am. – Lager, 1942–4, Rechtsabteilung, PAAA; Guatemalan Police Department, "Datos Personales," 7 Feb 1942, and "Con-versation with Tabu (Zillmer)," 12 Feb 1942, in folder "Zillmer, Theolinde," Naval Attaché – Guatemala City, Personality Files 1940–6, Box 45, ONI, RG38, NA; Lafoon to Warren, 18 Apr 1942, 740.00115EW1939/2643, RG59, NA; Zillmer-Zosel's postwar file in Name Files of Interned Enemy Aliens, alphabetical, Boxes 31–50, Special War Problems Division (hereafter SWP), RG59, NA.

61. Bohnenberger interview. Russian courses also mentioned in M. A. Cardinaux (IRC), *Camp Kenedy,* "Kenedy '43–'44," Inspection Reports on War Relocation Centers, 1942–6, Box 20, SWP, RG59, NA.

62. Margarete Langenbeck to DoS, 19 Aug 1943, in folder "El Salvador, A," Subject Files 1939–54, Box 69, SWP, RG59, NA.

63. Censorship report on Carmela Groskorth to Ernst Julius Groskorth, 9 Jul 1943, in folder "El Salvador, A," Subject Files 1939–54, Box 69, SWP, RG59, NA.

64. Franz Amrhein, "A," Name Files of Enemy Aliens, 1942–8, Box 31, SWP, RG59, NA, contains the testimonials. The wives' campaign is mentioned in Carlos Calvo Gamboa, *Costa Rica en la segunda guerra mundial, 1939–1945* (San José: Editorial Universidad Estatal a Distancia, 1985), 37–8.

65. Carlos Humberto Cuestas Gomez, *Cotito, Crónica de un Crimen Olvidado* (Panama: n.p., 1993), 23–5.

66. Brauchle postwar reports in Name Files of Interned Enemy Aliens, alphabetical, Boxes 31–50, SWP, RG59, NA.
67. Hull to Biddle, 9 Nov 1942, 740.00115EW1939/4570, RG59, NA.
68. Schofield to Attorney General, 27 Mar 1942, 740.00115EW1939/2426, RG59, NA; Schroetter to AA, 6 Apr 1942, R41856, Deutsche Zivilgefangene in Panama, 1941–4, Rechtsabteilung, PAAA; DoS to Swiss Legation Washington, 31 Oct 1942, Band 4, Noten von und an Staatsdepartement, Sept.–Okt. 1942, E2200 Washington/15, SBA; Hull to AmLegBern, 24 Nov 1942, 740.00115EW1939/5093, RG59, NA; Hull to AmEmbLima, 22 Jan 1943, 740.00115EW1939/5848, RG59, NA; Department of State, "Policy of the United States Government in removing dangerous Axis nationals from the other American republics," 28 May 1943, in folder "711.5," Costa Rica: San José Embassy Confidential File, Box 26, RG84, NA; Sakowsky to Theiss, 10 Mar 1944, R41879, Deutsche Zivilgefangene in den V. St. v. Am., Rechtsabteilung, PAAA.
69. Trueblood to Secretary of State, 7 Oct 1943, 740.00115EW1939/7464, RG59, NA.
70. Boaz Long to Secretary of State, 26 Oct 1943, 740.00115EW1939/7572, RG59, NA.

Chapter 6   Justice

1. Raymond Ickes, interview by author, Berkeley, CA, 18 Sep 1997.
2. Fred L. Israel, ed., *The War Diary of Breckinridge Long: Selections from the Years 1939–1944* (Lincoln: University of Nebraska Press, 1966), 216, 225, 243, 261, 270. See also Keeley to Long, 19 Nov 1942, "Olshansky, Andrew, Panama," Name Files of Interned Enemy Aliens from Latin America, 1942–8, Box 45, Special War Problems Division (hereafter SWP), RG59, National Archives, College Park, Maryland (hereafter NA); Long to Welles, 29 Jun 1943, "Special Division, Internees [Axis], 1942–4," Subject File, State Department, 1939–44, Box 204, Long Papers, Manuscript Division, Library of Congress, Washington, DC (hereafter LC); Breckinridge Long to Wilson, 8 Aug 1942, 740.00115EW1939/2792, RG59, NA; Long to Berle and Dunn, 26 Jun 1940, Box 211, Long Papers; David S. Wyman, *Paper Walls: America and the Refugee Crisis 1938–1941* (New York: Pantheon Books, 1985), 173–94.
3. Breckinridge Long memo, 4 Nov 1942, 740.00115EW1939/4442, RG59, NA, emphasis in original; Jewish internees identified in "German Nationals Deported from the Other American Republics Who Are Presently Detained in the US," Oct 1945, in folder "Statistics," Subject Files 1939–54, Box 70, SWP, RG59; Campbell to Hull, 27 Jul 1942, 740.00115EW1939/4215, RG59; Henkin, *Confidential: Heinz Luedeking (Nicaragua),* 2 Jan 1946, "Luedeking, Heinz, Nicaragua," Name Files of Interned Enemy Aliens from Latin America, 1942–8, Box 43, SWP, RG59, NA; and individual camp rosters in SWP.
4. Israel, *The War Diary of Breckinridge Long,* xvi, 243, 261; Dean Acheson, *Present at the Creation: My Years in the State Department* (New York: W. W. Norton & Co., 1969), 12.
5. See, for example, David S. Wyman, *The Abandonment of the Jews: America and the Holocaust 1941–1945* (New York: Pantheon Books, 1984), 125, 192.

6. Immigration and Naturalization Service Commissioner Earl G. Harrison, whose border patrol officers operated the camps, was praised by the German Interests Section of the Swiss Embassy in Washington as "sincere" and "idealistic." Swiss Legation Washington to Swiss Foreign Ministry, May 1944, B.24.A.(8)51, Band 83, E2001-02/17, Schweizerisches Bundesarchiv, Bern (hereafter SBA).

7. *New York Times* obituary, 9 Jan 1990, D22; Ennis to Biddle, "Memorandum for the Attorney General," 14 Feb 1942, in folder "146-13-2-0 Section 5," Closed Legal Case Files, Box 5, Alien Enemy Control Unit, War Division, DoJ, RG60, NA; public complaints and AECU form responses in same folder. Justice Department procedures regarding U.S. resident Germans and Italians are described in Arnold Krammer, *Undue Process: The Untold Story of America's German Alien Internees* (New York: Rowman and Littlefield, 1997), 46–9. Timothy J. Holian, *The German-Americans and World War II: An Ethnic Experience* (New York: Lang, 1996); Stephen Fox, *The Unknown Internment: An Oral History of the Relocation of Italian Americans during World War II* (Boston: Twayne, 1990) and idem, *America's Invisible Gulag: A Biography of German American Internment & Exclusion in World War II* (New York: Peter Lang, 2000); and Arthur Jacobs, *The Prison Called Hohenasperg* (Parkland, FL: Universal Publishers, 1999) also criticize the domestic internment program. My reading of the evidence suggests that while the legal domestic program was certainly flawed and trapped some innocent persons, it never reached the level of errors and abuses that characterized the illegal Latin American program, and that the treatment meted out to Japanese no matter what their citizenship was consistently less discriminate.

8. Long to Biddle, 12 Mar 1942, Biddle to Welles, 19 Mar 1942, and Schofield to Attorney General, 27 Mar 1942, 740.00115EW1939/2426, RG59, NA.

9. Jerre Mangione, *An Ethnic at Large* (New York: G. P. Putnam's Sons, 1978), 327.

10. Mangione, *An Ethnic at Large,* 321.

11. Harvey Strum, "Jewish Internees in the American South, 1942–1945," *American Jewish Archives* 42 (1990): 27–48, esp. 33.

12. Lafoon memo, 21 Sep 1942, 740.00115EW1939/4565, RG59, NA.

13. Scotten to Secretary of State, 22 Sep 1942, in folder "711.5," Costa Rica, San José Legation: Confidential File, Box 18, RG84, NA. See also Brandt, 20 Oct 1942, "V," Name Files of Interned Enemy Aliens from Latin America, 1942–8, Box 35, SWP, RG59, NA; Ennis to Keeley, 12 Nov 1942, 740.00115EW1939/4130, RG59, NA; Clattenburg to Ennis, 22 Dec 1942, 740.00115EW1939/5130, RG59, NA; Edward G. Trueblood, 7 Oct 1943, "711.5," Costa Rica: San José Embassy Confidential File, Box 26, RG84, NA; Charles D. Ameringer, *Don Pepe: A Political Biography of José Figueres of Costa Rica* (Albuquerque: University of New Mexico Press, 1978), 11.

14. Keeley to Moore, 12 Nov 1942, and Keeley to Long, 19 Nov 1942, in folder "Olshansky, Andrew, Panama," Name Files of Interned Enemy Aliens from Latin America, 1942–8, Box 45, SWP, RG59, NA.

15. Laurence A. Knapp, *CPD Projects Weekly Report,* 13 Feb 1943, "SWPU Latin American Section," Classified Records, Box 17, Special War Policies Unit, RG60, NA.

16. DoS to Swiss Legation Washington, 16 Jun 1943, Band 5, Noten von und an Staatsdepartement, April–Juni 1943, E2200 Washington/15, SBA, Bern.

17. Raymond Ickes, interview by author, Berkeley, CA, 18 Sep 1997. Ickes also spoke Navajo and Ojibwa. See the obituary by Carolyn Jones, "Raymond Ickes," *San Francisco Chronicle*, 6 Mar 2000.

18. Raymond Ickes, interview by author, Berkeley, CA, 18 Sep 1997.

19. Raymond Ickes, interview by author, Berkeley, CA, 18 Sep 1997.

20. Norweb to Nester, 13 Mar 1943, in folder "711," Ecuador: Quito Embassy, Confidential File, Box 10, RG84, NA.

21. Long to SD, 8 Feb 1943, in folder "Special Division, Internees [Axis] 1942–1944," Subject File, State Department, 1939–44, Box 206, Long Papers, FDR Library; Long to Nester, 11 Feb 1943, folder 711, Ecuador: Quito Embassy, Confidential File, Box 10, RG84.

22. Raymond Ickes, interview by author, Berkeley, Calif., 18 Sep 1997.

23. Raymond W. Ickes, *Memorandum to the Minister,* 30 Mar 1943, "711.5," Costa Rica: San José Embassy Confidential File, Box 26, RG84, NA, emphasis added.

24. Ickes, *Memorandum to the Minister,* 30 Mar 1943, "711.5," Costa Rica: San José Embassy Confidential File, Box 26, RG84, NA.

25. Bell to Ennis, 7 Dec 1943, "711.5," Costa Rica: San José Embassy Confidential File, Box 26, RG84, NA.

26. Raymond Ickes, interview by author, Berkeley, Calif., 18 Sep 1997.

27. Ickes's passport from 1943, made available to the author, contains entry visas for every Latin American country involved except Ecuador; despite the missing stamp, Ickes wrote a memorandum while in Quito: Ickes to Nester, 18 Mar 1943, "711," Ecuador: Quito Embassy Confidential File, Box 10, RG84, NA.

28. On methodological concerns in evaluating oral history, see the author's "Private Memory, Public Records, and Contested Terrain: Weighing Oral Testimony in the Deportation of Germans from Latin America During World War II," *Oral History Review* 27: 1 (Winter/Spring 2000): 1–16.

29. Author analysis of 531 Alien Enemy Control Section reports from 1946 in Name Files of Interned Enemy Aliens from Latin America, SWP, RG59, NA. See Chapter 4 for more details.

30. Among the 4,058 deportees were 8 individuals who were suspected of spying on the basis of hard evidence, or who confessed to espionage. See Chapter 2 for their names.

31. Raymond Ickes, interview by author, Berkeley, CA, 18 Sep 1997.

32. "Ickes' Son Is Decorated," *New York Times* 30 Nov 1945, 8.

33. Ennis to Keeley, 4 Sep 1943, 740.00115EW1939/7593, RG59, NA.

34. Heath to SecState, 20 Sep 1943, *FRUS 1943*, V: 821–2.

35. Berle forwards DoJ memo on the history of the conflict to U.S. missions in Latin America in "'Internment at Large' Program of Department of Justice," 27 Jun 1944, in folder "711.5," Costa Rica: San José Embassy, Confidential File, Box 32, RG84, NA.

36. Long to Biddle, 6 Apr 1943, and attached memo by Lafoon, 740.00115PW/1392, RG59, NA.

37. Berle, "'Internment at Large' Program of Justice," 27 Jun 1944, in folder "711.5," Costa Rica: San José Embassy, Confidential File, Box 32, RG84, NA.

38. Long to Welles, 29 Jun 1943, "Special Division, Internees [Axis], 1942–1944," Subject File, State Department, 1939–44, Box 204, Long Papers; Bell to Ennis, 9 Jun 1943, in folder "A8-5(1-Costa Rica) Germans," Naval Attaché – Guatemala

City, Personality Files 1940–6, Box 45, ONI, RG38, NA; Boaz Long to SecState, 5 May 1944, 740.00115EW1939/6-2344, RG59, NA.

39. Winings memo, 23 May 1944, in folder "711.5," Costa Rica: San José Embassy, Confidential File, Box 32, RG84, NA; Berle, "'Internment at Large' Program of Department of Justice," 27 Jun 1944, in folder "711.5," Costa Rica: San José Embassy, Confidential File, Box 32, RG84, NA.

40. Glover, "Arne Minden Aas (Panama)," 24 Jan 1946, in folder "Aas, Arne Minden, Panama," Name Files of Interned Enemy Aliens from Latin America, 1942–8, Box 35, SWP, RG59, NA.

41. Bingham, "Confidential: Leon Fuerst (Honduras)," 25 Jan 1946, in folder "Fuerst, Leon, Honduras," Name Files of Interned Enemy Aliens from Latin America, 1942–8, Box 39, SWP, RG59, NA.

42. *Justice Department Summary,* 1946, "Kugler, Otto Berthold," Name Files of Interned Enemy Aliens from Latin America, 1942–8, Box 42, SWP, RG59, NA.

43. Davis to Spaeth, *Confidential: Eric Rath,* 9 Nov 1945, "Rath, Eric, Ecuador," Name Files of Interned Enemy Aliens from Latin America, 1942–8, Box 45, SWP, RG59, NA; "Records of the War Department on KAPPEL, Werner Julius," in folder "Kappel, Werner. Panama," Name Files of Interned Enemy Aliens from Latin America, 1942–8, Box 41, SWP, RG59, NA.

44. Gordon to Hudson, 29 May 1942, and Bingham, "Confidential: Emmanuel Gordon (Dominican Republic)," 18 Feb 1946, in folder "Gordon, Emmanuel, Dom. Republic," Name Files of Interned Enemy Aliens from Latin America, 1942–8, Box 40, SWP, RG59, NA; Scotten to Secretary of State, *Internment of Settlers at Sosua, Dominican Republic,* 26 Dec 1941, 740.00115EW1939/1674, RG59, NA.

Chapter 7   Expropriation

1. JM Cabot to Special Division, 24 Nov 1943, in folder "Important Papers," Name Files of Enemy Aliens 1942–8, Box 31, Special War Problems Division (hereafter SWP), RG59, National Archives, College Park, Maryland (hereafter NA).

2. AmEmbGuatemala to Secretary of State, "Despatch no. 844," 19 Nov 1945, in folder "Kaltwasser, Hermann, Guatemala," Name Files of Interned Enemy Aliens from Latin America, 1942–8, Box 41, SWP, RG59, NA. Emphasis added. Dates of birth and arrival in Guatemala in individual internment records in Name Files of Interned Enemy Aliens from Latin America, Boxes 31–50, SWP, RG59, NA. For the commercial history of the four families mentioned see Regina Wagner, *Los Alemanes en Guatemala, 1828–1944* (Guatemala: Afanes, 1996).

3. AmEmbGuatemala to Secretary of State, "Despatch no. 844," 19 Nov 1945, in folder "Kaltwasser, Hermann, Guatemala," Name Files of Interned Enemy Aliens from Latin America, 1942–8, Box 41, SWP, RG59, NA.

4. Bingham, *Confidential: Martin Knoetzsch, Guatemala,* 6 Dec 1945, "Knoetzsch, Martin Hermann, Guatemala," Name Files of Interned Enemy Aliens from Latin America, 1942–8, Box 42, SWP, RG59, NA; the school protest is in *Denkschrift,* 28 Dec 1935, special file, German deportees collection, German Embassy, Guatemala City, and described in Ernesto Schaeffer, *Memoiren* (Guatemala City: n.p., n.d.), 71–3.

5. Guatemalan Police Department, *Datos Personales,* 21 Dec 1941, "Guatemala Photos of Deported Germans, 1936–47," Box 18, Naval Attaché, General Correspondence, ONI, RG38, NA.

6. AmEmbGuatemala, *Despatch no. 844,* 19 Nov 1945, "Sapper, Helmuth (Schilling), Guatemala," Name Files of Interned Enemy Aliens from Latin America, 1942–8, Box 46, SWP, RG59, NA.

7. AmEmbGuatemala to Secretary of State, "Despatch no. 844," 19 Nov 1945, in folder "Kaltwasser, Hermann, Guatemala," Name Files of Interned Enemy Aliens from Latin America, 1942–8, Box 41, SWP, RG59, NA.

8. Victor Bulmer-Thomas, *The Political Economy of Central America Since 1920* (Cambridge: Cambridge University Press, 1987), 91–2.

9. Martin Domke, "Western Hemisphere Control Over Enemy Property: A Comparative Survey," *Law and Contemporary Problems* 11:1 (Winter–Spring 1945): 3–16, quoted at 6.

10. Military Intelligence Division, *Axis Espionage and Propaganda in Latin America* (Washington, DC: War Department, 1946), 20–2.

11. The Allied effort to pursue German flight capital abroad was known as the "Safehaven" program.

12. Bonsal to Welles, *The Proclaimed List,* 2 Jan 1942, "General Memoranda Jan–Feb 1942," Memoranda Relating to General Latin American Affairs, Box 6, Division of American Republics (hereafter ARA), RG59, NA.

13. FBI, *Costa Rica Today,* p. 64, Sep 1943, "FBI Reports – Costa Rica," Box 142, Hopkins Papers, FDR Library.

14. Lieutenant Colonel E. Andino, "Foreign Capital – Total Assets Declared by Enemy Aliens," 13 Apr 1942, in folder "A8-5(1-Costa Rica) Germans," Naval Attaché – Guatemala City, Personality Files 1940–6, Box 45, ONI, RG38, NA.

15. See the genealogical chart in Eugenio Herrera Balharry, *Los alemanes y el estado cafetalero* (San José: Editorial Universidad Estatal a Distancia, 1988), 197ff.

16. Jacobo Schifter Sikora, *Las alianzas conflictivas: las relaciones de Estados Unidos y Costa Rica desde la Segunda Guerra Mundial a la guerra fría* (San José: Libro Libre, 1986), 59; Thomas M. Leonard, "The United States and German Nationals in Costa Rica on the Eve of World War II," paper delivered at the Southeastern Council on Latin America Studies Conference, San José, Costa Rica, 1997, 5. Efinger's role in rejecting visa applications from Jewish refugees has led to claims of Nazi influence. But such overt anti-Jewish immigrant sentiment as did exist in Costa Rica came principally from Lebanese, Spanish, and Costa Rican retail merchants, whose prices were undercut by the *buhoneros,* pushcart vendors who avoided license fees and taxes and who included most of the five hundred Jews who came to Costa Rica in the decade before the war. The German community did not engage in antiimmigrant propaganda, perhaps because, as an economic elite, they did not compete in the small retail sector. Jacobo Schifter Sikora, *El Judío en Costa Rica* (San José: Editorial Universidad Estatal a Distancia, 1979), 94, 150, 160.

17. Charles D. Ameringer, *Don Pepe: A Political Biography of José Figueres of Costa Rica* (Albuquerque: University of New Mexico Press, 1978), 17–20.

18. Jackson to Gordon, 25 July 1941, 164.12/4539 1/2, RG59, NA.

19. Woodbury S. Ober, 15 Jul 1942, 740.00115EW1939/4202, RG59, NA. Learning from mob violence, the State Department requested from its mission in San José a list of the businesses whose windows were broken, so it could add the targets to the Proclaimed List. Scotten to SecState, 7 Aug 1942, 740.00112AEW1939/15624, RG59, NA.

20. Ameringer, *Don Pepe,* 17–20.

21. Carlos Calvo Gamboa, *Costa Rica en la segunda guerra mundial, 1939–1945* (San José: Editorial Universidad Estatal a Distancia, 1985), 44.

22. Leslie E. Reed, *Suggestions for Control of Alien Property,* 27 Feb 1942, "711.3," Costa Rica, San José Legation: Confidential File, Box 18, RG84, NA.

23. Lane to Piza, 19 Feb 1942, 378, Sig. 264, Junta de Custodia, Archivo Nacional, San José, Costa Rica (hereafter AN); Lieutenant Colonel Andino, "Military Attaché Report," 26 Mar 1942, in folder "711.3," Costa Rica, San José Legation: Confidential File, Box 18, RG84, NA.

24. Reed to Secretary of State, 26 Mar 1942, in folder "711.3," Costa Rica, San José Legation: Confidential File, Box 18, RG84, NA.

25. Soley to Zweig, 5 May 1942, in folder "711.3," Costa Rica, San José Legation: Confidential File, Box 18, RG84, NA.

26. Hull to AmLegSan José, 8 Jun 1942, in folder "711.3," Costa Rica, San José Legation: Confidential File, Box 18, RG84, NA.

27. Hull to AmLegSan José, 13 Aug 1942, in folder "711.3," Costa Rica, San José Legation: Confidential File, Box 18, RG84, NA.

28. Soley Güell to Scotten, 18 Aug 1942, 10, Sig. 32, Junta de Custodia, AN; Scotten to Secretary of State, 27 Jul 1942, in folder "711.3," Costa Rica, San José Legation: Confidential File, Box 18, RG84, NA.

29. Calvo Gamboa, *Costa Rica,* 44.

30. Van der Laat to Heck, 22 Jul 1942, 308, Sig. 264, Junta de Custodia, AN.

31. Leslie E. Reed to Juan Trejos, 1 Aug 1942, 300, Sig. 264, Junta de Custodia, AN.

32. Tomás Soley Güell, 11 Dec 1942, 15, Sig. 32, Junta de Custodia, AN.

33. Trueblood to Secretary of State, 27 Sep 1943, in folder "711.2," Costa Rica: San José Embassy Confidential File, Box 25, RG84, NA.

34. Heck to van der Laat, Oct (?) 1942, 261, Sig. 264, Junta de Custodia, AN.

35. Eugene Desvernine, *Strictly Confidential Memorandum,* 2 Mar 1943, "711.2," Costa Rica: San José Embassy Confidential File, Box 25, RG84, NA.

36. Eugene Desvernine, *Memorandum of Interview with the Junta de Custodia,* 23 Jan 1943, "711.2," Costa Rica: San José Embassy Confidential File, Box 25, RG84, NA; Trueblood to SecState, 7 Jan 1944, "711.3," Costa Rica: San José Embassy, Confidential File, Box 32, RG84, NA.

37. Calvo Gamboa, *Costa Rica,* 147.

38. Some of the administrators are named in Soley Güell to Raúl Guzmán, 1 Dec 1942, 21, Sig. 32, Junta de Custodia, AN; Picado to Herrera González, 11 Aug 1945, 28.5, Sig. 508, Junta de Custodia, AN.

39. Kyle Longley, *The Sparrow and the Hawk: Costa Rica and the United States during the Rise of José Figueres* (Tuscaloosa: University of Alabama Press, 1997), 34; Schifter Sikora, *Las alianzas conflictivas,* 32; Ameringer, *Don Pepe,* 10–11.

40. Stettinius to Johnson, 2 Apr 1945, *FRUS 1945,* IX: 305–6.

41. Calvo Gamboa, *Costa Rica,* 40–51; Leonard, "The United States and German Nationals."
42. Eugene Desvernine, "Strictly Confidential Memorandum," 2 Mar 1943, in folder "711.2," Costa Rica: San José Embassy Confidential File, Box 25, RG84, NA.
43. Picado to Rafael Arias, 26 Dec 1944, 48, Sig. 508, Junta de Custodia, AN.
44. Ernst Ludwig Lohrengel to Reichsbauernführer, 25 Mar 1944, 3601000222, Lohrengel, Ernst Ludwig, Rückwandereramt der AO, Bundesarchiv, Berlin-Lichterfelde. Lohrengel was asking the agricultural ministry for aid in starting a farm in Germany until he could return to claim his property in Costa Rica after the war. The AO representative for Costa Rica included a letter of reference saying that Lohrengel's behavior in Costa Rica was above reproach.
45. Victor C. Heck, 5 Sep 1942, in folder "711.3/711.2," Costa Rica: San José Legation, Confidential File, Box 18, RG84, NA; Eugene Desvernine, "Strictly Confidential Memorandum," 2 Mar 1943, in folder "711.2," Costa Rica: San José Embassy Confidential File, Box 25, RG84, NA.
46. Senate Committee on Military Affairs, *Nazi Party Membership Records,* Senate Committee Prints 79/2/46, Part 2, March 1946, and Part 3, September 1946, S1535-S1538 (Washington, DC: U.S. Government Printing Office, 1946).
47. See Niehaus folders in alphabetical Name Files of Interned Enemy Aliens from Latin America, Boxes 31–50, SWP, RG59, NA.
48. Victor C. Heck, 5 Sep 1942, "711.3/711.2," Costa Rica: San José Legation, Confidential File, Box 18, RG84, NA.
49. Eugene Desvernine, *Strictly Confidential Memorandum,* 2 Mar 1943, "711.2," Costa Rica: San José Embassy Confidential File, Box 25, RG84, NA.
50. Coit MacLean to van der Laat, 8 Sep 1943, 20, Sig. 264, Junta de Custodia, AN.
51. Hull to AmLegSan José, 16 Nov 1942, "711.5," Costa Rica, San José Legation: Confidential File, Box 18, RG84, NA.
52. Reed to SecState, 2 Nov 1942, in folder "711.5," Costa Rica: San José Legation, Confidential File, Box 18, RG84, NA; Behrens information in Tenney, *Emil Albrecht Behrens,* 3 Jan 1946, "Behrens, Emil Albrecht, Costa Rica," Name Files of Interned Enemy Aliens from Latin America, 1942–8, Box 36, SWP, RG59, NA.
53. Tenney, *Confidential: Ernesto Gerothwol [sic] (Costa Rica),* 18 Jan 1946, "Gerothwol, Ernesto, Costa Rica," Name Files of Interned Enemy Aliens from Latin America, 1942–8, Box 39, SWP, RG59, NA; Ernesto Gerothwohl, 13 Jan 1943, 8, Sig. 141, Junta de Custodia, AN.
54. John Moors Cabot, *First Line of Defense: Forty Years' Experiences of a Career Diplomat* (Washington, DC: School of Foreign Service, Georgetown University, 1980[?]), 15.
55. Major F. M. June, *Confidential and Private Intelligence Report,* 25 Jan 1942, "US-Guatemalan Relations C-9-b/18685-B," Intelligence Division Confidential Reports of Naval Attaches 1940–6, Box 428, ONI, RG38, NA.
56. Major F. M. June, *Private and Confidential Intelligence Report,* 25 Feb 1942, "US-Guatemalan Relations C-9-b/18685-B," Intelligence Division Confidential Reports of Naval Attaches 1940–46, Box 428, ONI, RG38, NA. Major June thought Des Portes was incompetent, but June wanted more, not less,

interference in Guatemalan affairs. "We must dominate the entire situation in Guatemala," he wrote, suggesting the "removal of cabinet ministers who are known to be insincere to the United States and friendly to the Nazi philosophy" as "a symbol that we are bossing this show."

57. Des Portes to Secretary of State, 12 Aug 1943, "711.5," Costa Rica: San José Embassy Confidential File, Box 26, RG84, NA.

58. Trueblood to Secretary of State, 13 Sep 1943, "711.5," Costa Rica: San José Embassy Confidential File, Box 26, RG84, NA.

59. J. D. Tomlinson, 23 Sep 1943, "711.5," Costa Rica: San José Embassy Confidential File, Box 26, RG84, NA.

60. Trueblood to Secretary of State, 20 Sep 1943, in folder "711.5," Costa Rica: San José Embassy Confidential File, Box 26, RG84, NA; Ickes quote from Raymond W. Ickes, *Memorandum to the Minister,* 30 Mar 1943, "711.5," Costa Rica: San José Embassy Confidential File, Box 26, RG84, NA. See Chapter 6 for more on Ickes's criticisms.

61. Trueblood, 22 Oct 1943, "711.5," Costa Rica: San José Embassy Confidential File, Box 26, RG84, NA.

62. Trueblood, 22 Oct 1943, "711.5," Costa Rica: San José Embassy Confidential File, Box 26, RG84, NA.

63. Des Portes to Secretary of State, 29 Oct 1943, 734, "711.5," Costa Rica: San José Embassy Confidential File, Box 26, RG84, NA.

64. JMC to Wright and Bonsal, 15 Nov 1943, in folder "Important Papers," Name Files of Enemy Aliens 1942–8, Box 31, SWP, RG59, NA.

65. JM Cabot to Special Division, 24 Nov 1943, in folder "Important Papers," Name Files of Enemy Aliens 1942–8, Box 31, SWP, RG59, NA. In his memoirs, Cabot would explain his opposition to State Department interference in Latin America this way: "I had been brought up on the doctrine of non-intervention and I could recall various episodes in which intervention had ended disastrously." *First Line of Defense,* 24.

66. Andrés van der Laat to Desvernine, 22 Oct 1943, in folder "711.5," Costa Rica: San José Embassy Confidential File, Box 26, RG84, NA.

67. Trueblood to SecState, 11 Jul 1944, and Trueblood to SecState, 12 Jul 1944, in folder "711.5," Costa Rica: San José Embassy, Confidential File, Box 32, RG84, NA; *In the Matter of Franz Amrhein,* in folder "Costa Rica folder 3 of 6," Transcripts of Proceedings Before the Hearing Board, Alien Enemy Control Section, Department of State, 1946, Box 16, SWP, RG59, NA.

68. Executive Decree No. 2 of July 8, 1944 amending Art. 8 of Decreee 1, 18 Feb 1931, cited in Edward N. Barnhart, "Citizenship and Political Tests in Latin American Republics in World War II," *Hispanic American Historical Review* 42:3 (Aug 1962): 297–332, quote at 304.

69. All quotations in this paragraph from Tenney, *Gerhard Steinvorth (Costa Rica),* 7 Jan 1946, "Steinvorth, Gerhard, Costa Rica," Name Files of Interned Enemy Aliens from Latin America, 1942–8, Box 48, SWP, RG59, NA.

70. *Nazi Party Membership Records.*

71. Translation of Costa Rican government message on proposed deportations, 1943, in folder "Costa Rica AI 1943," Subject Files 1939–54, Box 69, SWP, RG59, NA.

72. Hans Bansbach *fils,* interview by author, San José, 23 Mar 1998.

73. Eberhard Steinvorth to Wilhelm Steinvorth, 21 Jan 1944, "Steinvorth, Eberhard, Costa Rica," Name Files of Interned Enemy Aliens from Latin America, 1942–48, Box 48, SWP, RG59, NA.

74. Cochran to SecState, 5 Mar 1942, 740.00115EW1939/2285, RG59, NA.

75. Cochran to SecState, 5 Mar 1942, 740.00115EW1939/2285, RG59, NA.

76. The sum in córdobas was worth approximately $340,000. William Krehm, *Democracies and Tyrannies of the Caribbean* (Westport, CT: Lawrence Hill, 1984), 114; Claribel Alegría and D. J. Flakoll, *Nicaragua: la revolución sandinista. Una crónica política 1855–1979* (México, D.F.: Ediciones Era, 1982), 120–1; Bernard Diederich, *Somoza* (London: Junction Books, 1982), 22.

77. Götz von Houwald, *Los alemanes en Nicaragua* (Managua: Editorial y Litografía San José, 1975), 151, 267.

78. Secretary of State to AmLegSan José, 24 Jul 1943, "711.2," Costa Rica: San José Embassy Confidential File, Box 25, RG84, NA; von Houwald, *Los alemanes en Nicaragua*, 150.

79. Randolph to DoS, Despatch 137, 715.00(W)/9-2252, cited in Mario Argueta, *Tiburcio Carías: anatomía de una época, 1923–1948* (Tegucigalpa: Editorial Guaymuras, 1989), 229.

80. Erwin to SecState, 31 May 1944, 740.00112RP/12, RG59, NA.

81. Erwin to SecState, 14 Oct 1944, 740.00112RP/10-1444, RG59, NA.

82. Segisfredo Infante et al., *Los Alemanes en el Sur, 1900–1947* (Tegucigalpa: Editorial Universitaria, 1993), 98. There was an Erwin Siercke on the Nazi Party Membership List for Honduras, and a Victor Siercke was deported from Honduras to internment in the United States. See *Nazi Party Membership Records* and *German Nationals Deported by the Other American Republics Who Were Deported Via the United States,* in folder of same name, Subject Files, 1939–54, Box 121, SWP, RG59, NA.

83. Grew to McGurk, 21 May 1945, *FRUS 1945,* IX: 335.

84. Military Intelligence Division, *Axis Espionage and Propaganda in Latin America* (Washington, DC: War Department, 1946), 110.

85. Argueta, *Tiburcio Carías,* 229.

86. Piero Gleijeses, *Shattered Hope: The Guatemalan Revolution and the United States, 1944–1954* (Princeton, New Jersey: Princeton University Press, 1991), 43.

87. Wagner, *Los Alemanes en Guatemala,* chart on page 391.

88. Moraht to Außenhandelsamt der AO, 30 Nov 1942, "Wirtschaftliche Beziehungen zu Deutschland. Süd- und Mittelamerika," R116258, Handelspolitische Abteilung IXb, Politisches Archiv des Auswärtigen Amtes, Bonn (hereafter PAAA).

89. Minutes, 3 Nov 1941, "Board of Economic Operations – Oct.–Dec.1941," Box 56, Berle Papers, FDR Library. Emphasis added.

90. Kenneth J. Grieb, "Guatemala and the Second World War," *Ibero-Amerikanisches Archiv* 3:4 (1977): 377–94.

91. Major F. M. June, *Private and Confidential Intelligence Report,* 25 Feb 1942, "US-Guatemalan Relations C-9-b/18685-B," Intelligence Division Confidential Reports of Naval Attaches 1940–6, Box 428, ONI, RG38, NA.

92. Bonsal to Long, 25 Apr 1942, "American Republics Affairs 1942," Subject File, State Department 1939–44, Box 188, Long Papers, Manuscript Division, Library of Congress, Washington, DC (hereafter LC).

93. Welles memo of conversation, 19 May 1942, Box 178, folder 2, Welles Papers.

94. SecState to Boaz Long, 28 Feb 1944, *FRUS,* VII.

95. Boaz Long to SecState, 13 Jun 1944, *FRUS,* VII: 1163.

96. Paul Dosal, *Power in Transition: The Rise of Guatemala's Industrial Oligarchy, 1871–1994* (Westport, CT: Praeger, 1995), 130.

97. J. Landahl to Latein-Amerikanischer Verein, 29 Sep 1944, "Berichte und Schriftwechsel über die Lage des Deutschtums und die Wirtschaftsver-hältnisse in den einzelnen Staaten Süd- und Mittelamerikas," R 64 III/4, Lateinamerikanischer Verein, Bundesarchiv.

98. Sharon Y. Clifford, "The Germans in Guatemala during World War II" (Master's thesis, Florida Atlantic University, 1974), 55.

99. "Guatemala Takes German Land," *New York Times,* 23 Jul 1945, 5; "'End of War' Act Aids Guatemala," *New York Times,* 25 Nov 1956.

100. Susanne Jonas and David Tobis, eds., *Guatemala* (Berkeley, CA: NACLA, 1974), 46.

101. Grew to McGurk, 21 May 1945, *FRUS 1945,* IX: 343.

102. Alfredo Schlesinger, *Comentarios alrededor de la ley de liquidación de asuntos de guerra* (Guatemala City: n.p., 1955). A self-published compilation of Schlesinger's columns for the newspaper *La Hora* in 1948.

103. Jonas and Tobis, *Guatemala,* 49.

104. See Gleijeses, *Shattered Hope;* Stephen Schlesinger and Stephen Kinzer, *Bitter Fruit: The Untold Story of the American Coup in Guatemala* (New York: Doubleday, 1982); Richard H. Immerman, *The CIA in Guatemala: The Foreign Poicy of Intervention* (Austin: University of Texas Press, 1982).

105. Carlos Gehlert, interview by author, Guatemala City, 30 May 1996.

106. Thomas Melville and Marjorie Melville, *Guatemala: The Politics of Land Ownership* (New York: Free Press, 1971), 122–33.

107. Grew to McGurk, 21 May 1945, *FRUS 1945,* IX: 310–44.

108. Moraht to Außenhandelsamt der AO, 30 Nov 1942, "Wirtschaftliche Beziehungen zu Deutschland. Süd- und Mittelamerika," R116258, Handelspolitische Abteilung IXb, PAAA.

109. Swiss Legation Washington to Swiss Foreign Ministry, 28 Sep 1944, 103, B.24.A.(14)7, Band 67, E2001–02/17, Schweizerisches Bundesarchiv, Bern (hereafter SBA).

110. Robert I. Rotberg, *Haiti: The Politics of Squalor* (Boston: Houghton Mifflin, 1971), 169–70.

111. Thurston to SecState, 26 Jul and 27 Jul 1943, *FRUS 1943,* VI: 324–8; Grew to McGurk, 21 May 1945, *FRUS 1945,* IX: 310–44; Simmons to SecState, 24 Jul 1945, *FRUS 1945,* IX: 345.

112. Moraht to Außenhandelsamt der AO, 30 Nov 1942, "Wirtschaftliche Beziehungen zu Deutschland. Süd- und Mittelamerika," R116258, Handelspolitische Abteilung IXb, PAAA.

113. The phrase, variants of which often appear in the record, comes here from Assistant Secretary of State William L. Clayton, *Statement before the Subcommittee on War Mobilization of the Senate Committee on Military Affairs,* 25 Jun 1945, "CIAA Background Material," folder 20, Box 3, Record Group III 40, Nelson A. Rockefeller Personal Files, Washington, DC, Files, Rockefeller Family Archives, Rockefeller Archive Center, North Tarrytown, NY (hereafter RAC).

114. Graham D. Taylor, "The Axis Replacement Program: Economic Warfare and the Chemical Industry in Latin America, 1942–44," *Diplomatic History* 8:2 (1984): 145–64, quoted at 147.

115. Acheson, "United States Financial Assistance to Eliminate Undesirable Ownership and Control from Proclaimed List Firms," 18 Jun 1943, in folder "711.2," Costa Rica: San José Embassy Confidential File, Box 25, RG84, NA.

116. Acheson, *Replacement of Enemy Nationals,* 7 Dec 1943, 740.00112 RP/3, RG59, NA.

117. Acheson, *Axis Replacement Program,* 20 May 1943, "711.2," Costa Rica: San José Embassy Confidential File, Box 25, RG84, NA.

118. Elliott Bowles to Rubin, 11 Dec 1943, 740.00112RP/4, RG59, NA.

119. McConaughy to SecState, 8 Jul 1944, 740.00112RP/7-844, RG59, NA.

120. Draft to HM Representative, Washington, DC, copy all Latin American posts, May 44, /38164, cited in Ronald C. Newton, *The 'Nazi Menace' in Argentina, 1931–1947* (Stanford, CA: Stanford University Press, 1992), 349.

121. Wells, 10 May 1945, 740.2112RP/5-1045, RG59, NA; John C. Wiley, 8 Nov 1945, in folder "Diplomatic Files: Colombia, 1944–1947," Box 5, Wiley Papers, FDR Library.

122. Graham D. Taylor, "The Axis Replacement Program: Economic Warfare and the Chemical Industry in Latin America, 1942–44," *Diplomatic History* 8:2 (1984): 145–64.

123. Raymond Ickes, interview by author, Berkeley, CA, 18 Sep 1997.

124. John K. Emmerson, *The Japanese Thread: A Life in the U.S. Foreign Service* (New York: Holt, Rinehart and Winston, 1978), 139–43.

125. Emmerson, *The Japanese Thread,* 137.

126. Acheson to Biddle, 22 Jun 1944, and Ennis to Acheson, 28 Jun 1944, "711.5," Costa Rica: San José Embassy, Confidential File, Box 32, RG84, NA.

127. See individual records in Name Files of Interned Enemy Aliens from Latin America, 1942–8, Box 41, SWP, RG59, NA.

Chapter 8   Repatriation

1. Barber to Cabot et al., "South American Passports for Refugees," 20 Mar 1944, in folder "General Memoranda Feb–April 1944," Memoranda Relating to General Latin American Affairs, Box 9, Division of American Republics (hereafter ARA), RG59, National Archives, College Park, Maryland (hereafter NA). Gordon was head of the Division of Foreign Activity Correlation.

2. Clattenburg, 25 May 1944, 840.48 Refugees/6406, M1284 reel 43, RG59, NA.

3. Copy of Bohnenberger's party card in Ortsgruppenkartei, reel B0072, Berlin Documents Center, NA. School role in FBI, *Guatemala Today,* July 1944, pp. 152–3, in folder "FBI Reports – Guatemala," Box 142, Hopkins Papers, FDR Library; and Werner Ascoli, interview by author, Guatemala City, 24 May 1996. On Bohnenberger's denial, see also the author's "Private Memory, Public Records, and Contested Terrain: Weighing Oral Testimony in the Deportation of Germans from Latin America During World War II," *Oral History Review* 27:1 (Winter/Spring 2000): 1–15.

4. Gerardo Bohnenberger, interview by author, Guatemala City, 18 May 1996.

5. Fred L. Israel, ed., *The War Diary of Breckinridge Long: Selections from the Years 1939–1944* (Lincoln: University of Nebraska Press, 1966), 245.

6. "German Nationals Deported by the Other American Republics Who Were Deported Via the United States," 25 Apr 1946, in folder "711.5," Ecuador: Quito Embassy Confidential File, Box 35, RG84, NA.

7. Albrecht to RAM, 2 Jul 1942, R41559, Zivilgefangenen-Austausch-Vereinigten Staaten von Amerika, Rechtsabteilung, Politisches Archiv des Auswärtigen Amtes, Bonn (hereafter PAAA). Alexandra-Eileen Wenck, *Zwischen Menschenhandel und "Endlösung": Das Konzentrationslager Bergen-Belsen* (Paderborn, Germany: Verlag Ferdinand Schöningh, 2000), 72–4.

8. Albrecht, 19 Sep 1941, "Zivilgefangenen-Austausch-Vereinigten Staaten von Amerika," R41555, Rechtsabteilung, PAAA.

9. Paltzo to Reichsminister for the Occupied Eastern Territories, 30(?) Sep 1942, "Zivilgefangenen-Austausch-Vereinigten Staaten von Amerika," R41564, Rechtsabteilung, PAAA.

10. Albrecht to RAM, 28 Jan 1942, "Deutsche Zivilgefangenen in den Verein. Staaten v. Amerika, 1941–1942," R41876, Rechtsabteilung, PAAA.

11. Albrecht to St.S & RAM, *Behandlung den Reichsdeutschen in Amerika and Deutsche Gegenmassnahmen,* 6 Feb 1942, "Deutsche Zivilgefangene in den Verein. Staaten. v. Amerika 1941–1942," R41876, Rechtsabteilung, PAAA; Albrecht to R IV, 26 Nov 1942, "Zivilgefangenen-Austausch-Vereinigten Staaten von Amerika," R41564, Rechtsabteilung, PAAA.

12. Correspondence in folder "British Objections – Lists 1 through 60 (our numbers)," Objections to the Repatriation of Enemy Aliens, 1942, Box 1 of 3, Special War Problems Division, Box 1, RG59, NA.

13. Eden to Winant, 12 Aug 1942, 740.00115EW1939/4302, RG59, NA.

14. Green to Long, 23 Jun 1942, "Special Division, General Correspondence," Subject File, State Department, 1939–44, Box 204, Manuscript Division, Library of Congress, Washington, DC (hereafter LC).

15. See Peter Gillman and Leni Gillman, *'Collar the Lot!' How Britain Interned and Expelled its Wartime Refugees* (London: Quartet Books, 1980); Louise London, *Whitehall and the Jews, 1933–1948: British Immigration Policy and the Holocaust* (Cambridge: Cambridge University Press, 2000).

16. Long to Messersmith, 26 Jun 1942, in folder "Messersmith, George S. Jan–Sept, 1942," Subject File, State Department 1939–44, Box 199, Long Papers, Manuscript Division, LC.

17. Green to Long, 23 Jun 1942, "Special Division, General Correspondence," Subject File, State Department, 1939–44, Box 204, Manuscript Division, LC.

18. Hull to AmEmbBogotá, 30 Jan 1942, 740.00115EW1939/1765, RG59, NA; Hull to AmEmbBogotá, 11 Feb 1942, 740.00115EW1939/1766, RG59, NA.

19. AmLegQuito to MRE, 31 Mar 1942, Serie B, Embajada de Estados Unidos, Ministerio de Relaciones Exteriores (hereafter MRE), Archivo Histórico de Quito (hereafter AHQ).

20. Green to Long, 17 Apr 1942, 740.00115EW1939/2608, RG59, NA; Joseph C. Green, 22 Jul 1942, 701.0010/523 1/2, RG59, NA.

21. Boaz Long to SecState, 31 Aug 1942, 740.00115EW1939/4439, RG59, NA.

22. Boaz Long to Guarderas, 29 Oct 1942, Serie B, Embajada de Estados Unidos, MRE, AHQ.

23. Long to Fahy, 10 Jul 1942, 740.00115EW1939/4307, RG59, NA.
24. Albrecht to St.S & RAM, *Behandlung den Reichsdeutschen in Amerika and Deutsche Gegenmassnahmen,* 6 Feb 1942, "Deutsche Zivilgefangene in den Verein. Staaten. v. Amerika 1941–1942," R41876, Rechtsabteilung, PAAA.
25. Clattenburg to Wright, 16 Jun 1942, 740.00115EW1939/4242, RG59, NA.
26. Clattenburg to Wright, 16 Jun 1942, 740.00115EW1939/4242, RG59, NA. A year later, Latin Americans interned at Bad Godesberg would add another plea to the U.S. government: to apprise the Air Force of their location, since aerial bombing of the Cologne area was getting uncomfortably close. The State Department made no promises. JWG to Guarderas, 4 Aug 1943, "711.5," and Hull to AmEmbQuito, 1 Sep 1943, "711," Ecuador: Quito Embassy, Confidential File, Box 10, RG84, NA. One camp holding U.S. and Latin American internees was bombed twice, without injuries, although it was lit up to alert air crews. Tait to Secretary of State, 20 Sep 1943, 740.00115EW1939/7472, RG59, NA.
27. Long to Messersmith, 26 Jun 1942, "Messersmith, George S. Jan–Sept, 1942," Subject File, State Department 1939–44, Box 199, Long Papers.
28. Clattenburg to Wright, 16 Jun 1942, 740.00115EW1939/4242, RG59, NA.
29. Albrecht to RAM, 2 Jul 1942, R41559, Zivilgefangenen-Austausch-Vereinigten Staaten von Amerika, Rechtsabteilung, PAAA; Wenck, *Menschenhandel,* 72–4.
30. "German Nationals Deported by the Other American Republics Who Were Deported Via the United States," 25 Apr 1946, in folder "711.5," Ecuador: Quito Embassy Confidential File, Box 35, RG84, NA.
31. Theiss, 9 Jul 1942, "Zivilgefangenen-Austausch-Vereinigten Staaten von Amerika," R41560, Rechtsabteilung, PAAA.
32. Attorney General to Secretary of State, 14 Aug 1942, "Special Division: Objections of Various Agencies 1942," Subject File, State Department 1939–44, Box 208, Long Papers.
33. Hull to President, 27 Aug 1942, 740.00115EW1939/4476, RG59, NA.
34. Long to Green, 15 Jun 1942 and Long to Green, 18 Jun 1942, "Special Division, General Correspondence," Subject File, State Department, 1939–44, Box 204, Manuscript Division, LC; Breckinridge Long, 29 Jun 1942, "Special Division: Obejctions of Various Agencies 1942," Subject File, State Department 1939–44, Box 208, Long Papers.
35. Hull to President, 27 Aug 1942, 740.00115EW1939/4476, RG59, NA.
36. Jean Duras to AA, 18 May 1942, "Zivilgefangenen-Austausch-Vereinigten Staaten von Amerika," R41557, Rechtsabteilung, PAAA.
37. Herbert Gompertz to AA, 14 Jul 1942, "Zivilgefangenen-Austausch-Vereinigten Staaten von Amerika," R41561, Rechtsabteilung, PAAA. Emphasis in original.
38. Else Schulz to "The Führer of Gross Deutschland," 6 Aug 1942, "Zivilgefangenen-Austausch-Vereinigten Staaten von Amerika," R41563, Rechtsabteilung, PAAA.
39. Roosevelt to Hull, 15 Aug 1942, 740.00115EW1939/4348, RG59. Copy in folder "Dept. of State July–Dec 1942," OF 20, Box 10, FDR Library.
40. Hull to President, 27 Aug 1942, 740.00115EW1939/4476, RG59, NA; copy in "Roosevelt, F.D. 1942," General Correspondence 1942, Box 144, Long Papers. The situation of the Japanese was different, Long wrote. In contrast to the U.S. citizens who might be brought back from Europe, the more than three thousand

U.S. citizens in Japanese-occupied China included important businesspeople and missionaries. Obtaining their return was urgent, and it could be done only by sending out an equal number of Japanese. In order to get more bodies for a hostage exchange, Long requested – and received – permission to "Continue our efforts to remove *all* the Japanese from these American Republics countries for internment in the United States." Thus FDR authorized, too, the mass deportation and internment measures taken against the Japanese of Latin America.

41. "German Nationals Deported by the Other American Republics Who Were Deported Via the United States," 25 Apr 1946, in folder "711.5," Ecuador: Quito Embassy Confidential File, Box 35, RG84, NA.

42. *Memorandum regarding activities of the United States Government in removing from the other American Republics dangerous subversive aliens,* 3 Nov 1942, p. 3, in Subject Files, Box 180, Special War Problems Division (hereafter SWP), RG59, NA. Emphasis added.

43. Emil Prüfert to Thomsen, 1 Jun 1942, R41559, Zivilgefangenen-Austausch-Vereinigten Staaten von Amerika, Rechtsabteilung, PAAA.

44. *Men Who Have Requested Repatriation But Who Are Not Considered to Be Dangerous,* in folder "Untitled Folder 2 of 2," Objections to the Repatriation of Enemy Aliens, 1942, Box 3, SWP, RG59, NA; Jellefsen, *Report of Alien Enemy,* 24 Jan 1945, "Behrens, Francisco Alfredo," Records Relating to German Civilian Internees During World War II, Box 8, Alien Enemy Information Bureau, Provost Marshal General, RG389, NA; Federico Knebusch, interview by author, Guatemala City, 26 May 1996.

45. Compare *Men Who Have Requested Repatriation But Who Are Not Considered to Be Dangerous,* in folder "Untitled Folder 2 of 2," Objections to the Repatriation of Enemy Aliens, 1942, Box 3, SWP, RG59, NA, to total list of Guatemalan deportees from individual internee reports plus *German Nationals Deported By The Other American Republics Who Were Deported By The United States,* in folder of same name, Subject Files 1939–54, Box 121, SWP, RG59, NA.

46. Bonsal to Welles, *Repatriation of Axis Nationals in the Western Hemisphere,* 26 Jun 1942, "General Memoranda May–June 1942," Memoranda Relating to General Latin American Affairs, Box 7, ARA, RG59, NA.

47. German Colony Colombia to German Embassy Madrid, 7 Mar 1942, 740.00115EW1939/2779, in folder "Declassification Folder #1," RG59, NA.

48. Swiss Legation Washington to DoS, 28 May 1942, "Noten von und an Staatsdepartement, Dez. 1941–Juni 1942," Band 3, E2200 Washington/15, Schweizerisches Bundesarchiv, Bern (hereafter SBA); Jobst-H. Floto, *Die Beziehungen Deutschlands zu Venezuela 1933 bis 1958* (Frankfurt: Peter Lang, 1991), 154.

49. See, for example, Patterson to SecState, 22 May 1942, 740.00115EW1939/3177, RG59, NA.

50. Albrecht to St.S., 1 Sep 1942, "Zivilgefangenen-Austausch-Vereinigten Staaten von Amerika," R41563, Rechtsabteilung, PAAA.

51. This policy is stated to have applied "since repatriation program was initiated" in Stettinius to AmEmbLima, 1 Mar 1944, in folder "Peru 1945 – Germans + Japs," Subject Files 1939–54, Box 194, SWP, RG59, NA. But see the comment about Breckinridge Long and the Jewish internees later in this chapter.

52. Juan Niemann, interview by author, Guatemala City, 30 May 1996.

53. Walter Sommer, interview by author, Bogotá, 13 Mar 1998.

54. Gotthold Heinrich Carl Busch-Beckemeyer, *Statement*, 26 May 1942, "146-13-2-0 Section 16," Closed Legal Case Files, Box 6, Alien Enemy Control Unit, War Division, DoJ, RG60, NA.

55. *German Nationals Deported By The Other American Republics Who Were Deported By The United States*, in folder of same name, Subject Files 1939–54, Box 121, SWP, RG59, NA.

56. Breckinridge Long to Mohler, 24 Sep 1942, "W," Name Files of Interned Enemy Aliens from Latin America, 1942–8, Box 35, SWP, RG59, NA.

57. Ennis to Green, 27 Jun 1942, 740.00115EW1939/4543, RG59, NA.

58. To my knowledge, only two of the repatriated Germans from Latin America had Jewish origins. Enrique Ascoli of Nicaragua was half Jewish, but apparently agreed to repatriation. Ascoli died in the Allied bombing; in an interview, his nephew was unable to explain why he might have agreed to return to Germany. Werner Ascoli, interview by author, Guatemala City, 24 May 1996. Friedrich Karl Kaul, a Jewish lawyer and member of the Communist Party, was repatriated in accordance with his wishes – but only in late 1945, after the war was over. *German Nationals Deported from the Other American Republics Who Are Presently Detained in the US*, Oct 1945, "Statistics," Subject Files 1939–54, Box 70, SWP, RG59, NA. See also entry on Kaul in Gabriele Baumgartner and Dieter Hebig, eds., *Biographisches Handbuch der SBZ/DDR 1945–1990* (Munich: K. G. Saur, 1996), and Kaul's fictionalized memoir, *Es wird Zeit, dass Du nach Hause kommst* (Berlin: Das Neue Berlin, 1959).

59. Long to Messersmith, 26 Jun 1942, "Messersmith, George S. Jan-Sept, 1942," Subject File, State Department 1939–44, Box 199, Long Papers.

60. A copy of the oath can be found in "Vol. 22, Protection, Exchanges of Civilian Nationals + Disabled POWs by Opposing Belligerents," Folder 1 of 2, Policy Books, 1939–45, Box 8, SWP, RG59, NA. The statement signed by Americans is quoted as "Declaration of Obligation. I hereby expressly obligate myself by my own signature not to bear arms during the war." See also Long to Green, 24 Jun 1942, "Special Division, General Correspondence," Subject File, State Department, 1939–44, Box 204, Manuscript Division, LC.

61. Gunter Beckmann, interview by author, Quito, 21 Jan 1998; Hackworth to Yingling, 22 Dec 1941, 740.00115EW1939/2054 1/3, RG59, NA.

62. Lafoon, 8 Feb 1945, 711.62115AR/2-845, RG59, NA.

63. SWP to War Department, 30 Jun 1944, and response, 21 Aug 1944, folder 1 of 2, Policy Books, 1939–45, Box 8, SWP, RG59, NA.

64. Lautz to Oberkommando der Wehrmacht, 9 Jul 1942, "Zivilgefangenen-Austausch-Vereinigten Staaten von Amerika," R41559, Rechtsabteilung, PAAA.

65. Canaris, *Militärdienst für Auslandsdeutsche aus Amerika*, 3 Aug 1942, "Zivilgefangenen-Austausch-Vereinigten Staaten von Amerika," R41562, Rechtsabteilung, PAAA.

66. SS-Gruppenführer Gosserger to AA, 3 Nov 1942, and Sethe to Reichsführer SS and Chef des SS-Headquarters, 18 Nov 1942, "Zivilgefangenen-Austausch-Vereinigten Staaten von Amerika," R41564, Reichsabteilung, PAAA.

67. Reichsminister der Luftfahrt und Oberbefehlshaber der Luftwaffe to AA, 25 Jul 1942, and Theiss to Reichsminister der Luftfahrt und Oberbefehlshaber der

Luftwaffe, 10 Aug 1942, "Zivilgefangenen-Austausch-Vereinigten Staaten von Amerika," R41561, Rechtsabteilung, PAAA.

68. Walter Maul, interview by author, Guatemala City, 30 May 1996.

69. Walter Sommer, interview by author, Bogotá, 13 Mar 1998.

70. Franz Spillmann to AA, 18 Aug 1942, and Albrecht to Spillmann, 26 Aug 1942, "Zivilgefangenen-Austausch-Vereinigten Staaten von Amerika," R41562, Rechtsabteilung, PAAA.

71. Georg Brückner to German repatriates from Guatemala, 20 May 1944, "Heimkehrerberichte über Südamerika," R64 III/6, Lateinamerikanischer Verein, Bundesarchiv.

72. Hans Kolter, interview by author, Guatemala City, 27 May 1996; Gunter Beckmann, interview by author, Quito, 21 Jan 1998.

73. Walter Maul, interview by author, Guatemala City, 30 May 1996.

74. Otto Stetzelberg to Gestapo, 6 Apr 1944, "Deutsche Zivilgefangene in den Ver.St.v.Amerika – Lager, 1942–1944," R42003, Rechtsabteilung, PAAA.

75. W. R. Asmus to Latein-Amerikanischer Verein, 28 Mar 1944, R64 III/6, Heimkehrberichte über Südamerika, Lateinamerikanischer Verein, Bundesarciv, Koblenz.

76. Carlos Gehlert, interview by author, Guatemala City, 30 May 1996.

77. Werner Ascoli, "Memoirs," unpublished manuscript, Guatemala City, n.d., 6; Götz von Houwald, *Los alemanes en Nicaragua* (Managua: Editorial y Litografía San José, 1975), 359.

78. Hans Joachim Schaer, interview by author, San José, 26 Mar 1998.

79. "Crueldad rusa llegó a extremos terribles no solo con los alemanes sin con ciudadaños de Naciones Unidas," *El Telegrafo,* 29 Sep 1946.

80. Hugo Droege, interview by author, Guatemala City, 22 May 1996.

81. Gerardo Bohnenberger, interview by author, Guatemala City, 18 May 1996.

82. Hugo Droege, interview by author, Guatemala City, 22 May 1996.

83. Hugo Droege, interview by author, Guatemala City, 22 May 1996.

84. There are an additional fifteen names on the refusal list that are nearly identical to those of repatriates but for minor changes in spelling; however, I have not included those here. Along with Droege, the other eleven were Max Emil Berger, Goerg Willy Bodechtel, and Friedrich Wilke of Peru; Alfons Andreas Hupp and Golmar von der Goltz of Honduras; Paul Wilhelm Lottmann and Walter Nagel Lottmann of Guatemala; Carl Friedrich Joerns of Colombia; Wilhelm A. Schmidt-Kreinert and Ulla Schmidt-Kreinert of El Salvador; and Kurt Garlef Jarren, country not specified. Compare *German Nationals Who Do Not Wish to be Repatriated* in Kelly to Keeley, 1 Jan 1944, in folder "Important Papers," Name Files of Enemy Aliens 1942–8, Box 31, SWP, RG59, NA, to *German Nationals Deported By The Other American Republics Who Were Deported By The United States,* in folder of same name, Subject Files 1939–54, Box 121, SWP, RG59, NA. (Jarren is not on the second list, but next to his name on the list of those who refused repatriation is the marginal note, "Repatriated 4/2/44.")

85. See, for example, Christopher R. Browning, *Nazi Policy, Jewish Workers, German Killers* (Cambridge: Cambridge University Press, 2000).

86. See Nathan Stoltzfus, *Resistance of the Heart: Intermarriage and the Rosenstrasse Protest in Nazi Germany* (New York: W. W. Norton, 1996).

87. Yehuda Bauer, *Jews for Sale? Nazi-Jewish Negotiations, 1933–1945* (New Haven, CT: Yale University Press, 1994); Richard Breitman and Shlomo Aronson, "The End of the 'Final Solution'?: Nazi Plans to Ransom Jews in 1944," *Central European History* 25:2 (1992): 177–203; Breitman, "A Deal with the Nazi Dictatorship: Himmler's Alleged Peace Emissaries in the Fall of 1943," *Journal of Contemporary History* 30, no. 3 (July 1995): 411–30.

88. Himmler to SS-Gruppenführer Müller (RSHA), Dec 1942, quoted in Eberhard Kolb, *Bergen-Belsen: Vom "Aufenthaltslager" zum Konzentrationslager, 1943–1945* (Göttingen: Vandenhoeck & Ruprecht, 1988), 20.

89. Bergmann to RSHA 2 Mar 1943, in Kolb, *Bergen-Belsen,* 19.

90. Von Gerlach to Theiss, 6 Jun 1942; Soldati to Theiss, 6 Jun 1942; Sethe to Halter, 12 Jun 1942; Sethe to von Gerlach, 15 Jun 1942; all in R41557, Zivilgefangenen-Austausch-Vereinigten Staaten von Amerika, Rechtsabteilung, PAAA; Sethe to Reichskommissar for the Eastern Territories, 31 Jul 1942, "Zivilgefangenen-Austausch-Vereinigten Staaten von Amerika," R41561, Rechtsabteilung, PAAA.

91. Sethe to Foreign Ministry Representative of Reichsprotektor in Böhmen und Mähren, 30 Jun 1942, R41559, Zivilgefangenen-Austausch-Vereinigten Staaten von Amerika, Rechtsabteilung, PAAA.

92. Wenck, *Menschenhandel,* 14, 56–7, 241 n. 382.

93. Kröning even released two people suspected of espionage after an examination of their case. Kröning to AA, 11 Jul 1942 and 15 Jul 1942, "Zivilgefangenen-Austausch-Vereinigten Staaten von Amerika," R41560, Rechtsabteilung, PAAA; Wenck, *Menschenhandel,* 64, 67, 388–9.

94. Wenck, *Menschenhandel,* 240–3, 389.

95. Hitler, *Erlaß des Führers und Reichskanzlers zur Festigung deutschen Volkstums,* 7 Oct 1939, "Reichskommisar für die Festigung deutschen Volkstums," R67423, Kulturabteilung, PAAA; Wenck, *Menschenhandel,* 76–7.

96. *Angehörige der Republik Nicaragua,* photostat dated 25 Mar 1943, pp. 6–8, R41524, Zivilgefangenen-Austausch-Nicaragua, Rechtsabteilung, PAAA. According to Nathan Eck, such documents cost between $200 and $300 in New York. He mentions the Honduran consul and an employee of the Salvadoran consulate, Mandel-Mantello, both in Geneva, as especially helpful in supplying *promesas* at little or no cost. See Eck, "The Rescue of Jews with the Aid of Passports and Citizenship Papers of Latin American States," *Yad Vashem Studies* I (1957): 125–52, esp. 134, 145.

97. Chief among them were Agudat Israel and the organization RELICO headed by Dr. Abraham Silberschein in Geneva. Eck, "The Rescue," 139–40.

98. Kolb, *Bergen-Belsen,* 23.

99. Eck, "The Rescue," 140.

100. Abraham Shulman, *The Case of Hotel Polski: An Account of One of the Most Enigmatic Episodes of World War II* (New York: Holocaust Library, 1982), 63.

101. Shulman, *Hotel Polski,* 80; Wenck, *Menschenhandel,* 147–150.

102. Wenck, *Menschenhandel,* 158.

103. Wenck, *Menschenhandel,* 157–8. The comparison to Theresienstadt is appropriate in another way, in that some of the camp personnel were transferred from the showcase camp in Czechoslovakia to help run Bergen-Belsen. Ibid., 82.

104. Kolb, *Bergen-Belsen,* 27; Wenck, *Menschenhandel,* 146, 150.

105. Kolb, *Bergen-Belsen,* 25.
106. Hartmann to AA, 31 Jan 1944, R41571, Amerikanische Zivilinternierte in Deutschland, Rechtsabteilung, PAAA.
107. Wenck, *Menschenhandel,* 247. Another 463 were exchanged for Germans held by the British in South Africa, Egypt, and Palestine. "The Nazis had 4,000 more Jews cleared to go, but the British lacked exchangeable German citizens." David S. Wyman, *The Abandonment of the Jews: America and the Holocaust 1941–1945* (New York: Pantheon Books, 1984), 277.
108. Breitman and Aronson, "The End of the 'Final Solution'?"
109. Leonard Dinnerstein, *Antisemitism in America* (New York: Oxford University Press, 1994), 83.
110. Dinnerstein, *Antisemitism,* 109.
111. David S. Wyman, *Paper Walls: America and the Refugee Crisis, 1938–1941* (New York: Pantheon Books, 1968, 1985), 22.
112. Richard Breitman and Alan M. Kraut, *American Refugee Policy and European Jewry, 1933–1945* (Bloomington: Indiana University Press, 1987), 58.
113. Samuel Lubell, "War by Refugee," in *Saturday Evening Post,* 29 Mar 1941, 12.
114. The Under Secretary of State (Welles) to President Roosevelt, 21 Dec 1940, in *FRUS 1940,* II: 245.
115. Presidential Press Conferences, June 5, 1940, *Complete Presidential Press Conferences of Franklin D. Roosevelt* (New York: Da Capo, 1972) 15: 495–6; Breitman and Kraut, *American Refugee Policy,* 121.
116. *FRUS 1940,* II: 231–2.
117. Long diary, 1940, p. 140, cited in Wyman, *Paper Walls,* 174.
118. Breckinridge Long to Adolf A. Berle, Jr., and James C. Dunn, June 26, 1940, Long Papers, Box 211; cited in Wyman, *Paper Walls,* 173.
119. Breckinridge Long Diary, August 30, 1942, Box 5, Manuscript Division, LC, cited in Breitman and Kraut, *American Refugee Policy,* 138.
120. Wyman, *Abandonment,* 132.
121. Braden memcon, 24 Apr 1942, *FRUS 1942,* I: 457.
122. This information comes from Thomas Schoonover, Sagera Professor of History at the University of Louisiana at Lafayette, who is currently engaged in research on Lüning. Another agent, Herbert Bahr, arrived on the first voyage of the *Drottningholm,* pretending to be a repatriating American; after he drew the suspicion of other passengers, he was arrested before he left the ship and indicted for espionage. See "'Refugee' Arrested as Spy," *New York Times,* 10 Jul 1942, 1, and Wyman, *Abandonment,* 132. Wyman reasonably suggests that the miniscule spy threat could have been addressed by screening or perhaps interning refugees upon arrival, rather than leaving them to their fate in Europe.
123. Hull to all missions in the other American republics, 2 Jan 1942, 800.20210/994, RG59, NA.
124. AmLegQuito to MRE, 9 Apr 1942, Serie B, Embajada de Estados Unidos, MRE, AHQ.
125. Leahy to SecState, 13 Jan 1942, 862.20200/48, and Hawley to Everett, 5 Jan 1942, 862.20200/53, LM195 reel 8, RG59, NA.
126. Matthews to Dunn, 27 Mar 1942, 740.00115EW1939/2636, RG59, NA.
127. Matthews to Dunn, 27 Mar 1942, 740.00115EW1939/2636, RG59, NA.
128. Dunn to Matthews, 16 May 1942, 740.00115EW1939/2636, RG59, NA.

129. Lubell, "War by Refugee," 89.
130. Lubell claimed he based the story on "more than 1000 reports and letters from abroad, many of them diplomatic and confidential," and on interviews with State Department officials. "Though my authorities cannot be quoted, I can say every statement in this article has been checked against official sources," he assured his readers. Ibid., 13.
131. Kessel to AA, 21 Jan 1943, "Zivilgefangene-Austausch-Nicaragua," R41524, Rechtsabteilung, PAAA; Hull to AmReps, 27 Mar 1943, and Ecuadoran Foreign Ministry to Boaz Long, 29 Apr 1943, 802.02, in folder "711," Ecuador: Quito Embassy, Confidential File, Box 10, RG84, NA; Echandi to Des Portes, 17 Feb 1944, in folder "711.5," Records of the San José, Costa Rica, Legation and Embassy: General Records, 1936–49, Box 97, RG84, NA.
132. Clattenburg, 13 Jul 1943, 740.00115EW1939/7121, RG59, NA.
133. Wyman, *Abandonment,* 178–206, quote at 207.
134. John Moors Cabot, *First Line of Defense: Forty Years' Experiences of a Career Diplomat* (Washington, DC: School of Foreign Service, Georgetown University, 1980[?]), 18. The exculpatory clause is wishful hindsight: the average newspaper reader, let alone such well-informed officials, had known about the death camps since November 1942.
135. Barber to Cabot et al., "South American Passports for Refugees," 20 Mar 1944, in folder "General Memoranda Feb–April 1944," Memoranda Relating to General Latin American Affairs, Box 9, ARA, RG59, NA. Gordon was head of the Division of Foreign Activity Correlation.
136. Ibid.
137. Hartmann to AA, 31 Jan 1944, R41571, Amerikanische Zivilinternierte in Deutschland, Rechtsabteilung, PAAA.
138. Wyman, *Abandonment,* 278–9.
139. Eck, "The Rescue," 150.
140. SecState to US missions in Latin America, 11 Apr 1944, *FRUS 1944,* I: 1026–7.
141. Clattenburg, 25 May 1944, 840.48 Refugees/6406, M1284 reel 43, RG59, NA.
142. Committee for Political Defense, "Resolution XXIV: Exchange of Persons Between the American Republics and Germany," 31 May 1944, in folder "711.5," Costa Rica: San José Embassy, Confidential File, Box 32, RG84, NA.
143. War Refugee Board estimate in its official history, cited in Wyman, *Abandonment,* 279.
144. Stettinius to AmEmbMontevideo, 6 Jun 1944, in folder "711.5," Costa Rica: San José Embassy, Confidential File, Box 32, RG84, NA.
145. Maney to SecState, 18 Sep 1944, in folder "711.5," Costa Rica: San José Embassy, Confidential File, Box 32, RG84, NA.
146. Jobst-H. Floto, *Die Beziehungen Deutschlands zu Venezuela 1933 bis 1958* (Frankfurt: Peter Lang, 1991), 127.
147. Marcy, "Information concerning conditions at Bergen Belsen," 25 Feb 1945, in folder "United States and German Internment Camps Comparative Report," Subject Files, 1939–54, Box 124, SWP, RG59, NA.
148. *FRUS 1943,* I: 143.
149. Wyman, *Abandonment,* 98.
150. Leonardo Senkman, "Parias und Privilegierte: Die jüdischen und spanischen Flüchtlinge in Mexiko und Argentinien 1939–1945. Eine vergleichende Studie,"

in *Alternative Lateinamerika: Das deutsche Exil in der Zeit des Nationalsozialismus,* Karl Kohut and Patrik von zur Mühlen, eds. (Frankfurt: Vervuert Verlag, 1994), 54–78.

151. Franco's government interned them in a North African camp, whence they later departed for Palestine. Kolb, *Bergen-Belsen,* 28–9; Wenck, *Menschenhandel,* 163–99.

152. Wenck, *Menschenhandel,* 396.

Chapter 9   Epilogue

1. Newbegin to Trueblood, 5 Dec 1946, 710.62115/12-546, RG59, National Archives, College Park, Maryland (hereafter NA).
2. Clattenburg to Keeley, 11 Sep 1943, 740.00115EW1939/7318 1/2, RG59, NA.
3. Clattenburg to Keeley, 11 Sep 1943, 740.00115EW1939/7318 1/2, RG59, NA.
4. Alfredo Brauer, interview by author, Quito, 5 Feb 1998.
5. *Von Heymann* v. *Watkins,* 159 F. 2d. 650; *Citizens Protective League* v. *Clark* App. D.C. 1946, 155 F. 2d. 290.
6. Presidential Proclamation No. 2662, 8 Sep 1945.
7. Summary by George Gray, 9 Feb 1948, 710.62115/10-246, RG59, NA; see also Senator William Langer to Marshall, 16 Apr 1947, 711.62115AR/4-1647, RG59, NA, and Langer's introduction of a resolution calling for hearings before deportation, Congressional Record, Senate, vol. 93, pt. 8, 80th Congress, 1st sess., 9466, 9488.
8. Summary by George Gray, 9 Feb 1948, 710.62115/10-246, RG59, NA; author analysis of AECS records in Name Files of Enemy Aliens, SWP Boxes 31–50, RG59, NA.
9. Ibid.
10. Watrous to SecState, 31 Aug 1945, "711.5," Costa Rica: San José Embassy, Confidential File, Box 39, RG84, NA.
11. *La Prensa Libre,* San José, 17 Sep 1945, cited in Karl Franz Merz to Swiss Legation Washington, "Verhaftung von Schweizern in Panama," N 9.1, Band 9, E2200 Washington/16, Schweizerisches Bundesarchiv, Bern (hereafter SBA).
12. Wood to Gibson, 4 Sep 1945, "711.5," Costa Rica: San José Embassy, Confidential File, Box 39, RG84, NA.
13. Ponce to Byrnes, 5 Sep 1945, Serie F, Documentos sobre Subditos de las Naciones del Eje, 1941 a 1946, Box 669 [38], Ministerio de Relaciones Exteriores (hereafter MRE), Archivo Histórico de Quito (hereafter AHQ).
14. Tittmann to Secretary of State, 29 Aug 1947, "Reinbold, Georges, Haiti," Name Files of Interned Enemy Aliens from Latin America, 1942–8, Box 46, Special War Problems Division (hereafter SWP), RG59, NA.
15. MRE, *Documentos Sobre Juicios de Expulsión del Ecuador a Súbditos del Eje, 1946,* 3 Oct 1946, Serie F, Documentos sobre Subditos de las Naciones del Eje, 1941 a 1946, Box 669 [38], MRE, AHQ.
16. Mann to Spaeth, 13 Nov 1945, "General Memoranda Nov–Dec 1945," Memoranda Relating to General Latin American Affairs, Box 10, Office of American Republics Affairs (hereafter ARA), RG59, NA.
17. Galo Plaza to SecState, *FRUS 1945,* IX: 285–6.
18. Clattenburg, 25 Apr 1945, 740.00115EW/4-2545, RG59, NA.

19. Briggs to Johnson, 26 Dec 1945, "711.5," Costa Rica: San José Embassy, Confidential File, Box 39, RG84, NA; see also DoS to Galo Plaza, 28 Dec 1945, Serie F, Documentos sobre Subditos de las Naciones del Eje, 1941 a 1946, Box 669 [38], MRE, AHQ.

20. Figures on the Jews from Harvey Strum, "Jewish Internees in the American South, 1942–1945," *American Jewish Archives* 42 (1990): 42–3, except for the returnee to Germany, Friedrich Karl Kaul, whom Strum missed, from Kaul's SWP records. See also C. Harvey Gardiner, *Pawns in a Triangle of Hate: The Peruvian Japanese and the United States* (Seattle: University of Washington Press, 1981), 170–1.

21. Major Richard N. Thompson to HQ Berlin Command, *Confiscation and Destruction of DP Identity Papers,* 19 Nov 1946, 340.1015/12–446, RG59, NA.

22. "Crueldad rusa llegó a extremos terribles no solo con los alemanes sin con ciudadaños de Naciones Unidas," *El Telégrafo,* 29 Sep 1946.

23. Owen to Dreier, 24 Feb 1947, 862.20210/2-2447, RG59, NA.

24. Flack to SecState, 12 Jan 1947, 340.1015/1-1147, RG59, NA.

25. Byrnes to AmReps, 31 Oct 1946, "711.5," Ecuador: Quito Embassy Confidential File, Box 34, RG84, NA.

26. Muccio to SecState, 31 Jan 1947, 340.1015/1-3147, RG59, NA; AmEmbParis to SecState, 10 Feb 1948, 711.62115AR/2-1048, RG59, NA.

27. "Crueldad rusa llegó a extremos terribles no solo con los alemanes sin con ciudadaños de Naciones Unidas," *El Telégrafo,* 29 Sep 1946.

28. Hugo Droege, interview by author, Guatemala City, 22 May 1996; Davis to SecState, 16 Jun 1948, 862.20210/6-1648, RG59, NA.

29. Knapp to Braden, 23 Sep 1946, 862.20210/9-2346, RG59, NA.

30. Linda Hunt, *Secret Agenda: the United States Government, Nazi Scientists, and Project Paperclip, 1945–1990* (New York: St. Martin's Press, 1991).

31. Christopher Simpson, *Blowback: The First Full Account of America's Recruitment of Nazis, and Its Disastrous Effect on Our Domestic and Foreign Policy* (New York: Weidenfeld & Nicholson, 1988).

32. Newbegin to Trueblood, 5 Dec 1946, 710.62115/12-546, RG59, NA.

33. Snow to Wright, 15 Aug 1947, 711.62115AR/8-1547, RG59, NA.

34. Lowell to Chappell, 28 Jan 1947, 711.62115AR/1-2847, RG59, NA.

35. Quoted in George C. Dix, *Totalitarians in the State Department,* Sep 1947(?), 710.62115/10-1146, RG59, NA. Dix was a lawyer representing many of the internees. This publication is predictably partisan and should be treated with care.

36. Clark to Marshall, 18 Sep 1947, 711.62115AR/9–1847, RG59, NA.

37. Dreier to Woodward, 25 Jul 1949, FW 840.48 Refugees/6-1049, M1284 reel 70, RG59, NA.

38. Martin to Barber, 27 Jul 1949, FW 840.48 Refugees/6-1049, M1284 reel 70, RG59, NA.

39. Mills to Woodward, 28 Jul 1949, FW 840.48 Refugees/6-1049, M1284 reel 70, RG59, NA. There were echoes here of a pre-1933 appreciation for Germans' "racial" contribution to Latin American development. For example, Woodrow Wilson's closest adviser, Colonel Edward House, believed that "the German population would be in every way preferable to the population now in the majority of South American countries." Cited in Lars Schoultz, *Beneath the*

United States: A History of U.S. Policy Toward Latin America (Cambridge, MA: Harvard University Press, 1998), 223.

40. Laurence Whitehead, "Bolivia," in *Latin America between the Second World War and the Cold War, 1944–1948,* Leslie Bethell and Ian Roxborough, eds. (Cambridge: Cambridge University Press, 1992),

41. Steve Lewontin, "'A Blessed Peace': Honduras under Carías," in *Honduras: Portrait of a Captive Nation,* Nancy Peckenham and Annie Street, eds. (New York: Praeger, 1985), 87.

Conclusion

1. Sumner Welles, "Intervention and Interventions," *Foreign Affairs* 26:1 (1947): 116–33, quoted at 116.

2. Sources on comparative internment practices are to be found in the Bibliography.

3. Federal law 50 U.S.C. 21.

4. The last applies to those Japanese and German civilians who were forced to clear tropical jungle and construct their own internment camp in the Panama Canal Zone, where they were held en route to the United States. See Chapter 5.

5. Article 23 of the 1907 Hague Convention on Laws and Customs of War on Land, for example, includes a prohibition "to declare abolished, suspended, or inadmissible in a court of law the rights and actions of the nationals of the hostile party." See Natsu Taylor Saito, "Justice Held Hostage: U.S. Disregard for International Law in the World War II Internment of Japanese Peruvians – A Case Study," *Boston College Law Review* 40: 1 (December 1998): 275–348.

6. Albrecht to St.S & RAM, *Behandlung den Reichsdeutschen in Amerika and Deutsche Gegenmassnahmen,* 6 Feb 1942, "Deutsche Zivilgefangene in den Verein. Staaten. v. Amerika 1941–1942," R41876, Rechtsabteilung, Politisches Archiv des Auswärtigen Amtes, Bonn (hereafter PAAA); Albrecht to R IV, 26 Nov 1942, "Zivilgefangenen-Austausch-Vereinigten Staaten von Amerika," R41564, Rechtsabteilung, PAAA.

7. Roosevelt to Hull, 15 Aug 1942, 740.00115EW1939/4348, RG59. Copy in folder "Dept. of State July–Dec 1942," OF 20, Box 10, FDR Library.

8. See Chapter 6. Clattenburg continued to insist even after the war was over that the Jewish internees should be returned to Germany because, he said, there was no longer any anti-Semitism in that country, and he claimed that every one of the Jewish internees from Panama had pro-Nazi feelings. Harvey Strum, "Jewish Internees in the American South, 1942–1945," *American Jewish Archives* 42 (1990): 27–48, cited at 41.

9. Bonsal to Brandt and Long, *Internment of Dangerous Aliens in the United States Now at Large in the Other American Republics,* 14 Jun 1943, "General Memoranda May–June 1943," Memoranda Relating to General Latin American Affairs, Box 8, ARA, RG59, National Archives, College Park, Maryland (NA).

Glossary

TERMS AND ABBREVIATIONS

Abwehr	German military intelligence
ACLU	American Civil Liberties Union
AECS	Alien Enemy Control Section, DoS
AECU	Alien Enemy Control Unit, DoJ
AHQ	Archivo Histórico de Quito, Ecuador
AMRE	Archivo General del Ministerio de Relaciones Exteriores, Bogotá, Colombia
AN	Archivo Nacional, San José, Costa Rica
ARA	Division of American Republics, DoS; renamed the Office of American Republic Affairs in 1944.
Auslandsdeutsche	Germans abroad, both citizens and noncitizens
Auslandsorganisation (AO)	Nazi Party Foreign Organization
Auswärtiges Amt (AA)	German Foreign Ministry
BA-K	Bundesarchiv Koblenz
BA-L	Bundesarchiv Berlin-Lichterfelde
BDC	Berlin Documents Center
CIAA	Coordinator of Inter-American Affairs
CIRMA	Centro de Investigaciones Regionales de Meso America, Antigua, Guatemala
COI	Coordinator of Information
CPD	Emergency Advisory Committee for Political Defense
Deutsche Arbeiter Front (DAF)	Nazi trade union
DoJ	Department of Justice
DoS	Department of State
FC	Division of Foreign Activity Correlation, DoS

finca	plantation or farm
G-2	Military Intelligence Division (also MID)
HJ	*Hitlerjugend*; Hitler Youth
Landesgruppenleiter	leader of countrywide Nazi organization
LC	Library of Congress
legation	diplomatic post not yet having embassy status
minister	ranking diplomatic envoy in a legation
MNR	Movimiento Nacional Revolucionario
MRE	Ministerio de Relaciones Exteriores (Foreign Ministry)
NSDAP	official abbreviation of the Nazi Party: *Nationalsozialistische Deutsche Arbeiterpartei* (German National Socialist Workers Party)
ONI	Office of Naval Intelligence
Ortsgruppenleiter	leader of local Nazi Party group
OSS	Office of Strategic Services
PAAA	Politisches Archiv des Auswärtigen Amtes, Bonn
Parteigenosse (Pg.)	Party member
PL	Proclaimed List of Certain Blocked Nationals
RAC	Rockefeller Archive Center
Reichsdeutsche	German citizen
RSHA	*Reichssicherheitshauptamt*; Reich Security Main Office
SBA	Schweizerisches Bundesarchiv, Bern
SCADTA	Sociedad Colombo-Alemana de Transportes Aéreos
SD	Special Division, DoS
SEDTA	Sociedad Ecuatoriana de Transportes Aéreos
SWP	Special War Problems Division, DoS
Volksdeutsche	ethnic German without German citizenship
WRB	War Refugee Board
WTI	Division of World Trade Intelligence, DoS

Select Bibliography

This study is based on documentary research in sixteen archives in seven countries, supplemented by interviews with more than forty participants and witnesses. Documents found in Latin American, German, and Swiss archives proved essential to reaching a balanced understanding of events without repeating the error of U.S. policymakers, whose perspectives so often remained firmly rooted in Washington.

I chose to approach both oral and written sources skeptically, reading them against one another. Recorded memory can be just as selective, or obfuscatory, as spoken memory and often needs correction – although in this case the highly charged nature of the topic made questioning an especially delicate process. A few interviewees, confronted for the first time in fifty years with evidence of their Nazi Party membership, reacted in ways that were admittedly more dramatic than informative. More often, interviewees were cooperative and helped illuminate the paper trail. In the small-town atmosphere of the German communities of Guatemala, Ecuador, Costa Rica, and Colombia, it was usually possible to find several people who had experienced the same event, and whose independent recollections could be compared with one another and with the written sources.

One of the key documentary sources referred to frequently in this study is my own tabulation and analysis of the records of 531 postwar investigations of individual cases conducted by the Alien Enemy Control Section of the State Department in late 1945 and early 1946 (Name Files of Enemy Aliens, SWP Boxes 31–50). During this period, the AECS compiled all the information about each German internee from Latin America still in U.S. custody at the end of the war that could be obtained from an array of government departments, including the embassies and intelligence agencies, and held hearings for the internees for the first time. Although these reports are not free of errors, they represent the most reliable official records available for discussing individual cases; taken together, they provide a detailed look at a cross-section of the internee population and at the German communities from which they were drawn.

Translations of foreign-language documents and interviews are the author's unless otherwise noted.

ARCHIVES

Colombia

Bogotá
Archivo General del Ministerio de Relaciones Exteriores (AMRE)
  Actividades Nazis
  Embajada de Colombia en Washington
  Estados Unidos – Embajadas – Consulados 1940–42
  Informes Confidenciales – Nazis
  Listas Negras – 1941
  Reclamación Sobre Bienes de Alemanes, Años 1939–61

Costa Rica

San José
Archivo Nacional (AN)
  Junta de Custodia

Ecuador

Quito
Archivo Histórico de Quito (AHQ)
Ministerio de Relaciones Exteriores (MRE)
  Embajada de Estados Unidos
  Embajada del Ecuador en Washington
  Documentos sobre Subditos de las Naciones del Eje, 1941 a 1946

Germany

Bonn
Politisches Archiv des Auswärtigen Amtes (PAAA)
  Rechtsabteilung
    Zivilgefangene
    Zivilinternierte
    Austausch
  Inland II g: Südamerika
    SD-Meldungen
    Tätigkeit des SD, d- Abwehr, d- Agenten und Polizeiattachés
  Kulturabteilung
    Rückwanderung aus Südamerika – Allgemeines
    Reichskommisar für die Festigung deutschen Volkstums
  Chef A/O (Auslandsorganisation)
  Handelspolitische Abteilung IX b

Koblenz
Bundesarchiv Koblenz (BA-K)

Nachlasse Kraske
R 64 III/4: Lateinamerikanischer Verein

Berlin
Bundesarchiv Berlin-Lichterfelde (BA-L)
   Auslandsorganisation der NSDAP
     Rückwandereramt der AO
     Statistik
Ibero-Amerikanisches Institut Preußischer Kulturbesitz
   Monographs and serials on German communities in Latin America
   Newspaper clip files

Guatemala

Antigua
Centro de Investigaciones Regionales de Meso America (CIRMA)

Guatemala City
German Embassy
   German deportees collection, special file

Switzerland

Bern
Schweizerisches Bundesarchiv (SBA)
   E2200 Washington/15
   E2001-02/17

United States

College Park, Maryland
National Archives (NA)
   RG38 Office of Naval Intelligence (ONI)
   RG59 State Department
     Special War Problems Division (SWP)
     Division of American Republics (ARA)
     Foreign Activity Correlation (FC)
     Central Decimal Files, especially:
       711.62115AR: German civilian prisoners from American Republics
       740.00112RP: Axis Replacement Program, expropriation
       740.00115EW1939: civilian exchanges, European War
       740.00115PW: civilian exchanges, Pacific War
       800.202xx: general subversive activities in country xx
       862.202xx: German subversive activities in country xx
       8xx.00N: Nazi activities in country xx
       862.20210 [Lastname, Firstname]: reports of German subversive activity by
         individuals

RG60 Justice Department
   Alien Enemy Control Unit – Closed Legal Case Files
   Special War Policies Unit – Latin American Section
RG84 Post Records (Embassies and Consulates)
   Bolivia
   Colombia
   Costa Rica
   Ecuador
RG165 Military Intelligence Division (MID or G-2)
   Latin American Branch
RG226 Office of Strategic Services (OSS)
RG229 Office of the Coordinator of Inter-American Affairs (CIAA)
RG242 Berlin Documents Center (BDC)
RG319 Army Staff
   Army Intelligence Decimal File
      Entry 47C Military Attachés, country
         intelligence
RG389 Provost Marshal General
   Alien Enemy Information Bureau

Hyde Park, New York
Franklin D. Roosevelt Library
   President's Secretary File (PSF)
   President's Personal File (PPF)
   President's Official File (OF)
   Map Room File (MR)
   Harry Hopkins Papers
   Sumner Welles Papers
   Henry Morgenthau, Jr., Papers and Diary
   James Rowe Papers
   John C. Wiley Papers
   Adolf Berle Papers
   Francis Biddle Papers
   Francis Corrigan Papers

Independence, Missouri
Harry S. Truman Library
   Merwin L. Bohan
   John M. Cabot

New Haven, Connecticut
Manuscripts and Archives, Yale University Library
   Arthur Bliss Lane Papers

New York City
Columbia University Oral History Research Project
   Spruille Braden
   Nelson Rockefeller

North Tarrytown, New York
Rockefeller Archive Center (RAC)
  Nelson A. Rockefeller Personal Files
  Nelson A. Rockefeller Washington, DC, Files

Washington, DC
Library of Congress (LC)
  Manuscript Division
    Philip W. Bonsal Papers
    Cordell Hull Papers
    Breckinridge Long Papers
    Josephus Daniels Diary
  Prints and Photographs Division
    German War Propaganda for Latin America
Georgetown University Foreign Affairs Oral History Collection
  W. Tapley Bennett, Jr.
  William Belton
  Ralph N. Clough
  Larue R. Lutkins

PUBLISHED DOCUMENTS

Auswärtiges Amt. *Akten zur deutschen auswärtigen Politik, 1918–1945*. Series D
  (1937–41). 13 vols. Baden, Frankfurt am Main, Bonn: Imprimerie Nationale,
  P.~Keppler Verlag, Gebr. Hermes, 1950–64. Series E (1941–45). 8 vols.
  Göttingen: Vanderhoeck & Rupprecht, 1969–79.
Auswärtiges Amt. *Documents on German Foreign Policy, 1918–45*. Series D (1937–45).
  13 vols. Washington and London: GPO/HMSO, 1949–64.
Commission on Wartime Relocation and Internment of Civilians. *Personal Justice
  Denied*. Washington, DC: Government Printing Office, 1982.
Department of State. *Bulletin*. 1939–47.
Department of State. Emergency Advisory Committee for Political Defense of the
  Hemisphere. *Annual Reports*.
Department of State. *Foreign Relations of the United States: Diplomatic Papers [FRUS]*,
  1939–1946. Washington, DC: Government Printing Office, 1967–69.
Military Intelligence Division. *Axis Espionage and Propaganda in Latin America*.
  Washington, DC: War Department, 1946.
Ministerio de Relaciones Exteriores. *Memoria presentada al Congreso Nacional*.
  Bogotá: Imprenta Nacional, 1939–48.
Senate Committee on Military Affairs. *Nazi Party Membership Records*. Senate Com-
  mittee Prints 79/2/46, Part 2, Mar 1946, and Part 3, Sep 1946, S1535–S1538.
  Washington, DC: U.S. Government Printing Office, 1946.

AUTHOR'S INTERVIEWS

Anonymous member of Jewish community, Guatemala City, 29 May 1996.
Werner Ascoli, Guatemala City, 24 May 1996.
Hans Bansbach, San José, Costa Rica, 23 Mar 1998.

Gunter Beckmann, Quito, 21 Jan 1998.
Eva Bloch, Guayaquil, 18 Feb 1998.
Gerardo Bohnenberger, Guatemala City, 18 May 1996.
Alfredo Brauer, Quito, 5 Feb 1998.
Hardy de von Campe, Guayaquil, 16 Feb 1998.
Jochen Chrambach, Quito, 23 Jan 1998.
Marianne Chrambach, Quito, 23 Jan 1998.
Hugo Droege, Guatemala City, 22 May 1996.
Oda Droege, Guatemala City, 22 May 1996.
Carlos Gehlert, Guatemala City, 30 May 1996.
Hans Griesbach, Quito, 8 Feb 1998.
Ilse Grossman, Quito, 30 Jan 1998.
Roberto Hahn, Guayaquil, 16 Feb 1998.
Walter Held, Bogotá, 9 Mar 1998.
Carlos Heymann Albán, Guayaquil, 18 Feb 1998.
Charlie Hirtz, Quito, 22 Jan 1998.
Sabine Hirtz, Quito, 22 Jan 1998.
Raymond Ickes, Berkeley, CA, 18 Sep 1997.
Werner J. Kappel (telephone), Sun City Center, FL, 30 Mar 1999, 25 Feb 2000.
Barbara Knebusch, Guatemala City, 26 May 1996.
Federico Knebusch, Guatemala City, 26 May 1996.
Hans Kolter, Guatemala City, 27 May 1996.
Gunter Lisken, Guayaquil, 17 Feb 1998.
Gerardo López, Bogotá, 6 Mar 1998.
Heinz Luedeking (telephone), Miami, 25 Feb 2000, 7 Jul 2000.
Walter Maul, Guatemala City, 30 May 1996.
Hans Niemann, Guatemala City, 30 May 1996.
Goetz Pfeil-Schneider, Bogotá, 15 Mar 1998.
Carl Riemann, Guayaquil, 16 Feb 1998.
Nina Roppel, Bogotá, 17 Mar 1998.
Hans Joachim Schaer, San José, Costa Rica, 26 Mar 1998.
Inge von Schröter, San José, Costa Rica, 26 Mar 1998.
Ilse Schwark, Quito, 28 Jan 1998.
Otto Luis Schwarz, Guayaquil, 16 Feb 1998.
Eva Sello, Guatemala City, 27 May 1996.
Joe Sello, Guatemala City, 27 May 1996.
Walter Sommer, Bogotá, 13 Mar 1998.
Hans Ungar, Bogotá, 16 Mar 1998.
Regina Wagner, Guatemala City, 17 May 1996.
Frank Weilbauer, Quito, 27 Jan 1998.

BOOKS

Abecia Baldivieso, Valentín. *Las relaciones internacionales en la historia de Bolivia.*
    2 vols. Vol. 2. La Paz: Editorial los Amigos del Libro, 1979.
Acheson, Dean. *Present at the Creation: My Years in the State Department.* New York:
    W. W. Norton & Co., 1969.

Aguilar Bulgarelli, Oscar R. *Costa Rica y sus hechos políticos de 1948. Problemática de una década*. San José: Editorial Costa Rica, 1969.

Alfaro, Ricardo J. *Medio siglo de relaciones entre Panamá y los Estados Unidos*. Panama [Secretaría de Información de la Presidencia de la República], 1959.

Allen, William Sheridan. *The Nazi Seizure of Power: The Experience of a Single German Town, 1930–1935*. New York: New Viewpoints, 1973.

Ameringer, Charles D. *Democracy in Costa Rica*. New York: Praeger, 1982.

   Don Pepe: A Political Biography of José Figueres of Costa Rica. Albuquerque: University of New Mexico Press, 1978.

Anderson, Thomas P. *Matanza: El Salvador's Communist Revolt of 1932*. Lincoln: University of Nebraska Press, 1971.

Andrade, Victor. *My Missions for Revolutionary Bolivia, 1944–1962*. Pittsburgh: University of Pittsburgh Press, 1976.

Argueta, Mario. *Tiburcio Carías: anatomía de una época, 1923–1948*. Tegucigalpa: Editorial Guaymuras, 1989.

Aron, Werner and Gert Aron. *The Halo of the Jungle*. Quito: n.p., 1967, rev. 1996.

Ascoli, Werner. Unpublished memoirs. Guatemala City: n.p., 1980–96.

Atkins, George Pope and Larman C. Wilson. *The United States and the Trujillo Regime*. New Brunswick, NJ: Rutgers University Press, 1972.

Bade, Klaus J., ed. *Population, Labour and Migration in 19th and 20th Century Germany*. New York: St. Martin's, 1987.

Bankier, David. *The Germans and the Final Solution: Public Opinion under Nazism*. Boston: Blackwell, 1996.

Bauer, Yehuda. *Jews for Sale? Nazi-Jewish Negotiations, 1933–1945*. New Haven, CT: Yale University Press, 1994.

Beals, Carleton. *The Coming Struggle for Latin America*. Philadelphia: Lippincott, 1938.

   Dawn over the Amazon. New York: Duell, Sloan and Pearce, 1943.

Behrendt, Richard F. *The Economic Defense of the Western Hemisphere: A Study in Conflicts*. Washington, DC: American Council on Public Affairs, 1941.

Bemis, Samuel Flagg. *The Latin American Policy of the United States*. New York: Harcourt, Brace & Co., 1943.

Berle, Adolf A. *Latin America: Diplomacy and Reality*. New York: Harper & Row, 1962.

Bessel, Richard. *Political Violence and the Rise of Nazism*. New Haven, CT: Yale University Press, 1984.

Bethell, Leslie and Ian Roxborough, eds. *Latin America between the Second World War and the Cold War, 1944–1948*. Cambridge: Cambridge University Press, 1992.

Bickelmann, Hartmut. *Die deutsche Überseeauswanderung in der Weimarer Zeit*. Wiesbaden: Steiner, 1980.

Biddle, Francis. *In Brief Authority*. New York: Doubleday and Co., 1962.

Bidwell, Percy. *Economic Defense of Latin America*. Boston: World Peace Foundation, 1941.

Bischoff, Ralph F. *Nazi Conquest Through German Culture*. Cambridge, MA: Harvard University Press, 1942.

Black, George. *The Good Neighbor: How the United States Wrote the History of Central America and the Caribbean*. New York: Pantheon Books, 1988.

Blancpain, Jean-Pierre. *Les Allemands au Chili, 1816–1945.* Cologne: Böhlau Verlag, 1974.

    Migrations et mémoires germaniques en Amérique Latine. Strasbourg: Presses Universitaires de Strasbourg, 1994.

Blasier, Cole. *The Hovering Giant: U.S. Responses to Revolutionary Change in Latin America 1910–1985.* Pittsburgh: University of Pittsburgh Press, 1985.

Blum, John Morton. *From the Morgenthau Diaries.* New York: Houghton Mifflin, 1959.

Bowers, Claude G. *Chile through Embassy Windows, 1939–1953.* New York: Simon & Schuster, 1958.

Braden, Spruille. *Diplomats and Demagogues.* New Rochelle, NY: Arlington House, 1971.

Breitman, Richard and Alan M. Kraut. *American Refugee Policy and European Jewry, 1933–1945.* Bloomington: Indiana University Press, 1981.

Brepohl de Magalhães, Marionilde. *Pangermanismo e Nazismo: A trajetória alemã rumo ao Brasil.* Campinas, Brazil: Editora da UNICAMP/FAPESP, 1998.

Briggs, Ellis. *Farewell to Foggy Bottom: The Recollections of a Career Diplomat.* New York: David McKay, 1964.

Brooks, Roy L., ed. *When Sorry Isn't Enough: The Controversy over Apologies and Reparations for Human Injustice.* New York: New York University Press, 1999.

Browning, Christopher R. *The Final Solution and the German Foreign Office.* New York: Holmes & Meier Publishers, 1978.

Brustein, William. *The Logic of Evil: The Social Origins of the Nazi Party, 1925–1933.* New Haven, CT: Yale University Press, 1996.

Buchheit, Gerd. *Der deutsche Geheimdienst: Geschichte der militärischen Abwehr.* Munich: List, 1966.

Buhite, Russell D. and David W. Levy, eds. *FDR's Fireside Chats.* Norman: University of Oklahoma Press, 1992.

Bulmer-Thomas, Victor. *The Political Economy of Central America Since 1920.* Cambridge: Cambridge University Press, 1987.

Burden, William. *The Struggle for Airways in Latin America.* New York: Arno Press, 1977.

Burdrick, Charles B. *An American Island in Hitler's Reich: The Bad Neuheim Internment.* Menlo Park, CA: Markgraf, 1987.

Burr, Robert N. and Roland D. Hussey, eds. *Documents on Inter-American Cooperation, 1881–1948.* 2 vols. Vol. 2. Philadelphia: University of Pennsylvania Press, 1955.

Bushnell, David. *Eduardo Santos and the Good Neighbor 1938–1942.* Gainesville: University of Florida Press, 1967.

Bussmann, Claus. *Treu Deutsch und Evangelisch: Die Geschichte der Deutschen Evangelischen Gemeinde zu Asunción/Paraguay von 1893–1963.* Stuttgart: Franz Steiner Verlag Wiesbaden GMBH, 1989.

Cabot, John Moors. *First Line of Defense: Forty Years' Experiences of a Career Diplomat.* Washington, DC: School of Foreign Service, Georgetown University, 1980[?].

Callcott, Wilfrid Hardy. *The Western Hemisphere: Its Influence on United States Policies to the End of World War II.* Austin: University of Texas Press, 1968.

Calvo Gamboa, Carlos. *Costa Rica en la segunda guerra mundial, 1939–1945.* San José: Editorial Universidad Estatal a Distancia, 1985.

Canedy, Susan. *America's Nazis: A History of the German American Bund*. Menlo Park, CA: Markgraf, 1990.

Cesarani, David and Tony Kushner, eds. *The Internment of Aliens in Twentieth Century Britain*. London: Frank Cass, 1993.

Céspedes, Augusto. *El presidente colgado: historia boliviana*. Buenos Aires: Jorge Alvarez, 1966.

Chan, Sucheng. *Asian Americans: An Interpretive History*. Boston: Twayne Publishers, 1991.

Childers, Thomas. *The Nazi Voter: The Social Foundations of Fascism in Germany, 1919–1933*. Chapel Hill: University of North Carolina Press, 1983.

Christgau, John. *Enemies: World War II Alien Internment*. Ames: Iowa State University Press, 1985.

Compton, James V. *The Swastika and the Eagle: Hitler, the United States, and the Origins of the Second World War*. London: Bodley, 1968.

Conn, Stetson and Byron Fairchild. *The Framework of Hemisphere Defense*. Washington, DC: Office of the Chief of Military History, Department of the Army, 1960.

Conn, Stetson, Rose C. Engleman and Byron Fairchild. *Guarding the United States and Its Outposts*. Washington, DC: Office of the Chief of Military History, Department of the Army, 1964.

Connell-Smith, Gordon. *The Inter-American System*. New York: Oxford University Press, 1966.

   The United States and Latin America: An Historical Analysis of Inter-American Relations. New York: John Wiley and Sons, 1974.

Conniff, Michael L. *Panama and the United States: The Forced Alliance*. Athens: University of Georgia Press, 1992.

Corbett, P. Scott. *Quiet Passages: The Exchange of Civilians between the United States and Japan during the Second World War*. Kent, OH: Kent State University Press, 1987.

Cousségal, Raymond Mériguet. *Antinazismo en Ecuador años 1941–1944*. Quito: R. Mériguet Cousségal, 1988.

Crassweller, Robert D. *Trujillo: The Life and Times of a Caribbean Dictator*. New York: Macmillan, 1966.

Cronon, E. David. *Josephus Daniels in Mexico*. Madison: University of Wisconsin Press, 1960.

Cuestas Gomez, Carlos Humberto. *Cotito, Crónica de un Crimen Olvidado*. Panama: n.p., 1993.

Cull, Nicholas John. *Selling War: The British Propaganda Campaign Against American 'Neutrality' in World War II*. New York: Oxford University Press, 1995.

Dallek, Robert. *Franklin D. Roosevelt and American Foreign Policy, 1932–1945*. Oxford: Oxford University Press, 1979.

Daniels, Roger. *Asian America: Chinese and Japanese in the United States since 1850*. Seattle: University of Washington Press, 1988.

   Concentration Camps USA. New York: Holt, Rinehart and Winston, 1971.

   The Decision to Relocate the Japanese Americans. Philadelphia: J. B. Lippincott, 1975.

DeConde, Alexander. *Herbert Hoover's Latin America Policy*. Stanford, CA: Stanford University Press, 1951.

De Jong, Louis. *The German Fifth Column in the Second World War*. Chicago: University of Chicago Press, 1956.

Deutsch, Sandra McGee. *Las Derechas: The Extreme Right in Argentina, Brazil, and Chile, 1890–1939*. Stanford, CA: Stanford University Press, 1999.

Deutsche Vereine im Ausland. *Wir Deutsche in der Welt*. Berlin: Verlagsanstalt Otto Stollberg, 1935.

Deutsches Auslands Institut. *Deutsche in Übersee*. Stuttgart: DAI, 1938.

Diamond, Sander A. *The Nazi Movement in the United States, 1924–1941*. Ithaca, NY: Cornell University Press, 1974.

Diederich, Bernard. *Somoza and the Legacy of U.S. Involvement in Central America*. London: Junction Books, 1982.

Dodd, Jr., William E. and Martha Dodd, eds. *Ambassador Dodd's Diary*. New York: Harcourt, Brace, and Co., 1941.

Dorwart, Jeffrey M. *Conflict of Duty: The U.S. Navy's Intelligence Dilemma, 1919–1945*. Annapolis, MD: Naval Institute Press, 1983.

Dosal, Paul. *Power in Transition: The Rise of Guatemala's Industrial Oligarchy, 1871–1994*. Westport, CT: Praeger, 1995.

Döscher, Hans-Jürgen. *Das Auswärtige Amt im Dritten Reich: Diplomatie im Schatten der Endlösung*. Berlin: Siedler Verlag, 1987.

Dozer, Donald. *Are We Good Neighbors? Three Decades of Inter-American Relations, 1930–1960*. Gainseville: University of Florida Press, 1959.

Drake, Paul. *Socialism and Populism in Chile 1932–1952*. Urbana: University of Illinois Press, 1978.

Drekonja, Gerhard. *Retos de la política exterior colombiana*. Bogotá: Fondo Editorial Cerec, 1983.

Dubois, Jules. *Danger over Panama*. Indianapolis, IN: Bobbs-Merrill, 1964.

Duggan, Laurence. *The Americas: The Search for Hemisphere Security*. New York: Henry Holt and Co., 1949.

Dunkerley, James. *The Long War: Dictatorship and Revolution in El Salvador*. London: Verso, 1982.

Power in the Isthmus: A Political History of Modern Central America. London: Verso, 1988.

Ebel, Arnold. *Das Dritte Reich und Argentinien: Die diplomatischen Beziehungen unter besonderer Berücksichtigung der Handelspolitik, 1933–1939*. Köln: Böhlau, 1971.

Elkin, Judith Laikin. *Jews of the Latin American Republics*. Chapel Hill: University of North Carolina Press, 1980.

Elkin, Judith Laikin and Gilbert W. Merkx, eds. *The Jewish Presence in Latin America*. Boston: Allen & Unwin, 1987.

Emmerson, John K. *The Japanese Thread: A Life in the U.S. Foreign Service*. New York: Holt, Rinehart and Winston, 1978.

Farago, Ladislas. *The Game of the Foxes: The Untold Story of German Espionage in the United States and Great Britain during World War II*. New York: David McKay, 1971.

Feingold, Henry L. *The Politics of Rescue: The Roosevelt Administration and the Holocaust, 1938–1945*. New Brunswick, NJ: Rutgers University Press, 1970.

Fellmann Velarde, José. *Victor Paz Estenssoro: el hombre y la revolución*. La Paz: Burillo, 1955.

Fernández Artucio, Hugo. *The Nazi Underground in South America.* New York: Farrar & Rinehart, 1942.

Fiebig-von Hase, Ragnhild. *Lateinamerika als Konfliktherd der deutsch-amerikanischen Beziehungen 1890–1903: Vom Beginn der Panamapolitik bis zur Venezuelakrise von 1902/03.* 2 vols. Göttingen: Vandenhoeck & Ruprecht, 1986.

Findling, John E. *Close Neighbors, Distant Friends: United States-Central American Relations.* New York: Greenwood Press, 1987.

Floto, Jobst-H. *Die Beziehungen Deutschlands zu Venezuela 1933 bis 1958.* Frankfurt: Peter Lang, 1991.

Fox, Stephen. *America's Invisible Gulag: A Biography of German American Internment & Exclusion in World War II.* New York: Peter Lang, 2000.

  The Unknown Internment: An Oral History of the Relocation of Italian Americans during World War II. Boston: Twayne, 1990.

Francis, Michael Jackson. *The Limits of Hegemony: United States Relations with Argentina and Chile during World War II.* Notre Dame, IN: University of Notre Dame Press, 1977.

Frank, Gary. *Struggle for Hegemony in South America: Argentina, Brazil, and the United States during the Second World War.* Miami: Center for Advanced International Studies, University of Miami, 1979.

Fröschle, Hartmut, ed. *Die Deutschen in Lateinamerika: Schicksal und Leistung.* Tübingen: Horst Erdmann Verlag, 1979.

Frye, Alton. *Nazi Germany and the American Hemisphere.* New Haven, CT: Yale University Press, 1967.

Funke, Manfred, ed. *Hitler, Deutschland und die Mächte. Materialien zur Außenpolitik des Dritten Reiches.* Düsseldorf: Droste Verlag, 1978.

Furtado Kestler, Izabela Maria. *Die Exilliteratur und das Exil der deutschsprachigen Schiftsteller und Publizisten in Brasilien.* Frankfurt: P. Lang, 1992.

Galvis, Silvia and Alberto Donadio. *Colombia Nazi, 1939–1945: Espionaje alemán, la cacería del FBI, Santos, López, y los pactos secretos.* Bogotá: Planeta Colombiana Editorial S.A., 1986.

Gantenbein, James, ed. *The Evolution of Our Latin American Policy: A Documentary Record.* New York: Columbia University Press, 1950.

Gardiner, C. Harvey. *Pawns in a Triangle of Hate: The Peruvian Japanese and the United States.* Seattle: University of Washington Press, 1981.

Gardner, Lloyd C. *Economic Aspects of New Deal Diplomacy.* Madison: University of Wisconsin Press, 1964.

Gaudig, Olaf and Peter Veit. *Der Widerschein des Nazismus: Das Bild des Nationalsozialismus in der deutschsprachigen Presse Argentiniens, Brasiliens und Chiles 1932–1945.* Berlin: Wissenschaftlicher Verlag, 1997.

Gellman, Irwin F. *Good Neighbor Diplomacy: United States Policies in Latin America, 1933–1945.* Baltimore: Johns Hopkins University Press, 1979.

  Roosevelt and Batista: Good Neighbor Diplomacy in Cuba, 1933–1945. Albuquerque: University of New Mexico Press, 1973.

  Secret Affairs: Franklin Roosevelt, Cordell Hull, and Sumner Welles. Baltimore: Johns Hopkins University Press, 1995.

Gertz, René. *O fascismo no sul de Brasil. Germanismo – Nazismo – Integralismo.* Porto Alegre: Mercado Aberto, 1987.

O perigo alemao. Porto Alegre: Editora da Universidade Federal do Rio Grande do Sul, 1991.

Gillman, Peter and Leni Gillman. *'Collar the Lot!' How Britain Interned and Expelled its Wartime Refugees*. London: Quartet Books, 1980.

Giudici, Ernesto. *Hitler conquista América*. Buenos Aires: Editorial Acento, 1938.

Gleijeses, Piero. *Shattered Hope: The Guatemalan Revolution and the United States, 1944–1954*. Princeton, NJ: Princeton University Press, 1991.

Goda, Norman J. W. *Tomorrow the World: Hitler, Northwest Africa, and the Path toward America*. College Station: Texas A&M University Press, 1998.

Gordon, David L. and Royden Dangerfield. *The Hidden Weapon: The Story of Economic Warfare*. New York: Harper, 1947.

Graff, Frank. *Strategy of Involvement: A Diplomatic Biography of Sumner Welles*. New York: Garland, 1988.

Graham, Richard, ed. *The Idea of Race in Latin America, 1870–1940*. Austin: University of Texas Press, 1990.

Green, David. *The Containment of Latin America: a History of the Myths and Realities of the Good Neighbor Policy*. Chicago: Quadrangle Books, 1971.

Grieb, Kenneth J. *Guatemalan Caudillo: The Regime of Jorge Ubico, Guatemala 1931–1944*. Athens: Ohio University Press, 1979.

Grodzins, Morton. *Americans Betrayed: Politics and the Japanese Evacuation*. Chicago: University of Chicago Press, 1949.

Grothe, Hugo. *Die Deutschen in Übersee, eine Skizze ihres werdens, ihrer Verbreitung und Kulturarbeit*. Berlin: Zentralverlag, 1932.

Grow, Michael. *The Good Neighbor Policy and Authoritarianism in Paraguay: United States Economic Expansion and Great-Power Rivalry in Latin America during World War II*. Lawrence: Regents Press of Kansas, 1981.

Gruening, Ernest. *Many Battles: The Autobiography of Ernest Gruening*. New York: Liveright, 1973.

Guerrant, Edward O. *Roosevelt's Good Neighbor Policy*. Albuquerque: University of New Mexico Press, 1950.

Gunther, John. *Inside Latin America*. New York: Harper & Brothers, 1941.

Haglund, David. *Latin America and the Transformation of U.S. Strategic Thought*. Albuquerque: University of New Mexico Press, 1984.

Hamilton, Richard. *Who Voted for Hitler?* Princeton, NJ: Princeton University Press, 1982.

Handy, Jim. *Revolution in the Countryside: Rural Conflict and Agrarian Reform in Guatemala, 1944–1954*. Chapel Hill: University of North Carolina Press, 1994.

Harms-Baltzer, Käte. *Die Nationalisierung der deutschen Einwanderer und ihrer Nachkommen in Brasilien als Problem der deutsch-brasilianischen Beziehungen 1930–1938*. Berlin: Colloquium Verlag, 1970.

Hassel, Georg von. *Die Auslandsdeutsche. Ihr Schaffen und ihre Verbreitung über die Erde*. Berlin (?), 1926.

Hastedt, Pedro Guillermo. *Deutsche Direktinvestionen in Lateinamerika: ihre Entwicklung seit dem Ersten Weltkrieg und ihre Bedeutung für die Industrialisierung des Subkontinents*. Göttingen: Otto Schwartz & Co., 1970.

Heinemann, Edgar A. *Lilric*. Guatemala City: Afanes, S.A., 1993.

Heinrichs, Waldo. *Threshold of War: Franklin D. Roosevelt and the American Entry into World War II*. New York: Oxford University Press, 1988.

Hellman, Florence S. *Nazi Fifth Column Activities: A List of References*. Washington, DC: Library of Congress, 1943.

Henderson, James D. *Conservative Thought in Twentieth Century Latin America: The Ideas of Laureano Gómez*. Athens: Ohio University Center for International Studies, 1988.

Herrera Balharry, Eugenio. *Los alemanes y el estado cafetalero*. San José: Editorial Universidad Estatal a Distancia, 1988.

Herring, Hubert. *Good Neighbors: Argentina, Brazil, Chile and Seventeen Other Countries*. New Haven, CT: Yale University Press, 1941.

Herzstein, Robert E. *Roosevelt and Hitler: Prelude to War*. New York: John Wiley & Sons, 1989.

Higashide, Seiichi. *Adios to Tears: The Memoirs of a Japanese-Peruvian Internee in U.S. Concentration Camps*. Honolulu: E & E Kudo, 1993.

Hildebrand, Klaus. *Deutsche Außenpolitik 1933–1945: Kalkül oder Dogma?* Stuttgart: Kohlhammer, 1973.

    Vom Reich zum Weltreich: Hitler, NSDAP und die koloniale Frage 1919–1945. München: W. Fink, 1962.

Hillgruber, Andreas, ed. *Staatsmänner und Diplomaten bei Hitler: Vertrauliche Aufzeichnungen über Unterredungen mit Vertretern des Auslandes 1942–1944*. Frankfurt: Bernard u. Graefe, 1970.

Hilton, Stanley E. *Brazil and the Great Powers, 1930–1939: The Politics of Trade Rivalry*. Austin: University of Texas Press, 1975.

    Hitler's Secret War in South America 1939–1945: German Military Espionage and Allied Counterespionage in Brazil. Baton Rouge: Louisiana State University Press, 1981.

    Oswaldo Aranha: uma biografia. Rio de Janeiro: Editorial Objetiva, 1994.

Holian, Timothy J. *The German-Americans and World War II: An Ethnic Experience*. New York: Lang, 1996.

Houwald, Götz von. *Los alemanes en Nicaragua*. Managua: Editorial y Litografía San José, 1975.

Hull, Cordell. *The Foreign Commercial Policy of the United States*. Washington, DC: U.S. Government Printing Office, 1935.

    The Memoirs of Cordell Hull. 2 vols. New York: Macmillan, 1948.

Humphreys, R. A. *Latin America and the Second World War*. 2 vols. London: Athlone, 1981–2.

Hunt, Linda. *Secret Agenda: The United States Government, Nazi Scientists, and Project Paperclip, 1945–1990*. New York: St. Martin's Press, 1991.

Hunt, Michael H. *Ideology and U.S. Foreign Policy*. New Haven, CT: Yale University Press, 1987.

Hutchinson, John and Anthony D. Smith, eds. *Nationalism*. Oxford: Oxford University Press, 1994.

Hyde, H. Montgomery. *The Quiet Canadian: The Secret Service Story of Sir William Stephenson*. London: Hamish Hamilton, 1962.

    Room 3603: The Story of the British Intelligence Center in New York During World War II. New York: Farrar and Straus, 1962.

Iacovetta, Franca et al. *Enemies Within: Italians and Other Internees in Canada and Abroad*. Toronto: University of Toronto Press, 2000.

Ickes, Harold L. *The Secret Diary of Harold L. Ickes*. 3 vols. New York: Simon and Schuster, 1953–4.

Inman, Samuel Guy. *Inter-American Conferences, 1826–1954: History and Problems.* Washington, DC: The University Press of Washington, 1965.

Latin America – Its Place in World Life. New York: Harcourt, Brace and Co., 1942.

Irons, Peter. *Justice at War.* New York: Oxford University Press, 1983.

Israel, Fred L., ed. *The War Diary of Breckinridge Long: Selections from the Years 1939–1944.* Lincoln: University of Nebraska Press, 1966.

Jackisch, Carlota. *El nazismo y los refugiados alemanes en la Argentina 1933–1945.* Buenos Aires: Editorial de Belgrano, 1989.

Jacobs, Arthur D. *The Prison Called Hohenasperg.* Parkland, FL: Universal Publishers, 1999.

Jacobs, Arthur D. and Joseph E. Fallon, eds. *The World War Two Experience: The Internment of German-Americans.* Vol. IV, *German-Americans in the World Wars,* ed. by Don H. Tolzmann. Munich: K. G. Saur, 1996.

Jacobsen, Hans-Adolf. *Nationalsozialistische Außenpolitik 1933–1938.* Frankfurt: Alfred Metzner Verlag, 1968.

Jacobsen, Ingrid and Karl Weidmann. *La Colonia Tovar.* Caracas: Oscar Todtmann Editores, 1992.

Jacob-Wendler, Gerhard. *Deutsche Elektroindustrie in Lateinamerika: Siemens und AEG, 1890–1914.* Stuttgart: Klett-Cotta, 1982.

Johnson, John J. *A Hemisphere Apart: The Foundations of United States Policy toward Latin America.* Baltimore: Johns Hopkins University Press, 1990.

Latin America in Caricature. Austin: University of Texas Press, 1993.

Jonas, Susanne and David Tobis, eds. *Guatemala.* Berkeley, CA: NACLA, 1974.

Josephson, Matthew. *Empire of the Air: Juan Trippe and the Struggle for World Airways.* New York: Harcourt, Brace and Co., 1944.

Junker, Detlev. *Der unteilbare Weltmarkt: Das ökonomische Interesse in der Außenpolitik der USA 1933–1941.* Stuttgart: E. Klett, 1975.

Kahle, Gunter. *Simón Bolívar und die Deutschen.* Berlin: Dietrich Reimer Verlag, 1980.

Kahn, David. *Hitler's Spies: German Military Intelligence in World War II.* New York: Da Capo, 1978.

Karlen, Stefan. *"Paz, progreso, justicia y honradez": das Ubico-Regime in Guatemala 1931–1944.* Stuttgart: Franz Steiner Verlag, 1991.

Kater, Michael. *The Nazi Party: A Social Profile of Members and Leaders, 1919–1945.* Oxford: Oxford University Press, 1983.

Katz, Barry M. *Foreign Intelligence: Research and Analysis in the Office of Strategic Services 1942–1945.* Cambridge, MA: Harvard University Press, 1989.

Kaul, Friedrich Karl. *Der Fall Eichmann.* Berlin: Das Neue Berlin, 1963.

Es wird Zeit, dass Du nach Hause kommst. Berlin: Das Neue Berlin, 1959.

Kershaw, Ian. *The Nazi Dictatorship: Problems and Perspectives of Interpretation.* London: Edward Arnold, 1989.

Kießling, Wolfgang. *Alemania Libre en Mexiko.* 2 vols. Berlin: Akademie-Verlag, 1974.

Exil in Lateinamerika. Frankfurt am Main: Verlag Philipp Reclam, 1984.

Klein, Herbert S. *Bolivia: The Evolution of a Multi-Ethnic Society.* New York: Oxford University Press, 1982.

Parties and Political Change in Bolivia, 1880–1952. London: Cambridge University Press, 1962.

Klich, Ignacio and Mario Rapoport, eds. *Discriminación y racismo en América Latina.* Buenos Aires: Grupo Editor Latinoamericano, 1997.

Kloosterhuis, Jürgen. *"Friedliche Imperialisten." Deutsche Auslandsvereine und auswärtige Kulturpolitik, 1906–1918.* Frankfurt: Lang, 1994.

Knapp, Manfred, Werner Link, Hans-Jürgen Schröder, and Klaus Schwabe. *Die USA und Deutschland 1918–1975. Deutsch-amerikanische Beziehungen zwischen Rivalität und Partnerschaft.* Munich: C. H. Beck, 1978.

Knudson, Jerry W. *The Press and the Bolivian National Revolution.* Lexington, KY: Journalism Monographs, 1973.

Koch, Conrad. *La Colonia Tovar: Geschichte und Kultur einer alemannischen Siedlung in Venezuela.* Geneva: Internationales Kulturinstitut, 1970.

Kohut, Karl, ed. *Deutsche in Lateinamerika – Lateinamerika in Deutschland.* Frankfurt: Vervuert Verlag, 1996.

Kohut, Karl and Patrik von zur Mühlen, eds. *Alternative Lateinamerika: Das deutsche Exil in der Zeit des Nationalsozialismus.* Frankfurt: Vervuert Verlag, 1994.

Kolb, Eberhard. *Bergen Belsen.* Hannover: Verlag für Literatur und Zeitgeschehen, 1962.

  Bergen-Belsen: Vom "Aufenthaltslager" zum Konzentrationslager, 1943–1945. Göttingen: Vandenhoeck & Ruprecht, 1988.

Krammer, Arnold. *Undue Process: The Untold Story of America's German Alien Internees.* New York: Rowman and Littlefield, 1997.

Krehm, William. *Democracies and Tyrannies of the Caribbean.* Westport, CT: Lawrence Hill, 1984.

Kreuter, María-Luise. *¿Dónde Queda el Ecuador? Exilio en un país desconocido desde 1938 hasta fines de los años cincuenta.* Quito: Abya-Yala, 1997.

Lael, Richard L. *Arrogant Diplomacy: U.S. Policy toward Colombia, 1903–1922.* Wilmington, DE: Scholarly Resources, 1988.

LaFeber, Walter. *Inevitable Revolutions: The United States in Central America.* New York: Norton, 1983.

  The Panama Canal: The Crisis in Historical Perspective. New York: Oxford University Press, 1989.

Langer, William L. and S. Everett Gleason. *The Challenge to Isolation, 1937–1940.* New York: Harper and Brothers, 1952.

Langhans, Paul. *Alldeutscher Atlas.* Gotha: Justus Perthes, 1900.

Langley, Lester D. *The Banana Wars: An Inner History of American Empire, 1900–1934.* Lexington: University Press of Kentucky, 1983.

  The United States and the Caribbean in the 20th Century. Athens: University of Georgia Press, 1982.

Lapper, Richard and James Painter. *Honduras: State for Sale.* London: Latin American Bureau, 1985.

Leonard, Thomas M. *Central America and the United States: The Search for Stability.* Athens: University of Georgia Press, 1991.

  The United States and Central America, 1944–1949: Perceptions of Political Dynamics. Tuscaloosa: University of Alabama Press, 1984.

Levine, Robert M. *Tropical Diaspora: The Jewish Experience in Cuba.* Gainesville: University Press of Florida, 1993.

Lleras Restrepo, Carlos. *Crónica de mi propia vida.* Vols. II–V. Bogotá: Stamato Editores, 1983.

Lombardo Toledano, Vicente. *Defensa: Una intriga nazi contra la defensa del continente americano*. Mexico, D.F.: Universidad Obrera, 1942.

National Sovereignty and Continental Defense: Nationalization of German and Italian Nazi-Fascist Properties in Latin America. Mexico, D.F.: n.p., 1941.

London, Louise. *Whitehall and the Jews, 1933–1948: British Immigration Policy and the Holocaust*. Cambridge: Cambridge University Press, 2000.

Longley, Kyle. *The Sparrow and the Hawk: Costa Rica and the United States during the Rise of José Figueres*. Tuscaloosa: University of Alabama Press, 1997.

López de Mesa, Luis. *Disertación Sociológica*. Medellín: Editorial Bedout, 1970.

López Michelsen, Alfonso. *Los Elegidos*. Bogotá: Tercer Mundo, 1967.

MacDonald, Norman P. *Hitler over Latin America*. London: Jarrolds, 1940.

MacDonnell, Francis. *Insidious Foes: The Axis Fifth Column and the American Home Front*. New York: Oxford University Press, 1995.

MacIntyre, Ben. *Forgotten Fatherland: The Search for Elizabeth Nietzsche*. New York: Farrar Straus Giroux, 1992.

Mader, Julius. *Hitlers Spionagegenerale sagen aus: Ein Dokumentarbericht über Aufbau, Struktur, Organisation des OKW Geheimdienstamtes*. Berlin: Verlag der Nation, 1979.

Malloy, James M. *Bolivia: The Uncompleted Revolution*. Pittsburgh: University of Pittsburgh Press, 1970.

Mangione, Jerre. *An Ethnic at Large*. New York: G. P. Putnam's Sons, 1978.

Manross, Lottie May. *Development of the Good Neighbor Policy (January 1942 to July 1945)*. Washington, DC: Library of Congress Legislative Reference Service, 1945.

Manvell, Roger and Heinrich Fraenkel. *The Canaris Conspiracy*. New York: David McKay, 1969.

Marschalck, Peter. *Deutsche Überseewanderung im 19. Jahrhundert*. Stuttgart: Ernst Klett, 1973.

McCann, Jr., Frank D. *The Brazilian-American Alliance, 1937–1964*. New York: Oxford University Press, 1973.

McKale, Donald M. *The Swastika Outside Germany*. Kent, OH: Kent State University Press, 1977.

Meding, Holger M., ed. *Nationalsozialismus und Argentinien: Beziehungen, Einflüsse und Nachwirkungen*. Frankfurt: Lang, 1995.

Meißner, Jochen and Boris Barth, eds. *Grenzenlose Märkte? Die deutsch-lateinamerikanischen Wirtschaftsbeziehungen vom Zeitalter des Imperialismus bis zur Weltwirtschaftskrise*. Münster: Lit, 1995.

Melville, Thomas and Marjorie Melville. *Guatemala: The Politics of Land Ownership*. New York: Free Press, 1971.

Millett, Richard. *Guardians of the Dynasty*. Maryknoll, NY: Orbis Books, 1977.

Mitchell, Christopher. *The Legacy of Populism in Bolivia: From the MNR to Military Rule*. New York: Praeger, 1977.

Mitchell, Nancy. *The Danger of Dreams. German and American Imperialism in Latin America*. Chapel Hill: University of North Carolina Press, 1999.

Möller, Horst, Andreas Wirsching and Walter Ziegler, eds. *Nationalsozialismus in der Region. Beitrage zur regionalen und lokalen Forschung und zum internationalen Vergleich*. Munich: Schriftenreihe der Vierteljahrshefte für Zeitgeschichte (Sondernummer), 1996.

Morris, James A. *Honduras: Caudillo Politics and Military Rulers*. Boulder, CO: Westview Press, 1984.

Müller, Jürgen. *Nationalsozialismus in Lateinamerika: Die Auslandsorganisation der NSDAP in Argentinien, Brasilien, Chile und Mexico, 1931–1945*. Stuttgart: Verlag Hans-Dieter Heinz, 1997.

Murphy, Raymond E. *National Socialism: Basic Principles, their Application by the Nazi Party's Foreign Organization, and the Use of Germans Abroad for Nazi Aims*. Washington, DC: Government Printing Office, 1943.

Newton, Ronald C. *German Buenos Aires, 1900–1933: Social Change and Cultural Crisis*. Austin: University of Texas Press, 1977.

  The 'Nazi Menace' in Argentina, 1931–1947. Stanford, CA: Stanford University Press, 1992.

Newton, Verne W., ed. *FDR and the Holocaust*. New York: St. Martin's Press, 1996.

Niblo, Stephen. *War, Diplomacy, and Development: The United States and Mexico, 1938–1954*, Wilmington, DE: Scholarly Resources, 1995.

Nunn, Frederick M. *Yesterday's Soldiers: European Military Professionalism in South America, 1890–1940*. Lincoln: University of Nebraska Press, 1983.

Panayi, Panakos, ed. *Minorities in Wartime: National and Racial Groupings in Europe, North America and Australia during the Two World Wars*. Oxford: Berg, 1993.

Pardo Sanz, Rosa María. *¡Con Franco hacia el Imperio! La política exterior española en América Latina, 1939–1945*. Madrid: Universidad Nacional de Educación a Distancia, 1995.

Payne, Stanley G. *Fascism in Spain, 1923–1977*. Madison: University of Wisconsin Press, 1999.

Paz, Maria Emilia. *Strategy, Security, and Spies: Mexico and the U.S. as Allies in World War II*. University Park: Pennsylvania State University Press, 1997.

Pérez Brignoli, Hector. *Breve historia de Centroamérica*. Madrid: Alianza Editorial, 1985.

Peukert, Detlev J. K. *Die Weimarer Republik*. Frankfurt: Suhrkamp, 1987.

  Inside Nazi Germany: Conformity, Opposition, and Racism in Everyday Life. New Haven, CT: Yale University Press, 1982.

Picard, Jacques. *Die Schweiz und die Juden, 1933–45*. Zurich: Chronos, 1994.

Pike, Fredrick B. *Chile and the United States, 1880–1962*. Notre Dame, IN: University of Notre Dame Press, 1963.

  FDR's Good Neighbor Policy: Sixty Years of Generally Gentle Chaos. Austin: University of Texas Press, 1995.

  The United States and Latin America: Myths and Stereotypes of Civilization and Nature. Austin: University of Texas Press, 1992.

  The United States and the Andean Republics: Peru, Bolivia, and Ecuador. Cambridge, MA: Harvard University Press, 1977.

Pohle, Fritz. *Das mexikanische Exil: Ein Beitrag zur Geschichte der politisch-kulturellen Emigration aus Deutschland, 1937–1946*. Stuttgart: J. B. Metzler, 1986.

Pommerin, Reiner. *Das Dritte Reich und Lateinamerika: Die deutsche Politik gegenüber Süd- und Mittelamerika, 1939–1942*. Düsseldorf: Droste Verlag, 1977.

Potashnik, Michael. *Nacismo: National Socialism in Chile, 1932–1938*. Los Angeles: University of California Press, 1974.

Powers, Richard Gid. *Secrecy and Power: The Life of J. Edgar Hoover*. New York: Free Press, 1987.

Prados, John. *Combined Fleet Decoded: The Secret History of American Intellignce and the Japanese Navy in World War II.* New York: Random House, 1995.

Pratt, Mary Louise. *Imperial Eyes: Travel Writing and Transculturation.* New York: Routledge, 1992.

Puttkammer, Ernst W. *Alien Friends and Alien Enemies in the United States: Public Policy Pamphlet #39.* Chicago: University of Chicago Press, 1943.

Randall, Stephen J. *Colombia and the United States: Hegemony and Interdependence.* Athens: University of Georgia Press, 1992.

Rapoport, Mario. *¿Aliados o Neutrales? La Argentina frente a la Segunda Guerra Mundial.* Buenos Aires: Editorial Universitaria de Buenos Aires, 1988.

Reich, Cary. *The Life of Nelson A Rockefeller: Worlds to Conquer 1908–1958.* New York: Doubleday, 1996.

Reichsstelle für das Auswanderungswesen. *Deutsche Vereine, Schulen, Kirchengemeinde und sonstige Anstalten und Einrichtungen in Sud-Amerika.* Berlin: Reichsverlagsamt, 1935.

Riley, Karen L. *Schools Behind Barbed Wire: The Untold Story of Wartime Internment and the Children of Arrested Enemy Aliens.* Lanham, MD: Rowman and Littlefield, 2002.

Rinke, Stefan. *"Der letzte freie Kontinent": Deutsche Lateinamerikapolitik im Zeichen transnationaler Beziehungen, 1918–1933.* 2 vols. Stuttgart: Hans-Dieter Heinz, 1996.

Rippy, James Fred. *Globe and Hemisphere.* Chicago: Henry Regnery Co., 1958.

Latin America and the Industrial Age. New York: G. P. Putnam's Sons, 1947.

Ritter, Ernst. *Das Deutsche Ausland-Institut in Stuttgart 1917–1945, Ein Beispiel der deutschen Volkstumsarbeit zwischen den Weltkriegen.* Wiesbaden: Franz Steiner Verlag, 1976.

Roche, Jean. *La colonisation allemande et le Rio Grande do Sul.* Paris: Institut des hautes études de l'Amérique latine, 1959.

Rock, David, ed. *Latin America in the 1940s: War and Postwar Transitions.* Berkeley: University of California Press, 1994.

Rojas Suárez, Juan Francisco, ed. *Costa Rica en la Segunda Guerra Mundial: 7 de diciembre de 1941 – 7 de diciembre de 1943.* San José: Imprenta Nacional, 1943.

Roorda, Eric Paul. *The Dictator Next Door: The Good Neighbor Policy and the Trujillo Regime in the Dominican Republic, 1930–1945.* Durham, NC: Duke University Press, 1998.

Rout, Jr., Leslie B. and John F. Bratzel. *The Shadow War: German Espionage and United States Counterespionage in Latin America during World War II.* Frederick, MD: University Publications of America, 1986.

Saint Sauveur-Henn, Anne. *Un siècle d'émigration allemande vers l'Argentine 1853–1945.* Köln: Böhlau, 1995.

ed. *Zweimal verjagt: die deutschsprachige Emigration und der Fluchtweg Frankreich-Lateinamerika, 1933–1945.* Berlin: Metropol-Verlag, 1998.

Schaefer, Ernesto. Unpublished manuscript. Guatemala City, 1950[?].

Schaefer, Jürgen. *Deutsche Militärhilfe an Südamerika: Militär- und Rüstungsinteressen in Argentinien, Bolivien und Chile vor 1914.* Düsseldorf: Bertelsmann, 1974.

Schifter Sikora, Jacobo. *El Judío en Costa Rica.* San José: Editorial Universidad Estatal a Distancia, 1979.

Las alianzas conflictivas: las relaciones de Estados Unidos y Costa Rica desde la Segunda Guerra Mundial a la guerra fría. San José: Libro Libre, 1986.

Schlesinger, Alfredo. *Comentarios alrededor de la ley de liquidación de asuntos de guerra*. Guatemala City: n.p., 1955.

El Arma Secreta: La Quinta Columna. Guatemala City: n.p., 1940.

Schmitz, David F. *Thank God They're on Our Side. The United States and Right-Wing Dictatorships, 1921–1965*. Chapel Hill: University of North Carolina Press, 1999.

Schobert, Kurt. *Soziale und kulturelle Integration am Beispiel der deutschen Einwanderung und Deutsch-Chilenen in Süd-Chile*. 2 vols. München: Kurt Schobert Verlag, 1983.

Schoonover, Thomas. *Germany in Central America: Competitive Imperialism, 1821–1929*. Tuscaloosa: University of Alabama Press, 1998.

Schoultz, Lars. *Beneath the United States: A History of U.S. Policy toward Latin America*. Cambridge, MA: Harvard University Press, 1998.

National Security and United States Policy Toward Latin America. Princeton, NJ: Princeton University Press, 1987.

Schrader, Achim and Karl Heinrich Rengstorf, eds. *Europaische Juden in Lateinamerika*. St. Ingbert: Werner J. Rohrig Verlag, 1989.

Schröder, Hans-Jürgen. *Deutschland und die Vereinigten Staaten, 1933–1939. Wirtschaft und Politik in der Entwicklung des deutsch-amerikanischen Gegensatzes*. Wiesbaden: Franz Steiner Verlag, 1970.

Schuler, Friedrich E. *Mexico between Hitler and Roosevelt: Mexican Foreign Relations in the Age of Lázaro Cárdenas, 1934–1940*. Albuquerque: University of New Mexico Press, 1998.

Schwarz, Jordan A. *Liberal: Adolf A. Berle and the Vision of an American Era*. New York: The Free Press, 1987.

Schwarz, Simone. *Chile im Schatten faschistischer Bewegungen: der Einfluß europäischer und chilenischer Strömungen in den 30er und 70er Jahren*. Frankfurt: Verlag für Akademische Schriften, 1997.

Schwarz Wilde, Otto. *Memorias de la Guerra*. Guayaquil: n.p., 1960.

Seabury, Paul. *The Wilhelmstrasse: A Study of German Diplomats Under the Nazi Regime*. Berkeley: University of California Press, 1954.

Segisfredo Infante et al. *Los Alemanes en el Sur, 1900–1947*. Tegucigalpa: Editorial Universitaria, 1993.

Seiferheld, Alfredo M. *Nazismo y fascismo en el Paraguay: los años de la guerra 1939–1945*. 2 vols. Asunción: Editorial Histórica, 1986.

Senkman, Leonardo. *Argentina, la segunda guerra mundial, y los refugiados indeseables 1933–1945*. Buenos Aires: Grupo Editor Latinoamericano, 1991.

Shulman, Abraham. *The Case of Hotel Polski: An Account of One of the Most Enigmatic Episodes of World War II*. New York: Holocaust Library, 1982.

Simpson, A. W. Brian. *In the Highest Degree Odious: Detention without Trial in Wartime Britain*. New York: Oxford University Press, 1993.

Simpson, Christopher. *Blowback: The First Full Account of America's Recruitment of Nazis, and Its Disastrous Effect on Our Domestic and Foreign Policy*. New York: Weidenfeld & Nicholson, 1988.

Singer, Kurt. *Germany's Secret Service in South America*. New York: Background, 1942.

Smith, Arthur L. *The Deutschtum of Nazi Germany and the United States*. The Hague: M. Nijhoff, 1965.

Smith, Bradley F. *The Shadow Warriors: O.S.S. and the Origins of the C.I.A.* New York: Basic Books, 1983.

Smith, Peter H. *Talons of the Eagle: Dynamics of U.S.-Latin American Relations*. New York: Oxford University Press, 1996.

Smith, R. Harris. *OSS: The Secret History of America's First Central Intelligence Agency.* Berkeley: University of California Press, 1972.

Sontheimer, Kurt. *Antidemokratisches Denken in der Weimarer Republik. Die politischen Ideen des deutschen Nationalismus zwischen 1918 und 1933.* München: Nymphenburger Verlagshandlung, 1962.

Spitta, Arnold. *Paul Zech im südamerikanischen Exil 1933–1946: Ein Beitrag zur Geschichte der deutschen Emigration in Argentinien.* Berlin: Colloquium Verlag, 1978.

Spitzer, Leo. *Hotel Bolivia: The Culture of Memory in a Refuge from Nazism.* New York: Hill and Wang, 1998.

 Lives in Between: Assimilation and Marginality in Austria, Brazil, West Africa, 1780–1945. Cambridge: Cambridge University Press, 1989.

Stent, Ronald. *A Bespattered Page? The Internment of 'His Majesty's Most Loyal Enemy Aliens'.* London: Andre Deutsch, 1980.

Stephan, Alexander. *Im Visier des FBI: Deutsche Exilschriftsteller in den Akten amerikanischer Geheimdienste.* Stuttgart: Verlag J. B. Metzler, 1995. [Published in English as *"Communazis": FBI Surveillance of German Emigré Writers.* New Haven, CT: Yale University Press, 2000.]

Stephenson, William S., ed. *British Security Coordination: The Secret History of British Intelligence in the Americas 1940–1945.* New York: Fromm International Publishing, 1998.

Stevenson, William. *A Man Called Intrepid: The Secret War.* New York: Harcourt, Brace, Jovanovich, 1976.

Steward, Dick. *Trade and Hemisphere: the Good Neighbor Policy and Reciprocal Trade.* Columbia: University of Missouri Press, 1975.

Strasser, Otto. *The Gangsters around Hitler – with a Tropical Postcript: Nazi Gangsters in South America.* London: W. H. Allen & Co., 1942.

Tannenberg, Otto Richard. *Groß-Deutschland: die Arbeit des 20. Jahrhunderts.* Leipzig: Bruno Bolger, 1911.

Tateishi, John, ed. *And Justice for All: An Oral History of the Japanese American Detention Camps.* New York: Random House, 1984.

Tejera, Adolfo. *Penetración Nazi en America Latina.* Montevideo: Editorial Nueva América, 1938.

Tella, Guido di and D. Cameron Watt, eds. *Argentina between the Great Powers, 1939–1946.* London: Macmillan, 1989.

tenBroek, Jacobus, Edward N. Barnhart and Floyd W. Matson. *Prejudice, War and the Constitution.* Berkeley: University of California Press, 1954.

Theoharis, Athan G. and John Stuart Cox. *The Boss: J. Edgar Hoover and the Great American Inquisition.* Philadelphia: Temple University Press, 1988.

Tinajero, Fernando. *Itinerario de un acercamiento: Colegio Alemán, 1917–1992.* Quito: Asociación Ecuatoriana-Alemana de Cultura y Educación, 1992.

Tirado Mejía, Alvaro, ed. *Nueva Historia de Colombia*. Bogotá: Planeta Colombiana Editorial, 1989.

Torres-Rivas, Edelberto, ed. *Historia general de Centroamérica*. 6 vols. Madrid: FLACSO, 1993.

Trindade, Hélgio. *Integralismo (o fascismo brasileiro na década de 30)*. Porto Alegre: Difel, 1979.

Troy, Thomas F. *Donovan and the CIA: A History of the Establishment of the Central Intelligence Agency*. Frederick, MD: University Publications of America, 1981.

Tulchin, Joseph S. *Argentina and the United States: A Conflicted Relationship*. Boston: Twayne Publishers, 1990.

Vagts, Alfred. *Deutschland und die Vereinigten Staaten in der Weltpolitik*. 2 vols. New York: Dornan, 1935.

Van Valkenburg, Carol. *An Alien Place: The Fort Missoula, Montana, Detention Camp, 1941–1944*. Missoula, MT: Pictorial Histories Publishing Company, 1995.

Varon, Benno Weise. *Professions of a Lucky Jew*. New York: Cornwall Books, 1992.

Vega, Bernardo. *Nazismo, fascismo y falangismo en la República Dominicana*. Santo Domingo: Amigo del Hogar, 1989.

Villacres Moscoso, Jorge W. *Historia diplomática de la república del Ecuador*. 5 vols. Vol. 4. Guayaquil: Impr. de la Universidad de Guayaquil, 1987.

Volberg, Heinrich. *Auslandsdeutschen und Drittes Reich: Der Fall Argentinien*. Cologne: Böhlau Verlag, 1981.

Volker, Nitz. *Unser Grenz- und Auslanddeutschtum*. Munich: Verlag F. Eher, 1931.

Volland, Klaus. *Das Dritte Reich und Mexiko: Studien zur Entwicklung des deutsch-mexikanischen Verhältnisses 1933–1942 unter besonderer Berücksichtigung der Ölpolitik*. Frankfurt: Peter Lang, 1976.

von Wehrenalp, Erwin Barth. *Deutsche in Übersee*. Leipzig: Lühe & Co., 1939.

Wagner, Regina. *Los Alemanes en Guatemala, 1828–1944*. Guatemala: Afanes, 1996.

Walter, Knut. *The Regime of Anastasio Somoza, 1936–1946*. Chapel Hill: University of North Carolina Press, 1993.

Watson, Mark Skinner. *Chief of Staff. Prewar Plans and Preparations. United States Army in World War II*. Washington, DC: Department of the Army, 1950.

Weglyn, Michi. *Years of Infamy: The Untold Story of America's Concentration Camps*. New York: Morrow, 1976.

Wehler, Hans-Ulrich. *Das deutsche Kaiserreich, 1871–1918*. Göttingen: Vandenhoeck und Ruprecht, 1973.

Weil, Martin. *A Pretty Good Club*. New York: Norton, 1978.

Weilbauer, Arthur. *Ein Weiter Weg*. Quito: n.p., 1982.

   Los Alemanes en el Ecuador. Quito: Colegio Alemán, 1975.

Weinberg, Gerald. *The Foreign Policy of Hitler's Germany*. Chicago: University of Chicago Press, 1980.

Welles, Sumner. *Where are We Heading?* New York: Harper and Brothers, 1946.

Welles, Sumner, et al. *Laurence Duggan, 1905–1948: In Memoriam*. Stamford, CT: Overbrook Press, 1949.

Wenck, Alexandra-Eileen. *Zwischen Menschenhandel und "Endlösung": Das Konzentrationslager Bergen-Belsen*. Paderborn, Germany: Verlag Ferdinand Schöningh, 2000.

Whitaker, Arthur P., ed. *Inter-American Affairs: An Annual Survey . . . 1941–1945.* 5 vols. New York: Columbia University Press, 1942–1946.

The United States and South America: The Northern Republics. Cambridge, MA: Harvard University Press, 1948.

The Western Hemisphere Idea: Its Rise and Decline. Ithaca, NY: Cornell University Press, 1954.

Whitehead, Donald F. *The FBI Story.* New York: Random House, 1956.

Williams, William Appleman. *The Tragedy of American Diplomacy.* 2nd revised ed. New York: Dell Publishing Co., 1959, 1972.

Wojak, Irmtrud. *Exil in Chile: Die deutsch-jüdische und politische Emigration während des Nationalsozialismus, 1933–1945.* Berlin: Metropol Verlag, 1994.

Wood, Bryce. *The Dismantling of the Good Neighbor Policy.* Austin: University of Texas Press, 1985.

The Making of the Good Neighbor Policy. New York: Columbia University Press, 1961.

Woods, Randall Bennett. *The Roosevelt Foreign-Policy Establishment and the 'Good Neighbor': The United States and Argentina, 1941–1945.* Lawrence: Regents Press of Kansas, 1979.

Wyman, David S. *The Abandonment of the Jews: America and the Holocaust 1941–1945.* New York: Pantheon Books, 1984.

Paper Walls: America and the Refugee Crisis, 1938–1941. New York: Pantheon Books, 1968, 1985.

zur Mühlen, Patrik von. *Fluchtziel Lateinamerika: Die deutsche Emigration 1933–1945: politische Aktivitäten und soziokulturelle Integration.* Bonn: Verlag Neue Gesellschaft, 1988.

ARTICLES

Atkins, George Pope and Larry V. Thompson. "German Military Influence in Argentina, 1921–1940." *Journal of Latin American Studies* 4:2 (1972): 257–74.

Avni, Haim. "Peru y Bolivia – dos naciones andinas – y los refugiados judios durante la era nazi." In *El Genocidio ante la Historia y la Naturaleza Humana*, ed. by Beatriz Gurevich and Carlos Escudé. Buenos Aires: Universidad Torcuato Di Tella: Grupo Editor Latinoamericano, 1994.

"The Role of Latin America in Immigration and Rescue during the Nazi Era 1933–1945." *The Wilson Center Colloquium Paper* (1986).

"The War and the Possibilities of Rescue." In *The Shoah and the War*, ed. by Asher Cohen, Yehoyakim Cochavi and Yoav Gelber. New York: Peter Lang, 1992.

Baecker, Thomas. "Deutschland im karibischen Raum im Spiegel amerikanischer Akten (1898–1914)." *Jahrbuch für Geschichte von Staat, Wirtschaft und Gesellschaft Lateinamerikas* 11 (1974): 167–237.

Bankier, David. "Die Beziehungen zwischen deutschen jüdischen Flüchtlingen und deutschen politischen Exilierten in Südamerika." In *Europaische Juden in Lateinamerika*, ed. by Achim Schrader and Karl Heinrich Rengstorf. St. Ingbert: Werner J. Rohrig Verlag, 1989.

Barnhart, Edward N. "Citizenship and Political Tests in Latin American Republics in World War II." *Hispanic American Historical Review* 42:3 (Aug 1962): 297–332.

"Japanese Internees from Peru." *Pacific Historical Review* 31:2 (May 1962): 169–78.

Bartelt, Dawid. "'Fünfte Kolonne' ohne Plan. Die Auslandsorganisation der NSDAP in Brasilien, 1931–1939." *Ibero-Amerikanisches Archiv* 19:1–2 (1993): 3–35.

Batista i Roca, J. M. "Nazi Intrigues in Latin America." *Contemporary Review* 159:903 (Mar 1941): 308–15.

Beals, Carleton. "Swastika Over the Andes: German Penetration in Latin America." *Harper's Magazine* 177 (1938): 176–86.

"Totalitarian Inroads in Latin America." *Foreign Affairs* 17 (1938): 78–89.

Bell, Leland V. "The Failure of Nazism in America: The German-American Bund, 1936–1941." *Political Science Quarterly* 85:4 (Dec 1970): 585–99.

Bernecker, Walther L. and Thomas Fischer. "Deutsche in Lateinamerika." In *Deutsche im Ausland – Fremde in Deutschland: Migration in Geschichte und Gegenwart*, ed. by Klaus J. Bade. Munich: C. H. Beck, 1992.

"Deutschland und Lateinamerika im Zeitalter des Imperialismus, 1871–1914." *Ibero-Amerikanisches Archiv* 21:3–4 (1995): 273–302.

Bidwell, Percy. "Latin America, Germany, and the Hull Program." *Foreign Affairs* 17 (Jul 1939): 374–96.

Bieber, León E. "La Política Militar Alemana en Bolivia, 1900–1935." *Latin American Research Review* 29:1 (1994): 85–106.

Biermann, Enrique. "Flüchtlinge und Emigranten." In *Die Deutschen in Kolumbien*, ed. by Claudia Tapias. Bogotá: Editorial Nomos S.A., 1994.

Blancpain, Jean-Pierre. "Des visées pangermanistes au noyautage hitlérien: Le nationalisme allemand et l'Amérique latine (1890–1945)." *Revue historique* 281:2 (1990): 433–82.

"L'Armée chilienne et les instructeurs allemands en Amérique latine (1885–1914)." *Revue Historique* 285:2 (1991): 347–94.

Blasier, Cole. "The United States, Germany, and the Bolivian Revolutionaries (1941–1946)." *Hispanic American Historical Review* 52:1 (Feb 1972): 26–54.

Bohle, Ernst. "The Foreign Organization of the NSDAP." *Almanach der Nationalsozialistischen Revolution (Berlin)* (1934): 90ff.

Böhm, Günter. "Jüdische Aspekte des lateinamerikanischen Exils." In *Alternative Lateinamerika: Das deutsche Exil in der Zeit des Nationalsozialismus*, ed. by Karl Kohut and Patrik von zur Mühlen. Frankfurt: Vervuert Verlag, 1994.

Bratzel, John F. and Leslie B. Rout, Jr. "FDR and the 'Secret Map'." *Wilson Quarterly* 9:1 (1985): 167–73.

Breitman, Richard. "Himmler and Belsen." In *Belsen in History and Memory*, ed. by Joanne Reilly, David Cesarani, Tony Kushner and Colin Richmond. London: Frank Cass, 1996.

Breitman, Richard and Shlomo Aronson. "The End of the 'Final Solution'?: Nazi Plans to Ransom Jews in 1944." *Central European History* 25:2 (1992): 177–203.

Brunn, Gerhard. "Deutscher Einfluss und deutsche Interessen in der Professionalisierung einiger lateinamerikanischer Armeen vor dem 1. Weltkrieg (1885–1914)." *Jahrbuch für Geschichte von Staat, Wirtschaft und Gesellschaft Lateinamerikas* 6 (1969): 278–336.

Burton, Wilbur. "South American Grab-Bag: Italy, Germany and Japan Are Making Attempts to Spread the Fascist Doctrine among our Neighbors." *Current History* 46 (Nov 1937): 54–8.

Cane, James A. "'Unity for the Defense of Culture': AIAPE and the Cultural Politics of Argentine Anti-Fascism, 1935–1943," *Hispanic American Historical Review*, 77:3 (Aug 1997): 443–82.

Cepeda Ulloa, Fernando and Rodrigo Pardo García-Peña. "La política exterior colombiana 1930–1946." In *Nueva Historia de Colombia*, ed. by Alvaro Tirado Mejía. Bogotá: Planeta Colombiana Editorial, 1989.

Child, John. "From 'Color' to 'Rainbow': U.S. Strategic Planning for Latin America, 1919–1945." *Journal of Inter-American Studies and World Affairs* 21:2 (1979): 233–59.

Ciccarelli, Orazio A. "Fascist Propaganda and the Italian Community in Peru during the Benavides Regime, 1933–1939." *Journal of Latin American Studies* 20 (1988): 361–88.

Clayton, Will, "Security Against Renewed German Aggression." *Department of State Bulletin* 13:314 (1 Jul 1945): 21–37.

Clementi, Hebe. "El negro en América Latina." In *Discriminación y racismo en América Latina*, ed. by Ignacio Klich and Mario Rapoport. Buenos Aires: Grupo Editor Latinoamericano, 1997.

Craig, Gordon A. "The German Foreign Office from Neurath to Ribbentrop." In *The Diplomats, 1919–1939*, ed. by Gordon A. Craig and Felix Gilbert. Princeton, NJ: Princeton University Press, 1953.

Culley, John Joel. "The Santa Fe Internment Camp and the Justice Department Program for Enemy Aliens." In *Japanese Americans from Relocation to Redress*, ed. by Roger Daniels et al. Salt Lake City: University of Utah Press, 1986.

"Trouble at the Lordsburg Internment Camp." *New Mexico Historical Review* 60 (1985): 225–48.

"A Troublesome Presence: World War II Internment of German Sailors in New Mexico." *Prologue* 28 (Winter 1996): 179–95.

Daniels, Roger. "L'Internamento di 'Alien Enemies' negli Stati Uniti durante la seconda guerra mondiale." *Acoma: Rivista Internazionale di Studi Nordamericani* 11 (1997): 39–49.

da Silveira, Helder Gordim. "A Ofensiva Política dos EUA Sobre a América Latina na Visão Alemá: Uma Face do Confronto Interimperialista (1938)." *Estudos Ibero-Americanos* 18:1 (Jul 1992): 19–27.

Domke, Martin. "Western Hemisphere Control Over Enemy Property: A Comparative Survey." *Law and Contemporary Problems* 11:1 (Winter–Spring 1945): 3–16.

Duggan, Laurence. "Background for Revolution." *Inter-American* 5:9 (Sep 1946): 15ff.

Eck, Nathan. "The Rescue of Jews with the Aid of Passports and Citizenship Papers of Latin American States." *Yad Vashem Studies* I (1957): 125–52.

Effron, David. "Latin America and the Fascist 'Holy Alliance'." *Annals* 204 (1939): 17–25.

Ellis, Mark and Panikos Panayi. "German Minorities in World War I: A Comparative Study of Britain and the USA." *Ethnic and Racial Studies* 17:2 (1994): 238–59.

Etchepare, Jaime Antonio and Hamish I. Stewatt. "Nazism in Chile: A Particular Type of Fascism in South America." *Journal of Contemporary History* 30:4 (Oct 1995): 577–606.

Fortmann, Michel and David G. Haglund. "Public Diplomacy and Dirty Tricks: Two Faces of United States 'Informal Penetration' of Latin America on the Eve of World War II." *Diplomacy and Statecraft* 6:2 (1995): 536–77.

Fox, Stephen. "The Deportation of Latin American Germans, 1941–1947: Fresh Legs for Mr. Monroe's Doctrine." *Yearbook of German-American Studies* (1997): 117–44.

Francis, Michael J. "The United States and Chile during the Second World War: The Diplomacy of Misunderstanding." *Journal of Latin American Studies* 9:1 (1977): 91–113.

"The United States at Rio, 1942: The Strains of Pan Americanism." *Journal of Latin American Studies* 6:1 (1974): 77–95.

Frey, Martin. "Ergänzungen zu dem Buch von Adrian Kösch, 'Allerlei aus der Verapaz'." In *Deutschtum in der Alta Verapaz*. Stuttgart: Deutsches Verein zu Coban, 1938.

Friedman, Max Paul. "Private Memory, Public Records, and Contested Terrain: Weighing Oral Testimony in the Deportation of Germans from Latin America during World War II." *The Oral History Review* 27:1 (Winter/Spring 2000): 1–16.

"Specter of a Nazi Threat: United States-Colombian Relations, 1939–1945." *The Americas: A Quarterly Review of Inter-American Cultural History* 56:4 (Apr 2000): 563–89.

Gallego, Ferrán. "Notas sobre el gobierno de Enrique Peñaranda en Bolivia (1940–43)." *Ibero-Amerikanisches Archiv* (1987).

Galvis, Silvia. "Peripecias de los Nazis Criollos." *Credencial Historia* 67 (Jul 1995): 12–15.

Gardiner, C. Harvey. "The Japanese and Central America." *Journal of Inter-American Studies and World Affairs* 14 (May 1972): 15–47.

Gaudig, Olag and Peter Veit. "El Partido Alemán Nacionalsocialista en Argentina, Brasil y Chile frente a las comunidades alemanas: 1933–1939." *Estudios Interdisciplinarios de América Latina y el Caribe (Tel Aviv)* 6:1 (1995): 71–87.

Gojman de Backal, Alicia. "Deutsche Beteiligung an der Bewegung der 'Goldhemden' im Mexiko der 30er Jahre." In *Europaische Juden in Lateinamerika*, ed. by Achim Schrader and Karl Heinrich Rengstorf. St. Ingbert: Werner J. Rohrig Verlag, 1989.

Grieb, Kenneth. "The Fascist Mirage in Central America: Guatemalan-United States Relations and the Yankee Fear of Fascism, 1936–1944." In *Perspectives in American Diplomacy*, ed. by Jules Davids. New York: Arno Press, 1976.

"Guatemala and the Second World War." *Ibero-Amerikanisches Archiv* 3:4 (1977): 377–94.

"The United States and the Rise of General Maximiliano Hernández Martínez." *Journal of Latin American Studies* 3:2 (Nov 1971): 151–72.

Haglund, David G. "'De-lousing' SCADTA: the Role of Pan American Airways in US Aviation Diplomacy in Colombia, 1939–1940." *Aerospace Historian* 30:3 (Sep 1983): 170–90.

Haines, Gerald K. "Under the Eagle's Wing: The Franklin Roosevelt Administration Forges an American Hemisphere." *Diplomatic History* 1 (1977): 373–8.

Hall, Melvin and Peck Walter. "Wings for the Trojan Horse: German and Italian Airplanes over South America." *Foreign Affairs* 19:2 (1941): 347–69.

Herwig, Holger H. "Prelude to *Weltblitzkrieg*: Germany's Naval Policy toward the United States of America, 1939–41." *Journal of Modern History* 43 (Dec 1971): 649–68.

Hilton, Stanley E. "Acção Integralista Brasileira: Fascism in Brazil, 1932–1938." *Luso-Brazilian Review* 9 (1972): 3–29.

Hoover, J. Edgar. "Alien Enemy Control." *Iowa Law Review* 29 (1944): 396–408.

Houner, Milan. "Did Hitler Want a World Dominion?" *Journal of Contemporary History* 13 (Jan 1978): 15–32.

Illi, Manfred. "Die deutsche Auswanderung nach Lateinamerika. Eine Literaturübersicht." *Lateinamerika-Studien* 2 (1977): 1–176.

Irizarry y Puente, J. "Exclusion and Expulsion of Aliens in Latin America." *American Journal of International Law* 36 (1942): 252–70.

Jacobsen, Hans-Adolf. "Die Gründung der Auslandsabteilung der NSDAP (1931–1933)." In *Gedenkschrift für Martin Göhring*, 353–368. Wiesbaden, 1968.

———. "Zur Struktur der NS-Außenpolitik 1933–1945." In *Hitler, Deutschland und die Mächte. Materialien zur Außenpolitik des Dritten Reiches*, ed. by Manfred Funke. Düsseldorf: Droste Verlag, 1978.

Kappe, Walter. "Juden gegen das Deutschtum in Übersee." *Deutschtum im Ausland* 22:2–3 (1939): 77–82.

Katz, Friedrich. "Einige Grundzüge der Politik des deutschen Imperialismus in Lateinamerika von 1898 bis 1941." In *Der deutsche Faschismus in Lateinamerika, 1933–1943*, ed. by Heinz Sanke. Berlin: Humboldt-Universität zu Berlin, 1966.

Kellenbenz, Hermann and Jürgen Schneider. "La emigración alemana a América Latina desde 1821 hasta 1930." *Jahrbuch für Geschichte von Staat, Wirtschaft und Gesellschaft Lateinamerikas* 13 (1976): 386–403.

Klich, Ignacio. "The Nazis in Argentina: Deconstructing Some Myths." *Patterns of Prejudice* 29:4 (1995): 53–66.

Klubock, Thomas Miller. "From Welfare Capitalism to the Free Market in Chile: Gender, Culture, and Politics in the Copper Mines." In *Close Encounters of Empire: Writing the Cultural History of U.S.-Latin American Relations*, ed. by Gilbert M. Joseph, Catherine C. LeGrande and Ricardo D. Salvatore. Durham, NC: Duke University Press, 1998.

Kossok, Manfred. "'Sonderauftrag Südamerika': Zur deutschen Politik gegenüber Lateinamerika 1938 bis 1942." In *Lateinamerika Zwischen Emanzipation und Imperialismus, 1810–1960*, ed. by Kurt Büttner and Manfred Kossok. Berlin: Akademie Verlag, 1961.

Kramer-Kaske, Lieselotte. "Zur Politik der deutschen Faschisten in Kolumbien 1933 bis 1945." In *Der deutsche Faschismus in Lateinamerika, 1933–1943*, ed. by Heinz Sanke. Berlin: Humboldt-Universität zu Berlin, 1966.

Krammer, Arnold. "Feinde ohne Uniform: deutsche Zivilinternierte in den USA während des Zweiten Weltkrieges." *Vierteljahrshefte für Zeitgeschichte* 44:4 (1996): 581–603.

———. "In Splendid Isolation: Enemy Diplomats in WWII." *Prologue* 17:1 (Spring 1985): 25–43.

Kraus, Theresa L. "Clipping Axis Wings." *Air Power History* 37:1 (1990): 19–26.

Langley, Lester D. "The World Crisis and the Good Neighbor Policy in Panama, 1936–1941." *The Americas* 24:2 (Oct 1967): 137–52.

Leonard, Thomas M. "The United States and German Nationals in Costa Rica on the Eve of World War II." Paper delivered at Southeastern Council on Latin America Studies Conference, San José, Costa Rica, 1997.

Leopold, Werner F. "Der Deutsche in Costa Rica." *Hamburger Wirtschaftschronik* 3 (Oct 1966): 133–214.

Lewontin, Steve. "'A Blessed Peace': Honduras under Carías." In *Honduras: Portrait of a Captive Nation*, ed. by Nancy Peckenham and Annie Street. New York: Praeger, 1985.

Maack, Reinhard. "The Germans of South Brazil: A German View." *Journal of Inter-American Relations* I:3 (1939): 5–23.

MacDonnell, Francis. "The Search for a Second Zimmerman Telegram: FDR, BSC, and the Latin American Front." *International Journal of Intelligence and Counterintelligence* 4:4 (Winter 1990): 487–505.

Madders, Kevin J. "Internment." In *Encyclopedia of Public International Law*, 225–33. Amsterdam: Max Planck Institute for Comparative Public Law and International Law, 1985.

Mann, Thomas C. "Elimination of Axis Influence in This Hemisphere: Measures Adopted at the Mexico City Conference." *Department of State Bulletin* 12 (20 May 1945): 924–6.

Martin, Lawrence and Sylvia Martin. "Nazi Intrigues in Central America." *The American Mercury* 53:211 (Jul 1941): 66–73.

McCann, Frank D. "Brazil and World War II: The Forgotten Ally." *Estudios Interdisciplinarios de América Latina y el Caribe* 6:2 (1995): 35–70.

"Vargas and the Destruction of the Brazilian Integralista and Nazi Parties." *The Americas* 26 (1969/70): 15–34.

Millett, Richard and Marvin A. Soloman. "Trujillo violó una mujer en una iglesia." *Ahora* 492 (16 Apr 1973): 2–10.

Mitchell, Nancy. "Protective Imperialism Versus Weltpolitik in Brazil." *International History Review* 18:2 (1996): 253–78; 18:3 (1996): 546–72.

Monteforte Toledo, Mario. "Bean of Contention." *The Inter-American* 2 (Mar 1943): 22–4.

Moran, William T. "Our Latin American Trade Faces Difficulties." *Annals* 211 (1940): 173–9.

Mugnaini, Marco. "L'Italia e l'America latina (1930–1936): alcuni aspetti della politica estera fascista." *Storia delle Relazioni Internazionali* 2:2 (1986): 199–244.

Müller, Jürgen. "El NSDAP en México: historia y percepciones, 1931–1940." *Estudios Interdisciplinarios de América Latina y el Caribe (Tel Aviv)* 6:2 (1995): 89–107.

"Entwicklung und Aktivitäten der NSDAP in Argentinien, 1931–1945." In *Nationalsozialismus und Argentinien: Beziehungen, Einflüsse und Nachwirkungen*, ed. by Holger M. Meding. Frankfurt: Lang, 1995.

"Hitler, Lateinamerika und die Weltherrschaft." *Ibero-Amerikanisches Archiv* 18:1/2 (1992): 67–101.

Nagler, Jörg. "Victims of the Home Front: Enemy Aliens in the United States During the First World War." In *Minorities in Wartime: National and Racial Groupings in Europe, North America and Australia during the Two World Wars*, ed. by Panikos Panayi. Oxford: Berg, 1993.

Newton, Ronald C. "El fascismo y la colectividad italo-argentina (1922–1945)." In *Discriminación y racismo en América Latina*, ed. by Ignacio Klich and Mario Rapoport. Buenos Aires: Grupo Editor Latinoamericano, 1997.

"'Graue Eminenzen und schiefe Existenzen': Die deutschsprachigen Berater der Alliierten in Argentinien während des Zweiten Weltkrieges." In *Alternative Lateinamerika: Das deutsche Exil in der Zeit des Nationalsozialismus*, ed. by Karl Kohut and Patrik von zur Mühlen. Frankfurt: Vervuert Verlag, 1994.

"Italienischer Faschismus und deutscher Nationalsozialismus in Argentinien. Eine vergleichende Analyse." In *Nationalsozialismus und Argentinien: Beziehungen, Einflüsse und Nachwirkungen*, ed. by Holger M. Meding. Frankfurt: Lang, 1995.

"The 'Nazi Menace' in Argentina Revisited." *Patterns of Prejudice* 31:3 (1997): 7–15.

"The United States, the German-Argentines, and the Myth of the Fourth Reich, 1943–47." *Hispanic American Historical Review* 64:1 (1984): 81–103.

Nunn, Frederick M. "Emil Körner and the Prussianization of the Chilean Army: Origins, Process, and Consequences, 1885–1920." *Hispanic American Historical Review* 50:2 (1970): 300–22.

"European Military Influence in South America: The Origins and Nature of Professional Militarism in Argentina, Brazil, Chile and Peru, 1890–1940." *Jahrbuch für Geschichte von Staat, Wirtschaft und Gesellschaft Lateinamerikas* 12 (1975): 230–52.

Pach, Jr., Chester. "The Containment of U.S. Military Aid to Latin America, 1944–49." *Diplomatic History* 6:3 (Jul 1982): 225–44.

Pade Werner. "Deutsche als Ausländer: das Beispiel Lateinamerika." *Apuntes Latinoamericanos (Rostock)* 4 (1993): 18–31.

"Deutschland und Lateinamerika nach Versailles oder ein ex-Reichskanzler auf Resien." *Lateinamerika* 24:2 (1989): 124–30.

"Guerra mundial, revolución de noviembre y nueva expansión." *Lateinamerika* 20:2 (1985): 133–8.

"Relaciones alemanas con América Latina: algunas consideraciones acerca de los resultados y las tareas de su investigación en el ejemplo de la república de Weimar." *Lateinamerika* 25:2 (1990): 77–91.

Pardo Sanz, Rosa Maria. "Antifascismo en América Latina: España, Cuba y Estados Unidos durante la Segunda Guerra Mundial." *Estudios Interdisciplinarios de América Latina y el Caribe* 6:1 (1995): 51–73.

Pommerin, Reiner. "Überlegungen des 'Dritten Reiches' zur Rückholung deutscher Auswanderer aus Lateinamerika." *Jahrbuch für Geschichte von Staat, Wirtschaft und Gesellschaft Lateinamerikas* 16 (1979): 365–77.

Prien, Hans-Jürgen. "Die 'Deutsch-Evangelische Kirche' in Brasilien im Spannungsbogen von nationaler Wende (1933) und Kirchenkampf." *Jahrbuch für Geschichte von Staat, Wirtschaft und Gesellschaft Lateinamerikas* 25 (1988): 511–34.

Prisco, Salvatore. "Vampire Diplomacy: Nazi Economic Nationalism in Latin America, 1934–40." *Diplomacy and Statecraft* 2:1 (1991): 173–81.

Randall, Stephen J. "Ideology, National Security, and the Corporate State: The Historiography of U.S.-Latin American Relations." *Latin American Research Review* 27:1 (1991): 205–17.

Rinke, Stefan H. "Deutsche Lateinamerikapolitik, 1918–1933: Modernisierungsan-sätze im Zeichen transnationaler Beziehungen." *Jahrbuch für Geschichte von Staat, Wirtschaft und Gesellschaft Lateinamerikas* 34 (1997): 355–83.

Ríos, Fernando de los. "Nazi Infiltration in Ibero-America." *Social Research* 7 (1940): 389–409.

Rossi, Luigi. "L'etnia italiana nelle Americhe: la strategia statunitense durante la seconda guerra mondiale." *Nuova Rivista Storica* 79:1 (1995): 115–42.

Rout, Jr., Leslie B. and John F. Bratzel. "Heinrich Jürges and the Cult of Disinforma-tion." *International History Review* 6 (1984): 611–23.

Saito, Natsu Taylor. "Justice Held Hostage: U.S. Disregard for International Law in the World War II Internment of Japanese Peruvians – A Case Study." *Boston College Law Review* 40:1 (Dec 1998): 275–348.

Samhaber, Ernst. "Südamerika und der Krieg." *Monatshefte für Auswärtige Politik* 6 (1939): 1047–50.

Schlenther, Ursula. "Rassenideologie der Nazis in der ethnographischen Literatur über Lateinamerika." In *Der deutsche Faschismus in Lateinamerika, 1933–1943*, ed. by Heinz Sanke. Berlin: Humboldt-Universität zu Berlin, 1966.

Schönwald, Matthias. "Nationalsozialismus im Aufwind? Das politische Leben der deutschen Gemeinschaft Argentiniens in den frühen zwanziger Jahren des 20. Jahrhunderts." In *Nationalsozialismus und Argentinien: Beziehungen, Einflüsse und Nachwirkungen*, ed. by Holger M. Meding. Frankfurt: Lang, 1995.

Schoonover, Thomas. "Germany in Central America, 1820s to 1929: An overview." *Jahrbuch für Geschichte von Staat, Wirtschaft und Gesellschaft Lateinamerikas* 25 (1988): 33–59.

"Statistics for an Understanding of Foreign Intrusions into Central America from the 1920s to 1930." *Anuario de Estudios Centroamericanos* 15:1 (1989): 93–117.

Schröder, Hans-Jürgen. "Das Dritte Reich, die USA und Lateinamerika 1933–1941." In *Hitler, Deutschland und die Mächte. Materialien zur Außenpolitik des Dritten Reiches*, ed. by Manfred Funke. Düsseldorf: Athenäum/Droste Taschenbücher, 1978.

"Die 'Neue deutsche Südamerikapolitik.' Dokumente zur nationalsozialistischen Wirtschaftspolitik in Lateinamerika von 1934 bis 1936." *Jahrbuch für Geschichte von Staat, Wirtschaft und Gesellschaft Lateinamerikas* VI (1969): 337–451.

"Die Vereinigten Staaten und die nazionalsozialistische Handelspolitik gegenüber Lateinamerika." *Jahrbuch für Geschichte von Staat, Wirtschaft und Gesellschaft Lateinamerikas* 7 (1970): 309–71.

"Hauptprobleme der deutschen Lateinamerikapolitik, 1933–1941." *Jahrbuch für Geschichte von Staat, Wirtschaft und Gesellschaft Lateinamerikas* 12 (1975): 408–33.

Schuler, Friedrich Englebert. "Germany, Mexico and the United States during the Second World War." *Jahrbuch für Geschichte von Staat, Wirtschaft und Gesellschaft Lateinamerikas* 22 (1985): 457–76.

Seelisch, Winfried. "Jüdische Emigration nach Bolivien Ende der 30er Jahre." In *Europaische Juden in Lateinamerika*, ed. by Achim Schrader and Karl Heinrich Rengstorf. St. Ingbert: Werner J. Rohrig Verlag, 1989.

Senkman, Leonardo. "Parias und Privilegierte: Die jüdischen und spanischen Flüchtlinge in Mexiko und Argentinien 1939–1945. Eine vergleichende Studie."

In *Alternative Lateinamerika: Das deutsche Exil in der Zeit des Nationalsozialismus*, ed. by Karl Kohut and Patrik von zur Mühlen. Frankfurt: Vervuert Verlag, 1994.

Small, Melvin. "The United States and the German 'Threat' to the Hemisphere, 1905–1914." *Americas* 28:3 (1972): 252–70.

Smith, Robert Freeman. "Latin America, the United States, and the European Powers, 1830–1930." In *The Cambridge History of Latin America*, ed. by Leslie Bethell. Cambridge: Cambridge University Press, 1982–1993.

Spaeth, Carl B. and Sanders William. "The Emergency Advisory Committee for Political Defense." *American Journal of International Law* 38:2 (Apr 1944): 218–41.

Strauss, Herbert A. "Jewish Emigration from Germany: Nazi Policies and Jewish Reponses (II)." *Leo Baeck Institute Year Book* 26 (1981): 343–409.

Strum, Harvey. "Jewish Internees in the American South, 1942–1945." *American Jewish Archives* 42 (1990): 27–48.

Strunck, G. "Deutschland und USA im Kampf um die mittelamerikanischen Märkte." *Ibero-Amerikanische Rundschau* 4:10 (1937): 245–50.

Stuart, Graham H. "Special War Problems Division." *Department of State Bulletin* 11 (2 Jul 1944): 6–12.

"Special War Problems Division: Internees Section." *Department of State Bulletin* 11 (16 Jul 1944): 63–74.

"Special War Problems Division: Representation of Foreign Interests." *Department of State Bulletin* 11 (6 Aug 1944): 142–7.

Taylor, Graham D. "The Axis Replacement Program: Economic Warfare and the Chemical Industry in Latin America, 1942–44." *Diplomatic History* 8:2 (1984): 145–64.

Thompson, John A. "Exaggeration of American Vulnerability: The Anatomy of a Tradition." *Diplomatic History* 16:1 (Winter 1992): 28–30.

Tirado Mejía, Alvaro. "Colombia: Siglo y medio de bipartidismo." In *Colombia Hoy*, ed. by Mario Arrubla. Bogotá: Siglo Veintiuno Editores, 1978.

Trotz, Joachim. "Zur Tätigkeit der deutschen 5. Kolonne in Lateinamerika 1933–1945." *Wissenschaftliche Zeitschrift der Universität Rostock, Geschichtliche und sprachwissenschaftliche Reihe* 14 (1965): 119–32.

Trueblood, Howard J. "Economic Defense of the Americas." *Foreign Policy Reports* 16 (1940): 126–36.

"Trade Rivalries in Latin America." *Foreign Policy Reports* 13 (1937): 154–64.

"War and United States-Latin American Trade." *Foreign Policy Reports* 15 (1939): 218–28.

Vannucci, Albert P. "Elected by Providence: Spruille Braden in Argentina in 1945." In *Ambassadors in Foreign Policy: The Influence of Individuals on U.S.-Latin American Policy*, ed. by C. Neale Ronning and Albert P. Vannucci. New York: Praeger, 1987.

"The Influence of Latin Governments on United States Foreign Policy: The Case of US-Argentine Relations, 1943–1948." *Journal of Latin American Studies* 18 (Nov 1986): 355–82.

Welles, Sumner. "Intervention and Interventions." *Foreign Affairs* 26 (1947): 116–33.

Whitehead, Laurence. "Bolivia." In *Latin America between the Second World War and the Cold War, 1944–1948*, ed. by Leslie Bethell and Ian Roxborough. Cambridge: Cambridge University Press, 1992.

"The Imposition of Democracy." In *Exporting Democracy: The United States and Latin America*, ed. by Abraham F. Lowenthal. Baltimore: Johns Hopkins University Press, 1991.

Wilhelm, Cornelia. "'Deutschamerika' zwischen Nationalsozialismus und Amerikanismus." In *Nationalsozialismus in der Region*, ed. by Horst Möller, Andreas Wirsching and Walter Ziegler. Munich: R. Oldenbourg Verlag, 1996.

Wolff, Reinhard and Hartmut Fröschle. "Die Deutschen in Bolivien." In *Die Deutschen in Lateinamerika: Schicksal und Leistung*, ed. by Hartmut Fröschle. Tübingen: Horst Erdmann Verlag, 1979.

Young, George F. W. "German Banking and German Imperialism in Latin America in the Wilhelmine Era." *Ibero-Amerikanisches Archiv* 18:1/2 (1992): 31–66.

"German Capital Investment in Latin America in World War I." *Jahrbuch für Geschichte von Staat, Wirtschaft und Gesellschaft Lateinamerikas* 25 (1988): 215–39.

"Jorge González von Marées – Chief of Chilean Nacism." *Jahrbuch für Geschichte von Staat, Wirtschaft und Gesellschaft Lateinamerikas* 11 (1974): 309–33.

Zariz, Ruth. "Officially Approved Emigration From Germany After 1941: A Case Study." *Yad Vashem Studies* 18 (1987): 275–91.

Zeuske, Max and Ulrich Strulik. "Die Geschichte der deutsch-lateinamerikanischen Beziehungen vom Ende des 19. Jahrhunderts bis 1945 im Spiegel der DDR-Historiographie." *Jahrbuch für Geschichte von Staat, Wirtschaft und Gesellschaft Lateinamerikas* 25 (1988): 807–30.

Zinsser, Christian. "Diplomatische Mission in Honduras." *Jahrbuch für Geschichte von Staat, Wirtschaft und Gesellschaft Lateinamerikas* 12 (1975): 434–55.

Zipser, Ekkehard and Hartmut Fröschle. "Die Deutschen in Guatemala." In *Die Deutschen in Lateinamerika: Schicksal und Leistung.*, ed. by Hartmut Fröschle. Tübingen: Horst Erdmann Verlag, 1979.

Zu Putlitz, Wolfgang. "Your German-American Neighbor and the Fifth Column." *Harper's Magazine* (Feb 1942): 324.

zur Mühlen, Patrik von. "Politisches Engagement und jüdische Identität im lateinamerikanischen Exil." In *Europaische Juden in Lateinamerika*, ed. by Achim Schrader and Karl Heinrich Rengstorf. St. Ingbert: Werner J. Rohrig Verlag, 1989.

THESES

Bales, Peter R. "Nelson Rockefeller and His Quest for Inter-American Unity." Ph.D. diss., State University of New York at Stony Brook, 1982.

Blumenthal, Michael D. "The Economic Good Neighbor: Aspects of United States Economic Policy toward Latin America in the Early 1940's as Revealed by the Activities of the Office of Inter-American Affairs." Ph.D. diss., University of Wisconsin, 1969.

Clifford, Sharon Y. "The Germans in Guatemala during World War II." Master's thesis, Florida Atlantic University, 1974.

Connell, Thomas. "The Internment of Latin-American Japanese in the United States during World War II: The Peruvian Japanese Experience." Ph.D. diss., Florida State University, 1995.

Converse, Christel K. "The Rise and Fall of Nazi Influence among the German-Chileans." Ph.D. diss., Georgetown University, 1990.

Erb, Claude Curtis. "Nelson Rockefeller and United States–Latin American Relations, 1940–1945." Ph.D. diss., Clark University, 1982.

Hanson, Gail. "Sumner Welles and the American System." Ph.D. diss., State University of New York, Stony Brook, 1990.

Höbbel, Georg-Alexander. "Das 'Dritte Reich' und die Good Neighbor Policy: die nationalsozialistische Beurteilung der Lateinamerikapolitik Franklin D Roosevelts, 1933–1941." Ph.D. diss., Hamburg, 1997.

Langley, Lester D. "The United States and Panama, 1933–1941: A Study in Strategy and Diplomacy." Ph.D. diss., University of Kansas, 1965.

Magnus, Arthur W. "Die neue Phase der Monroedoktrin angesichts der Bedrohung Lateinamerikas durch die totalitären Staaten, 1933–1945." Ph.D. diss., Freie Universität, Berlin, 1956.

Maxwell, Allen Brewster. "Evoking Latin American Collaboration in the Second World War: A Study of the Office of the Coordinator of Inter-American Affairs (1940–1946)." Ph.D. diss., Fletcher School of Law and Diplomacy, 1971.

Náñez Falcón, Guillermo. "Erwin Paul Dieseldorff, German Entrepreneneur in the Alta Verapaz of Guatemala, 1889–1937." Ph.D. diss., Tulane University, 1970.

Rawls, Shirley N. "Spruille Braden: A Political Biography." Ph.D. diss., University of New Mexico, 1976.

Schmitz, John Eric. "Democracy Under Stress: The Internment of German-Americans in World War II." Ph.D. diss., North Carolina State University, 1993.

Tag, Lutz Steffen. "Die Entwicklung der Beziehungen zwischen Deutschland und Peru in der Zeit von 1933 bis 1945, unter besonderer Berücksichtigung der Rolle der IG-Farbenindustrie AG in Peru." Diss. A., Leipzig, 1974.

AUDIOVISUAL MATERIAL

Alien Enemy Detention Facility. Immigration and Naturalization Service, 1946. Accession Number N3-85-86-1, Control Number NWDNM(m)-85.1, National Archives. 16mm, videocassette copy.

Amateur footage of shipboard election off Ecuadorian coast. 1938. Courtesy Hardy de von Campe, Guayaquil, Ecuador. 8mm.

Campos de concentración. Siete Días, Canal 7, San José, Costa Rica. 12 Jan 1998. Videocassette.

Thompson, Lea. *Roundup*. Produced by Chris Scholl. Dateline NBC, 30 Nov 1994. Videocassette.

Index